Wine For Dummies, 3rd Edition

BESTSELLING BOOK SERIES

Cheat Sheet

O9-AHW-548

Quick Pronunciation Guide to Common Wine Names

The stressed syllable in each word is capitalized; if no syllable is capitalized, all syllables carry equal weight.

Auslese	OUSE lay seh
Beaujolais	boh jhoe lay
Bourgogne	bor guh nyeh
Brut	brute
Cabernet Sauvignon	cab er nay saw vee nyon
Chablis	shah blee
Chardonnay	shar dohn nay
Châteauneuf-du-Pape	shah toe nuf-doo-pahp
Côte Rotie	coat roe tee
Gewürztraminer	geh VAIRTZ trah mee ner
Haut-Brion	oh bree ohn
Hermitage	er mee tahj
Loire	lwahr
Mâcon	mah cawn
Merlot	mer loh
Meursault	muhr so
Moët	moh ett
Montepulciano d'Abruzzo	mon tay pul CHA noh dah BREWTZ zoh
Montrachet	mon rah shay
Mosel-Saar-Ruwer	MOH zel-zar-ROO ver
Muscadet	moos cah day
Pauillac	poy yac
Perrier-Jouët	per ree yay-joo ett
Pinot Grigio	pee noh GREE joe
Pinot Noir	pee noh nwahr
Pouilly-Fuissé	pwee fwee say
Riesling	REESE ling
Rioja	ree OH hah
Sancerre	sahn sehr
Spätlese	SHPATE lay seh
Viognier	vee oh nyay
Vosne Romanée	vone roh mah nay
Willamette Valley	wil LAM ette

Ten Most Useful Wine Descriptors

1. **Aroma or bouquet:** The smell of a wine. *Bouquet* applies particularly to the aroma of older wines.
2. **Body:** The apparent weight of a wine in your mouth (light, medium, or full)
3. **Crisp:** A wine with refreshing acidity
4. **Dry:** Not sweet
5. **Finish:** The impression a wine leaves as you swallow it
6. **Flavor intensity:** How strong or weak a wine's flavors are
7. **Fruity:** A wine whose aromas and flavors suggest fruit; does not imply sweetness
8. **Oaky:** A wine that has oak flavors (smoky, toasty)
9. **Soft:** A wine that is smooth and not crisp
10. **Tannic:** A red wine that is firm and leaves the mouth feeling dry

For Dummies: Bestselling Book Series for Beginners

Guide to Wine Vintages

Like any vintage wine chart, this must be considered only a rough guide. Many wines will be exceptions to the vintage's rating.

Wine Region	1993	1994	1995	1996	1997	1998	1999	2000	2001
Bordeaux: Médoc, Graves	80c	85c	90b	90a	85b	85a	85a	95a	85a
Bordeaux: Pomerol, St Emilion	80c	85b	90b	85a	85b	95a	85a	95a	85a
Côte de Nuits-Red Burgundy	80c	75d	90a	90a	90c	85b	90b	85b	85b
Côte Beaune-Red Burgundy	70d	75d	90a	90a	85c	80b	90b	75c	80b
Burgundy, White	75d	80d	90b	90b	85c	85c	85b	85c	85b

Cut out this card and carry it in your wallet as a handy guide to picking out the best wines!

Wine For Dummies, 3rd Edition

Instant Wine Identifier

Wine Name	Grape or Place	Wine Color
Barbera	Grape	Red
Bardolino	Place/Italy	Red
Barolo	Place/Italy	Red
Beaujolais	Place/France	Red
Bordeaux	Place/France	Red or white
Burgundy (Bourgogne)	Place/France	Red or white
Cabernet Sauvignon	Grape	Red
Chablis	Place/France	White
Champagne	Place/France	White or rosé
Chardonnay	Grape	White
Chianti	Place/Italy	Red
Côtes du Rhône	Place/France	Red or white
Dolcetto	Grape	Red
Merlot	Grape	Red
Mosel	Place/Germany	White
Pinot Grigio/Pinot Gris	Grape	White
Pinot Noir	Grape	Red
Port (Porto)	Place/Portugal	Red (fortified)
Pouilly-Fuissé	Place/France	White
Rhine (Rheingau, Rheinhessen)	Place/Germany	White
Riesling	Grape	White
Rioja	Place/Spain	Red or white
Sancerre	Place/France	White
Sauternes	Place/France	White (dessert)
Sauvignon Blanc	Grape	White
Sherry	Place/Spain	White (fortified)
Soave	Place/Italy	White
Syrah/Shiraz	Grape	Red
Valpolicella	Place/Italy	Red
Zinfandel	Grape	Red or pink

Positive Thinking for Wine Shoppers

No one in the world knows everything about wine.

Smart people aren't afraid to ask "dumb" questions.

The purpose of wine is to be enjoyed.

Expensive doesn't necessarily mean better.

I am my own best judge of wine quality.

Most wines are good wines.

Experimentation is fun.

Advice is free for the asking.

Every bottle of wine is a live performance.

I'll never know . . . until I try it!

Wine Region	1993	1994	1995	1996	1997	1998	1999	2000	2001
Northern Rhône	60d	85c	90a	85b	90b	90a	95a	85b	90a
Southern Rhône	80d	85d	90a	80c	80c	95b	90b	95b	90a
Champagne	80b	NV	85b	95a	80b	95a	80b	80b	NV
Germany	85c	90a	85c	95b	85c	85c	85c	85b	90b
Rioja (Spain)	85c	90c	90c	85c	80c	85b	85b	85b	95b
Piedmont (Italy)	80c	75c	85b	95a	90c	90a	95a	90a	90a
Tuscany (Italy)	75d	85c	90b	75c	95c	85c	90b	90a	85a
Calif. N. Coast Cab. Sauvignon	85b	95c	90b	90b	90c	85c	85a	85b	95a

Vintage Key:

100 = Outstanding	85 = Good	70 = Below Average
95 = Excellent	80 = Fairly Good	65 = Poor
90 = Very Good	75 = Average	50–60 = Very Poor

a = Too young to drink   b = Can be consumed now, but will improve with time

c = Ready to drink   d = May be too old   NV = Non-vintage year

Copyright © 2003 Wiley Publishing, Inc.
All rights reserved.

Item 2544-1.

For more information about Wiley Publishing, call 1-800-762-2974.

For Dummies: Bestselling Book Series for Beginners

Praise for Wine For Dummies

"This book is not just for wine 'dummies,' but for everyone who loves wine or wants to know more about it. Ed and Mary have made understanding wine entertaining as well as educational — rather than stuffy or intimidating. I've always felt that the more you know about wine, the more it adds to your meals and your life."

> — Robert Mondavi, Chairman Emeritus
> Robert Mondavi Winery

"The book has a marvelously refreshing point of view; it is enjoyable to read, straightforward, and full of common sense. I recommend it not only to beginners, but to experts as well. The beginners will find it enlightening, while the experts will benefit from the refresher course and wry wine humor."

> — Larry S. Maguire, president and CEO
> Far Niente

"Wine For Dummies is a tremendous 'door opener' for people who now will be able to enjoy wine with their meal and not be intimidated by all the hype."

> — Jack Cakebread, Proprietor
> Cakebread Winery

"Mary and Ed are born educators. They have truly added to the understanding of wine in the United States and around the world. This For Dummies book will help people to trust their own tastes and enjoyment of wine."

> — Jess Jackson, Proprietor
> Kendall-Jackson, Jackson Family Farms

"A delightfully formatted compendium of everything you need to know about wine . . . This book will appeal to all wine drinkers, from the occasional drinker to the seasoned pro."

> — Piero Antinori, Proprietor
> Marchesi Antinori Winery
> Florence, Italy

Praise for French Wine For Dummies

"This is an extraordinarily detailed yet easy-to-understand look at the world of French wine written from a loving perspective. Full of useful information as well as down-to-earth facts, I found myself pondering just which French wines I wanted to drink as I read the book."

> — Todd Hess, Wine Director, Sam's Wine & Spirits, Chicago

"Ed McCarthy and Mary Ewing-Mulligan are well-informed wine experts, and this is an original, accurate, and essential book for anyone willing to learn about French wine."

> — Jacques Lardière, Technical Director, Maison Louis Jadot

"Whether you are an avid collector or wine novice, this book offers an extensive resource in an accessible format."

> — Charlie Trotter, Acclaimed Chef, Award-Winning Restaurant Owner, and Author

Praise for Italian Wine For Dummies

"Almost anything you could want to know about Italian wine is there, at just about every level from the most basic to the highly sophisticated. In fact, at the level of knowledge to which *Italian Wine For Dummies* can take you, the title becomes a bravura piece of reverse snobbery. If this is information for dummies, what's left for experts?"

> — Tom Maresca, *Wine & Spirits Magazine*

"The esteem in which I hold the authors of *Italian Wine For Dummies* is boundless. I have known Ed and Mary, individually and as a team, for over 30 years and am able to say that I have yet to encounter more knowledgeable guides to the ins and outs of Italian wine."

> — Piero Antinori, Proprietor, Marchesi Antinori Winery Florence, Italy

"A must-have book for anyone who is serious about Italian wines. Cin cin."

> — Lidia Bastianich, Restaurateur (Felidia, Becco, Lidia's K.C., Lidia's Pittsburgh), Cookbook Author (*Lidia's Italian American Kitchen*), and TV Host (*Lidia's Italian Table*)

Wine

FOR

DUMMIES®

3RD EDITION

Wine
FOR
DUMMIES®
3RD EDITION

**by Ed McCarthy and
Mary Ewing-Mulligan MW**

Foreword by Piero Antinori
Proprietor, Marchesi Antinori Winery, Florence, Italy

Wiley Publishing, Inc.

Wine For Dummies®, 3rd Edition

Published by
Wiley Publishing, Inc.
111 River Street
Hoboken, NJ 10022
www.wiley.com

For general information on our other products and services or to obtain technical support, please contact our Customer Care Department within the U.S. at 800-762-2974, outside the U.S. at 317-572-3993, or fax 317-572-4002.

Wiley also publishes its books in a variety of electronic formats. Some content that appears in print may not be available in electronic books.

Library of Congress Cataloging-in-Publication Data:

Library of Congress Control Number: 2003105676

ISBN: 0-7645-2544-1

Manufactured in the United States of America

10 9 8 7 6 5 4

3O/QX/QY/QT/IN

About the Authors

Ed McCarthy and **Mary Ewing-Mulligan** are two wine lovers who met at an Italian wine tasting in New York City's Chinatown in 1981. Two years later, they formally merged their wine cellars and wine libraries when they married. They have since co-authored six wine books in the *Wine For Dummies* series of books (including their latest two, *French Wine For Dummies* and *Italian Wine For Dummies*), taught hundreds of wine classes together, visited nearly every wine region in the world, run five marathons, and raised ten cats. Along the way, they have amassed more than half a century of professional wine experience between them.

Mary grew up in Pennsylvania and attended the University of Pennsylvania, where she majored in English literature. She got started in the wine business right out of college, by complete chance, when she accepted a position with the Italian Trade Commission. Today, her true love in wine is still Italian. Mary runs International Wine Center, a New York City–based wine school, where she and her staff teach classes mainly for wine professionals; she's also wine columnist for the *NY Daily News.* Perhaps Mary's most impressive credential is that she's the first female Master of Wine (MW) in the United States, and one of only 19 MW's in the country (with 240 worldwide).

Ed, a New Yorker, graduated from City University of NY with a master's degree in psychology. He taught high school English in another life, while working part-time in wine shops to satisfy his passion for wine and to subsidize his growing wine cellar. That cellar is especially heavy in his favorite wines — Bordeaux, Barolo, and Champagne. Besides co-authoring six wine books in the *For Dummies* series with Mary, Ed went solo as author of *Champagne For Dummies,* a topic on which he's especially expert.

Ed and Mary also share wine columns in *Nation's Restaurant News* and in *Beverage Media,* a trade publication. Ed also writes for *Wine Enthusiast Magazine* and *Decanter.* He and Mary are both accredited as Certified Wine Educators (CWE).

When they are not writing, teaching, or visiting wine regions, Mary and Ed maintain a busy schedule of speaking, judging at professional wine competitions, and tasting as many new wines as possible. They admit to leading thoroughly unbalanced lives in which their only non-wine pursuits are hiking in the Berkshires and the Italian Alps. At home, they wind down to the tunes of Bob Dylan and Neil Young, in the company of their feline roommates, Brunello, Dolcetto, Black & Whitey, and Pinot.

Dedication

We dedicate this book to all of you readers who made our first two editions of *Wine For Dummies* such a success; you are the reason that this book exists.

Authors' Acknowledgments

The wine world is dynamic; it's constantly changing. Because it's been five years since the second edition of *Wine For Dummies,* we decided to revise and update the book. We especially felt an obligation to write this third edition because of all of you readers who have personally told us how valuable *Wine For Dummies* has been to you. We are grateful that we've been able to contribute to your knowledge about this wonderful beverage, wine.

But this book would not have been possible without the team at John Wiley & Sons. We sincerely thank Publisher Jennifer Feldman who engaged us to write the third edition of *Wine For Dummies,* along with Acquisitions Editors Pam Mourouzis and Norman Crampton. Really special thanks go to our Project Editor Joan Friedman, who made excellent suggestions to improve the text.

We thank our technical reviewer, colleague Chris Cree MW, for his expertise. It's a better, more accurate book because of you.

Special thanks to Steve Ettlinger, our agent and friend, who brought us to the *For Dummies* series in the first place, and who is always there for us.

We thank all of our friends in the wine business for your information and kind suggestions for our book; the book reviewers, whose criticism has been so generous; and our readers, who have encouraged us with your enthusiasm for our previous books in this series.

Thanks also to Elise McCarthy, E.J. and Bernadette McCarthy, Cindy McCarthy Tomarchio and her husband David for their encouragement and support.

Publisher's Acknowledgments

We're proud of this book; please send us your comments through our Dummies online registration form located at www.dummies.com/register/.

Some of the people who helped bring this book to market include the following:

Acquisitions, Editorial, and Media Development

Project Editor: Joan Friedman

(Previous Edition: Mary Goodwin)

Acquisitions Editor: Norm Crampton, Pam Mourouzis

Acquisitions Coordinator: Holly Gastineau-Grimes

Technical Editor: Christopher Cree MW

Editorial Manager: Michelle Hacker

Media Development Manager: Laura VanWinkle

Editorial Assistant: Elizabeth Rea

Cartoons: Rich Tennant, www.the5thwave.com

Production

Project Coordinators: Courtney MacIntyre, Nancee Reeves

Layout and Graphics: Seth Conley, LeAndra Hosier, Jacque Schneider

Special Art: © 2003 Akira Chiwaki

Proofreaders: Laura Albert, John Tyler Connoley, Andy Hollandbeck, Brian H. Walls, TECHBOOKS Production Services

Indexer: TECHBOOKS Production Services

Publishing and Editorial for Consumer Dummies

    Diane Graves Steele, Vice President and Publisher, Consumer Dummies

    Joyce Pepple, Acquisitions Director, Consumer Dummies

    Kristin A. Cocks, Product Development Director, Consumer Dummies

    Michael Spring, Vice President and Publisher, Travel

    Brice Gosnell, Associate Publisher, Travel

    Kelly Regan, Editorial Director, Travel

Publishing for Technology Dummies

    Andy Cummings, Vice President and Publisher, Dummies Technology/General User

Composition Services

    Gerry Fahey, Vice President of Production Services

    Debbie Stailey, Director of Composition Services

Contents at a Glance

Table of Contents

· ·

Foreword

*I*t is my privilege to have been asked to write the foreword to Ed McCarthy and Mary Ewing-Mulligan's book. I've known them for 30 years and can wholeheartedly vouch for their knowledge, their enthusiasm, and their pure pleasure in the joy of wine. I honestly can't think of anyone whose talents are better suited to *Wine For Dummies*.

I consider it particularly appropriate that wine was among the first *For Dummies* books written for a subject other than computers, since many people consider winespeak as foreign and intimidating as computerese. Ed and his wife Mary prove in this down-to-earth, humorous yet thorough book that nothing could be further from the truth.

In everyday language (something missing from most wine literature), they explain all that you ever wanted to know about wine: where and how to buy it, how to read wine labels and speak the language of wine, how to taste wine, how to recognize a bad one, how to navigate restaurant wine lists, and even how to open a bottle. They cover every topic from the most basic to the more advanced. Truly a delightfully formatted compendium of everything you need to know about wine. And its timing is perfect.

These days, wine production is at an all-time high, as is wine quality. More varieties of wine are coming from more regions than ever before, creating more confusion in consumers' minds (though I hope that my wines, from Italy's regions of Tuscany and Umbria, do not add to that confusion!). Anyway, we now have the spirited and personal assistance of *Wine For Dummies*.

Wine is for everyone, after all, and we should not treat it as if it were something reserved for a mystical elite. Producers such as myself must support the effort to help the uninitiated and the intimidated.

This book will appeal to all wine drinkers, from the occasional drinker to the seasoned pro. Whether you read this book from cover to cover, dip into it for an occasional bit of knowledge, or turn to it in a moment of crisis, you will be rewarded with the wit and wisdom of two expert teachers. To your health!

Piero Antinori, Proprietor
Marchesi Antinori Winery
Florence, Italy

Piero Antinori's family has been making wine since 1385; his wines are prized by connoisseurs the world over. He also owns Atlas Peak winery in Napa, California, is part owner of Col Solare winery in Washington state, and has an interest in a Hungarian winery. He has been honored by many of the leading international wine organizations and has often acted as a spokesman for the Italian wine industry.

Introduction

● ●

*W*e love wine. We love the way it tastes, we love the fascinating variety of wines in the world, and we love the way wine brings people together at the dinner table. We believe that you and everyone else should be able to enjoy wine — regardless of your experience or your budget.

But we'll be the first to admit that wine people, such as many wine professionals and really serious connoisseurs, don't make it easy for regular people to enjoy wine. You have to know strange names of grape varieties and foreign wine regions. You have to figure out whether to buy a $16 wine or a $6 wine that seems to be pretty much the same thing. You even need a special tool to open the bottle once you get it home!

All this complication surrounding wine will never go away, because wine is a very rich and complex field. But you don't have to let it stand in your way. With the right attitude and a little understanding of what wine is, you can begin to buy and enjoy wine. And if, like us, you decide that wine is fascinating, you can find out more and turn it into a wonderful hobby.

Welcome to Our Third Edition

If you already have the original *Wine For Dummies,* or the second edition, you might be wondering whether you need this book. We believe that you do. We wrote the second edition of *Wine For Dummies* in 1998, and the world of wine has changed a lot since then:

- ✔ Dozens of wineries have opened, a few have gone out of business, many have improved, and a few have slipped. Web sites on wine have come and gone. The wine auction scene bears almost no resemblance to what it was. Our recommendations reflect all these changes.

- ✔ Remember those prices that we listed for your favorite wines in our earlier editions? Well, big surprise: Just about all of those prices have increased. But we point out some bargains, especially in Part III.

- ✔ Several new vintages have occurred; we give you the lowdown on them throughout the book, and especially in our vintage chart in Appendix C.

- ✔ Great wine regions of yesterday, such as Hungary and Greece, have revitalized themselves, and we tell you about them.

Also in this edition, we've expanded coverage of France's wine regions, adding much-needed sections on the South and Southwest, and have updated the wine regions of Italy, California, Chile, and Argentina, among others.

How to Use This Book

This book is a wine textbook of sorts, a user's manual, and a reference book, all in one. We've included very basic information about wine for readers who know nothing (or next to nothing) about wine — but we have also included tips, suggestions, and more sophisticated information for seasoned wine drinkers who want to take their hobby to a more advanced level. Depending on where you fall on the wine-knowledge gradient, different chapters will be relevant to you.

Part I: Getting Started with Wine

The five chapters in Part I get you up and sipping even if you've never tasted wine in your life. We tell you the basic types of wine, how to taste it, which grapes make wine, why winemaking matters, and how wines are named.

Part II: Close Encounters of the Wine Kind

This part deals with practical wine matters — in the wine shop, in the restaurant, and in your home. Find out how to handle snooty wine clerks, restaurant wine lists, and those stubborn corks. In addition, we show you how to decipher cryptic wine labels.

Part III: Around the World of Wine

Visit this part, the heart of the book, for a tour of the major wine regions of the world and the wines they produce. France, Italy, and the U.S. have their own chapters, as do sparkling wines and dessert wines, but even tiny regions such as Austria's and New Zealand's are stops on the tour.

Part IV: When You've Caught the Bug

You find a wealth of practical advice in this part, including recommendations on where and how you can buy wine beyond your local wine shops. We also tell you how to describe and rate wines you taste, how to pair food and wine, how to store wine properly — and even how you can pursue your love and knowledge of wine beyond this book.

Part V: The Part of Tens

What *For Dummies* book would be complete without this final part? It's a synopsis of interesting tips and recommendations about wine to reinforce our suggestions earlier in the book. We're particularly happy to debunk ten prevalent myths about wine so that you can become a savvier consumer and a more satisfied wine drinker.

Part VI: Appendixes

In Part VI, we show you how to pronounce foreign wine words, and you can look up unfamiliar wine terms in our glossary. You can also consult our vintage chart to check out the quality and drinkability of your wine.

Icons Used in This Book

This odd little guy is a bit like the two-year-old who constantly insists on knowing "Why, Mommy, why?" But he knows that you might not have the same level of curiosity that he has. Where you see him, feel free to skip over the technical information that follows. Wine will still taste just as delicious.

Advice and information that will make you a wiser wine drinker or buyer is marked by this bull's-eye so that you won't miss it.

There's very little you can do in the course of moderate wine consumption that can land you in jail — but you could spoil an expensive bottle and sink into a deep depression over your loss. This symbol warns you about common pitfalls.

Some issues in wine are so fundamental that they bear repeating. Just so you don't think we repeated ourselves without realizing it, we mark the repetitions with this symbol.

Wine snobs practice all sorts of affectations designed to make other wine drinkers feel inferior. But you won't be intimidated by their snobbery if you see it for what it is. (And you can learn how to impersonate a wine snob!)

A bargain's not a bargain unless you really like the outfit, as they say. To our tastes, the wines we mark with this icon are bargains because we like them, we believe them to be of good quality, and their price is low compared to other wines of similar type, style, or quality. You can also interpret this logo as a badge of genuineness, as in "This Chablis is the real deal."

Unfortunately, some of the finest, most intriguing, most delicious wines are made in very small quantities. Usually, those wines cost more than wines made in large quantities — but that's not the only problem; the real frustration is that those wines have very limited distribution, and you can't always get your hands on a bottle even if you're willing to pay the price. We mark such wines with this icon, and hope that your search proves fruitful.

Wine Is for Everyone

Because we hate to think that wine, which has brought so much pleasure into our lives, could be the source of anxiety for anyone, we want to help you feel more comfortable around wine. Some knowledge of wine, gleaned from the pages of this book and from our shared experiences, will go a long way toward increasing your comfort level.

But ironically, what will *really* make you feel comfortable about wine is accepting the fact that you'll never know it all — and that you've got *plenty* of company.

You see, after you really get a handle on wine, you discover that *no one* knows everything there is to know about wine. There is just too much information, and it's always changing. And when you know that, you can just relax and enjoy the stuff.

Part I
Getting Started with Wine

The 5th Wave   By Rich Tennant

"Oh, come on, you're just drinking it! You're not even tasting it ..."

In this part . . .

To grasp the material in this part of the book, it helps to have some preliminary knowledge: what a grape is, and where your tongue and nose are located.

If you've got those bases covered, you're ready to begin understanding and enjoying wine — even if you've never tasted wine before in your life. We'll start slowly so that you can enjoy the scenery along the way.

Chapter 1

Wine 101

*W*e visit wineries all the time, and when we do, we usually end up talking with the winemaker about how he makes his wine. One of us is thrilled by these conversations because they're opportunities to learn more about why wines taste the way they do. But the other gets bored very quickly, because who cares how wine is made, as long as it's delicious?

It seems that there are two types of wine lovers in the world: the *hedonists,* who just want to enjoy wine and find more and more wines they can enjoy; and the *thinkers,* who are fascinated by how wine happens. (The hedonists call the thinkers *wine nerds.*) Our family has one of each.

If you're a thinker, you'll enjoy discovering what's behind the differences in wines. And even if you're a hedonist, a little knowledge can help you discover more wines that you'll enjoy. Of course, this is the thinker speaking.

How Wine Happens

The recipe for turning fruit into wine goes something like this:

1. **Pick a large quantity of ripe grapes from grapevines.**

   You could substitute raspberries or any other fruit, but 99.9 percent of all the wine in the world is made from grapes, because they make the best wines.

2. **Put the grapes into a clean container that doesn't leak.**

3. **Crush the grapes somehow to release their juice.**

   Once upon a time, feet performed this step.

4. **Wait.**

In its most basic form, winemaking is that simple. After the grapes are crushed, *yeasts* (tiny one-celled organisms that exist naturally in the vineyard and, therefore, on the grapes) come into contact with the sugar in the grapes' juice and gradually convert that sugar into alcohol. Yeasts also produce carbon dioxide, which evaporates into the air. When the yeasts are done working, your grape juice is wine. The sugar that was in the juice is no longer there — alcohol is present instead. (The riper and sweeter the grapes, the more alcohol the wine will have.) This process is called *fermentation*.

What could be more natural?

Fermentation is a totally natural process that doesn't require man's participation at all, except to put the grapes into a container and release the juice from the grapes. Fermentation occurs in fresh apple cider left too long in your refrigerator, without any help from you. In fact we read that milk, which contains a different sort of sugar than grapes do, develops a small amount of alcohol if left on the kitchen table all day long.

Speaking of milk, Louis Pasteur is the man credited with discovering fermentation in the nineteenth century. That's discovering, not inventing. Some of those apples in the Garden of Eden probably fermented long before Pasteur came along. (Well, we don't think it could have been much of an Eden without wine!)

Modern wrinkles in winemaking

Now if every winemaker actually made wine in as crude a manner as we just described, we'd be drinking some pretty rough stuff that would hardly inspire us to write a wine book.

But today's winemakers have a bag of tricks as big as George Foreman's appetite. That's one reason why no two wines ever taste exactly the same.

The men and women who make wine can control the type of container they use for the fermentation process (stainless steel and oak are the two main materials), as well as the size of the container and the temperature of the juice during fermentation — and every one of these choices can make a big difference in the taste of the wine. After fermentation, they can choose how long to let the wine *mature* (a stage when the wine sort of gets its act together) and in what kind of container. Fermentation can last three days or three months, and the wine can then mature for a couple of months or a couple of years or anything in between. If you have trouble making decisions, don't ever become a winemaker.

The main ingredient

Obviously, one of the biggest factors in making one wine different from the next is the nature of the raw material, the grape juice. Besides the fact that riper, sweeter grapes make a more alcoholic wine, different *varieties* of grapes (Chardonnay, Cabernet Sauvignon, or Merlot, for example) make different wines. Grapes are the main ingredient in wine, and everything the winemaker does, he does to the particular grape juice he has. Chapter 3 covers specific grapes and the kinds of wine they make.

What Color Is Your Appetite?

Your inner child will be happy to know that when it comes to wine, it's okay to like some colors more than others. You can't get away with saying "I don't like green food!" beyond your sixth birthday, but you can express a general preference for white, red, or pink wine for all your adult years.

(Not exactly) white wine

Whoever coined the term "white wine" must have been colorblind. All you have to do is look at it to see that it's not white, it's yellow. But we've all gotten used to the expression by now, and so *white wine* it is. (Let's hope that person didn't live in a snowy city.)

White wine is wine without any red color (or pink color, which is in the red family). This means that *White Zinfandel,* a popular pink wine, isn't white wine. But yellow wines, golden wines, and wines that are as pale as water are all white wines.

Wine becomes white wine in one of two ways. First, white wine can be made from white grapes — which, by the way, are not white. (Did you see that one coming?) *White* grapes are greenish, greenish yellow, golden yellow, or sometimes even pinkish yellow. Basically, white grapes include all the grape types that are not dark red or bluish. If you make a wine from white grapes, it's a white wine.

The second way a wine can become white is a little more complicated. The process involves using red grapes — but only the *juice* of red grapes, not the grape skins. The juice of most red grapes has no red pigmentation — only the skins do — so a wine made with only the juice of red grapes can be a white wine. In practice, though, very few white wines are made from red grapes. (Champagne is one exception; Chapter 15 addresses the use of red grapes to make Champagne.)

In case you're wondering, the skins are removed from the grapes by either *pressing* large quantities of grapes so that the juice flows out and the skins stay behind — sort of like squeezing the pulp out of grapes, the way kids do in the cafeteria — or by *crushing* the grapes in a machine with a huge screw that breaks the skins and lets the juice drain away.

Is white always right?

You can drink white wine anytime you like — which for most people means as a drink without food or with lighter foods.

The skinny on sulfites

Sulfur dioxide, a compound formed from sulfur and oxygen, occurs naturally during fermentation in very small quantities. Winemakers add it, too. Sulfur dioxide is to wine what a combination of aspirin and vitamin E is to humans — a wonder drug that cures all sorts of afflictions and prevents others. Sulfur dioxide is an antibacterial, preventing the wine from turning to vinegar. It inhibits yeasts, preventing sweet wines from refermenting in the bottle. It's an antioxidant, keeping the wine fresh and untainted by the demon oxygen. Despite these magical properties, winemakers try to use as little sulfur dioxide as possible because many of them share a belief that the less you add to wine, the better (just as many people prefer to ingest as little medication as possible).

Now here's a bit of irony for you:

Today — when winemaking is so advanced that winemakers need to rely on sulfur dioxide's help less than ever before — most wine labels in America state "Contains Sulfites" (meaning sulfur dioxide). That's because Congress passed a law in 1988 requiring that phrase on the label.

So now many wine drinkers think that there's *more* sulfur in the wine than there used to be; but, in reality, sulfur dioxide use is probably at an all-time low.

Approximately 5 percent of asthmatics are extremely sensitive to sulfites. To protect them, Congress mandated that any wine containing more than 10 parts per million of sulfites carry the "Contains Sulfites" phrase on its label. Considering that about 10 to 20 parts per million occur naturally in wine, that covers just about every wine. (The exception is organic wines, which are intentionally made without the addition of sulfites; some of them are low enough in sulfites that they don't have to use the mandated phrase.)

Actual sulfite levels in wine range from about 100 to 150 parts per million (about the same as in dried apricots); the legal max in the U.S. is 350. White dessert wines have the most sulfur — followed by medium-sweet white wines and blush wines — because those types of wine need the most protection. Dry white wines generally have less, and dry reds have the least.

White wine styles: There's no such thing as just plain white wine

White wines fall into three general taste categories, not counting sparkling wine or the really sweet white wine you drink with dessert (see Chapter 16 for more on those). If the words we use to describe these taste categories sound weird, take heart — they're all explained in Chapter 2. Here are the three broad categories:

✔ Some white wines are *dry and crisp, with no sweetness and no oaky character.* (Turn to Chapter 3 for the lowdown on oak.) Most Italian white wines, like Soave and Pinot Grigio, and some French whites, like Sancerre and some Chablis wines, fall into this category.

✔ Some white wines are *dry, or fairly dry, and full-bodied with oaky character.* Most California and Australian Chardonnays and many French wines — like most of those from the Burgundy region of France — fall into this group.

✔ Finally, some white wines are *off-dry* (that is, not bone-dry). Examples include many of the less expensive American wines (under $10 a bottle in the U.S.) as well as a lot of German wines, especially the least expensive ones.

White wines are often considered *apéritif* wines, meaning wines consumed before dinner, in place of cocktails, or at parties. (If you ask the officials who busy themselves defining such things, an apéritif wine is a wine that has flavors added to it, as vermouth does. But unless you're in the business of writing wine labels for a living, don't worry about that. In common parlance, an apéritif wine is just what we said.)

Lots of people like to drink white wines when the weather is hot because they are more refreshing than red wines, and they are usually drunk chilled (the wines, not the people).

We serve white wines cool, but not ice-cold. Sometimes restaurants serve white wines too cold, and we actually have to wait a while for the wine to warm up before we drink it. If you like your wine cold, fine; but try drinking your favorite white wine a little less cold sometime, and we bet you'll discover it has more flavor that way.

For suggestions of foods to eat with white wine, turn to Chapter 20; for really detailed information about white wine and food (and white wine itself, for that matter), refer to our book *White Wine For Dummies* (John Wiley Publishing, Inc.).

Red wine styles: There's no such thing as just plain red wine, either

Here are just three of the many red wine styles:

- *Light-bodied red wines with not much tannin* (like Beaujolais Nouveau wine from France, Valpolicella from Italy, and many U.S. wines selling for less than $10 a bottle)

- *Medium-bodied, moderately tannic red wines* (like less expensive wines from Bordeaux, in France; Italian Chianti; many Australian red wines; and some American Merlots)

- *Full-bodied, tannic reds* (such as the most expensive California Cabernets; Barolo, from Italy; the most expensive Australian reds; and lots of other expensive reds)

Red, red wine

In this case, the name is correct. Red wines really are red. They can be purple red, ruby red, or garnet, but they're red.

Red wines are made from grapes that are red or bluish in color. So guess what wine people call these grapes? Black grapes! We suppose that's because black is the opposite of white.

The most obvious difference between red wine and white wine is color. The red color occurs when the colorless juice of red grapes stays in contact with the dark grape skins during fermentation and absorbs the skins' color. Along with color, the grape skins give the wine *tannin,* a substance that's an important part of the way a red wine tastes. (See Chapter 2 for more about the taste of tannin.) The presence of tannin in red wines is actually the most important taste difference between red wines and white wines.

Red wines vary in style more than white wines do. This is partly because winemakers have more ways of adjusting their red-winemaking to achieve the kind of wine they want. For example, if winemakers leave the juice in contact with the skins for a long time, the wine becomes more *tannic* (firmer in the mouth, like strong tea; tannic wines can make you pucker). If winemakers drain the juice off the skins sooner, the wine is softer and less tannic.

Red wine tends to be consumed more often as part of a meal than as a drink on its own.

Thanks to the wide range of red wine styles, you can find red wines to go with just about every type of food and every occasion when you want to drink wine (except the times when you want to drink a wine with bubbles, because most bubbly wines are white or pink). In Chapter 20, we give you some tips on matching red wine with food. You can also consult our book about red wine, *Red Wine For Dummies* (John Wiley Publishing, Inc.).

One sure way to spoil the fun in drinking most red wines is to drink them cold. Those tannins can taste really bitter when the wine is cold — just as in a cold glass of very strong tea. On the other hand, many restaurants serve red wines too warm. (Where do they store them? Next to the boiler?) If the bottle feels cool to your hand, that's a good temperature. For more about serving wine at the right temperature, see Chapter 8.

A rose is a rose, but a rosé is "white"

Rosé wines are pink wines. Rosé wines are made from red grapes, but they don't end up red because the grape juice stays in contact with the red skins for a very short time — only a few hours, compared to days or weeks for red wines. Because this *skin contact* (the period when the juice and the skins intermingle) is brief, rosé wines absorb very little tannin from the skins. Therefore, you can chill rosé wines and drink them as you would white wines.

Of course, not all rosé wines are called rosés. (That would be too simple.) Many rosé wines today are called *blush* wines — a term invented by wine marketers to avoid the word *rosé,* because back in the '80s pink wines weren't very popular. Lest someone figures out that *blush* is a synonym for *rosé,* the labels call these wines *white*. But even a child can see that White Zinfandel is really pink.

The blush wines that call themselves *white* are fairly sweet. Wines labeled *rosé* can be sweetish, too, but some wonderful rosés from Europe (and a few from America, too) are *dry* (not sweet). Although hard-core wine lovers hardly ever drink rosé wine, we love to drink dry rosés in the summer.

Red wine sensitivities

Some people complain that they can't drink red wines without getting a headache or feeling ill. Usually, they blame the sulfites in the wine. We're not doctors or scientists, but we can tell you that red wines contain far less sulfur than white wines. That's because the tannin in red wines acts as a preservative, making sulfur dioxide less necessary. Red wines do contain histamine-like compounds and other substances derived from the grape skins that could be the culprits. Whatever the source of the discomfort, it's probably not sulfites.

Ten occasions to drink rosé (and defy the snobs)

1. When she's having fish and he's having meat (or vice versa)

2. When a red wine just seems too heavy

3. With lunch — hamburgers, grilled cheese sandwiches, and so on

4. On picnics on warm, sunny days

5. To wean your son/daughter, mate, friend (yourself?) off cola

6. On warm evenings

7. To celebrate the arrival of spring or summer

8. With ham (hot or cold) or other pork dishes

9. When you feel like putting ice cubes in your wine

10. On Valentine's Day (or any other pink occasion)

Other Ways of Categorizing Wine

There's a game we sometimes play with our friends. "Which wine," we ask them, "would you want to have with you if you were stranded on a desert island?" In other words, which wine could you drink for the rest of your life without getting tired of it? Our own answer is always Champagne, with a capital *C* (more on the capitalization later in this section).

In a way, it's an odd choice because, as much as we love Champagne, we don't drink it *every day* under normal circumstances. We welcome guests with it, we celebrate with it after our team wins a Sunday football game, and we toast our cats with it on their birthdays. We don't need much of an excuse to drink Champagne, but it's not the type of wine we drink every night.

What we drink every night is regular wine — red, white, or pink — without bubbles. There are various names for these wines. In America, they're called *table* wines, and in Europe they're called *light* wines. Sometimes we refer to them as *still* wines, because they don't have bubbles moving around in them.

In the following sections, we explain the differences between three categories of wines: table wines, dessert wines, and sparkling wines.

Table wine

Table wine, or light wine, is fermented grape juice whose alcohol content falls within a certain range. Furthermore, table wine is not bubbly. (Some table wines have a very slight carbonation, but not enough to disqualify them as table wines.) According to U.S. standards of identification, table wines may have an alcohol content no higher than 14 percent; in Europe, light wine must contain from 8.5 percent to 14 percent alcohol by volume (with a few exceptions). So unless a wine has more than 14 percent alcohol or has bubbles, it's a table wine or a light wine in the eyes of the law.

The regulations-makers didn't get the number 14 by drawing it from a hat. Historically, most wines contained less than 14 percent alcohol — either because there wasn't enough sugar in the juice to attain a higher alcohol level, or because the yeasts died off when the alcohol reached 14 percent, halting the fermentation. That number, therefore, became the legal borderline between wines that have no alcohol added to them (table wines) and wines that do have alcohol added to them (see "Dessert wine," in the next section).

Today, however, the issue isn't as clear-cut as it was when the laws were written. Many grapes are now grown in warm climates where they become so ripe, and have so much natural sugar, that their juice attains more than 14 percent alcohol when it's fermented. The use of gonzo yeast strains that continue working even when the alcohol exceeds 14 percent is another factor. Many red Zinfandels, Cabernets, and Chardonnays from California now have 14.5 or even 15.5 percent alcohol. Wine drinkers still consider them table wines, but legally they don't qualify. Which is just to say that laws and reality don't always keep pace.

Here's our own, real-world definition of table wines: They are the normal, non-bubbly wines that most people drink most of the time.

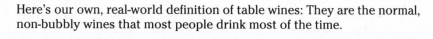

How to (sort of) learn the alcohol content of a wine

Regulations require wineries to state a wine's alcohol percentage on the label (again, with some minor exceptions). It can be expressed in *degrees,* like 12.5 degrees, or as a percentage, like 12.5 percent. If a wine carries the words "Table Wine" on its label in the U.S., but not the alcohol percentage, it should have less than 14 percent alcohol by law.

For wines sold within the U.S. — whether the wine is American or imported — there's a big catch, however. The labels are allowed to lie.

U.S. regulations give wineries a 1.5 percent leeway in the accuracy of the alcohol level. If the label states 12.5 percent, the actual alcohol level can be as high as 14 percent or as low as 11 percent. The leeway does not entitle the wineries to exceed the 14 percent maximum, however.

If the alcohol percentage is stated as a number that's neither a full number nor a half-number — 12.8 or 13.2, for example, instead of 12.5 or 13 — odds are it's precise.

Dessert wine

Many wines have more than 14 percent alcohol because alcohol was added during or after the fermentation. That's an unusual way of making wine, but some parts of the world, like the Sherry region in Spain and the Port region in Portugal, have made quite a specialty of it.

Dessert wine is the legal U.S. terminology for these wines, probably because they're usually sweet and often enjoyed after dinner. We find that term misleading, because dessert wines are not *always* sweet and not *always* consumed after dinner. (Dry Sherry is categorized as a dessert wine, for example, but it's dry, and we drink it before dinner.)

In Europe, this category of wines is called *liqueur wines,* which carries the same connotation of sweetness. We prefer the term *fortified,* which suggests that the wine has been strengthened with additional alcohol. But until we get elected to run things, the term will have to be *dessert wine* or *liqueur wine.*

Sparkling wine (and a highly personal spelling lesson)

Sparkling wines are wines that contain carbon dioxide bubbles. Carbon dioxide gas is a natural byproduct of fermentation, and winemakers sometimes decide to trap it in the wine. Just about every country that makes wine also makes sparkling wine.

In the U.S., Canada, and Europe, *sparkling wine* is the official name for the category of wines with bubbles. Isn't it nice when everyone agrees?

Popular white wines

These types of white wine are available almost everywhere in the U.S. We describe these wines in Part III of this book.

- **Chardonnay:** Can come from California, Australia, France, or almost any other place

- **Sauvignon Blanc:** Can come from California, France, New Zealand, South Africa, and other places

- **Riesling:** Can come from Germany, California, New York, Washington, France, Austria, Australia, and other places

- **Pinot Grigio** or **Pinot Gris:** Can come from Italy, France, Oregon, California, and other places

- **Soave:** Comes from Italy

Popular red wines

You'll find descriptions and explanations of these popular and widely available red wines all through this book.

- ✔ **Cabernet Sauvignon:** Can come from California, Australia, France, and other places

- ✔ **Merlot:** Can come from California, France, Washington, New York, Chile, and other places

- ✔ **Pinot Noir:** Can come from California, France, Oregon, New Zealand, and other places

- ✔ **Beaujolais:** Comes from France

- ✔ **Lambrusco:** Usually comes from Italy

- ✔ **Chianti:** Comes from Italy

- ✔ **Zinfandel:** Usually comes from California

- ✔ **Côtes du Rhône:** Comes from France

- ✔ **Bordeaux:** Comes from France

Champagne (with a capital C) is the most famous sparkling wine — and probably the most famous *wine,* for that matter. Champagne is a specific type of sparkling wine (made from certain grape varieties and produced in a certain way) that comes from a region in France called Champagne. It is the undisputed Grand Champion of Bubblies.

Unfortunately for the people of Champagne, France, their wine is so famous that the name *champagne* has been borrowed again and again by producers elsewhere, until the word has become synonymous with practically the whole category of sparkling wines. In the U.S., for example, winemakers can legally call any sparkling wine *champagne* — even with a capital C, if they want — as long as the carbonation was not added artificially. (They do have to add a qualifying geographic term such as *American* or *Californian* before the word Champagne, however.)

For the French, limiting the use of the name *champagne* to the wines of the Champagne region has become a *cause célèbre.* European Union regulations not only prevent any other member country from calling its sparkling wines *champagne* but also prohibit the use of terms that even *suggest* the word *champagne,* such as fine print on the label saying that a wine was made using the "champagne method." What's more, bottles of sparkling wine from countries outside the European Union that use the word champagne on the label are banned from sale in Europe. The French are that serious.

To us, this seems perfectly fair. You'll never catch us using the word *champagne* as a generic term for wine with bubbles. We have too much respect for the people and the traditions of Champagne, France, where the best sparkling wines in the world are made. That's why we stress the capital "C" when we say Champagne. *Those* are the wines we want on our desert island, not just any sparkling wine from anywhere that calls itself champagne.

When someone tries to impress you by serving a "Champagne" that's not French, don't be impressed. In places such as the U.S. where it's legal to call sparkling wines champagne, usually only inexpensive, low quality wines actually use that name. Most of the top sparkling wine companies in America, for example, won't call their wines champagne — even though it's legal — out of respect for their French counterparts. (Of course, many of California's top sparkling wine companies are actually owned by the French — so it's no surprise that *they* won't call their wines champagne — but many other companies won't use the term, either.)

Chapter 2

These Taste Buds Are for You

*O*ur friends who are normal people (as opposed to our friends who are wine people) like to mock us when we do things like bring our own wine to a party or drive all the way from New York to Boston to go wine shopping. Most of the time, we don't even try to defend ourselves. We realize how ridiculous our behavior must seem.

In our early days as wine drinkers, we, too, used to think that all wines tasted more or less the same. Wine was wine. All that changed when we started to taste wine the way the pros do.

The Special Technique for Tasting Wine

We know you're out there — the cynics who are saying, right about now, "Hey, I already know how to taste. I do it every day, three to five times a day. All that wine-tasting humbug is just another way of making wine seem fancy."

And you know, in a way, those cynics are right. Anyone who can taste coffee or a hamburger can taste wine. All you need are a nose, taste buds, and a brain. Unless you're like our friend who lost his sense of smell from the permanent-wave solution he used every day as a cosmetology teacher back in the '60s, you, too, have all that it takes to taste wine properly.

You also have all that it takes to speak Mandarin. Having the ability to do something is different from knowing how to do it and applying that know-how in everyday life, however.

Two very complicated rules of wine tasting

You drink beverages every day, tasting them as they pass through your mouth. In the case of wine, however, drinking and tasting are not synonymous. Wine is much more complex than other beverages: There's more going on in a mouthful of wine. For example, most wines have lots of different (and subtle) flavors, all at the same time, and they give you multiple sensations when they're in your mouth, such as softness and sharpness together.

If you just drink wine, gulping it down the way you do soda, you miss a lot of what you paid for. But if you *taste* wine, you can discover its nuances. In fact, the more slowly and attentively you taste wine, the more interesting it tastes.

And with that, we have two of the fundamental rules of wine tasting:

1. Slow down.
2. Pay attention.

The appearance of the wine

We enjoy looking at the wine in our glass, noticing how brilliant it is and the way it reflects the light, trying to decide precisely which shade of red it is and whether it will stain the tablecloth permanently if we tilt the glass too far.

Most books tell you that you look at the wine to determine whether it is clear (because cloudiness generally indicates a flawed wine). That advice dates itself, though. Ever since high technology infiltrated the wine industry, visual flaws in wine are as rare as a winning lottery ticket. You could probably drink wine every night for a year without encountering a cloudy wine.

But look at the wine for a moment, anyway. Tilt your (half-full) glass away from you and look at the color of the wine against a white background, such as the tablecloth or a piece of paper (a colored background distorts the color of the wine). Just notice how dark or how pale the wine in your tilted glass is and what color it is, for the record. Eventually, you'll begin to notice differences from one wine to the next; but for now, just observe.

Tips for smelling wine

1. Be bold. Stick your nose right into the air-space of the glass where all the aromas are captured.

2. Don't wear a strong scent; it will compete with the smell of the wine.

3. Don't knock yourself out smelling a wine when there are strong food aromas around. The tomatoes you smell in the wine could really be the tomato in someone's pasta sauce.

4. Become a smeller. Smell every ingredient when you cook, everything you eat, the fresh fruits and vegetables you buy at the supermarket, even the smells of your environment — like leather, wet earth, fresh road tar, grass, flowers, your wet dog, shoe polish, and your medicine cabinet. Stuff your mental database with smells so that you'll have aroma memories at your disposal when you need to draw on them.

5. Try different techniques of sniffing. Some people like to take short, quick sniffs, while others like to inhale a deep whiff of the wine's smell. Keeping your mouth open a bit while you inhale can help you perceive aromas. (Some people even hold one nostril closed and smell with the other, but we think that's a bit kinky, especially in family restaurants.)

If you have time to kill, at this point you can also swirl the wine around in your glass (see the following section, "The nose knows") and observe the way the wine runs back down the inside of the glass. Some wines form *legs* or *tears* that flow slowly down. Once upon a time, these legs were interpreted as the sure sign of a rich, high-quality wine. Today, we know that a wine's legs are a complicated phenomenon having to do with the surface tension of the wine and the evaporation rate of the wine's alcohol. If you're a physicist, this is a good time to show off your expertise and enlighten your fellow wine tasters — but if you're not, don't bother drawing much conclusion from the legs.

The nose knows

Now we get to the really fun part of tasting wine: swirling and sniffing. This is when you can let your imagination run wild, and no one will ever dare to contradict you. If you say that a wine smells like wild strawberries to you, how can anyone prove that it doesn't?

Before we explain the smelling ritual, and the tasting technique that goes along with it (described in the next section), we want to assure you that: a) you don't have to apply this procedure to every single wine you drink; b) you won't look foolish doing it, at least in the eyes of other wine lovers (we can't speak for the other 90 percent of the human population); and c) it's a great trick at parties to avoid talking with someone you don't like.

To get the most out of your sniffing, swirl the wine in the glass first. But don't even *think* about swirling your wine if your glass is more than half full.

Keep your glass on the table and rotate it so that the wine swirls around inside the glass and air mixes with the wine. Then bring the glass to your nose quickly. Stick your nose as far as it will go into the airspace of the glass without actually touching the wine, and smell the wine. Free-associate. Is the aroma fruity, woodsy, fresh, cooked, intense, light? Your nose tires quickly, but it recovers quickly, too. Wait just a moment and try again. Listen to your friends' comments and try to find the same things they find in the smell.

You can revitalize your nose more quickly by smelling something else, like your water, a piece of bread, or your shirt sleeve — but be prepared for the odd looks you'll get from everyone around you.

As you swirl, the aromas in the wine vaporize, and you can smell them. Wine has so many *aromatic compounds* that whatever you find in the smell of a wine is probably not merely a figment of your imagination.

The point behind this whole ritual of swirling and sniffing is that what you smell should be pleasurable to you, maybe even fascinating, and that you should have fun in the process. But what if you notice a smell that you don't like?

Hang around wine geeks for a while, and you'll start to hear words like *petrol, manure, sweaty saddle, burnt match,* and *asparagus* used to describe the aromas of some wines. "Yuck!" you say? Of course you do! Fortunately, the wines that exhibit such smells are not the wines you'll be drinking for the most part — at least not unless you really catch the wine bug. And when you do catch the wine bug, you might discover that those aromas, in the right wine, can really be a kick. Even if you don't learn to enjoy those smells (some of us do, honest!), you'll appreciate them as typical characteristics of certain regions or grapes.

Wines have noses

With poetic license typical of wine tasters, someone once dubbed the smell of a wine its *nose* — and the expression took hold. If someone says that a wine has a huge nose, he means that the wine has a very strong smell. If he says that he detects lemon *in the nose* or *on the nose,* he means that the wine smells like lemons.

In fact, most wine tasters rarely use the word *smell* to describe how a wine smells because the word *smell* (like the word *odor*) seems pejorative. Wine tasters talk about the wine's nose or aroma. Sometimes they use the word *bouquet,* although that word is falling out of fashion.

Wines have palates, too

Just as a wine taster might use the term *nose* for the smell of a wine, he might use the word *palate* in referring to the taste of a wine. A wine's palate is the overall impression the wine gives in your mouth, or any isolated aspect of the wine's taste — as in "This wine has a harmonious palate," or "The palate of this wine is a bit acidic." When a wine taster says that he finds raspberries *on the palate,* he means that the wine has the flavor of raspberries.

Then there are the bad smells that nobody will try to defend. It doesn't happen often, but it does happen, because wine is a natural, agricultural product with a will of its own. Often when a wine is seriously flawed, it shows immediately in the nose of the wine. Wine judges have a term for such wines. They call them DNPIM — Do Not Put In Mouth. Not that you'll get ill, but why subject your taste buds to the same abuse that your nose just took? Sometimes it's a bad cork that's to blame, and sometimes it's some other sort of problem in the winemaking or even the storage of the wine. Just rack it up to experience and open a different bottle.

While you're choosing the next bottle, make up your own acronyms: SOTYWE (Serve Only To Your Worst Enemies) for example, or ETMYG (Enough To Make You Gag), or our own favorite, SLADDR (Smells Like A Dirty Dish Rag).

When it comes to smelling wine, many people are concerned that they aren't able to detect as many aromas as they think they should. Smelling wine is really just a matter of practice and attention. If you start to pay more attention to smells in your normal activities, you'll get better at smelling wine.

The mouth action

After you've looked at the wine and smelled it, you're finally allowed to taste it. This is when grown men and women sit around and make strange faces, gurgling the wine and sloshing it around in their mouths with looks of intense concentration in their eyes. You can make an enemy for life if you distract a wine taster just at the moment when he is focusing all his energy on the last few drops of a special wine.

Here's how the procedure goes. Take a medium-sized sip of wine. Hold it in your mouth, purse your lips, and draw in some air across your tongue, over the wine. (Be utterly careful not to choke or dribble, or everyone will strongly suspect that you're not a wine expert.) Then swish the wine around in your mouth as if you are chewing it. Then swallow it. The whole process should take several seconds, depending on how much you are concentrating on the wine. (Wondering what to concentrate on? The next two sections tell you, along with the section "Parlez-Vous Winespeak?" later in this chapter.)

Feeling the tastes

Different parts of the tongue specialize in registering different sensations; sweetness is perceived most keenly on the front of the tongue, sourness is triggered principally on the sides, and bitterness is detected particularly across the rear of the tongue. (The tongue can also detect saltiness, but that taste is uncommon in wine.) By moving the wine around in your mouth, you give it a chance to hit all of these places so that you don't miss anything in the wine (even if sourness and bitterness sound like things you wouldn't mind missing).

As you swish the wine around in your mouth, you are also buying time. Your brain needs a few seconds to figure out what the tongue is tasting and make some sense of it. Any sweetness in the wine registers in your brain first because the sensation of sweetness corresponds to the first place the wine hits in your mouth; the *acidity* registers next (acidity, by the way, is what normal people call sourness), and then the bitterness. While your brain is working out the relative impressions of sweetness, acidity, and bitterness, you can be thinking about how the wine feels in your mouth — whether it's heavy, light, smooth, rough, and so on.

Tasting the smells

Until you cut your nose in on the action, that's all you can taste in the wine — those three sensations of sweetness, acidity, and bitterness and a general impression of weight and texture. Where have all the wild strawberries gone?

Ten aromas (or flavors) associated with wine

1. Fruits
2. Herbs
3. Vegetables
4. Earth
5. Flowers

6. Grass
7. Tobacco
8. Toast
9. Smoke
10. Coffee, mocha, or chocolate

Ten odors not associated with wine

1. Paint
2. New car
3. Fax paper
4. Glue
5. Gorgonzola

6. Cannabis
7. Magic Marker
8. Elephant dung
9. Chanel No. 5
10. Fabric softener

They're still there in the wine, right next to the chocolate and plums. But — to be perfectly correct about it — these flavors are actually *aromas* that you taste, not through tongue contact, but by inhaling them up an interior nasal passage in the back of your mouth called the *retronasal passage* (see Figure 2-1). When you draw in air across the wine in your mouth, you are vaporizing the aromas just as you did when you swirled the wine in your glass. (There's a method to this madness.)

Figure 2-1: Most wine flavors are actually aromas that vaporize in your mouth; you perceive them through the rear nasal passage.

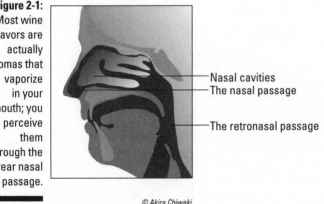

Nasal cavities
The nasal passage

The retronasal passage

© Akira Chiwaki

After you go through all this rigmarole, it's time to reach a conclusion: Do you like what you tasted? The possible answers are yes, no, an indifferent shrug of the shoulders, or "I'm not sure, let me take another taste," which means that you have serious wine-nerd potential.

Parlez-Vous Winespeak?

Now we have to confess that there is one step between knowing how to taste wine and always drinking wine that you like. And it's a doozy. That step is putting taste into words.

We wouldn't have to bother with this detail if only we could choose our wines the way that customers choose cheese in a gourmet shop. ("Can I try that one? No, I don't like it; let me taste the one next to it. Good. I'll take half a pound.")

"Like/Don't Like" is a no-brainer once you have the wine in your mouth. But most of the time you have to buy the stuff without tasting it first. So unless you want to drink the same wine for the rest of your life, you're going to have to decide what it is that you like or don't like in a wine and communicate that to another person who can steer you in the right direction.

There are two hurdles here: Finding the words to describe what you like or don't like, and then getting the other person to understand what you mean. Naturally, it helps if we all speak the same language.

Unfortunately, Winespeak is a dialect with an undisciplined and sometimes poetic vocabulary whose definitions change all the time, depending on who is speaking. In case you really want to get into this wine thing, we treat you to some sophisticated wine language in Chapters 5 and 19. For now, a few basic words and concepts should do the trick.

The tastes of a wine actually reveal themselves sequentially as the tongue detects them. We recommend that you follow this natural sequence when you try to put words to what you're tasting.

Sweetness

Right there, on the tip of your tongue, as soon as you put the wine into your mouth, you can notice sweetness or the lack of it. In Winespeak, *dry* is the opposite of sweet. Classify the wine you're tasting as either *dry, off-dry* (in other words, somewhat sweet), or *sweet.*

Acidity

All wine contains acid (mainly *tartaric acid,* which exists in grapes), but some wines are more acidic than others. Acidity is more of a taste factor in white wines than in reds. For white wines, acidity is the backbone of the wine's taste

TIP

Is it sweetness or fruitiness?

Beginning wine tasters sometimes describe dry wines as sweet because they confuse fruitiness with sweetness. A wine is *fruity* when it has distinct aromas and flavors of fruit. You smell the fruitiness with your nose; in your mouth, you "smell" it through your retronasal passage.

Sweetness, on the other hand, is a tactile impression on your tongue. When in doubt, try holding your nose when you taste the wine; if the wine really is sweet, you'll be able to taste the sweetness despite the fact that you can't smell the fruitiness.

(it gives the wine firmness and structure in your mouth). White wines with a good amount of acidity taste *crisp*, and those without enough acidity taste *fat* and *flabby*. The sides of the tongue trigger your perception of acidity. You can also sense the consequences of acidity (or the lack of it) in the overall style of the wine — whether it's a tart little number or a soft and generous sort, for example. Classify the wine you're tasting as *tart, crisp, soft,* or "couch potato."

Tannin

Tannin is a substance that exists naturally in the skins, seeds (or *pips*), and stems of grapes. Because red wines are fermented with their grape skins and pips, tannin levels are far higher in red wines than in white wines. Oak barrels can also contribute tannin to wines. Have you ever taken a sip of a red wine and rapidly experienced a drying-out feeling in your mouth, as if someone had shoved a blotter in there? That's tannin.

To generalize a bit, tannin is to a red wine what acidity is to a white: a backbone. Because tannin sometimes tastes bitter, you sense tannin near the back of your tongue, but you can detect it elsewhere, too — on the inside of your cheeks and between your cheeks and gums — if the amount of tannin in a wine is high. Depending on the amount and nature of its tannin, a red wine can be called *astringent, firm,* or *soft*.

Body

A wine's body is an impression you get from the whole of the wine — not at any one place on your tongue. It's the impression of the weight and size of the wine in your mouth, which is usually attributable principally to a wine's alcohol. We say "impression" because, obviously, one ounce of any wine will occupy exactly the same space in your mouth and weigh the same as one ounce of any other wine. But some wines *seem* fuller, bigger, or heavier in the mouth than others. Think about the wine's fullness and weight as you taste it. Don't tell your friends that you're doing this, but imagine that your tongue is a tiny postal scale and judge how much the wine is weighing it down. Classify the wine as *light-bodied, medium-bodied,* or *full-bodied.*

Flavors

Wines have flavors (er, we mean *mouth aromas*), but wines don't come in a specific flavor. While you might enjoy the suggestion of chocolate in a red wine that you're tasting, you wouldn't want to go to a wine store and ask for a chocolatey wine, unless you don't mind the idea of people holding their hands over their mouths and trying not to laugh aloud at you.

Instead, you should refer to *families of flavors* in wine. There are your *fruity wines* (the ones that make you think of all sorts of fruit when you smell them or hold the wine in your mouth), your *earthy wines* (these make you think of mushrooms, walks in the forest, turning the earth in your garden, dry leaves, and so on), your *spicy wines* (cinnamon, cloves, black pepper, or Indian spices, for example), your *herbal wines* (mint, grass, hay, rosemary, and so on), and so on, and so on. There are so many flavors in wine that we could go on and on (and we often do!), but you get the picture, don't you?

If you like a wine and want to try another wine that's similar but different (and it will always be different, we guarantee you), one method is to decide what families of flavors in the wine you like and mention that to the person selling you your next bottle. In Part III, you'll find wines that fit these specific flavors.

Touchy-feely

Softness and firmness are actually *textural impressions* a wine gives you as you taste it. Just as your mouth feels temperature in a liquid, it feels texture. Some wines literally *feel* soft and smooth in your mouth, while others feel hard, rough, or coarse. In white wines, acid is usually responsible for impressions of hardness or firmness (or crispness); in red wines, tannin is usually responsible. Low levels of either substance can make a wine feel pleasantly soft — or too soft, depending on the wine and your taste preferences. Unfermented sugar also contributes to an impression of softness, and alcohol can, too. But very high alcohol — which is fairly common in wines these days — can give a wine an edge of hardness.

Is it acid or tannin?

Red wines have acid as well as tannin, and distinguishing between the two as you taste a wine can be a real challenge. When you're not sure whether it's mainly tannin or acid you're perceiving, pay attention to how your mouth feels *after* you've swallowed the wine. Both tannin and acid will make your mouth feel dry, but acid makes you salivate in response to the dry feeling (saliva is alkaline, and it neutralizes the acid). Tannin just leaves your mouth dry.

Now you have 13 words — and a whole community of families — that allow you to explain what kind of wine you like. (If you're superstitious, consider *couch* and *potato* as separate words, and you have 14.) In Chapter 19, we elaborate on Winespeak and show you how to describe a wine as *round and supple, regal but unpretentious, gutsy yet not overbearing.*

The Quality Issue: What's a Good Wine?

Did you notice, by any chance, that nowhere on the list of terms we use to describe wines are the words *great, very good,* or *good*? Instead of worrying about crisp wines, earthy wines, and medium-bodied wines, wouldn't it just be easier to walk into a wine shop and say, "Give me a very good wine for dinner tonight"? Isn't *quality* the ultimate issue — or at least, quality within your price range, also known as *value?*

Well, quality is so important that, our cats will tell you with some embarrassment, we sometimes argue at the dinner table about the quality of the wine we're drinking. It's not that we don't know a great wine when we find one; in fact, we usually agree on whether the wine we are drinking is good. What we debate is *how* good the wine is or isn't — because it's a matter of personal taste.

The instruments that measure the quality of a wine are a human being's nose and mouth, and because we're all different, we all have different opinions on how good a wine is. The combined opinion of a group of trained, experienced palates (also known as wine experts) is usually considered a definitive judgment of a wine's quality. (Turn to "Rating Wine Quality" in Chapter 19 for more about expert opinion.) But there's no guarantee that you will *like* the wine that the experts agree is very good. We've purchased highly rated wines and ended up pouring them down the sink because we didn't think they were very good at all.

We know it sounds like we're describing some kind of anarchy here, with everyone deciding for himself what's good and what isn't. But that's the way it is. When the primary purpose of a wine is to taste good, the person tasting the wine is the only one who can decide whether a particular wine works.

Of course, there are degrees of good and bad. Our old clunker worked when it got us where we were going, but it probably wasn't considered a good car because we felt every bump in the road. Somewhere along the way, someone established quality standards for cars that say that the best cars are quiet, ride smoothly, and are easy to steer — and ours wasn't.

Quality standards exist for wine, too. What's frustrating is that there's no Detroit testing ground where scientific instruments can measure each wine against these quality standards. The measurement rests with your own palate.

So, what's a good wine? It is, above all, a wine that you like enough to drink. After that, how good a wine is depends on how it measures up to a set of (more or less) agreed-upon standards of performance established by experienced, trained experts. These standards involve mysterious concepts like *balance, length, depth, complexity,* and *trueness to type* (*typicity* in Winespeak, *typicité* in Snobwinespeak). None of these concepts are objectively measurable, by the way.

Balance

Three words we talk about in the "Parlez-Vous Winespeak?" section in this chapter — sweetness, acidity, and tannin — represent three of the major *components* (parts) of wine. The fourth is alcohol. Besides being one of the reasons we usually want to drink a glass of wine in the first place, alcohol is an important element of wine quality.

Balance in action

For firsthand experience of how the principle of taste balance works, try this. Make a very strong cup of tea. When you sip it, the tea will taste bitter, because it's very tannic. Now add lemon juice; the tea will taste astringent (constricting and drying out your mouth), because the acid of the lemon and the tannin of the tea are accentuating each other. Now add lots of sugar to the tea. The sweetness should counterbalance the acid–tannin impact, and the tea will taste softer than it did before.

Balance is the relationship of these four components to one another. A wine is balanced when nothing sticks out as you taste it, like harsh tannin or too much sweetness. Most wines are balanced to most people. But if you have any pet peeves about food — if you really hate anything tart, for example, or if you never eat sweets — you might perceive some wines to be unbalanced. If you perceive them to be unbalanced, then they are unbalanced for you. (Professional tasters know their own idiosyncrasies and adjust for them when they judge wine.)

Tannin and acidity are *hardening elements* in a wine (they make a wine taste firmer in the mouth), while alcohol and sugar (if any) are *softening elements*. The balance of a wine is the interrelationship of the hard and the soft aspects of a wine, and a key indicator of quality.

Length

When we call wines *long* or *short,* we're not referring to the size of the bottle or how quickly we empty it. *Length* is a word used to describe a wine that goes all the way on the palate — you can taste it across the full length of your tongue — and doesn't stop short halfway through your tasting of it. A wine with good length hits all the taste centers on your tongue. Many wines today are very up-front on the palate — they make a big impression as soon as you taste them — but they are short. Length is a sure sign of quality.

Depth

This is another subjective, unmeasurable attribute of a high-quality wine. We say a wine has *depth* when it does not taste flat and one-dimensional in your mouth but instead seems to have underlying layers of taste. A flat wine can never be great.

Complexity

There's nothing wrong with a simple, straightforward wine any more than there's something wrong with Homer Simpson — both are just what they are. But a wine that keeps revealing different things about itself, always showing you a new flavor or impression — a wine that has *complexity* — is usually considered better quality. Some experts use the term *complexity* specifically to indicate that a wine has a multiplicity of aromas and flavors, while others use it in a more holistic sense, to refer to the total impression a wine gives you.

Finish

The impression a wine leaves in the back of your mouth and in your throat after you have swallowed it is its *finish* or *aftertaste*. In a good wine, you can still perceive the wine's flavors — such as fruitiness or spiciness — at that point. Some wines might finish *hot,* because of high alcohol, or *bitter,* because of tannin — both shortcomings. Or a wine might have nothing much at all to say for itself after you swallow.

Typicity

In order to judge whether a wine is true to its type, you have to know how that type is supposed to be. So you have to know the textbook characteristics of wines made from the major grape varieties and wines of the world's classic wine regions. (For example, the Cabernet Sauvignon grape typically has an aroma and flavor of blackcurrants, and the French white wine called Pouilly-Fumé typically has a slight gunflint aroma.) Turn to Chapter 3 and Chapters 10 through 16 for all those details.

What's a Bad Wine?

Strangely enough, the right to declare a wine "good" just because you like it does not carry with it the right to call a wine "bad" just because you don't. In this game, you get to make your own rules, but you don't get to force other people to live by them.

The fact is there are very few bad wines in the world today compared to even 20 years ago. And many of the wines we could call bad are actually just bad *bottles* of wine — bottles that were handled badly, so that the good wine inside them got ruined.

Here are some characteristics that everyone agrees indicate a bad wine. Let's hope you never meet one. You might not.

- ✔ **Moldy fruit:** Have you ever eaten a raspberry from the bottom of the container that had a dusty, cardboardy taste to it? That same taste of rot can be in a wine if the wine was made from grapes that were not completely fresh and healthy when they were harvested. Bad wine.

- ✔ **Vinegar:** In the natural evolution of things, wine is just a pit stop between grape juice and vinegar. Most wines today remain forever in the wine stage because of technology or careful winemaking. If you find a wine that has crossed the line toward vinegar, it's bad wine.

- ✔ **Chemical or bacterial smells:** The most common are acetone (nail polish thinner) and sulfur flaws (rotten eggs, burnt rubber, bad garlic). Bad wines.

- ✔ **Oxidized wine:** This wine smells flat, weak, or maybe cooked, and it tastes the same. It might have been a good wine once, but air — oxygen — got in somehow and killed the wine. Bad bottle.

- ✔ **Cooked aromas and taste:** When a wine has been stored or shipped in heat, it can actually taste cooked or baked as a result. Often there's tell-tale leakage from the cork, or the cork is pushed up a little. Bad bottle. (Unfortunately, every other bottle of that wine that experienced the same shipping or storage will also be bad.)

- ✔ **Corky wine:** The most common flaw, *corkiness* comes across as a smell of damp cardboard that gets worse with air. It's caused by a bad cork, and even the best wines in the world are not immune to it. Bad bottle.

The Final Analysis: Do You Like It?

Let's not dwell too long on what can go wrong with a wine. If you find a bad wine or a bad bottle — or even a wine that is considered a good wine, but you don't like it — just move on to something you like better. Drinking a so-called great wine that you don't enjoy is as stupid as watching foreign films that bore you. Change the channel. Explore.

Chapter 3

Pinot Envy and Other Secrets about Grape Varieties

In This Chapter

▶ Descriptions of major grape varieties and their wines

▶ Genus, species, variety, clone, and other grape terms

▶ Endangered species and mixed marriages

▶ Soils that grapes love

*W*e love to visit wine country — which for us means "anywhere in the world where vineyards are." Gazing across manicured rows of grapevines in Napa Valley or pondering craggy terraces of rugged vines on the hillsides of Portugal inspires us — and reinforces for us the fact that wine is an agricultural product, born of the earth, the grapevine, and the hard work of humans. Literally and emotionally, grapes are the link between the land and the wine.

Grapes also happen to give us one of the easiest ways of classifying wine and making sense of the hundreds of different types of wine that exist.

It's the Grape Whodunit

If anyone were to invent a mystery game about wine, it would probably be a big flop because there's no real mystery in knowing what makes most wines taste the way they do. The grapes done it. With Mother Nature and a wine-maker as accomplices, the grapes are responsible for the style and personality of every wine, and sometimes the quality, because they are the starting point of the wine. The grapes dictate the genetic structure of a wine and how it will respond to everything that is done to it.

Think back to the last wine you drank. What color was it? If it was white, the odds are that's because it came from white grapes; if it was pink or red, that's because the wine came from red grapes.

Did it smell herbal or earthy or fruity? Whichever, those aromas came from the grapes. Was it firm and tannic or soft and voluptuous? Thank the grapes (with a nod to their co-conspirators, Nature and the winemaker).

The specific grape variety (or varieties) that makes any given wine is largely responsible for the sensory characteristics the wine offers — from its appearance to its aromas, its flavors, and its alcohol–tannin–acid profile.

Of genus and species

By *grape variety,* we mean the fruit of a specific type of grapevine: the fruit of the Cabernet Sauvignon vine, for example, or of the Chardonnay vine.

The term *variety* actually has specific meaning in scientific circles. A variety is a subdivision of a species. Most of the world's wines are made from grape varieties that belong to the species *vinifera* — itself a subdivision of the genus *Vitis.* This species originated in Europe and western Asia; other distinct species of *Vitis* are native to North America.

Grapes of other species can also make wine; for example, the Concord grape, which makes Concord wine as well as grape juice and jelly, belongs to the native American species *Vitis labrusca.* But the grapes of this species have a very different flavor from vinifera grapes — *foxy* is the word used to describe that taste. The number of non-vinifera wines is small because their flavor is unpopular in wine.

A variety of varieties

Snowflakes and fingerprints aren't the only examples of Nature's infinite variety. Within the genus *Vitis* and the species *vinifera,* there are as many as 10,000 varieties of wine grapes. If wine from every one of these varieties were commercially available and you drank the wine of a different variety every single day, it would take you more than 27 years to experience them all!

Not that you would want to. Within those 10,000 varieties are grapes that have the ability to make extraordinary wine, grapes that tend to make very ordinary wine, and grapes that only a parent could love. Most varieties are obscure grapes whose wines rarely enter into international commerce.

The phylloxera threat

If endangered species lists had existed at the end of the nineteenth century, *Vitis vinifera* certainly would have been on them. The entire species was nearly eradicated by a tiny louse called *phylloxera* that immigrated to Europe from America and proceeded to feast on the roots of vinifera grapevines, wiping out vineyards across the continent.

To this day, no remedy has been found to protect vinifera roots from phylloxera. What saved the species was grafting vinifera vines onto rootstocks of native American species that are resistant to the bug. The practice of grafting the fruit-bearing part of *Vitis vinifera* onto the rooting part of other, phylloxera-resistant species continues today everywhere in the world where phylloxera is present and fine wine is made. (The fruit-bearing part is called a *scion,* and the rooting plant is called a *rootstock.*) Miraculously, each grape variety maintains its own character despite the fact that its roots are alien.

An extremely adventuresome grape nut who has plenty of free time to explore the back roads of Spain, Portugal, Italy, and Greece might be able to encounter 1,500 different grape varieties (only four years' worth of drinking) in his lifetime. The grape varieties you might encounter in the course of your normal wine enjoyment probably number fewer than 50.

How the grape done it

All sorts of attributes distinguish each grape variety from the next. These attributes fall into two categories: personality traits and performance factors. *Personality traits* are the characteristics of the fruit itself — its flavors, for example. *Performance factors* refer to how the grapevine grows, how its fruit ripens, and how quickly it can get from 0 to 60 miles per hour. Both types of characteristics affect the ultimate taste and style of wines made from a specific grape variety.

Personality traits of grape varieties

Skin color is the most fundamental distinction among grape varieties. Every grape variety is considered either a white variety or a red (or "black") one, according to the color of its skins when the grapes are ripe. (A few red-skinned varieties are further distinguished by having red pulp rather than white pulp.)

Individual grape varieties also differ from one another in other ways.

- ✔ **Aromatic compounds:** Some grapes (like Muscat) contribute floral aromas and flavors to their wine, for example, while other grapes contribute herbaceous notes (as Sauvignon Blanc does) or fruity character. Some grapes have very neutral aromas and flavors and, therefore, make fairly neutral wines.

- ✔ **Acidity levels:** Some grapes are naturally disposed to higher acid levels than others, which influences the wine made from those grapes.

- ✔ **Thickness of skin and size of the individual grapes (called *berries*):** Black grapes with thick skins naturally have more tannin than grapes with thin skins; ditto for small-berried varieties compared to large-berried varieties, because their skin-to-juice ratio is higher. More tannin in the grapes translates into a firmer, more tannic red wine.

The composite personality traits of any grape variety are fairly evident in wines made from that grape. A Cabernet Sauvignon wine is almost always more tannic and slightly lower in alcohol than a Merlot wine, for example, because that's the nature of those two grapes.

Performance factors of grape varieties

The performance factors that distinguish grape varieties are vitally important to the grape grower because those factors determine how easy or challenging it will be for him to cultivate a specific variety in his vineyard — if he can even grow it at all. The issues include

- ✔ How much time a variety typically needs to ripen its grapes. (In regions with short summers, early-ripening varieties do best.)

- ✔ How dense and compact the bunches of grapes are. (In warm, damp climates, grape varieties with dense bunches can have mildew problems.)

- ✔ How much vegetation a particular variety tends to grow. (In fertile soils, a vine that's disposed to grow lots of leaves and shoots could have so much vegetation that the grapes don't get enough sun to ripen.)

How grapes ripen

When grapes are not yet ripe, they contain high amounts of acid and very little sugar — which is true for any fruit — and their flavor is tart. As ripening progresses, they become sweeter and less acidic (although they always retain some acid), and their flavors become richer and more complex. Their skins get thinner, and even their seeds and stems "ripen," sometimes changing color from green to brown. In red grape varieties, the tannin in the skins, stems, and pips becomes richer and less astringent. Because grapes are the raw material of wine, the stage of ripeness that the grapes attain by harvest time dictates the style of the wine.

Chardonnay, do you take this limestone soil?

One important factor in how a grape variety performs is the soil in the vineyard. Over the centuries, some classic compatibilities between grape varieties and types of soil have become evident: Chardonnay in limestone or chalk, Cabernet Sauvignon in gravelly soil, Pinot Noir in limestone, and Riesling in slatey soil. At any rate, these are the soils of the regions where these grape varieties perform at their legendary best.

Soil affects a grapevine in several ways (besides simply anchoring the vine): It provides nutrition for the grapevine; it can influence the temperature of the vineyard; and it is a water-management system for the plant.

A safe generalization is that the best soils are those that have good drainage and are not particularly fertile. (An extreme example is the soil — if we can call it that — of the Châteauneuf-du-Pape district in France's Rhône Valley: It's just stones.) The wisdom of the ages dictates that the grapevine must struggle to produce the best grapes — and well-drained, less fertile soils challenge the vine to struggle, regardless of what variety the grapevine is.

The reasons some grape varieties perform brilliantly in certain places (and make excellent wine as a result) are so complex that grape growers haven't figured them all out yet. The amount of heat and cold, the amount of wind and rain (or lack of it), and the slant of the sun's rays on a hillside of vines are among the factors affecting a vine's performance. In any case, no two vineyards in the world have precisely the same combination of these factors — precisely the same *terroir* (see Chapter 4). The issue simply defies simple generalizations.

Like grape, like wine

There are things a winemaker can do to change the nature of his grape juice, and therefore his wine — to an extent. In places where it's legal, he can add acid to the juice if the grapes are too ripe, for example, or add sugar to the juice if the grapes aren't ripe enough. (That added sugar will ferment into alcohol.) If he decides to put the juice or wine into oak barrels, he can create oaky aromas and flavors in the wine that go beyond what the grapes themselves brought to the table.

But for the most part, what the grapes give is what the wine is. The personality traits of each grape variety, tempered by its performance wherever it's grown, more or less define the nature of each wine.

Grape Royalty and Commoners

Bees have their queens, wolves have their alpha males, gorillas have their silverbacks, and humans have their royal families. In the grape kingdom, there are nobles, too — at least as interpreted by the human beings who drink the wine made from those grapes.

Noble grape varieties (as wine people call them) have the potential to make great — not just good — wine. Every noble grape variety can claim at least one wine region where it is the undisputed king. The wines made from noble grapes on their home turf can be so great that they inspire winemakers in far-flung regions to grow the same grape in their own vineyards. The noble grape might prove itself noble there, too — but frequently the grape does not. Adaptability is not a prerequisite of nobility.

Classic examples of noble grape varieties at their best are

- The Chardonnay grape and the Pinot Noir grape in Burgundy, France
- The Cabernet Sauvignon grape in Bordeaux, France
- The Syrah grape in France's Northern Rhône Valley
- The Chenin Blanc grape in France's Loire Valley
- The Nebbiolo grape in Piedmont, Italy
- The Sangiovese grape in Tuscany, Italy
- The Riesling grape in the Mosel and Rheingau regions of Germany

Cloning the perfect grapevine

If you hang around wine people long enough, you're sure to hear them talk about *clones* or *clonal selection* of grape varieties. Has the Brave New World of grape growing arrived?

Not really. In botanical terms, a *clone* is a subdivision of a variety. Remember all those things we said about how every grape variety is different from the next? Well, individuality doesn't end with the grape variety. Even within a single variety, such as Chardonnay, there can be differences from one plant to the next. Some vines ripen their fruit slightly more quickly, for example, or produce grapes with slightly different aromas and flavors than the next vine.

Nurseries usually propagate grapevines asexually, by taking cuttings from a *mother plant* and allowing those cuttings to root (until the new plant is mature enough to be grafted onto a phylloxera-resistant rootstock). The new plants are genetically identical to the mother plant. Naturally, grape growers or nursery managers choose the most ideal plants (in terms of ripening, fruit flavor, disease resistance, heartiness — or whatever it is they're looking for) to use as the mother plants. Voilá! They have made a clonal selection.

A Primer on White Grape Varieties

This section includes descriptions of the 12 most important white *vinifera* varieties today. In describing the grapes, naturally we describe the types of wine that are made from each grape. These wines could be varietal wines, or place-name wines that don't mention the grape variety anywhere on the label (a common practice for European wines; see Chapter 4). These grapes could also be blending partners for other grapes, in wines made from multiple grape varieties. (Turn to Chapter 2 for a quick review of some of the descriptors we use in this section.)

Chardonnay

Today's darling white grape, Chardonnay, is quite a regal grape, producing the greatest dry white wines in the world — white Burgundies. Chardonnay is also one of the main grapes of Champagne.

The Chardonnay grape grows in practically every wine-producing country of the world, for two reasons: It's relatively adaptable to a wide range of climates; and the name Chardonnay on a wine label is, these days, a sure-fire sales tool.

Because the flavors of Chardonnay are very compatible with those of oak — and because white Burgundy (the great prototype) is generally an oaked wine, and because many wine drinkers love the flavor of oak — most Chardonnay wine receives some oak treatment either during or after fermentation. (For the best Chardonnays, oak treatment means expensive barrels of French oak; but for lower-priced Chardonnays it could mean soaking oak chips in the wine or even adding liquid essence of oak. See Chapter 5 for more on oak.) Except for Northeastern Italy and France's Chablis and Mâconnais districts, where oak is usually not used for Chardonnay, oaky Chardonnay wine is the norm and unoaked Chardonnay is the exception.

Oaked Chardonnay is so common that some wine drinkers confuse the flavor of oak with the flavor of Chardonnay. If your glass of Chardonnay smells or tastes toasty, smoky, spicy, vanilla-like, or butterscotch-like, that's the oak you're perceiving, not the Chardonnay!

Chardonnay itself has fruity aromas and flavors that range from apple — in cooler wine regions — to tropical fruits, especially pineapple, in warmer regions. Chardonnay also can display subtle earthy aromas, such as mushroom or minerals. Chardonnay wine has medium to high acidity and is generally full-bodied. Classically, Chardonnay wines are dry. But most inexpensive Chardonnays these days are actually a bit sweet.

Aliases and a.k.a.'s

The same grape variety will often go by different names in different countries or even in different districts within the same country. Often it's just a case of traditional local synonyms. But sometimes, grape growers call one variety by the name of another because they think that's what they're growing (until a specialized botanist called an *ampelographer* examines their vines and tells them otherwise). In California, for example, some of the so-called Pinot Blanc is really another grape entirely: the Melon de Bourgogne. In Chile, much of what grape growers call Merlot is really the Carmenère grape — while in the Friuli region of Italy, some of what is called Cabernet Franc is actually Carmenère.

For more tales of viticultural intrigue, read Jancis Robinson's classic book on grape varieties, *Vines, Grapes and Wines* (Alfred A. Knopf), an indispensable and fascinating reference.

Chardonnay is a grape that can stand on its own in a wine, and the top Chardonnay-based wines (except for Champagne and similar bubblies) are 100 percent Chardonnay. But less expensive wines that are labeled *Chardonnay* — those selling for less than $8 a bottle in the U.S., for example — are likely to have some other, far less distinguished grape blended in. That's because blending in wine from an ordinary grape like Colombard helps reduce the cost of making the wine. Anyway, it's perfectly legal. And who can even tell if it's all Chardonnay or not, behind all that oak?

Riesling

The great Riesling wines of Germany have put the Riesling grape on the charts as an undisputedly noble variety. Riesling shows its real class only in a few places outside of Germany, however. The Alsace region of France, Austria, and the Finger Lakes district of New York are among the few.

Riesling wines are as unpopular today as Chardonnay is popular. Maybe that's because Riesling is the antithesis of Chardonnay. While Chardonnay is usually gussied up with oak, Riesling never is; while Chardonnay can be full-bodied and rich, Riesling is more often light-bodied and refreshing. Riesling's fresh, vivid personality can make many Chardonnays taste clumsy in comparison.

The common perception of Riesling wines is that they are sweet, and many of them are — but plenty of them aren't. Alsace Rieslings are normally dry, many German Rieslings are dry, and a few American Rieslings are dry. (Riesling can be vinified either way, according to the style of wine a producer wants to make.) Look for the word *trocken* (meaning dry) on German Riesling labels and the word *dry* on American labels if you prefer the dry style of Riesling.

High acidity, low to medium alcohol levels, and aromas/flavors that range from ebulliently fruity to flowery to minerally are trademarks of Riesling.

Riesling wines are sometimes labeled as *White Riesling* or *Johannisberg Riesling* — both synonyms for the noble Riesling grape. With wines from Eastern European countries, though, read the fine print: Olazrizling, Laskirizling, and Welschriesling are from another grape altogether.

If you consider yourself a maverick that hates to follow trends, check out the Riesling section of your wine shop instead of the Chardonnay aisle.

Sauvignon Blanc

While just about everybody likes Chardonnay, Sauvignon Blanc is controversial with wine drinkers. That's because it has such distinctive character.

For one thing, Sauvignon Blanc is high in acidity — great if you like crisp wines, but not so great otherwise. For another thing, its aromas and flavors can be herbaceous (suggestive of herbs or grass) — delicious and intriguing to some wine lovers, but too weird for others.

Sauvignon Blanc wines are light-bodied to medium-bodied and usually dry. European versions are unoaked more often than oaked, but in California the wines can be oaky and not fully dry — in the Chardonnay-wannabe style. Besides herbaceous character (sometimes referred to as *grassy*), Sauvignon Blanc wines display mineral aromas and flavors, vegetal character, or — in certain climates — fruity character, such as ripe melon, figs, or passion fruit.

France has two classic wine regions for the Sauvignon Blanc grape: Bordeaux and the Loire Valley. The Bordeaux wine is called Bordeaux Blanc (white Bordeaux), and the two best known of the Loire wines are called Sancerre or Pouilly-Fumé (all described in Chapter 10). In Bordeaux, Sauvignon Blanc is sometimes blended with Sémillon (described in Table 3-1); some of the wines that are blended about 50–50 from the two grapes are among the great white wines of the world. Sauvignon Blanc is also important in New Zealand, Northeastern Italy, South Africa, and parts of California.

Pinot Gris/Pinot Grigio

Pinot Gris (*gree*) is one of several grape varieties called *Pinot:* There's Pinot Blanc (white Pinot), Pinot Noir (black Pinot), Pinot Meunier (we don't know how that one translates), and Pinot Gris (gray Pinot), which is called *Pinot Grigio* in Italian. Pinot Gris is believed to have mutated from the black Pinot Noir grape. Although it's considered a white grape, its skin color is unusually dark for a white variety.

Wines made from Pinot Gris can be deeper in color than most white wines — although Italy's Pinot Grigio wines are quite pale. Pinot Gris wines are medium- to full-bodied, with rather low acidity and fairly neutral aromas. Sometimes the flavor and aroma can suggest the skins of fruit, such as peach skins or orange rind.

Pinot Gris is an important grape throughout Northeastern Italy and also grows in Germany, where it is called Ruländer. The only region in France where Pinot Gris is important is in Alsace, where it really struts its stuff. Oregon has had good success with Pinot Gris, and more and more winemakers in California are now taking a shot at it.

Other white grapes

Table 3-1 describes some other grapes whose names you see on wine labels, or whose wine you could drink in place-name wines without realizing it.

Table 3-1	Other White Grapes and Their Characteristics
Grape Type	*Characteristics*
Albariño	An aromatic grape from the northwestern corner of Spain — the wine region called Rias Baixas — and Portugal's northerly Vinho Verde region, where it's called *Alvarinho.* It makes medium-bodied, crisp, unoaked, appley-tasting white wines whose high glycerine gives them silky texture.
Chenin Blanc	A noble grape in the Loire Valley of France, for Vouvray and other wines. The best wines have high acidity and a fascinating oily texture (they feel rather viscous in your mouth). Some good dry Chenin Blanc comes from California, but so does a ton of ordinary off-dry wine. In South Africa, Chenin Blanc is often called *Steen.*
Gewürztraminer *(geh-VAIRTZ-trah-mee-ner)*	A wonderfully exotic grape that makes fairly deep-colored, full-bodied, soft white wines with aromas and flavors of roses and lychee fruit. France's Alsace region is the classic domain of this variety; the wines have pronounced floral and fruity aromas and flavors, but are actually dry — as fascinating as they are delicious. The most commercial style of U.S. Gewürztraminer is light, sweetish, and relatively insipid, but a few wineries in California, Oregon, and New York do make good, dry Gewürztraminer.

Grape Type	*Characteristics*
Grüner Veltliner	A native Austrian variety that boasts complex aromas and flavors (vegetal, spicy, mineral), rich texture, and usually substantial weight.
Muscat	An aromatic grape that makes Italy's sparkling Asti (which, incidentally, tastes *exactly* like ripe Muscat grapes). Extremely pretty floral aromas. In Alsace and Austria, makes a dry wine, and in lots of places (southern France, southern Italy, Australia) makes a delicious, sweet dessert wine through the addition of alcohol.
Pinot Blanc	Fairly neutral in aroma and flavors, yet can make characterful wines. High acidity and low sugar levels translate into dry, crisp, medium-bodied wines. Alsace, Austria, northern Italy, and Germany are the main production zones.
Sémillon *(seh-mee-yohn)*	Sauvignon Blanc's classic blending partner and a good grape in its own right. Sémillon wine is relatively low in acid (compared to Sauvignon Blanc, anyway) and has attractive but subtle aromas — lanolin sometimes, although it can be slightly herbaceous when young. A major grape in Australia, and southwestern France, including Bordeaux (where it is the key player in Sauternes).
Viognier (vee-ohn-yay)	A grape from France's Rhône Valley that's becoming popular in California and the south of France. Floral aroma, delicately apricot-like, medium- to full-bodied with low acidity.

A Primer on Red Grape Varieties

Here are descriptions of 12 important red vinifera grape varieties. You'll encounter these grapes in varietal wines and also in place-name wines. See Chapter 4 for a chart listing the grape varieties of major place-name wines.

Cabernet Sauvignon

Cabernet Sauvignon is not only a noble grape variety but also an adaptable one, growing well in just about any climate that isn't very cool. It became famous through the ageworthy red wines of the Médoc district of Bordeaux (which usually also contain Merlot and Cabernet Franc, in varying proportions; see Chapter 10). But today California is an equally important region for Cabernet Sauvignon — not to mention Washington, southern France, Italy, Australia, South Africa, Chile, Argentina, and so on.

The Cabernet Sauvignon grape makes wines that are high in tannin and are medium- to full-bodied. The textbook descriptor for Cabernet Sauvignon's aroma and flavor is *blackcurrants* or *cassis;* the grape can also contribute vegetal tones to a wine when or where the grapes are less than ideally ripe.

Like Chardonnay, Cabernet Sauvignon grows well in many different wine regions. As a result, Cabernet Sauvignon wines come in all price and quality levels, from numerous countries. The least-expensive versions are usually quite soft and nondescriptly fruity (not specifically blackcurrants), with medium body at best. The best wines are rich and firm with great depth and classic Cabernet flavor. Serious Cabernet Sauvignons can age for 15 years or more.

Because Cabernet Sauvignon is fairly tannic (and because of the blending precedent in Bordeaux), it is often blended with other grapes; usually Merlot — being less tannic — is considered an ideal partner. Australian winemakers have an unusual practice of blending Cabernet Sauvignon with Syrah. (More on that in the "Odd couples" sidebar in Chapter 13.)

Cabernet Sauvignon often goes by just its first name, Cabernet (although there are other Cabernets) or even by its nickname, *Cab.*

Merlot

Deep color, full body, high alcohol, and low tannin are the characteristics of wines made from the Merlot grape. The aromas and flavors can be plummy or sometimes chocolatey, or they can suggest tea leaves.

Some wine drinkers find Merlot easier to like than Cabernet Sauvignon because it's less tannic. (But some winemakers feel that Merlot is not satisfactory in its own right, and thus often blend it with Cabernet Sauvignon, Cabernet Franc, or both.)

Merlot is actually the most-planted grape variety in Bordeaux. Merlot is also important in Washington, California, the Long Island district of New York, Northeastern Italy, and Chile.

Pinot Noir

The late Andre Tchelitscheff, the legendary winemaker of some of California's finest Cabernets, once told us that if he could do it all over again, he'd make

Pinot Noir instead of Cab. He's probably not alone. Cabernet is the sensible wine to make — a good, steady, reliable wine that doesn't give the winemaker too much trouble and can achieve excellent quality — and Pinot Noir is finicky, troublesome, enigmatic, and challenging. But a great Pinot Noir can be one of the greatest wines ever.

The prototype for Pinot Noir wine is red Burgundy, from France, where tiny vineyard plots yield rare treasures of wine made entirely from Pinot Noir. Oregon, California, New Zealand, and parts of Australia also produce good Pinot Noir. But Pinot Noir's production is rather limited, because this variety is very particular about climate and soil.

Pinot Noir wine is lighter in color than Cabernet or Merlot. It has relatively high alcohol, medium-to-high acidity, and medium-to-low tannin (although oak barrels can contribute additional tannin to the wine). Its flavors and aromas can be very fruity — often like a mélange of red berries — or earthy and woodsy, depending on how it is grown and/or vinified. Pinot Noir is rarely blended with other grapes.

Syrah/Shiraz

The northern part of France's Rhône Valley is the classic home for great wines from the Syrah grape. Rhône wines such as Hermitage and Côte-Rôtie are the inspiration for Syrah's dissemination to Australia, California, Washington, Italy, and Spain.

Syrah produces deeply colored wines with full body, firm tannin, and aromas/flavors that can suggest berries, smoked meat, bell peppers, spice, tar, or even burnt rubber (believe it or not). In Australia, Syrah (called Shiraz) comes in several styles — some of them charming, medium-bodied wines with strawberry-like flavor that are quite the opposite of the Northern Rhône's powerful Syrahs. Turn to "Winemaking, grapes, and terroir" in Chapter 13 for more on Shiraz.

Syrah doesn't require any other grape to complement its flavors, although in Australia it is often blended with Cabernet, and in the Southern Rhône it is often part of a blended wine with Grenache and other varieties.

Zinfandel

White Zinfandel is such a popular wine — and so much better known than the red style of Zinfandel — that its fans might argue that Zinfandel is a white grape. But it's really red.

Zinfandel is one of the oldest grapes in California, and it therefore enjoys a certain stature there. Its aura is enhanced by its mysterious history: Although

Zinfandel is clearly a vinifera grape and not a native American variety, for decades authorities were uncertain where it came from. They have finally proven that Zinfandel is an obscure Croatian grape.

Zin — as lovers of red Zinfandel call it — makes rich, dark wines that are high in alcohol and medium to high in tannin. They can have a blackberry or raspberry aroma and flavor, a spicy character, or even a jammy flavor. Some Zins are lighter than others and meant to be enjoyed young, and some are serious wines with a tannin structure that's built for aging. (You can tell which is which by the price.)

Nebbiolo

Outside of scattered sites in Northwestern Italy — mainly the Piedmont region — Nebbiolo just doesn't make remarkable wine. But the extraordinary quality of Barolo and Barbaresco, two Piedmont wines, prove what greatness it can achieve under the right conditions.

The Nebbiolo grape is high in both tannin and acid, which can make a wine tough. Fortunately, it also gives enough alcohol to soften the package. Its color can be deep when the wine is young but can develop orangey tinges within a few years. Its complex aroma is fruity (strawberry and jam), earthy and woodsy (tar, truffles), herbal (mint, eucalyptus, anise), and floral (roses).

Lighter versions of Nebbiolo are meant to be drunk young — wines labeled Nebbiolo d'Alba, Roero, or Nebbiolo delle Langhe, for example — while Barolo and Barbaresco are wines that really deserve a *minimum* of eight years' age before drinking.

Sangiovese

This Italian grape has proven itself in the Tuscany region of Italy, especially in the Brunello di Montalcino and Chianti districts, and is increasingly popular in California. Sangiovese makes wines that are medium to high in acidity and firm in tannin; the wines can be light-bodied to full-bodied, depending on exactly where the grapes grow and how the wine is made. The aromas and flavors of the wines are fruity — especially cherry, often tart cherry — with floral nuances of violets and sometimes a slightly nutty character.

Tempranillo

Tempranillo is Spain's candidate for greatness. It gives wines deep color, low acidity, and only moderate alcohol. Modern renditions of Tempranillo from the Ribera del Duero region and elsewhere in Spain prove what color and fruitiness this grape has. In more traditional wines, such as those of the Rioja region, much of the grape's color and flavor is lost due to long wood aging and to blending with varieties that lack color, such as Grenache.

Other red grapes

Table 3-2 describes additional red grape varieties and their wines, which you could encounter either as varietal wines or as wines named for their place of production.

Table 3-2	Other Red Grapes and Their Characteristics
Grape Type	*Characteristics*
Aglianico	Little known outside of Southern Italy, where it makes Taurasi and other age-worthy, powerful red wines, high in tannin.
Barbera	Italian variety that, oddly for a red grape, has little tannin but very high acidity. When fully ripe, it can give big, fruity wines with refreshing crispness. Many producers age the wine in new oak to increase the tannin level of their wine.
Cabernet Franc	A parent of Cabernet Sauvignon, and often blended with it to make Bordeaux-style wines. Ripens earlier, and has more expressive, fruitier flavor (especially berries), as well as less tannin. A specialty of the Loire Valley in France, where it makes wines with place-names such as Chinon and Bourgeuil.
Gamay	Excels in the Beaujolais district of France. It makes grapey wines that can be low in tannin — although the Gamay grape itself is fairly tannic. Neither the grape called *Gamay Beaujolais* in California nor the grape called *Napa Gamay* is true Gamay.
Grenache	A Spanish grape by origin, called Garnacha there. (Most wine drinkers associate Grenache with France's southern Rhône Valley more than with Spain, however.) Sometimes Grenache makes pale, high-alcohol wines that are dilute in flavor. In the right circumstances, it can make deeply colored wines with velvety texture and fruity aromas and flavors suggestive of raspberries.

Chapter 4

Is It a Grape? Is It a Place?

*W*e remember a cartoon in *The New Yorker* some years ago that depicted the students of a private nursery school lined up for their class picture. The caption identified the children only by their first names. Every girl was Jennifer, and every boy was Scott.

When you walk into a wine shop these days, you'd think that the people who name wines have the same fixation as the parents of those nursery school children. More than half the white wines are named *Chardonnay,* and the majority of the red wines are named either *Cabernet Sauvignon* or *Merlot.*

Actually, one Merlot is no more identical to the next than one little Jennifer is identical to the next Jennifer. But to distinguish one Merlot from the other (without opening the bottles, that is), you need more information. You need to read the rest of the label.

What's in a Name

All sorts of names can appear on wine labels. These names often include

✔ The name of the *grape* from which the wine was made.

✔ A *brand name,* which is often the name of the company or person that made the wine (who is called the *producer*).

✔ Sometimes a special, invented name for that particular wine (called a *proprietary name*).

✔ The name of the *place,* or *places,* where the grapes grew (the wine region, and sometimes the name of the specific vineyard property).

Then there's the *vintage* year (the year the grapes were harvested), which is part of the wine's identity; and sometimes you see a descriptor like *reserve,* which either has specific legal meaning or means nothing at all, depending on where the wine came from.

Veteran wine lovers appreciate all this detailed information on wine labels because they know how to interpret it. But to anyone who is just discovering wine, the information embedded in wine names is more confusing than enlightening. Although we'd all agree that little Jennifer needs more than just the name *Jennifer* to identify herself in the world (unless she plans to become a rock star or comedienne), does she really need the equivalent of: Jennifer Smith, "Jenny," Caucasian female, upper middle class, produced by Don and Louise Smith, New York City, Upper West Side, 1995?

Of course she doesn't. But — we know you don't want to hear this — for bottles of wine the answer, frankly, is yes.

The Wine Name Game

Most of the wines that you find in your wine shop or on restaurant wine lists are named in one of two basic ways: either for their *grape variety* or for the *place where the grapes grew.* That information, plus the name of the producer, becomes the shorthand name we use in talking about the wine.

Robert Mondavi Cabernet Sauvignon, for example, is a wine made by Robert Mondavi Winery and named after the Cabernet Sauvignon grape. Fontodi Chianti Classico is a wine made by the Fontodi winery and named after the place called Chianti Classico.

You might recognize some names as grape names (see Chapter 3) and other names as place-names right off the bat; but if you don't, don't panic. That information is the kind of thing you can look up. (Chapters 10 through 16 will help.)

Hello, my name is Chardonnay

A *varietal* wine is a wine that is named after either the *principal* or the *sole* grape variety that makes up the wine.

Each country (and in the U.S., some individual states) has laws that dictate the minimum percentage of the named grape that a wine must contain if that wine wants to call itself by a grape name. The issue is truth in advertising.

U.S. federal regulations fix the legal minimum percentage of the named grape at 75 percent (which means that your favorite California Chardonnay could have as much as 25 percent of some *other* grape in it). In Oregon, the minimum is 90 percent (except for Cabernet, which can be 75 percent). In Australia, it's 85 percent. And in the countries that form the European Union (EU), the minimum is 85 percent.

Some varietal wines are made *entirely* from the grape variety for which the wine is named. There's no law against that anywhere.

Most of the time, the labels of varietal wines don't tell you whether other grapes are present in the wine, what those grapes are, or the percentage of the wine that they account for. You can only know that the wine contains at least the minimum legal percentage of the named variety. Interestingly, if a wine is named for two or more grape varieties — it's a Semillon-Chardonnay, for example — the label must state the percentages of each, and these percentages must total 100 percent. Now that's an honest varietal wine!

Why name a wine after a grape variety?

Grapes are the raw material of a wine. Except for whatever a wine absorbs from oak barrels (certain aromas and flavors, as well as tannin) and from certain winemaking processes described in Chapter 5, the juice of the grapes is what any wine *is*. So to name a wine after its grape variety is very logical.

Naming a wine for its grape variety is also very satisfying to exacting consumers. Knowing what grape a wine is made from is akin to knowing what type of oil is in the salad dressing, how many grams of fat are in the soup, and how much egg is in your egg roll.

From a producer's viewpoint, naming a wine by its grape variety enables the wine to gain a cut of whatever demand already exists for wines of the same name.

Most California (and other American) wines carry varietal names. Likewise, most Australian, South American, and South African wines are named using the *principal* principle. Even some countries that don't normally name their wines after grapes, like France, are jumping on the varietal-name bandwagon for certain wines that they especially want to sell to Americans.

The varietal name game

A common perception among some wine lovers is that a varietal wine is somehow *better* than a non-varietal wine. Actually, the fact that a wine is named after its principal grape variety is absolutely *no indication of quality*.

The most common place-names

Beaujolais	Chianti	Rioja
Bordeaux	Côtes du Rhône	Sancerre
Burgundy (Bourgogne)	Mosel	Sauternes
Chablis	Port (Porto)	Sherry
Champagne	Pouilly-Fuissé	Soave
Châteauneuf-du-Pape	Rhine (Rheingau, Rheinhessen)	Valpolicella

Many decades ago, when some California wineries began using varietal names for their wines instead of meaningless *generic* names (see the "Generic wines" section at the end of this chapter), intelligent wine drinkers felt more comfortable with the wines. Even if, in those days, the law said the wine had to contain only 51 percent of the named grape, we felt that we were drinking Known Entities rather than some labeling gimmick. The wineries that made varietal wines in those days were the most avant-garde wineries around, and they generally produced the best wines. That was then. Today, varietal wines are commonplace.

Hello, my name is Bordeaux

Unlike American wines, most European wines are named for the *region* (place) where their grapes grow rather than for the grape variety itself. Many of these European wines are made from precisely the same grape varieties as American wines (like Chardonnay, Cabernet Sauvignon, Sauvignon Blanc, and so on), but they don't say so on the label. Instead, the labels say Burgundy, Bordeaux, Sancerre, and so on: the *place* where those grapes grow.

Is this some nefarious plot to make wine incomprehensible to English-only wine lovers who have never visited Europe and flunked geography in school?

Au contraire! The European system of naming wines is actually intended to provide more information about each wine, and more understanding of what's in the bottle, than varietal naming does. The only catch is that to harvest this information, you have to learn something about the different regions from which the wines come. (Turn to Chapters 10 through 14 for some of that information.)

Why name a wine after a place?

Grapes, the raw material of wine, have to grow somewhere. Depending on the type of soil, the amount of sunshine, the amount of rain, the slope of the hill, and the many other characteristics that each *somewhere* has, the grapes will turn out differently. If the grapes are different, the wine is different. Each wine, therefore, reflects the place where its grapes grow.

Decoding common European place-names

Wine Name	*Country*	*Grape Varieties*
Beaujolais	France	Gamay
Bordeaux (red)	France	Cabernet Sauvignon, Merlot, Cabernet Franc, and others*
Bordeaux (white)	France	Sauvignon Blanc, Sémillon, Muscadelle*
Burgundy (red)	France	Pinot Noir
Burgundy (white)	France	Chardonnay
Chablis	France	Chardonnay
Champagne	France	Chardonnay, Pinot Noir, Pinot Meunier*
Châteauneuf-du-Pape*	France	Grenache, Mourvèdre, Syrah, and others*
Chianti	Italy	Sangiovese, Canaiolo, and others*
Côtes du Rhône*	France	Grenache, Mourvèdre, Carignan, and others*
Port (Porto)	Portugal	Touriga Nacional, Tinta Barroca, Touriga Francesa, Tinta Roriz, Tinto Cão, and others*
Pouilly-Fuissé, Macon, Saint Veran	France	Chardonnay
Rioja (red)	Spain	Tempranillo, Grenache, and others*
Sancerre/Pouilly-Fumé	France	Sauvignon Blanc
Sauternes	France	Sémillon, Sauvignon Blanc*
Sherry	Spain	Palomino
Soave	Italy	Garganega and others*
Valpolicella	Italy	Corvina, Molinara, Rondinella*

Indicates that a blend of grapes is used to make these wines.

The same type of grape, such as Chardonnay, can get riper in one place than another, for example. (The riper grapes make a wine higher in alcohol with riper fruit flavors.) Or the grapes (and wine) can have some subtle, unusual flavors — such as mineral flavors — attributable to a particular place. In one way or another, the place *always* affects the character of the grapes.

In Europe, grape growers/winemakers have had centuries to figure out which grapes grow best where. They've identified most of these grape–location match-ups and codified them into wine laws. Therefore, the name of a *place* where grapes are grown in Europe automatically connotes the grape (or grapes) used to make the wine of that place. The label on the bottle usually doesn't tell you the grape (or grapes), though. Which brings us back to our original question: Is this some kind of nefarious plot to make wine incomprehensible to non-Europeans?

The terroir name game

Terroir (pronounced *ter wahr*) is a French word that has no direct translation in English, so wine people just use the French word, for expediency (not for snobbery).

There's no fixed definition of *terroir;* it's a concept, and, like most concepts, people tend to define it more broadly or more narrowly to suit their own needs. The word itself is based on the French word *terre,* which means soil; so some people define *terroir* as, simply, dirt (as in "Our American dirt is every bit as good as their French dirt").

But *terroir* is really much more complex (and complicated) than just dirt. *Terroir* is the combination of immutable natural factors — such as topsoil, subsoil, climate (sun, rain, wind, and so on), the slope of the hill, and altitude — that a particular vineyard site has. Chances are that no two vineyards in the entire world have precisely the same combination of these factors. So we consider *terroir* to be the *unique* combination of natural factors that a particular vineyard site has.

Terroir is the guiding principle behind the European concept that wines should be named after the place they come from (thought we'd gotten off the track, didn't you?). The thinking goes like this: The name of the place connotes which grapes were used to make the wine of that place (because the grapes are dictated by law), and the place influences the character of those grapes in its own unique way. Therefore, the most accurate name that a wine can have is the name of the place where its grapes grew.

It's not some nefarious plot; it's just a whole different way of looking at things.

Place-names on American wine labels

France might have invented the concept that wines should be named after their place of origin, but neither France nor even greater Europe has a monopoly on the idea. Wine labels from non-European countries also tell you where a wine is made — usually by featuring the name of a place (called an *appellation of origin* in Winespeak) somewhere on the label. But there are a few differences between the European and non-European systems.

First of all, on an American wine label (or an Australian or Chilean or South African label, for that matter) you have to go to some effort to find the place-name on the label. The place of origin is not the fundamental name of the wine (as it is for most European wines); the grape usually is.

Second, place-names in the U.S. mean far less than they do in Europe. Okay, if the label says Napa Valley, and you've visited that area — and you loved eating at Mustards, and you'd like to spend the rest of your life in one of those houses atop a hill off the Silverado Trail — Napa Valley will mean something to you. But *legally,* the name Napa Valley only means that at least 85 percent of the grapes came from an area defined by law as the Napa Valley wine zone. The name Napa Valley does not define the type of wine, nor does it imply specific grape varieties, the way a European place-name does. (Good thing the grape name is there, as big as day, on the label.)

Place-names on labels of non-European wines, for the most part, merely pay lip service to the concept of *terroir.* In fact, some non-European appellations are ridiculously broad. We have to laugh when we think how European wine-makers must react to all those wine labels that announce a wine's place of origin simply as "California." *Great. This label says that this wine comes from a specific area that is 30 percent larger than the entire country of Italy! Some specific area!* (Italy has more than 300 specific wine zones.)

When the place on the label is merely *California,* in fact, that information tells you next to nothing about where the grapes grew. California's a big place, and those grapes could come from just about anywhere. Same thing for all those Australian wines labeled *South Eastern Australia* — an area only slightly smaller than France and Spain *combined.*

Wines named in other ways

Now and then, you might come across a wine that is named for neither its grape variety nor its region of origin. Such wines usually fall into three categories: *branded wines, wines with proprietary names,* or *generic wines.*

Bigger than a breadbasket

When we travel to other countries, we realize that people in different places have different ways of perceiving space and distance. If someone tells us that we'll find a certain restaurant "just up ahead," for example, we figure it's the equivalent of about three blocks away — but they might mean three miles.

Discussing place-names for European wines can be just as problematic. Some of the *places*

are as small as several acres, some are 100 square miles big, and others are the size of New Jersey. Certain words used to describe wine zones suggest the relative size of the place. In descending order of size and ascending order of specificity: country, region, district, subdistrict, commune, vineyard.

Branded wines

Most wines have brand names, including those wines that are named after their grape variety — like Simi (brand name) Sauvignon Blanc (grape) — and those that are named after their region of origin — like Masi (brand name) Valpolicella (place). These brand names are usually the name of the company that made the wine, called a *winery*. Because most wineries make several different wines, the brand name itself is not specific enough to be the actual name of the wine.

But sometimes a wine has *only* a brand name. For example, the label says *Salamandre* and *red French wine* but provides little other identification.

Wines that have *only* a brand name on them, with no indication of grape or of place — other than the country of production — are generally the most inexpensive, ordinary wines you can get. If they're from a European Union country, they won't even be *vintage dated* (that is, there won't be any indication of what year the grapes were harvested) because EU law does not entitle such wines to carry a vintage date.

Wines with proprietary names

You can find some pretty creative names on wine bottles these days: Tapestry, Conundrum, Insignia, Isosceles, Mythology, Trilogy. Is this stuff to drink, to drive, or to dab behind your ears?

Names like these are *proprietary names* (often trademarked) that producers create for special wines. In the case of American wines, the bottles with proprietary names usually contain wines made from a *blend* of grapes; therefore, no one grape name can be used as the name of the wine. (Remember

California's 75 percent policy?) In the case of European wines, the grapes used to make the wine were probably not the approved grapes for that region; therefore, the regional name could not be used on the label.

Although a brand name can apply to several different wines, a proprietary name usually applies to one specific wine. You can find Zinfandel, Cabernet Sauvignon, Chardonnay, and numerous other wines under the Fetzer brand from California, for example, and you can find Beaujolais, Pouilly-Fuissé, Mâcon-Villages, and numerous other wines under the Louis Jadot brand from France. But the proprietary name Luce applies to a single wine.

A producer who creates a wine with a proprietary name has high-minded motives. He is driven by artistic impulse, intellectual curiosity, or sheer ego to form a wine that surpasses the norm for his part of the world. The price tag on the bottle reflects the magnitude of his endeavor.

Wines with proprietary names usually are made in small quantities, are quite expensive ($30 to $75 or more a bottle), and are, in fact, high in quality. They particularly satisfy wine lovers who enjoy discovering new and unusual wines. Sometimes they draw rave reviews from the critics and end up as established successes that endure in the marketplace. Sometimes they take the route of old soldiers.

Generic wines

A generic name is a wine name that has been used inappropriately for so long that it has lost its original meaning in the eyes of the government (exactly what Xerox, Kleenex, and Band-Aid are afraid of becoming).

Grape names on European wines

Although most European wines are named after their place of origin, grape names do sometimes appear on labels of European wines.

In Italy, for example, several place-names routinely have grape names appended to them — the name Trentino (place) Pinot Grigio (grape) is an example. Or the official name of a wine could be a combination of place and grape — like the name Barbera d'Alba, which translates as Barbera (grape) of Alba (place).

In France, some producers have deliberately added the grape name to their labels even though the grape is already implicit in the wine name. For example, a white Bourgogne (place-name) might also have the word Chardonnay (grape) on the label, for those wine drinkers who don't know that white Bourgogne is 100 percent Chardonnay. And German wines usually carry grape names along with their official place-names.

But even if a European wine does carry a grape name, the most important part of the wine's name, in the eyes of the people who make the wine, is the place.

Burgundy, Chianti, Chablis, Champagne, Rhine wine, Sherry, Port, and Sauterne are all names that rightfully should apply only to wines made in those specific places. But these names have been usurped by very large and powerful wine companies. So now both the U.S. and Canadian governments recognize these names as broad *types* of wine rather than as wines from specific regions.

Most California wines carried generic names until the late '60s or early '70s when varietals came into vogue. Generics are still around, but they are less popular in the marketplace with every passing year.

When you buy a generic wine, you have absolutely no idea what you are getting except that it is a piece of history.

Chapter 5

Behind the Scenes of Winemaking

- -

In This Chapter

▶ Separating the meaningful wine terms from the mumbo jumbo

▶ *ML, pH,* and *stirred lees*

▶ Technical terms to wow your friends

- -

The most frustrating thing about wine has got to be the technical lingo. All you want is a crisp, fruity white wine to serve with tonight's fried chicken. But to find it, you have to fight your way through a jungle of jargon on the back labels of the wine bottles — as well as in the words the sales clerk uses to explain his recommendations, and on the signs all around the wine shop. Why on earth is everyone making wine so complicated?

Here's the story: Wine is two products. Some wine is just a beverage, and it should taste good — period. Other wine is an art form that fascinates and intrigues people. Complicated technical language is supposed to make you think that a wine is special, more than just a beverage. (This, of course, is what every winemaker wants you to believe about his wine.)

How much of this information (if any) is pivotal in helping you get the kind of wine you want, and how much is pretentious technobabble? Read on.

A Reality Check for Wine Jargon

Winemakers use numerous techniques to make wine. These techniques vary according to the grapes they have and the type of wine they are making. (If a winemaker is producing a huge quantity of a wine that will sell for $5.99 retail, for example, he probably won't put the wine into new oak barrels because the cost of the barrels could add $2 to the price of every bottle.)

No winemaking procedure is inherently good or inherently bad; it all depends on the grapes and the type of wine being made. How the wine tastes is the ultimate justification of the method: The procedures themselves are meaningless if they don't create a wine that is appealing to wine drinkers. Of course, different wines appeal to different wine drinkers at different times:

- ✔ Some wines are intended to taste good right away, while others are intended to taste good down the road, after the wine has aged (see Chapter 21).
- ✔ Some are intended to taste good to casual wine drinkers, while others are intended for more experienced wine lovers.

The *taste* of the wine involves the wine's aroma, body, texture, length, and so on (see Chapter 2), not just its flavors. And the taste of a wine is a subjective experience.

Every winemaking technique affects the taste of the wine in one way or another. Most of the technical words that are bandied about in wine circles therefore represent procedures that *are* relevant to the taste of a wine. But — here's the key point — these technical words each represent isolated elements in the making of the wine, which are only *parts* of the total picture that begins with the grapes and ends when you put the wine in your mouth.

Viti-vini

Producing wine actually involves two separate steps: the growing of the grapes, called *viticulture,* and the making of the wine, called *vinification.* (In some wine courses, students nickname the dual process *viti-vini.*)

Sometimes one company performs both steps, as is the case with *estate-bottled* wines (see Chapter 9). And sometimes the two steps are completely separate. Some large wineries, for example, buy grapes from private grape growers. These growers don't make wine; they just grow grapes and sell them to whatever wine company offers them the highest price per ton.

Vine-growing vernacular

Much more jargon is associated with the making of a wine than with the growing of its grapes. But a few technical terms relating to grape growing do crop up on wine labels or in wine descriptions. Here are the expressions that you're likely to encounter:

✔ **Low yields.** Generally speaking, the more grapes a grapevine grows (the higher its *yield* of grapes), the less concentrated the flavors of those grapes will be, and the lower in quality (and less expensive) their wine will be. Just about any wine producer anywhere can *claim* that his yields are low, because it's too complicated to prove otherwise. If the wine tastes thin or watery, we'd be suspicious.

✔ **Ripeness.** Harvesting grapes when they're perfectly ripe is one of the crucial points in wine production. (See the "How grapes ripen" sidebar in Chapter 3.) But ripeness is a subjective issue.

In cooler climates, a high degree of ripeness doesn't happen every year; wines from "riper" vintages should therefore be richer and fuller-bodied than the norm for that type of wine. In warmer climates, ripeness is almost automatic; the trick becomes not letting the grapes get too ripe too fast, which causes them to be physiologically mature but undeveloped in their flavors (like a physically precocious but immature teenager). There's no fixed definition of perfect ripeness.

✔ **Canopy.** Left untended, grapevines would grow along the ground, up trees, wherever. (They're *vines,* after all!) Commercial viticulture involves attaching the shoots of vines to wires or trellises in a systematic pattern. The purpose of *training* the vine — as this activity is called — is to position the grape bunches so that they get enough sun to ripen well and so that the fruit is easy for the harvesters to reach.

An *open canopy* is a trellising method that maximizes the sunlight exposure of the grapes. *Canopy management,* the practice of maneuvering the leaves and fruit into the best position for a given vineyard, is a popular buzzword.

✔ **Microclimate.** Every wine region has climatic conditions (the amount and timing of sun, rain, wind, humidity, and so on) that are considered the norm for that area. But individual locations within a region — the south-facing side of a particular hill, for example — can have a climatic reality that is different from neighboring vineyards. The unique climatic reality of a specific location is called its *microclimate.*

Winemaking wonder words

The vinification end of wine production falls into two parts:

✔ **Fermentation,** the period when the grape juice turns into wine

✔ **Maturation** (or *finishing*), the period following fermentation when the wine settles down, loses its rough edges, goes to prep school, and gets ready to meet the world

Depending on the type of wine being made, the whole process could take three months or five years — or even longer if the bank isn't breathing down the winery's neck.

Winemakers don't have as many options in making wine as chefs do in preparing food — but almost! Of all the jargon you're likely to hear, information about oak is probably the most common.

When wood becomes magic

Oak barrels, 60 gallons in size, are often used as containers for wine during either fermentation or maturation. The barrels lend oaky flavor and aroma to the wine, which many people find very appealing. The barrels are expensive — about $600 per barrel if they're made from French oak. (Most people consider French oak to be the finest.) We suppose the expense is one good reason to boast about using the barrels.

But not all oak is the same. Oak barrels vary in the origin of their oak, the amount of *toast* (a charring of the inside of the barrels) each barrel has, how often the barrels have been used (their oaky character diminishes with use), and even the size of the barrels. Even if all oak *were* the same, a wine could turn out differently depending on whether unfermented juice or actual wine went into the barrels, and how long it stayed there.

In fact, the whole issue of oak is so complex that anyone who suggests that a wine is better simply because it has been oaked is guilty of gross oversimplification.

Barrel-fermented versus barrel-aged

You don't have to venture very far into wine before you find someone explaining to you that a particular wine was barrel-fermented or barrel-aged. What in the world does he mean, and should you care?

The term *barrel-fermented* means that unfermented juice went into barrels (almost always oak) and changed into wine there. The term *barrel-aged* usually means that wine (already fermented) went into barrels and stayed there for a maturation period — from a few months to a couple of years. Because most wines that ferment in barrels remain there for several months after fermentation ends, *barrel-fermented* and *barrel-aged* are often used together. The term *barrel-aged* alone suggests that the fermentation happened somewhere other than the barrel — usually in stainless steel tanks.

Classic barrel-fermentation — juice into the barrel, wine out — applies mainly to white wines, and the reason is very practical. As we mention in Chapter 2, the juice of red wines ferments together with the grape skins in order to become red, and that's a mighty messy mixture to clean out of a barrel! Red wines usually ferment in larger containers — stainless steel tanks or even large wooden vats — and then *age* in small oak barrels after the wine has been drained off the grape skins. (Some light, fruity styles of red wine might not be oaked at all.) But these days, some winemakers drain partially-fermented red juice from the grape skins and let that juice finish its fermentation in barrels, without the skins; when a red wine is described as being barrel-fermented, that's usually the case.

Here's why you might care whether a white wine is barrel-fermented or just barrel-aged. Wines that ferment in barrels actually end up tasting *less* oaky than wines that simply age in barrels, even though they might have spent more time in oak. (A barrel-fermented and barrel-aged Chardonnay might have spent 11 months in oak, for example, and a barrel-aged Chardonnay may have spent only 5 months in oak.) That's because juice interacts differently with the oak than wine does.

Lots of people who are supposed to know more about wine than you do get the effects of the two processes backward and tell you that the barrel-fermented wine tastes oakier. If you have a strong opinion about the flavor of oak in your wine, be sure that you know the real story.

Other winemaking terms

Become a wine expert overnight and dazzle your friends with this amazing array of wine jargon. (Just don't fool yourself into believing that any one of the procedures described necessarily creates a high quality wine. The merit of each procedure depends on the particular wine being made.)

- ✔ **Lees.** *Lees* is the name for various solids that precipitate to the bottom of a white wine after fermentation. These solids can interact with the wine and create more complex flavors in the wine. (Sometimes the wine-maker stirs the lees around in the wine periodically to enhance this process.) A white wine with extended lees contact is usually richer in texture and tastes less overtly fruity than it would otherwise.

- ✔ **ML or malolactic.** *Malolactic,* nicknamed *ML* or *malo,* is a secondary fermentation that changes the nature of the acids in the wine. The net result is that the wine is softer and less acidic. ML usually happens naturally, but a winemaker can also incite it or prevent it.

  Red wines almost always undergo malolactic fermentation, but for white wines, ML is a stylistic judgment call on the winemaker's part. Sometimes, ML can contribute a buttery flavor to a white wine, but it diminishes the wine's fruitiness.

- ✔ **pH.** The chemical term *pH* means exactly the same thing for wine as it does in other scientific fields. ("Our facial cream is pH-balanced for sensitive skin.") If you want a technical explanation, look up your former chemistry teacher. If you'll settle for the general concept, pH is a measurement of acidity; wines with low pH (approximately 3.4 or less) have higher acidity, and wines with high pH have lower acidity.

✔ **Soft tannins.** Tannin in red wines varies not only in its quantity, but also in its nature. Some tannins give wines rich texture and an impression of substance without tasting bitter; other tannins are astringent and mouth-drying. *Soft tannins* is the buzzphrase for the good kind. Winemakers achieve soft tannins by harvesting fully ripe grapes, controlling fermentation time and temperature, and other techniques.

✔ **Fining** and **filtering.** Winemakers *fine* and *filter* most wines near the end of their maturation period. The purpose of these procedures is to *clarify* the wine — that is, to remove any cloudiness or solid matter in the wine — and to *stabilize* it — to remove any yeast, bacteria, or other microscopic critters that might change the wine for the worse after it is bottled.

There's a popular belief among anti-tech wine lovers that fining and filtration strip a wine of its character — and that unfined, unfiltered wines are inherently better, even if they're not brilliant in appearance. But it's a complex issue. (For one thing, there are *degrees* of fining and filtration, like *light* fining and *gentle* filtration.)

✔ **Blending.** This term usually applies to the process of making a wine from more than one grape variety. Winemakers usually ferment the different grapes separately and then blend their wines together.

The reasons for blending wines of different grapes are either to reduce costs — by diluting an expensive wine like Chardonnay with something else far less expensive, for example — or to improve the quality of the wine by using complementary grapes whose characteristics enhance each other. Many of Europe's traditional wines — such as red Rioja, red Bordeaux, Châteauneuf-du-Pape, and Champagne — are blended wines that owe their personalities to several grapes.

Part II
Close Encounters of the Wine Kind

In this part . . .

*W*ith some of the basics under your belt — such as grape varieties, wine types, and wine names — you're ready to apply your knowledge at the practical level. Corkscrews, wine glasses, restaurant wine lists, and wine shops won't be any challenge at all, once you get the hang of them by browsing through the pages of the chapters that follow. Even all those technical terms on wine labels will become as clear as day. We promise.

Chapter 6

Navigating a Wine Shop

*U*nless you enjoy a permanent, dependent relationship with an indulgent and knowledgeable wine lover, the day will come when you have to purchase a bottle of wine yourself. If you're lucky, the shop owner will just happen to be some enlightened fellow whose life purpose is to make good wine easy and accessible to others. If you're lucky, you'll also be awarded an honorary doctorate from Harvard and receive a tax-free inheritance from a great aunt you've never met. The odds are about equal.

Buying Wine Can Intimidate Anyone

Common sense suggests that buying a few bottles of wine should be less stressful than, say, applying for a bank loan or interviewing for a new job. What's the big deal? It's only grape juice.

But memories tell us otherwise. There was the time the wine shop wouldn't take back one of the two bottles of inexpensive wine that we bought the week before, even when we explained how awful the first bottle had been. (Were *we* wrong about the wine or were *they* arrogant? We wasted days wondering.) And the time we pretended we knew what we were doing and bought a full case — 12 bottles — of a French wine based on the brand's general reputation, not realizing that the particular vintage we purchased was a miserable aberration from the brand's usual quality. (Why didn't we just ask someone in the store?) Then there was all that time we spent staring at shelves lined with bottles whose labels might as well have been written in Greek, for all that we could understand from them.

Fortunately, our enthusiasm for wine caused us to persevere. We eventually discovered that wine shopping can be fun. We also discovered a strange thing about bottles of fermented grape juice: The prospect of buying or selling them can turn normally kind and sensitive individuals into victimizers or victims, depending on whether they are trying to show off what they know or are trying to hide what they don't know. But it doesn't have to be that way.

Too much information about wine is constantly changing — new vintages each year, hundreds of new wineries, new wines, advances in wine technology, and so on — for *anyone* to presume that he knows it all, or for anyone to feel insecure about what he doesn't know.

Our experience has taught us that the single most effective way to assure yourself of more good experiences than bad ones in buying wine is to come to terms with your knowledge — or lack thereof — of the subject. If we'd all quit pretending that we know more than we do and give up our defensiveness about what we don't know, buying wine would become the simple exchange that it should be.

Wine Retailers, Large and Small

There are four really great things about buying wine in a store to drink later at home. Stores usually have a much bigger selection of wines than restaurants do. The wine is less expensive than in restaurants. You can touch the bottles and compare the labels. And the guy who sells the wine to you can't watch you or listen to what you say when you're drinking it.

On the other hand, you have to provide your own wine glasses, and you have to open the bottle yourself (see Chapter 8 for the lowdown on all that). And that big selection can be downright daunting.

Supermarket survival tips

If you're shopping in a supermarket where there's no one to turn to for advice, do one of the following:

1. Try to remember the names of the recommended wines in the last wine article you read. Bring the article or list with you.

2. Call a wine-knowledgeable friend on your cell phone, or, better yet, bring him or her with you (assuming that his or her palate and yours get along).

3. Buy the wine with the prettiest label. What have you got to lose?

You can buy wine at all sorts of stores: supermarkets, wine superstores, discount warehouses, or small specialty wine shops. Each type of store has its own advantages and disadvantages in terms of selection, price, or service.

Because wine is a regulated beverage in many countries, governments often get involved in deciding where and how wine may be sold (and sometimes even when). So you will have more or fewer choices of where to buy your wine depending on where you live.

Some states within the U.S. and some provinces in Canada have raised government control of alcoholic beverage sales to a fine art. Some states and provinces not only decide _where_ you can buy wine, but they also decide _which wines_ will be available for you to buy. If you love wine and you live in one of those areas (you know who you are), take comfort in the fact that a) you have a vote; b) freedom of choice lies just across the border; and c) if the Berlin Wall and the Iron Curtain could topple, there's hope for change in your local government, too.

We'll assume a healthy, open-minded, free-market economy for wine in our discussion of retail wine sales. We hope that scenario applies where you live, because your enjoyment of wine will blossom all the more easily if it does.

Supermarkets

In truly _open_ wine markets, you can buy wine in supermarkets, like any other food product. Supermarkets make wine accessible to everyone.

When wine is sold in supermarkets, the mystique surrounding the product evaporates. (Who can waste time feeling insecure about a wine purchase when there are much more critical issues at hand, such as how much time is left before the kids turn into monsters and which is the shortest line at the checkout?) And the prices, especially in large stores, are usually quite reasonable.

The downside about buying wine in supermarkets is that your selection is often limited to wines produced by large wineries that generate enough volume to sell to supermarket chains. And you'll seldom get any advice on which wines to buy. Basically, you're on your own.

We know for a fact that some people in the wine business disapprove of the straightforward attitude toward wine in supermarkets; to them, wine is sacrosanct and should always be treated like an elite beverage. At least you won't run into _them_ as you browse the wine aisles in your supermarket.

Discount warehouses and superstores

Most discount warehouse chains sell wine on the scale of a supermarket. Along with your wine, you can pick up any spirits, beer, carbonated beverages, snack foods, or party supplies that you need — not to mention pantyhose and auto supplies. The stores are large and their prices are usually quite good.

But the same problems you often encounter at a supermarket — lack of service and limited selections — usually apply to these stores, as well.

To guide you on your wine-buying journey, many stores offer plenty of *shelf-talkers* (small signs on the shelves that describe individual wines). But the shelf-talkers should be taken with a very large grain of salt. They are often provided by the company selling the wine, which is more interested in convincing you to grab a bottle than in offering you information to help you understand the wine. Most likely, you'll find flowery phrases, hyperbolic adjectives, impressive scores (not always accurate) and safe, common-denominator stuff like "delicious with chicken." (*Any* chicken, cooked in *any* way?) The information will be biased and of limited value. We strongly recommend that you find a knowledgeable person from the store to help you, if at all possible, rather than rely on shelf-talkers.

The bottom line is that supermarkets and discount warehouses can be great places to buy everyday wine for casual enjoyment. But if what you really want is to learn about wine as you buy it, or if you want an unusually interesting variety of wines to satisfy your rapacious curiosity, you will probably find yourself shopping elsewhere.

Ten clues for identifying a store where you should *not* buy wine

1. The dust on the wine bottles is more than 1/8-inch thick.

2. Most of the white wines are light brown in color.

3. The most recent vintage in the store is 1992.

4. The colors on all the wine labels have faded from bright sunlight.

5. It's warmer than a sauna inside.

6. Most of the bottles are standing up.

7. All of the bottles are standing up!

8. The selection consists mainly of jug wines or "Bag-in-the-Box" wines.

9. The June Wine of the Month has a picture of Santa Claus on the label.

10. The owner resembles Darth Vader.

Of course, exceptions do exist: The Wine Club in San Francisco (and other locations) and Wine Warehouse in Los Angeles are two large discount stores that do offer knowledgeable service as well as an excellent variety of fine wines at reasonable prices. And a few more such high-end discount stores are starting to appear across the U.S.

Wine specialty shops

Wine specialty shops are small- to medium-sized stores that sell wine and liquor and, sometimes, wine books, corkscrews (see Chapter 8 for more on those), wine glasses, and maybe a few specialty foods. The foods sold in wine shops tend to be gourmet items rather than just run-of-the-mill snack foods.

If you decide to pursue wine as a serious hobby, shops like these are the ones where you'll probably end up buying your wine because they offer many advantages that larger operations cannot. For one thing, wine specialty shops almost always have wine-knowledgeable staffers on the premises. Also, you can usually find an interesting, varied selection of wines at all price levels.

Wine shops often organize their wines by country of origin and — in the case of classic wine countries, such as France — by region (Bordeaux, Burgundy, Rhône, and so on). Red wines and white wines are often in separate sections within these country areas. There might be a special section for Champagnes and other sparkling wines and another section for dessert wines.

Some wine shops have a special area (or even a special room) for the finer or more expensive wines. In some stores, it's a locked vault-like room. In others, it's the whole back area of the store.

Over in a corner somewhere, often right by the door to accommodate quick purchases, there's usually a *cold box,* a refrigerated cabinet with glass doors where bottles of best-selling white and sparkling wines sit. Unless you really *must* have an ice-cold bottle of wine immediately (the two of you have just decided to elope, the marriage minister is a mile down the road, and the wedding toast is only ten minutes away), avoid the cold box. The wines in there are usually too cold and, therefore, might not be in good condition. You never know how long the bottle you select has been sitting there under frigid conditions, numbed lifeless.

Near the front of the store you might also see boxes or bins of special *sale* wines. These sale displays are usually topped with *case cards* — large cardboard signs that stand above the open boxes of wine — or similar descriptive material. Our words of caution in the previous section on the credibility of shelf-talkers apply to case cards, too; but because case cards are a lot bigger, there's more of a chance that some useful information might appear on them.

Choosing the Right Wine Merchant

Sizing up a wine merchant is as simple as sizing up any other specialty retailer. The main criteria are fair prices, a wide selection, staff expertise, and service. Also, the shop must store its wines in the proper conditions.

No such species in your neighborhood? In Chapter 17, we talk about the advantages and disadvantages of buying wine by catalog, telephone, mail, or the Internet, which can be good alternatives if you don't have access to a decent wine shop where you live.

Putting price in perspective

When you're a novice wine buyer, your best strategy is to shop around with an eye to service and reliable advice more than to price. After you've found a merchant who has suggested several wines that you've liked, stick with him, even if he doesn't have the best prices in town. It makes better sense to pay a dollar or so more for wines that are recommended by a reliable merchant (wines that you'll probably like) than to buy wines in a cut-rate or discount store and save a buck, especially if that store has no special wine adviser or if the advice you receive is suspect.

When you have more knowledge of wine, you'll have enough confidence to shop at stores with the best prices. But even then, price must take a backseat to the storage conditions of the wine (see "Judging wine storage conditions," later in this chapter).

Evaluating selection and expertise

You won't necessarily know on your first visit whether a particular store's selection is adequate for you. If you notice many wines from many different countries at various prices, give the store's selection the benefit of the doubt. If you outgrow the selection as you learn more about wine, you can seek out a new merchant at that point.

Don't be too ready to give a merchant the benefit of the doubt when it comes to expertise, however. Some retailers are not only extremely knowledgeable about the specific wines they sell, but also extremely knowledgeable about wine in general. But some retailers know less than their customers. Just as you expect a butcher to know his cuts of meat, you should expect a wine merchant to know a lot more about wine than most of his customers do! Be free with your questions (such as, "Can you tell me something about this wine?" or "How are these two wines different?"), and judge how willing and able the merchant is to answer them.

Expect a wine merchant to have *personal* knowledge and experience of the wines he sells. These days, lots of retailers use the ratings of a few critics as a crutch in selling wines. They plaster their shelves with the critics' scores (usually a number like 90 on a scale of 100) and advertise their wines by these numbers (see "Wine magazines" and "Wine newsletters" in Chapter 18). We agree that selling by the numbers is one quick way of communicating an approximate sense of the wine's quality. (Remember, that doesn't mean you'll *like* the wine!) But the retailer's knowledge and experience of the wines simply must go beyond the critics' scores, or he's not doing his job properly.

Expecting service with a smile

Most knowledgeable wine merchants pride themselves in their ability to guide you through the maze of wine selections and help you find a wine that you will like. Trust a merchant's advice at least once or twice and see if his choices are good ones. If he's not flexible enough — or knowledgeable enough — to suggest wine that suits your needs, obviously you need another merchant. All it will have cost you is the price of a bottle or two of wine. (Much less costly than choosing the wrong doctor or lawyer!)

Speaking of service, any reputable wine merchant will accept a bottle back from you if he has made a poor recommendation or if the wine seems damaged. After all, he wants to keep you as a customer. But with the privilege comes responsibility: Be reasonable. You should return an *open* bottle only if you think the wine is defective (and then the bottle should be mostly full!). Hold on to the store's receipt. And don't wait several months before returning an unopened bottle of wine. By that time, the store might have a hard time reselling the wine. After a week or two, consider the wine yours — whether you like it or not.

Judging wine storage conditions

Here's a fact about wine that's worth learning early on: Wine is a perishable product. It doesn't go moldy like cheese, and it can't host e-coli bacteria, as meat can. In fact, some wines — usually the more expensive ones — can get better and better as they get older. But if wine is not stored properly, its taste can suffer. (For advice on storing wine in your own home, see "A Healthy Environment for Your Wines" in Chapter 21.)

In sizing up a wine shop, especially if you plan to buy a lot of wine or expensive wine, check out the store's wine storage conditions. What you don't want to see is an area that's warm — for example, wines stored near the boiler so that they cook all winter, or wines stored on the top floor of the building where the sun can smile on them all summer. The very best shops will have climate-controlled storerooms for wine — although, frankly, these shops are in the minority. If a shop does have a good storage system, the proprietor will be happy to show it off to you because he'll be rightfully proud of all the expense and effort he put into it.

In better wine shops, you'll see most of the bottles (except for the inexpensive, large, jug-like bottles) lying *in a horizontal position,* so that their corks remain moist, ensuring a firm closure. A dry cork can crack or shrink and let air into the bottle, which will spoil the wine.

Unfortunately, the problem of wine spoilage doesn't begin at the retail outlet. Quite frequently, the *wholesaler* or *distributor* — the company from which the retailer purchases wine — doesn't have proper storage conditions, either. And there have certainly been instances when wine has been damaged by extremes of weather even before it got to the distributor — for example, while sitting on the docks in the dead of winter (or the dead of summer) or while traveling through the Panama Canal. A good retailer will check out the quality of the wine before he buys it, or he will send it back if he discovers the problem after he has already bought the wine.

Strategies for Wine Shopping

When you get beyond all the ego-compromising innuendo associated with buying wine, you can really have fun in wine shops. We remember when we first caught the wine bug. We spent countless hours on Saturdays visiting different wine stores near our home. (To a passionate wine lover, 30 miles can be near.) Trips to other cities offered new opportunities to explore. So many wines, so little time. . . .

We discovered good, reliable stores — and stores that we would Recommend Only To Our Worst Enemies (ROTOWE). Naturally, we made our share of mistakes along the way, but we learned a lot of good lessons.

See a chance, take it

When we first started buying wine, our repertoire was about as broad as a two-year-old child's vocabulary. We'd buy the same brands again and again because they were safe choices, we knew what to expect from them, and we liked them well enough — all good reasons to buy a particular wine. But in retrospect, we let ourselves get stuck in a rut because we were afraid to take a chance on anything new.

If wine was really going to be fun, we realized, we had to be a little more adventuresome.

If you want to experience the wonderful array of wines in the world, experimenting is a must. New wines can be interesting and exciting. Now and then you might get a lemon, but at least you'll learn not to buy that wine again!

Explain what you want

The following scene — or something very much like it — occurs in every wine shop every day (and ten times every Saturday):

Customer: I remember that it's got a beige label. I had it in this little restaurant last week.

Wine Merchant: Do you know what country it's from?

Customer: No, but I think it has a flower on the label.

Wine Merchant: Do you recall the vintage?

Customer: I think it's young, but I'm not sure. Maybe if I walk around, I can spot it.

How to avoid encounters with poorly stored wine

If you don't know how a wine has been stored — and let's face it, most of the time you don't — you can do two things to minimize the risk of getting a bad bottle.

First, patronize retailers who seem to care about their wine and who provide their customers with good service. Second, be attentive to seasonal weather patterns when buying wine or when having it shipped to you. We're very cautious about buying wine at the end of, or during, a very hot summer, unless the store has a good climate-control system. And we never

have wine shipped to us (other than quick deliveries from our local shop) at the height of summer or winter.

Another way of knowing that the wine you are buying is sound is just to buy the best-selling, most popular wines — assuming you don't mind being a slave to taste trends. Wines that move through the distribution chain very quickly have less opportunity to be damaged along the way. Sometimes we wonder if the wines that sell the most just sell the most because they sell the most. . . .

In-store wine tastings

In general, we're all for tasting wines before buying them, whenever possible. But the wine tastings that some retailers arrange in their stores do have their limitations. In addition to the fact that you usually get a miniscule serving in a little plastic cup more suited to dispensing pills in a hospital, you get to taste only the wines that the wine merchant (or one of his suppliers) happens to be pushing that day. Sometimes it's a wine that the store made an especially good buy on (translation: The store is making a good profit), or a wine that a local distributor is particularly interested in selling. You might like or not like the wine, but in either case you might feel some pressure to buy it after trying it. Our advice to you is not to succumb to any conscious or unconscious sales pressure. Buy the wine only if you really like it — and even then, buy only one bottle to start. The wine might taste completely different to you when you're having dinner that night. If it tastes even better than you thought, you can always buy more bottles later.

Needless to say, most of the time that customer never finds the wine he or she is looking for.

TIP

When you come across a wine you like in a restaurant or at a friend's house, write down as much specific information about the wine from the label as you can. Don't trust your memory. By the time you arrive in your wine store, you might not recall many details about the wine if you haven't written them down. If your wine merchant can see the name, he can give you that wine or — if he doesn't have that exact wine — he might be able to give you something very similar to it.

Five questions you should ask in a wine shop

1. If a wine costs more than $10: What kind of storage has this wine experienced? Hemming and hawing on the part of the wine merchant should be taken to mean, "Poor."

2. How long has this wine been in your store? (This is especially important if the store does not have a climate-control system.)

3. What are some particularly good buys this month? (Provided you trust the wine merchant, and you don't think he's dumping some overstocked, closeout wine on you.)

4. If applicable: Why is this wine selling at such a low price? (The merchant might know that the wine is too old, or is otherwise defective; unless he comes up with a believable explanation, assume that's the case.)

5. Will this wine go well with the food I'm planning to serve?

It's clearly to your advantage to be able to tell your wine retailer anything you can about the types of wine that you have liked previously or that you want to try. Often, telling him about the food you are planning to have with the wine is helpful, too (see Chapter 20, "Marrying Wine with Food").

Name your price

Because the price of a bottle of wine can range from $3 to — literally — hundreds of dollars, it's a good idea to decide approximately how much you want to spend and to tell your wine merchant. A good retailer with an adequate selection should be able to make several wine suggestions in your preferred price category.

A good wine merchant is more interested in the repeat business he'll get by making you happy than he is in trading you up to a bottle of wine that's beyond your limits. If what you want to spend is $10 a bottle, just say so, and stand firm, without embarrassment. There are plenty of decent, enjoyable wines at that price.

Four easy steps to getting a wine you like

Step One

Decide how much you want to spend on a bottle

a) For everyday purposes (This figure might change over time; the $5 to $8 range you start with often rises to $12 to $18 as you discover better wines.)

b) For special occasions

Tell your wine merchant your price range; this will narrow the arena of wines to consider.

Step Two

Describe to your wine merchant the kind of wine you like in clear, simple terms. For example, for white wine, you might use such words as "crisp, dry," or "fruity, ripe, oaky, buttery, full-bodied." For red wines, you might say "big, rich, tannic," or "medium-bodied, soft." (Turn to Chapter 2 to learn other helpful descriptors.)

Step Three

Tell your wine merchant what kind of food you plan to have with the wine, if you know. This will narrow down your choices even more. The wine you drink with your filet of sole is probably not the one you want with spicy chili! A good wine merchant is invaluable in helping you match your wine with food.

Step Four

Ask for tasting samples, if they are available where you shop. (Stores often have wine samples available for tasting every Saturday, where legal.) Of course, the sample will probably come to you in a plastic cup and the temperature might not be ideal; therefore, the sample might not be truly indicative of the quality or taste of that wine. But at least you'll get a general idea of whether or not it's your cup of tea.

Chapter 7

Navigating a Restaurant Wine List

*W*hen you buy a bottle of wine in a restaurant, you get to taste it right then and there: instant gratification. If you've chosen well, you have a delicious wine that pairs beautifully with the food you've selected. You also can bask in the compliments of your family and friends during the whole meal and go home feeling good about yourself. If you haven't chosen well . . . well, we all know *that* feeling! Fortunately, practice *does* make perfect, at least most of the time.

The Restaurant Wine Experience

Here and there, you might come across a restaurant with a retail wine shop on the premises, a useful hybrid of a place where you can look over all the bottles, read the labels, browse through wine books and magazines, and then carry your chosen bottle to your table. Unfortunately, such establishments are rarer than four-leaf clovers. In most restaurants, you have to choose your wine from a menu that tells you only the names of the wines and the price per bottle — and manages to make even that little bit of information somewhat incomprehensible. Welcome to the *restaurant wine list*.

Restaurant wine lists can be infuriating: Typically, they don't tell you enough about the wines. Often, either there's nothing worth drinking, or the choice is so huge that you're immobilized. All too frequently, the lists simply are not accurate; you spend ten good minutes of your life deciding which wine to order, only to discover that it's "not available tonight" (and probably hasn't been for months).

When you eat out, you might not feel like wading through the restaurant's wine list at all, knowing that it can be an ego-deflating experience. But don't give up without a fight. With a little guidance and a few tips, you can navigate the choppy waters of the wine list.

How Wine Is Sold in Restaurants

Believe it or not, restaurateurs really do want you to buy their wine. They usually make a sizable profit on every sale, their servers earn bigger tips and become happier employees, and you enjoy your meal more, going home a happier customer.

But traditionally (and, we trust, unwittingly), many restaurants have done more to hinder wine sales than to encourage them. Fortunately, the old ways are changing. (*Un*fortunately, they're changing slowly.)

Wines available for sale in a restaurant these days generally fall into four categories:

✔ The *house wines,* usually one white and one red, and sometimes also a sparkling wine. These can be purchased *by the glass* or in a *carafe* (a wide-mouthed handle-less pitcher). They are the wines you get when you simply ask for a glass of white or a glass of red.

✔ *Premium* wines, available by the glass. These offer a wider selection than the house wines and are generally better quality. (These wines are usually available also by the bottle.)

✔ Wines available by the bottle from the restaurant's *regular,* or standard, *wine list.*

✔ Older or rarer wines available by the bottle from a special wine list, sometimes called a *reserve wine list.*

Keep in mind that not all restaurants offer wines in all four categories.

The choice of the house

The wine list looks so imposing that you finally give up laboring over it. You hand it back to the server and say (either a bit sheepishly, because you're acknowledging that you can't handle the list, or with defiant bravado, signifying that you're not going to waste your time on this nonsense), "I'll just have a glass of white wine (or, 'Chardonnay')." Smart move, or big mistake?

You'll probably know the answer to this question as soon as the house wine hits your lips. It might be just what you wanted — and you avoided the effort of plowing through that list. But in theory, we'd say, "Mistake."

The "wine-by-the-glass" trend

We're delighted to see that more and more restaurants these days are offering interesting selections of wine by the glass. In its annual survey of quality restaurants, *Wine & Spirits* magazine reported that in 2002, these restaurants offered, on average, 19 wines by the glass.

Wine by the glass is a growing trend despite the challenges that it presents to restaurateurs. Their main problem is preserving the wine in all of those open bottles. The more wines a restaurant offers by the glass, the greater the odds that there will be wine left over in each bottle at the end of the evening, and those wines won't be fresh enough to serve the next day. To solve this problem, restaurateurs must have some sort of wine preservation system — sometimes an attractive console behind the bar that injects inert gas into the open bottles to displace oxygen, or some simpler, behind-the-scenes gadget to protect the leftover wine from air. Otherwise, unless they're lucky enough to finish every bottle every night, they will waste an enormous amount of wine. Their wine profits will go right down the drain! (Or into the stew!)

Usually, a restaurant's *house wines* are some inferior stuff that the restaurant owner is making an enormous profit on. (Cost-per-ounce is usually a restaurant owner's main criterion in choosing a house wine.) House wines can range in price from $3 up to $8 a glass (with an average of $5 to $6). Often, the entire bottle costs the proprietor the price of one glass, or less! No wonder the "obliging" server fills your glass to the brim.

By the way, you usually will save money if you buy the house wine by the carafe — if it's offered that way. On the other hand, you might not want an entire carafe of the house wine!

We've found that only a small percentage of better restaurants — and wine-conscious restaurants, often located in enlightened places like Napa or Sonoma — offer a house wine worth drinking. And it's practically never a good value. Under most circumstances, avoid the house wine. For the same reasons, avoid asking for "a glass of Chardonnay" or "a glass of Merlot."

If circumstances are such that a glass of wine makes the most sense (if you're the only one in your group who's having wine with dinner, for example), chances are you'll need to order the house wine, unless you're at a restaurant that offers premium selections by the glass as well. If the house wine is your only option, ask the server what it is. Don't be satisfied with the response, "It's Chardonnay"; ask for specifics. Chardonnay from where? What brand? Ask to see the bottle. Either your worst fears will be confirmed (you've never heard of the wine, or it has a reputation for being inferior), or you'll be pleasantly surprised (you *have* heard of the wine, and it has a good reputation). At least you'll know what you're drinking, for future reference.

Premium pours

The word *premium* is used very loosely by the wine industry. You might think that it refers to a rather high-quality wine, but when annual industry sales statistics are compiled for the U.S., *premium* indicates any wine that sells for more than $7 a bottle in stores!

As used in the phrase *premium wines by the glass,* however, *premium* usually does connote better quality. These are red and white wines that a restaurant offers at a higher price than its basic house wines. (Oh, we get it: You pay a premium for them!) Premium wines are usually in the $6 to $12 price range per glass.

A restaurant might offer just one premium white and one red, or it might offer several choices. These premium wines are not anonymous beverages, like the house red and white, but are identified for you somehow — on the wine list, on a separate card, verbally, or sometimes even by a display of bottles. (Why would you ever pay a premium for them if you didn't know what they were?) In some informal restaurants, wines by the glass are listed on a chalkboard.

Ordering premium wines by the glass is a fine idea, especially if you want to have only a glass or two or if you and your guests want to experiment by trying several wines. Sometimes we order a glass of a premium white wine or glass of Champagne as a starter and then go on to a bottle of red wine.

Of course, there's a catch. Only a small percentage of restaurants — the "wine-conscious" ones — offer premium wines by the glass. Also, you'll end up paying more for the wine if you order a bottle's worth of individual glasses than you would if you ordered a whole bottle to begin with.

When the restaurant doesn't have an alcohol license — BYOB

In most places, establishments that sell alcohol beverages — both retail stores and restaurants — must be licensed by the government to assure that all appropriate taxes are paid and to aid in the enforcement of local laws. Sometimes a restaurant doesn't have a liquor license due to circumstance or choice, and it therefore cannot sell wine. In those restaurants, you can BYOB (bring your own bottle of wine) to enjoy with your meal. (If you're not sure of the restaurant's policy on BYOB, call ahead.)

Many Chinese restaurants fall into this category, for example. (Although it can be difficult to match Asian cuisine with wine, we have found that Champagne and sparkling wine generally go well, as does off-dry German Riesling or Alsace Gewürztraminer.) Other examples include restaurants that have recently opened and have not yet received their liquor licenses, or restaurants that for some reason do not qualify for a license (they may be located too close to a school or a church, for example).

If two or three of you are ordering the same wine by the glass — and especially if you might want refills — ask how many ounces are poured into each glass (usually five to eight ounces) and compare the price with that of a 25.4-ounce (750 ml) bottle of the same wine. (You do usually have the option of buying an entire bottle.) Sometimes, for the cost of only three glasses you can have the whole bottle.

Special, or reserve, wine lists

Some restaurants — only a few, and usually the fanciest — offer a special wine list of rare wines to supplement their regular wine list. These special lists appeal to two types of customers: very serious wine connoisseurs and "high rollers." If you're not in either category, don't even bother asking if the restaurant has such a list. Then again, if you're not paying for the meal or if you seriously want to impress a client or a date, you might want to look at it! Try to get help with the list from some knowledgeable person on the restaurant staff, though: Any mistake you make could be a costly one.

The (anything but) standard wine list

Most of the time, you'll probably end up turning to the restaurant's standard wine list to choose your wine. Lucky you.

We use the term *standard wine list* to distinguish a restaurant's basic wine list from its special, or reserve, wine list. Unfortunately, there's nothing standard about wine lists at all. They come in all sizes, shapes, degrees of detail, degrees of accuracy, and degrees of user-friendliness (the latter usually ranging from moderate to nil).

If you're still hung up on the emotional-vulnerability potential of buying wine, don't even pick up a wine list. (Instead, turn to Chapter 6 and re-read our pep talk about wine buying in the section, "Buying Wine Can Intimidate Anyone.") When you're ready, read the following section to get a wine you'll like — with minimum angst.

How to Scope Out a Wine List

Your first step in the dark encounter between you and the wine list is to size up the opposition. You can do this by noting how the wine list is organized.

Read the headings on the wine list the way you'd read the chapter titles in a book that you were considering buying. Figure out how the wines are categorized and how they are arranged within each category. Notice how much or how little information is given about each wine. Check out the style of the list: Does it seem pretentious or straightforward? Estimate the number of wines on it — there could be 12 or 200. (An indirect benefit of this procedure is that the purposeful look in your eyes as you peruse the list will convince your guests that you know what you're doing.)

Sometimes, you'll discover that the list is very small, with hardly any wines on it. It's tough to look purposeful for very long when you're studying a list like that.

Sizing up the organization of the list

There's no way of predicting exactly what you'll find on the list, other than prices. Generally speaking, though, you may discover the wines arranged in the following categories:

- ✔ Champagne and sparkling wines
- ✔ (Dry) white wines
- ✔ (Dry) red wines
- ✔ Dessert wines

Wine list power struggles

In many restaurants, the servers don't give you enough time to study the wine list. (Really good restaurants recognize that choosing a bottle of wine can take some time and, therefore, don't put you in this position.) If your waiter asks, somewhat impatiently, "Have you selected your wine yet?" simply tell him (firmly) that you need more time. Don't be bullied into making a hasty choice.

Usually, your table will receive only one wine list. An outmoded convention dictates that only the host (the masculine is intentional) needs to see the list. (It's part of the same, outmoded thinking that dictates that females should receive menus with no prices on them.) At our table of two, there are *two* thinking, curious, decision-making customers. We ask for a second list.

Invariably, the wine list is handed to the oldest or most important-looking male at the table. If you are a female entertaining business clients, this situation can be insulting and infuriating. Speak up and ask for a copy of the wine list for yourself. If it's important enough to you, slip away from the table and inform the server that you are the host of the table.

The lowdown on high prices

Most restaurateurs count on wine and liquor sales to provide a disproportionate percentage of their business profit. The typical restaurant, therefore, charges two to two-and-a-half (sometimes three!) times the retail store price for a bottle of wine. That means that the restaurant is earning *three to four times* the price it paid for the bottle.

Admittedly, restaurateurs incur costs for wine storage, glasses, breakage, service, and so on. But those costs don't justify such extraordinary markups in the eyes of most wine drinkers.

Some savvy restaurateurs have discovered that by marking up their wines less, they actually sell *more* wine and make *more money* in the end. We try to patronize *those* restaurants.

If you frequent restaurants in Canada, you should know that restaurateurs there have a serious disadvantage (except in the province of Alberta): They must purchase their wines from the provincial liquor control authorities *at the same price as you would purchase the wines* for drinking in your own home. There's no such thing as wholesale for them — and prices reflect that fact.

After-dinner drinks like Cognac, Armagnac, single-malt Scotches, grappas, or liqueurs usually will not appear on the list, or if they do, they'll have their own section near the back of the list.

Some restaurants further subdivide the wines on their list according to country, especially in the white and red wine categories: French red wines, Italian red wines, American reds, and so on. These country sections might then be subdivided by wine region. France, for example, might have listings of Bordeaux, Burgundy, and possibly Rhône all under *French red wines. USA reds* may be divided into California wines, Oregon wines, and Washington wines.

Or you might find that the categories under white wines and red wines are the names of grape varieties — for example, a Chardonnay section, a Sauvignon Blanc section, and a miscellaneous *other dry whites* section, all under the general heading of white wines. If the restaurant features a particular country's cuisine, the wines of that country might be listed first (and given certain prominence), followed by a cursory listing of wines from other areas.

We've noticed two recent trends in wine-conscious restaurants, and we applaud them both, because they make ordering easier and more fun:

✓ **The so-called progressive wine list, in which wines appear in a progressive sequence under each category heading.** For example, under "Chardonnays," the wines are arranged by weight and richness, progressing from the lightest wines to the most intense, regardless of price.

✔ **Lists that use wine styles as their basic form of organization.** In these lists, the category headings are neither varietal nor regional, but describe the taste of the wines in each category, such as "Fresh, crisp, unoaked whites," or "Full-bodied, serious reds."

Getting a handle on the pricing

Often you'll find that within each category, the wines are arranged in ascending order of price with the least expensive wine first. Many a restaurateur is betting that you won't order that first wine out of fear of looking cheap. They figure you'll go for the second, third, or fourth wine down the price column or even deeper if you're feeling insecure and need the reassurance that your choice is a good one. (Meanwhile, that least expensive wine might be perfectly fine.)

What the wine list should tell you

The more serious a restaurant is about its wine selection, the more information it gives you about each wine.

Here's some information that's likely to be on the wine list:

✔ An *item number* for each wine. These are sometimes called *bin numbers,* referring to the specific location of each wine in the restaurant's cellar or wine storage room.

Item numbers make it easier for the server to locate and pull the wine quickly for you, after you order it. They're also a crutch to help the server bring you the right wine in case he doesn't have a clue about wine. They're also a crutch for *you* in ordering the wine in case you don't have a clue how to pronounce what you've decided to drink. (And you can always pretend that you're using the number for the waiter's benefit.)

✔ The name of each wine. These names might be grape names or place-names (see Chapter 4), but they had better also include the name of each producer (Château this or that, or such-and-such Winery), or you'll have no way of knowing exactly which wine any listing is meant to represent.

✔ A vintage indication for each wine — the year that the grapes were harvested. If the wine is a blend of wines from different years, it might say *NV,* for *non-vintage.* (Chapter 9 tells you why non-vintage wines exist.) Sometimes, you'll see *VV,* which means that the wine is a vintage-dated wine, but you're not allowed to know *which* vintage it is unless you ask.

The restaurateur just doesn't want to bother changing the year on the list when the wine's vintage changes. We're always annoyed when we see lists that don't name the wine's vintage.

✔ Sometimes, a brief description of the wines — but this is unlikely if dozens of wines are on the list.

✔ Sometimes, suggestions from the restaurateur for certain wines to go with their dinner entrées. In our experience, this information is helpful at times, but you might not always like — or agree with — their wine suggestion.

✔ Prices. There will *always* be a price for each wine.

Assessing the list's style

Once upon a time, the best wine lists consisted of hand-lettered pages inside heavy leather covers embossed with the words *Carte des Vins* in gold. Today, the best wine lists are more likely to be laser-printed pages or cards that more than make up in functionality what they sacrifice in romance.

The more permanent and immutable a wine list seems, the less accurate its listings are likely to be — and the less specific. Such lists suggest that no one is really looking after wine on a day-to-day basis in that restaurant. Chances are that many of the wines listed will be out of stock.

Sometimes, the list of wines is actually included on the restaurant's menu, especially if the menu is a computer-printed page or two that changes from week to week or from month to month. Restaurants featuring immediate, up-to-date wine listings like this can be a good bet for wine.

Digital browsing

A few restaurants have dared to go where no wine list has gone before: into the digital realm. Their wine lists — at least a few copies of them — are on portable computer screens, or e-books, that enable you not only to see the list of available wines and their prices, but also to read background information by tapping a wine's name; you can even request a list of wines that are suitable for the food you're ordering. Of course, these lists have their down-side: They're so much fun that you risk offending your friends by playing with the list for too long!

Many more restaurants have published their wine lists on the Internet. Before a special meal, you can go to the restaurant's Web site and make a short list of possible wines for your meal — guaranteed to boost your comfort level.

The world's most complicated wine list

We've heard that there's a restaurant in Colorado whose wine list is like this:

1. White wine

2. Red wine

3. Rosé wine

To avoid confusing the waiter, please order your wine by number."

How to Ask for Advice

If, after sizing up the wine list, you decide that you are not familiar with most of the wines on it, ask for help with your selection.

If the restaurant is a fancy one, ask if there's a *sommelier* (pronounced *som-mel-yay*) — technically, a specially trained, high-level wine specialist who is responsible for putting the wine list together and for making sure that the wines offered on the list complement the cuisine of the restaurant. (Unfortunately, only a few restaurants employ one — usually the most wine-conscious.)

If the restaurant is not particularly fancy, ask to speak with the wine specialist. Often someone on the staff, frequently the proprietor, knows the wine list well.

If someone on the restaurant staff knows the wine list well, this person is your best bet to help you select a wine. He or she will usually know what wines go best with the food you are ordering. He will also be extremely appreciative of your interest in the list. For these reasons, even though we are familiar with wine, we often consult the sommelier, proprietor, or wine specialist for suggestions from the wine list.

Timing counts

As soon as your server comes to the table, ask to see the wine list. Besides communicating to the server that you feel comfortable with wine (whether it's true or not), your asking for the list quickly gives you more time to study it.

Order the wine at the same time that you order the food — if not sooner; otherwise, you might be sipping water with your first course.

Here are some face-saving methods of getting help:

- If you are not sure how to pronounce the wine's name, point to it on the list, or use the wine's item or bin number (if there is one).

- Point out two or three wines on the list to the sommelier or server and say, "I'm considering these wines. Which one do you recommend?" This is also a subtle way of communicating your price range.

- Ask to *see* one or two bottles; the labels might help you make up your mind.

- Ask if there are any half-bottles (375 ml) or 500 ml bottles available (sometimes they're not listed). Smaller bottles give you wider possibilities in ordering: For example, you might drink one half-bottle of white wine and a half or full (750 ml) bottle of red wine.

- Mention the food you plan to order and ask for suggestions of wines that would complement the meal.

How to Ace the Wine Presentation Ritual

In many restaurants, the wine presentation occurs with such solemnity and ceremony that you'd think you were involved in high church or temple services. The hushed tones of the waiter, the ritualized performance — the seriousness of it all can make you want to laugh (but that seems wrong — like laughing in church). At the very least, you might be tempted to tell your waiter, "Lighten up! It's just a bottle of fermented fruit juice!"

Twice the price

A few profit-minded restaurateurs train their servers to maximize wine sales in every way possible — even at the customers' expense. For example, some servers are trained to refill wine glasses liberally so that the bottle is emptied before the main course arrives. (This can happen all the more easily when the glasses are large.) Upon emptying the bottle, the server asks, "Shall I bring another bottle of the same wine?" Depending on how much wine is in everyone's glass and how much wine your guests tend to drink, you might not *need* another bottle, but your tendency will be to say yes to avoid looking stingy.

An even trickier practice is to refill the glasses starting with the host, so that the bottle runs dry before each of the guests has had a refill. How can you refuse a second bottle at the expense of your guests' enjoyment?! You'll have to order that second bottle — and you should let the manager know how you feel about it when you leave. (But remember, these nefarious restaurant practices are the exception rather than the rule.)

Safe wine choices in a restaurant

White Wine:

Soave, Pinot Grigio, or Sancerre (if you like crisp, dry wines that aren't too flavorful)

Sauvignon Blanc from South Africa and New Zealand (if you like dry white wines with assertive flavor)

Mâcon-Villages or Pouilly-Fuissé (if you prefer a medium-bodied, characterful, dry white wine)

California or Australian Chardonnay (if you want a full-bodied, rich white wine)

Meursault (if a dry, full-bodied wine with a honeyeyed, nutty character sounds good to you)

Chenin Blanc, Vouvray, or German Riesling (generally medium-dry wines, for times when you don't want a wine that's very dry)

Red Wine:

Beaujolais (especially from a reputable producer, like Louis Jadot or Georges Duboeuf, when you want an easy-drinking, inexpensive red)

California red Zinfandel (when you need a versatile, flavorful, relatively inexpensive red that can even stand up to spicy food)

Oregon or California Pinot Noir (for a lighter red that's delicious young and works with all sorts of light- and medium-intensity foods)

Bourgogne Rouge (the basic French version of Pinot Noir)

Barbera or Dolcetto (widely available in Italian restaurants; dry, spicy, grapey, and relatively inexpensive)

Chianti Classico (a very dry, medium-bodied red wine that's great with food)

For more information on all these wines, refer to Chapters 10 through 14.

Actually, though, there's some logic behind the Wine Presentation Ritual.

Step by step, the Ritual (and the logic) goes like this:

1. **The waiter or sommelier presents the bottle to you (assuming that you are the person who ordered the wine) for inspection.**

The point of this procedure is to make sure that the bottle *is* the bottle you ordered. Check the label carefully. In our experience, 15 to 20 percent of the time it's the wrong bottle. Feel the bottle with your hand, if you like, to determine whether its temperature seems to be correct. (This is also a good time for you to pretend to recognize something about the label, as if the wine is an old friend, even if you've never seen it before.) If you're satisfied with the bottle, nod your approval to the server.

2. The server then removes the cork and places it in front of you.

The purpose of this step is for you to determine, by smelling and visually inspecting the cork, whether the cork is in good condition, and whether the cork seems to be the legitimate cork for that bottle of wine.

In rare instances, a wine may be so corky (see Chapter 2) that the cork itself will have an unpleasant odor. On even rarer occasions, the cork might be totally wet and shriveled or very dry and crumbly — either situation suggesting that air has gotten into the wine and spoiled it.

Once in your life, you might discover a vintage year or winery name on your cork that is different from that on the label. (Quick! Call the wine fraud police!) But most of the time, the presentation of the cork is inconsequential.

If the cork does raise your suspicions, you should still wait to smell or taste the wine itself before rejecting the bottle.

Once, when one of our wise-guy friends was presented the cork by the server, he proceeded to put it into his mouth and chew it, and then he pronounced to the waiter that it was just fine!

3. If your wine needs decanting, the server will decant it at this point.

For more information on decanting, see "How to aerate your wine" in Chapter 8.

4. The server pours a small amount of wine into your glass and waits.

At this point, you're *not* supposed to say, "Is that all you're giving me?!" You're expected to take a sniff of the wine, perhaps a little sip, and then either nod your approval to the waiter or murmur, "It's fine." Actually, this is an important step of the Wine Presentation Ritual because if something is *wrong* with the wine, *now* is the time to return it (not after you've finished half of the bottle!). For a review of wine-tasting technique, turn to Chapter 2 before you head out to the restaurant.

If you're not really sure whether the condition of the wine is acceptable, ask for someone else's opinion at your table and then make a group decision; otherwise, you risk feeling foolish by either returning the bottle later when it's been declared defective by one of your guests, or by drinking the stuff when it becomes clear to you later that there's something wrong with it. Either way, you suffer. Take as long as you need to on this step.

If you do decide that the bottle is out of condition, describe to the server what you find wrong with the wine, using the best language you can. (*Musty* or *dank* are descriptors that are easily understood.) Be sympathetic to the fact that you're causing more work for him, but don't be overly apologetic. (Why should you be? You didn't make the wine!) Let him smell or taste the wine himself if he would like. But don't let him make you feel guilty.

Depending on whether the sommelier or captain agrees that it's a bad bottle or whether he believes that you just don't understand the wine, he might bring you another bottle of the same, or he might bring you the wine list so that you can select a different wine. Either way, the Ritual begins again from the top.

5. **If you do accept the wine, the waiter will pour the wine into your guests' glasses and then finally into yours. Now you're allowed to relax.**

Restaurant Wining Tips

Wining in restaurants requires so many decisions that you really do need a guidebook. Should you leave the wine in an ice bucket? What should you do if the wine is bad? And can you bring your own wine? Let the following tips guide you:

✔ **Can I kick the ice-bucket habit?** Most servers assume that an ice bucket is necessary to chill white wines and sparkling wines. But sometimes the bottle is already so cold when it comes to you that the wine would be better off warming up a bit on the table. If your white wine goes into an ice bucket and you think it's getting *too* cold, remove it from the bucket, or have the waiter remove it. Just because that ice bucket is sitting there on your table (or next to your table) doesn't mean that your bottle has to be in it!

Sometimes, a red wine that's a bit too warm can benefit from five or ten minutes in an ice bucket. (But be careful! It can get too cold very quickly.) If the server acts as if you're nuts to chill a red wine, ignore him.

✔ **What's with these tiny glasses?** When various glasses are available, you can exercise your right to choose a different glass from the one you were given. If the restaurant's red wine glass is quite small, a stemmed water glass might be more appropriate for the red wine.

✔ **Should the wine "breathe"?** If a red wine you ordered needs aeration to soften its harsh tannins (see Chapter 8), merely pulling the cork will be practically useless in accomplishing that (because the air space at the neck of the bottle is too small). Decanting the bottle or pouring the wine into glasses is the best tactic.

✔ **Where's my bottle?** We prefer to have our bottle of wine on or near our table, not out of our reach. We can look at the label that way, and we don't have to wait for the server to remember to refill our glasses, either. (Okay, call us controlling.)

✔ **What if the bottle is bad?** Refuse any bottle that tastes or smells unpleasant (unless you brought it yourself!). A good restaurateur will always replace the wine, even if he thinks there's nothing wrong with it.

✔ **May I bring my own wine?** Some restaurants allow you to bring your own wine — especially if you express the desire to bring a special wine, or an older wine. Restaurants will usually charge a *corkage* fee (a fee for wine service, use of the glasses, and so on) that can vary from $10 to even $25 a bottle, depending on the attitude of the restaurant. You should never bring a wine that is already on the restaurant's wine list; it's cheap and it's insulting. (Call and ask the restaurant when you're not sure whether the wine is on its list.) Anyway, you certainly should call ahead to determine whether it's possible to bring wine (in some places, the restaurant's license prohibits it) and to ask what the corkage fee is.

✔ **What if I'm traveling abroad?** If you journey to countries where wine is made, such as France, Italy, Germany, Switzerland, Austria, Spain, or Portugal, by all means try the local wines. They will be fresher than the imports, in good condition, and the best values on the wine list. It doesn't make sense to order French wines, such as Bordeaux or Burgundy, in Italy, for example. Or California Cabernets in Paris.

Wine bars

Wine bars are fairly popular in London, Italy, and Paris. They are establishments that offer an extensive choice of wines by the glass — from 12 to 100 — as well as simple food to accompany the wines. The wine bottles are usually either hooked up to an inert-gas injection system, which keeps the wine fresh, or are topped up with inert gas from a freestanding dispenser after each serving. The former system often makes a dramatic centerpiece behind the bar.

In wine bars, you are sometimes offered a choice of two different *sizes* of wines by the glass. You can have a *taste* of a wine (about two-and-a-half ounces) for one price, or a *glass* of a wine (often five ounces) for another price. And you can often order a *flight* of wines — several similar wines served side by side so that you can compare them.

Wine bars are catching on now in the United States, especially in a few major cities such as New York, Chicago, and San Francisco. Wine bars are the ideal way to try lots of different wines by the glass — an educational as well as a satisfying experience. Hopefully, their numbers will increase with the years.

Chapter 8

Everything You Need to Know about Serving and Using Wine

*H*ave you ever broken a cork while trying to extract it from the bottle, or taken an unusually long time to remove a stubborn cork, while your guests smiled at you uneasily? This has certainly happened to us from time to time and probably to just about everyone else who has ever pulled a cork out of a bottle of wine. It's enough to give anyone a case of corkophobia!

Removing the cork from a wine bottle is the first challenge that faces you in your quest to enjoy wine, and it's a big one. (Fortunately, once you get the hang of it, it's easy — most of the time.) Afterwards, there are the niggling details of wine service, such as which type of glass to use and what to do if you don't finish the whole bottle. But help is at hand for the wine-challenged!

Getting the Cork Out

Before you can even think about removing the cork from a wine bottle, you need to deal with whatever covers the cork. Most wine bottles have a colorful covering over the cork end of the bottle that's called a *capsule*. Wineries place capsules on top of the corks for two reasons: to keep the corks clean, and to create a fetching look for their bottles.

These days, most wineries use colored foil or plastic capsules rather than the traditional lead capsules. In keeping with the sheerness trend in fashion, some wineries use a transparent cellophane covering that lets the cork show through; often, the sheer look graces special *flange-top* bottles, a fancy wine bottle with a protruding, flat lip at the top. (Some flange-top bottles sport colorful plastic plugs on top of the cork instead of cellophane.)

Whether the capsule is plastic, foil, or cellophane, we usually remove the entire capsule, so that no wine can possibly come into contact with the covering when we pour. (We use the small knife that's part of most *corkscrews* — the devices that exist solely for opening wine bottles.) When we encounter a plastic plug atop the cork instead of a capsule, we just flick it off with the tip of a knife.

After removing the capsule or plug, we wipe clean the top of the bottle with a damp cloth. Sometimes the visible end of the cork is dark with mold that developed under the capsule, and in that case, we wipe all the more diligently. (If you encounter mold atop the cork, don't be concerned. That mold is actually a good sign: It means that the wine has been stored in humid conditions. See Chapter 21 for information on humidity and other aspects of wine storage.)

Sometimes wine lovers just can't bring themselves to remove the whole capsule out of respect for the bottle of wine that they are about to drink. (In fact, traditional wine etiquette dictates that you do not remove the entire capsule.) Many people use a gizmo called a foil cutter that sells for about $6 or $7 in wine shops, kitchen stores, or specialty catalogs. However, the foil cutter does not cut the capsule low enough, in our opinion, to prevent wine from dripping over the edge of the foil into your glass. If you want to leave the capsule on, cut the foil with a knife under the second lip of the bottle, which is approximately three-fourths of an inch below the top of the bottle.

The right tools

Corkophobia or not, anyone can conquer most corks with a good corkscrew.

We suspect it's probably wise not to mention that we actually use three different corkscrews, each for certain situations, or that we use certain corkscrews only in desperation, as a last resort. We don't want to sound like snobs or fanatics. After all, who cares what kind of corkscrew you use as long as you can extract the cork and drink the wine?

We agree that getting to the wine is the important thing. But the voyage to the wine is much smoother sailing with a good corkscrew. And struggling over a puny piece of cork with a second-rate corkscrew will surely put you in a miserable mood before you even pour a drop.

The corkscrew not to use

The one corkscrew we absolutely avoid happens to be the most common type of corkscrew around. We don't like it for one very simple reason: It mangles the cork, almost guaranteeing that brown flakes will be floating in your glass of wine. (We also don't like it because it offends our sense of righteousness that an inferior product should be so popular.)

That corkscrew is the infamous Wing Type Corkscrew, a bright silver-colored, metal device that looks something like a pair of pliers; when you insert this corkscrew into a cork, two "wings" open out from the side of the corkscrew. The major shortcoming of this device is its very short worm, or *auger* (the curly prong that bores into the cork), which is too short for many corks and overly aggressive on all of them. Unfortunately, the Wing Type is the most commonly found corkscrew in most stores. No wonder people have trouble with corks!

Rather than finding out the hard way that this corkscrew just doesn't cut it (or, literally, cuts it too much!), as we did, invest a few dollars in a decent corkscrew right off the bat. The time and hassle you'll save will be more than worth the investment. Of the many types of wine-bottle openers available, we recommend the three described in the following sections.

The corkscrew to buy

The one indispensable corkscrew for every household is the Screwpull. It was invented in the early 1980s by a renowned Houston scientist, Dr. Herbert Allen, who was apparently tired of having a ten-cent piece of cork get the better of him.

The Screwpull is about six inches long. It consists of an arched piece of plastic (which looks like a clothespin on steroids) straddling an inordinately long, 5-inch worm that's coated with Teflon (see Figure 8-1). To use this corkscrew, you simply place the plastic over the bottle top (having removed the capsule), until a lip on the plastic is resting on the top of the bottle. Insert the worm through the plastic, until it touches the cork. Hold on to the plastic firmly while turning the lever atop the worm clockwise. The worm descends into the cork. Then you simply keep turning the lever in the same clockwise direction, and the cork magically emerges from the bottle. To remove the cork from the Screwpull, simply turn the lever counterclockwise while holding on to the cork.

The Screwpull comes in many colors — burgundy, black, and China red being the most common — and costs in the $20 range in wine shops, kitchen stores, and specialty catalogs. It's very simple to use, does not require a lot of muscle, and is our corkscrew of choice for most of the corks that we encounter.

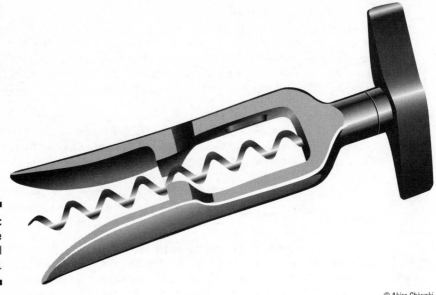

Figure 8-1:
The
Screwpull
corkscrew.

Other corkscrews worth owning

Did we say most? Well, you see, that's why we have two other corkscrews for the remaining corks that the Screwpull can't remove (or threatens to break itself on; after all, it is mostly plastic, and $20 is $20). Flange-top bottles, for example, really challenge the Screwpull because of their unusual width at the top.

Our two alternative corkscrews are smaller devices that — besides working better now and then — can conveniently fit into your pocket or apron. Their size is one reason that servers in restaurants favor them.

The two-pronged type that they use in California

One is called, unofficially, the Ah-So because (according to wine legend, anyway) when people finally figure out how it works, they say, "Ah, so that's how it works!" (It's also known as the "Butler's Friend" — but where are the butlers these days?)

It's a simple device made up of two thin, flat metal prongs, one slightly longer than the other (see Figure 8-2). To use it, you slide the prongs down into the tight space between the cork and the bottle (inserting the longer prong first), using a back-and-forth seesaw motion until the top of the Ah-So is resting on the top of the cork. Then you twist the cork while gently pulling it up.

One advantage of the Ah-So is that it delivers an intact cork, without a hole in it, that can be reused to close bottles of homemade vinegar, or to make cutesy bulletin boards.

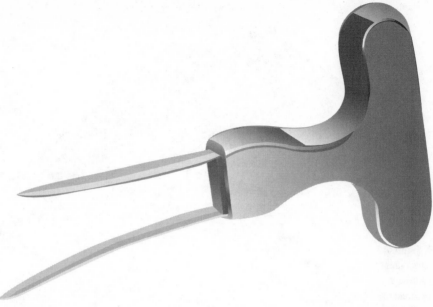

Figure 8-2:
The Ah-So
corkscrew.

Although more difficult to operate than the Screwpull, the Ah-So really comes into its own with very tight-fitting corks that no other corkscrews, including the Screwpull, seem to be able to budge. Also, the Ah-So can be effective with old, crumbly corks in which other corkscrews cannot get a proper grip.

The Ah-So is useless with loose corks that move around in the bottle's neck when you try to remove them. It just pushes those corks down into the wine. At that point, you'll need another tool called a *cork retriever* (which we describe in the "Waiter, there's cork in my wine!" section, later in this chapter).

The Ah-So sells for around $6 to $8. It seems to be especially popular in California for no particular reason that we've ever been able to figure out.

The most professional corkscrew of them all

Our final recommended corkscrew, probably the most commonly used corkscrew in restaurants all over the world, is simply called the Waiter's Corkscrew. A straight metal base holds three devices that fold into it, like a Swiss Army knife: a lever; a small, two-inch worm; and a little knife (see Figure 8-3). The latter is especially handy for removing the capsule from the bottle.

Figure 8-3:
The Waiter's
Corkscrew.

Using the Waiter's Corkscrew requires some practice. First, wrap a fist around the bottle's neck. The trick then is to guide the worm down through the center of the cork, by turning the corkscrew; turn slowly at first, until you're sure that the worm is descending down the middle of the cork rather than the side. After the worm is fully descended into the cork, place the lever on the lip of the bottle and push against the lever while lifting the cork up. Give a firm pull at the very end or wiggle the bottom of the cork out with your hand.

Why is my cork blue?

Have you ever opened a bottle of wine and discovered that the "cork" is not cork at all, but plastic — and brightly colored, to boot?

While we appreciate the touch of whimsy that an orange or blue cork contributes, we must admit that we are not fans of plastic corks. We can understand winemakers' disillusion with real cork, due to its potential to taint a wine with off-aromas. But if you're going to invent an alternative to cork, why invent yet another closure that sits in the bottle's neck as a rude barrier between wine drinkers and their wine, demanding the same, complicated tool as a cork does — and can be even more difficult to remove?! Fortunately, some new versions of synthetic corks are relatively user-friendly compared to earlier types. But screwcaps are even more so.

The comeback of the screwcap

Instead of imitation cork (see the sidebar "Why is my cork blue?"), we'd prefer to see real screwcaps on most wine bottles. Screwcaps are perfectly sound closures, technically speaking. And they prevent "cork taint," a chemical flaw affecting a small percentage of corks, and consequently the wine in those bottles. A "corky" wine — that is, one affected with cork taint — is damaged either slightly or flagrantly. In the worst-case scenarios, corky wines give off an offensive odor similar to moldy or damp cardboard.

Formerly, only the least expensive, lower-quality wines had screwcap closures. But in the last few years, as a reaction to the corky wine problem, more and more wine producers have been switching from corks to screwcaps. For example, a number of New Zealand and Australian wineries are now using screwcaps, especially for their white wines. Some Swiss producers have been using screwcaps for their quality wines for years now, especially for half-bottles. And now some California producers, notably Bonny Doon, are dressing their bottles with screwcaps. Is this the start of a movement? Fine with us.

If your cork ever breaks and part of it gets stuck in the neck of the bottle, the Waiter's Corkscrew is indispensable for removing the remaining piece. Use the method we just described, but insert the worm at a 45-degree angle instead. In most cases, you will successfully remove the broken cork.

The Waiter's Corkscrew sells for as little as $7, but designer versions can cost more than ten times that much.

Waiter, there's cork in my wine!

Every now and then, even if you've used the right corkscrew and used it properly, you can still have pieces of cork floating in your wine. They can be tiny dry flakes that crumbled into the bottle, actual chunks of cork, or even the entire cork.

Before you start berating yourself for being a klutz, you should know that Floating Cork has happened to all of us at one time or another, no matter how experienced we are. Cork won't harm the wine. And besides, there's a wonderful instrument called a *cork retriever* (no, it's not a small dog from the south of Ireland!) available in specialty stores and in catalogs, although it's considerably more difficult to find than a corkscrew.

The cork retriever consists of three 10-inch pieces of stiff metal wire with hooks on the ends. This device is remarkably effective in removing floating pieces of cork from the bottle. We have even removed a whole cork from the neck with a cork retriever (fearing the whole time that the bottle neck would explode when we tried to force the cork *and* the retriever back up through the tiny diameter).

Alternatively, you can just pick out the offending piece(s) of cork with a spoon after you pour the wine into your glass. (That's one occasion when it's rude to serve your guest first, because the first glass has more cork pieces in it.) Or you can pour the wine through a paper coffee filter (preferably rinsed with hot water, to remove the chemicals) into a decanter or pitcher to catch the remaining pieces of cork.

A Special Case: Opening Champagne and Sparkling Wine

Opening a bottle of sparkling wine is often an exciting occasion. Who doesn't enjoy the ceremony of a cold glass of bubbly? But you need to use a completely different technique than you'd use to open a regular wine bottle. The cork even looks different. Sparkling wine corks have a mushroom-shaped head that protrudes from the bottle and a wire cage that holds the cork in place against the pressure that's trapped inside the bottle.

Never, ever use a corkscrew on a bottle of sparkling wine. The pressure of the trapped carbonation, when suddenly released, could send the cork *and* corkscrew flying right into your eye.

Forget how the victors do it in locker rooms

If your bottle of bubbly has just traveled, let it rest for a while, preferably a day. Controlling the cork is difficult when the carbonation has been stirred up. (Hey, you wouldn't open a large bottle of soda that's warm and shaken up, either, would you? Sparkling wine has much more carbonated pressure than soda, and needs more time to settle down.)

If you're in the midst of a sparkling wine emergency and need to open the bottle anyway, one quick solution is to calm down the carbonation by submerging the bottle in an ice bucket for about 30 minutes. (Fill the bucket with one-half ice cubes and one-half ice-cold water.)

In any case, be careful when you remove the wire cage, and keep one hand on top of the cork as a precaution. (We had a hole in our kitchen ceiling from one adventure with a flying cork.) Be sure to point the bottle away from people and other fragile objects.

A sigh is better than a pop

If you like to hear the sparkling wine pop, just yank the cork out. When you do that, however, you'll lose some of the precious wine, which will froth out of the bottle. Also, the noise could interfere with your guests' conversation. Besides, it ain't too classy!

Removing the cork from sparkling wine with just a gentle sigh rather than a loud pop is fairly easy. Simply hold the bottle at a 45-degree angle with a towel wrapped around it if it's wet. (Try resting the base of the bottle on your hipbone.) Twist the bottle while holding on to the cork so that you can control the cork as it emerges. When you feel the cork starting to come out of the bottle, *push down against the cork* with some pressure as if you don't want to let it out of the bottle. In this way, the cork will emerge slowly with a hissing or sighing sound rather than a pop.

Every once in a while, you'll come across a really tight cork that doesn't want to budge. Try running the top of the bottle under warm water for a few moments, or wrapping a towel around it to create friction. Either one of these actions will usually enable you to remove the cork.

Another option is to purchase a fancy gadget resembling a pair of pliers (there are actually three gadgets: Champagne Pliers, a Champagne Star, and a Champagne Key) that you place around the part of the cork that's outside the bottle. Or you could probably try using regular pliers, although lugging in the toolbox will surely change the mood of the occasion.

Does Wine Really Breathe?

Most wine is alive in the sense that it changes chemically as it slowly grows older. Wine absorbs oxygen and, like our own cells, it oxidizes. When the grapes turn into wine in the first place, they give off carbon dioxide, just like us. So we suppose you could say that wine breathes, in a sense.

But that's not what the server means when he asks, "Shall I pull the cork and let the wine breathe, sir (or madam)?" The term *breathing* usually refers to the process of aerating the wine, exposing it to air. Sometimes the aroma and flavor of a very young wine will improve with aeration. But just pulling the cork out of the bottle and letting the bottle sit there is a truly ineffective way to aerate the wine. The little space at the neck of the bottle is way too small to allow your wine to breathe very much.

How to aerate your wine

If you really want to aerate your wine, do one or both of the following:

1. Pour the wine into a *decanter* (a fancy word for a glass container that is big enough to hold the contents of an entire bottle of wine).

2. Pour the wine into large glasses at least ten minutes before you plan to drink it.

Practically speaking, it doesn't matter what your decanter looks like or how much it costs. In fact, the very inexpensive, wide-mouthed carafes are fine.

Which wines need aerating?

Many red wines but only a few white wines — and some dessert wines — can benefit from aeration. You can drink most white wines upon pouring, unless they're too cold, but that's a discussion for later.

Young, tannic red wines

Young red wines, especially those that are high in tannin (see Chapter 2 for more on tannin) — such as Cabernet Sauvignons, Bordeaux, many wines from the Rhône Valley, and many Italian wines — actually taste better with aeration because their tannins soften and the wine becomes less harsh.

The younger and more tannic the wine is, the longer it needs to breathe. As a general rule, most tannic, young red wines soften up with one hour of aeration. A glaring exception to the one-hour rule would be many young Barolos or Barbarescos (red wines from Piedmont, Italy, which you can read about in Chapter 11); these wines are frequently so tannic that they can practically stand up by themselves without a decanter. They often can benefit from three or four hours of aeration.

Older red wines with sediment

Many red wines develop *sediment* (tannin and other matter in the wine that solidifies over time) usually after about eight years of age. The sediment can taste a bit bitter (remember, it's tannin). Also, the dark particles floating in your wine, usually near the bottom of your glass, don't look very appetizing.

To remove sediment, keep the bottle of wine upright at least a day or two before you plan to open it so that the sediment settles at the bottom of the bottle. Then decant the wine carefully: Pour the wine out of the bottle slowly into a decanter while watching the wine inside the bottle as it approaches the neck. You watch the wine so that you can stop pouring when you see cloudy wine from the bottom of the bottle making its way to the neck. When you stop pouring at the right moment, all the cloudy wine remains behind in the bottle.

To actually see the wine inside the bottle as you pour, you need to have a bright light shining through the bottle's neck. Candles are commonly used for this purpose, and they are romantic, but a flashlight standing on end works even better. (It's brighter, and it doesn't flicker.) Or simply hold the bottle up to a bright light, and pour slowly. Stop pouring the wine into the decanter when you reach the sediment, which should be toward the bottom of the bottle.

The older the wine, the more delicate it can be. Don't give old, fragile-looking wines excessive aeration. (Look at the color of the wine through the bottle before you decant; if it looks pale, the wine could be pretty far along its maturity curve.) The flavors of really old wines will start fading rapidly after 10 or 15 minutes of being exposed to air.

If the wine needs aeration after decanting (that is, it still tastes a bit harsh), let it breathe in the open decanter. If the wine has a dark color, chances are that it is still quite youthful and will need to breathe more. Conversely, if the wine has a brick red or pale garnet color, it probably has matured and might not need much more aeration.

A few white wines

Some very good, dry white wines — such as full-bodied white Burgundies and white Bordeaux wines, as well as the best Alsace whites — also get better with aeration. For example, if you open up a young Corton-Charlemagne (a great white Burgundy), and it doesn't seem to be showing much aroma or flavor, chances are that it needs aeration. Decant it and try it again in half an hour. In most cases, your wine will dramatically improve.

Vintage Ports

One of the most famous fortified wines is Vintage Port (properly called "Porto"). We discuss this wine and others like it in Chapter 16.

For now, we'll just say that, yes, Vintage Port needs breathing lessons, very much so indeed! Young Vintage Ports are so brutally tannic that they demand many hours of aeration (eight would not be too much). Even older Ports will improve with four hours or more of aeration. Older Vintage Ports require decanting for another reason: They are chock-full of sediment. (Often, large flakes of sediment fill the bottom 10 percent of the bottle.) Keep Vintage Ports standing for several days before you open them.

Exceptions to the "decant your red wines and Ports" rule

The exceptions prove the rule. The majority of red wines you drink do not require decanting, aeration, or any special preparation other than pulling the cork out and having a glass handy.

The following red wines *do not* need decanting:

- Lighter-bodied, less tannic red wines, such as Pinot Noirs, Burgundies, Beaujolais, and Côtes du Rhônes; lighter red Zinfandels; and lighter-bodied Italian reds, such as Dolcettos, Barberas, and lighter Chiantis. These wines don't have much tannin and, therefore, don't need much aeration.

- Inexpensive (less than $12) red wines. Same reason as preceding.

- Tawny ports — in fact, any other Ports except Vintage Ports. These wines should be free from sediment (which stayed behind in the barrels where the wine aged) and are ready to drink when you pour them.

Does the Glass Really Matter?

If you're just drinking wine as refreshment with your meal, and you aren't thinking about the wine much as it goes down, the glass you use probably doesn't matter in the least. A jelly glass? Why not? Plastic glasses? We've used them dozens of times on picnics, not to mention in airplanes (where the wine's quality usually doesn't demand great glasses, anyway).

But if you have a good wine, a special occasion, friends who want to talk about the wine with you, or the boss for dinner, *stemware* (glasses with stems) is called for. And it's not just a question of etiquette and status: Good wine tastes better out of good glasses. Really.

Compare wine glasses to stereo speakers. Any old speaker brings the music to your ears, just like any old glass brings the wine to your lips. But (assuming that you care to notice it) can't you appreciate the sound so much more, aesthetically and emotionally, from good speakers? The same principle holds true with wine and wine glasses. You can appreciate wine's aroma and flavor complexities so much more out of a fine wine glass. The medium is the message.

The right color: none

Good wine glasses are always clear. (It's okay for jelly glasses to have pictures of the Flintstones on them, as long as the background is clear.) Those pretty pink or green glasses may look nice in your china cabinet, but they interfere with your ability to distinguish the true colors of the wine.

Thin but not tiny

Believe it or not (we didn't always), the taste of a wine changes when you drink the wine out of different types of glasses. A riot almost broke out at one wine event we organized because the same wine tasted so different in different glasses that the tasters thought we served them different wines — and that we had just pretended it was all the same wine, to fool them. We learned that three aspects of a glass are important: its size, its shape, and the thickness of the glass.

Size

For dry red and white wine, small glasses are anathema — besides that, they're a pain in the neck. You just can't swirl the wine around in those little glasses without spilling it, which makes appreciating the aroma of the wine almost impossible. And furthermore, who wants to bother continually refilling them? Small glasses can work adequately only for sherry or dessert wines, which have strong aromas to begin with and are generally consumed in smaller quantities than table wines. But in most cases, larger is usually better.

- ✔ Glasses for red wines should hold a minimum of 12 ounces; many of the best glasses have capacities ranging from 16 to 24 ounces, or more.
- ✔ For white wines, 10 to 12 ounces should be the minimum capacity.
- ✔ For sparkling wines, an 8 to 12 ounce capacity is fine.

Thickness and shape

Stemware made of very thin, fine crystal costs a lot more than normal glasses. That's one reason why many people don't use it, and why some people do. The better reason for using fine crystal is that the wine tastes better out of it. We're not sure whether the elegant crystal simply heightens the aesthetic experience of wine drinking or whether there's some more scientific reason.

The shape of the bowl also matters. Some wine glasses have very round bowls, while others have more elongated, somewhat narrower bowls. Often, when we're having dinner at home, we like to try our wine in glasses of different shapes, just to see which glass works best for that wine. We discuss the functions of various glass shapes in the next section.

Tulips, flutes, trumpets, and other picturesque wine-glass names

You thought that a tulip was a flower and a flute was a musical instrument? Well, they also happen to be types of glasses designed for use with sparkling wine. The tulip is the ideally shaped glass for bubblies (see Figure 8-4). It is tall, elongated, and narrower at the rim than in the middle of the bowl. This shape helps hold the bubbles in the wine longer, not allowing them to escape freely (the way the wide-mouthed, sherbet-cuplike, so-called Champagne glasses do).

The flute is another good sparkling wine glass (see Figure 8-5); but it is less ideal than the tulip because it does not narrow at the mouth. The trumpet actually widens at the mouth, making it less suitable for sparkling wine but very elegant looking (see Figure 8-6). Another drawback of the trumpet glass is that, depending on the design, the wine could actually fill the whole stem, which means the wine warms up from the heat of your hand as you hold the stem. Avoid the trumpet glass; it has no useful purpose as a wine glass.

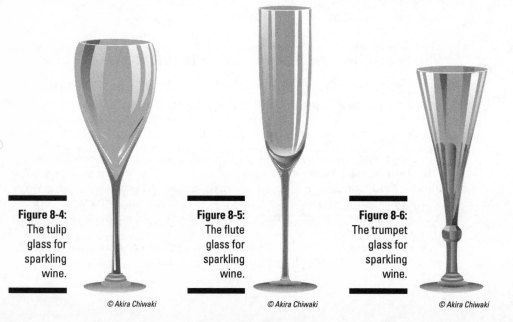

Figure 8-4:
The tulip glass for sparkling wine.

© Akira Chiwaki

Figure 8-5:
The flute glass for sparkling wine.

© Akira Chiwaki

Figure 8-6:
The trumpet glass for sparkling wine.

© Akira Chiwaki

An oval-shaped bowl that is narrow at its mouth (see Figure 8-7) is ideal for many red wines, such as Bordeaux, Cabernet Sauvignons, Merlots, Chiantis, and Zinfandels. On the other hand, some red wines, such as Burgundies, Pinot Noirs, and Barolos, are best appreciated in wider-bowled, apple-shaped glasses (see Figure 8-8). Which shape and size works best for which wine has to do with issues such as how the glass's shape controls the flow of wine onto your tongue. One glassmaker, Riedel Crystal, has designed a specific glass for every imaginable type of wine!

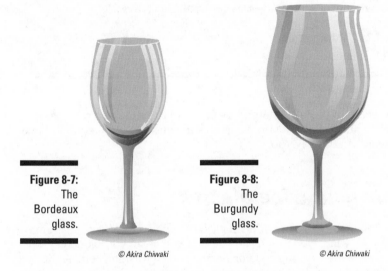

Figure 8-7:
The Bordeaux glass.

© Akira Chiwaki

Figure 8-8:
The Burgundy glass.

© Akira Chiwaki

How many glasses do I need, anyway?

So what's a wine lover to do: Buy different glasses for each kind of wine? Fortunately, some all-purpose red and white wine glasses combine the best features, in terms of size, thickness, and shape, of most glasses. And you don't have to pay a fortune for decent glassware. A company called St. George Crystal makes crystal glasses in all sizes and shapes that sell for about $4 apiece. They are available in most wine stores.

If you want something finer, try Riedel or Spiegelau Crystal. Riedel is an Austrian glass manufacturer that specializes in making the right wine glass for each kind of wine. (Spiegelau, a German company, operates similarly, but its glasses are less expensive than Riedel's). You can buy these glasses in many department stores, specialty shops, or glass companies, such as the Flemington Glass Company in Flemington, New Jersey.

Half empty or half full?

"Fill 'er up" might be the rule for your service station attendant, but not for the person pouring wine. It always annoys us when servers fill our glasses to the top. We guess they don't want to bother re-pouring the wine too often. Or maybe they want to give us our money's worth. But how can we stick our noses into full glasses without looking like idiots? Once a kid at a nearby table blurted out, "Look, Mom, that man is drinking with his nose!"

To leave some margin of safety for swirling and smelling the wine, fill the glass only partially. One-third capacity, at the most, is the best fill-level for serious red wines. (This goes back to that idea of aerating the wine.) White wine glasses can be filled halfway, while sparkling wines can be three-quarters full.

The more you care to pay attention to the flavor of the wine, the more you truly appreciate and enjoy wine from a good wine glass. If you just don't have an ear for music, that's okay, too.

Washing your wine glasses

Detergents often leave a filmy residue in glasses, which can affect the aroma and flavor of your wine. We strongly advise that you clean your good crystal glasses by hand, using washing soda or baking soda. (Washing soda is the better of the two; it doesn't cake up, like baking soda.) Neither product leaves any soapy, filmy residue in your glass. You can find washing soda in the soap/detergent section of supermarkets.

Serving Wine Not Too Warm, Not Too Cold

Just as the right glass will enhance your wine experience, serving wine at the ideal temperature is a vital factor in your enjoyment of wine. Frequently, we have tasted the same wine at different temperatures (and, believe it or not, at different barometric pressures) and have loved the wine on one occasion but disliked it the other time!

Most red wines are at their best at cool room temperature, 62° to 65°F (16° to 18°C). Once upon a time, in drafty old English and Scottish castles, that was simply room temperature. (Actually, it was probably *warm, high noon room temperature!*) Today when you hear room temperature, you think of a room that's about 70°F (21°C), don't you? Red wine served at this temperature can taste flat, flabby, lifeless, and often too *hot* — you get a burning sensation from the alcohol.

Ten or fifteen minutes in the fridge will do wonders to revive red wines that have been suffering from heat prostration. But don't let the wine get too cold. Red wines served too cold taste overly tannic and acidic, decidedly unpleasant. Light, fruity red wines, such as Beaujolais, are most delightful when served slightly chilled at about 58° to 60°F (14° to 15.5°C).

Are you wondering how to know when your bottle is 58° to 60°F? You could buy a nifty digital thermometer that wraps around the outside of the bottle and gives you a color-coded reading. Or you could buy something that looks like a real thermometer that you place into the opened bottle (in the bottle's mouth, you might say). We have both of those, and we never use them. Just feel the bottle with your hand and take a guess. Practice makes perfect.

Just as many red wines are served too warm, most white wines are definitely served too cold, judging by the service that we have received in many restaurants. The higher the quality of a white wine, the less cold it should be so that you can properly appreciate its flavor. Table 8-1 indicates our recommended serving temperatures for various types of wines.

Table 8-1	Serving Temperatures for Wine	
Type of wine	*Temperature °F*	*Temperature °C*
Most Champagnes and sparkling wines	45°F	7°C
Older or expensive, complex Champagnes	52°–54°F	11°–12°C
Inexpensive sweet wines	50°–55°F	10°–12.8°C
Rosés and blush wines	50°–55°F	10°–12.8°C
Simpler, inexpensive, quaffing-type white wines	50°–55°F	10°–12.8°C
Dry Sherry, such as fino or manzanilla	55°–56°F	12°–13°C
Fine, dry white wines	58°–62°F	14°–16.5°C

(continued)

Table 8-1 *(continued)*

Type of wine	Temperature °F	Temperature °C
Finer dessert wines, such as a good Sauternes	58°–62°F	14°–16.5°C
Light, fruity red wines	58°–60°F	14°–14.5°C
Most red wines	62°–65°F	16°–18°C
Sherry other than dry fino or manzanilla	62°–65°F	16°–18°C
Port	62°–65°F	16°–18°C

To avoid the problem of warm bubbly, keep an ice bucket handy. Or put the bottle back in the refrigerator between pourings.

Storing Leftover Wine

A sparkling-wine stopper, a device that fits over an opened bottle, is really effective in keeping any remaining Champagne or sparkling wine fresh (often for several days) in the refrigerator. But what do you do when you have red or white wine left in the bottle?

WARNING!

An aside about atmospheric pressure

File this under FYI ("For Your Information") — or maybe under "Believe It or Not."

Several years ago, we were enjoying one of our favorite red wines, an Italian Barbera, in the Alps. It was a perfect summer day in the mountains — crisp, clear, and cool. The wine was also perfect — absolutely delicious with our salami, bread, and cheese. A couple of days later, we had the very same wine at the seashore, on a cloudy, humid, heavy-pressure day. The wine was heavy, flat, and lifeless. What had happened to our wonderful mountain wine? We made inquiries among some of our wine-drinking friends and discovered that they had had similar experiences. For red wines, at least, atmospheric pressure apparently influences the taste of the wine: thin, light pressure, for the better; heavy pressure, heavy humidity, for the worse. So the next time one of your favorite red wines doesn't seem quite right, check the air pressure! Believe it or not.

You can put the cork back in the bottle if it still fits, and put the bottle into the refrigerator. (Even red wines will stay fresher there; just take the bottle out to warm up a couple of hours before serving it.) But four other methods are also reliable in keeping your remaining wine from oxidizing (these techniques are all the more effective if you put the bottle in the fridge after using them):

- ✓ If you have about half a bottle of wine left, you can simply pour the wine into a clean, empty half-sized wine bottle and recork the smaller bottle. We sometimes buy wines in half-bottles, just to make sure that we have the empty half-bottles around.

- ✓ There is a handy, inexpensive, miniature pump called a Vac-U-Vin that you can buy in most wine stores. This pump removes the oxygen from the bottle, and the rubber stoppers that come with it prevent additional oxygen from entering the bottle. It's supposed to keep your wine fresh for up to a week, but it doesn't always work that well, in our experience.

- ✓ You can buy small cans of inert gas in some wine stores. Just squirt a few shots of the gas into the bottle through a skinny straw, which comes with the can, and put the cork back in the bottle. The gas displaces the oxygen in the bottle, thus protecting the wine from oxidizing. Simple and effective. Private Preserve is one of the better brands; it is highly recommended.

- ✓ A new device, called WineSavor, is a flexible plastic disk that you roll up and insert down the bottle's neck. Once inside the bottle, the disk opens up and floats on top of the wine, blocking the wine from oxygen.

To avoid all this bother, just drink the wine! Or, if you're not too fussy, just place the leftover wine in the refrigerator and drink it in the next day or two — before it goes into a coma.

Entertaining with Wine

When you're hosting a dinner party, you'll probably serve more wines than you would in the course of a normal dinner. Instead of just one wine all through the meal, you might want to serve a different wine with every course. Many people serve two wines at the table: a white with the first course and a red with the entrée. (And if they love wine, they'll use a cheese course as an excuse to serve a second, knockout red.)

Because you want every wine to taste even better than the one before it — besides blending perfectly with the food you're serving — you should give some thought to the sequence in which the wines will be served. The classic guidelines are the following:

> ✔ White wine before red wine
>
> ✔ Light wine before heavy wine
>
> ✔ Dry wine before sweet wine
>
> ✔ Simple wine before complex, richly flavored wine

Each of these principles operates independently. You needn't go crazy trying to follow all of them together, or you'll be able to drink nothing but light, dry, simple whites and heavy, complex, sweet reds! A very light red wine served before a rich, full-bodied white can work just fine. If the food you're serving calls for only white wine, there's really no reason that both wines couldn't be white: a simpler, lighter white first and a richer, fuller-bodied white second. Likewise, both wines could be red, or you could serve a dry rosé followed by a red.

First things first

Even if you don't plan to serve hors d'oeuvres, you'll probably want to offer your guests a drink when they arrive to set a relaxing tone for the evening.

We like to serve Champagne (notice the capital C) as the apéritif because opening the bottle of Champagne is a ceremony that brings together everyone in the group. Champagne honors your guests. And a glass of Champagne is compelling enough that to spend a thoughtful moment tasting it doesn't seem rude; even people who think it's absurd to talk about wine understand that Champagne is too special to be ignored. Unlike many white wines, Champagne stands alone just fine, without food.

How much is enough

The necessary quantity of each wine depends on all sorts of issues, including the number of wines you serve (if there are several, you need less of each), the pace of service (if you plan a long, leisurely meal, you'll need more of each wine), and the size of your wine glasses. If you're using oversized glasses, you need more of each wine, because it's easy to pour more than you realize into each glass.

Assuming a full-blown dinner that includes an apéritif wine, two wines with dinner, and another with cheese — and guests who all drink moderately — we recommend that you plan to have one bottle of each wine for every four people. That gives each person four ounces of each wine, with plenty left over in the 25-ounce bottle for refills. When serving two wines, plan one bottle of each wine per couple.

One simpler rule is to figure, in total, a full bottle of wine per guest (total consumption). That quantity might sound high, but if your dinner is spread over several hours and you're serving a lot of food, it really isn't immoderate. If you're concerned that your guests might overindulge, be sure that their water glasses are always full so that they have an alternative to automatically reaching for the wine.

If your dinner party is special enough to have several food courses and several wines, we recommend giving each guest a separate glass for each wine. The glasses can be different for each wine, or they can be alike. All those glasses really look festive on the table. And with a separate glass for each wine, no guest feels compelled to empty each glass before going on to the next wine. (You also can tell at a glance who is drinking the wine and who isn't really interested in it, and you can adjust your pouring accordingly.)

Chapter 9

Judging a Wine by Its Label

. . . .

In This Chapter

▶ The language of the wine label

▶ The truth behind impressive terms like *reserve* and *estate-bottled*

▶ Vintage versus nonvintage wines

▶ AOC, DOC, DO, QbA, QWPSR, and other strange designations

. . . .

*W*e're standing at the immigration desk in some foreign airport, and a distrustful officer is studying our passports. We're disheveled after six hours of trying to sleep in seats too small to sit in. He needs to make a judgment about us, and all he has to go on is the sketchy information in our passports and our tired faces.

Do you sometimes feel like that immigration officer when you stand in front of an array of wine bottles and attempt to make a judgment about which to buy? To the untrained eye, the labels hardly say more than a passport, and the pretty pictures on the labels are even less relevant to what's inside the bottles than passport photos are to a traveler's true appearance.

The Wine Label and What It Tells You

Every bottle of wine must have a label, and that label must provide certain information about the wine. Some of the information on a wine label is required by the country where the wine is *made*. Other items of information are required by the country where the wine is *sold*. When the requirements are different in the two places, life can get very, very complicated for label writers!

The forward and backward of wine labels

Many wine bottles have two labels. The front label names the wine and grabs your eye as you walk down the aisle, and the back label gives you a little more information, ranging from really helpful suggestions like "this wine tastes delicious with food" to oh-so-useful data such as "this wine has a total acidity of 6.02 and a pH of 3.34."

Now, if you're really on your toes, you might be thinking: How can you tell the difference between front and back on a round bottle?

The government authorities in the U.S. apparently haven't thought that one through yet. They (and other governments) require certain information to appear on the front label of all wine bottles — basic stuff, such as the alcohol content, the type of wine (usually *red table wine* or *white table wine*), and the country of origin — but they don't define *front label*. So sometimes producers put all that information on the smaller of two labels and call that one the front label. Then the producers place a larger, colorful, dramatically eye-catching label — with little more than the name of the wine on it — on the *back* of the bottle. Guess which way the back label ends up facing when the bottle is placed on the shelf?

We don't feel at all outraged about this situation. We'd rather look at colorful labels on the shelf than boring information-laden ones any day. And we're not so lazy that we can't just pick up the bottle and turn it around to find out what we need to know. Besides, we enjoy the idea that wine producers and importers — whose every word and image on the label is scrutinized by the authorities — have found one small way of getting even with the government.

The mandatory sentence

The federal government mandates that certain items of information appear on labels of wines sold in the U.S. (see Figure 9-1). Such items are generally referred to as *the mandatory.* These include

- ✔ A brand name
- ✔ Indication of class or type (table wine, dessert wine, or sparkling wine)
- ✔ The percentage of alcohol by volume (unless it is implicit — for example, the statement "table wine" implies an alcohol content of less than 14 percent; see the section "Table wine" in Chapter 1)
- ✔ Name and location of the bottler
- ✔ Net contents (expressed in milliliters; the standard wine bottle is 750 ml, which is 25.6 ounces)
- ✔ The phrase *Contains Sulfites* (with very, very few exceptions)
- ✔ The government warning (that we won't dignify by repeating here; just pick up any bottle of wine and you'll see it)

Will the real producer please stand up?

Although U.S. and Canadian labeling laws require wine labels to carry the name and address of the bottler or dealer, respectively, this information doesn't necessarily tell you who made the wine.

Of the various phrases that may be used to identify the bottler on labels of wine sold in the U.S., only the words *produced by* or *made by* indicate the name of the company that actually fermented 75 percent or more of the wine (that is, who really *made* the wine); words such as *cellared by* or *vinted by* mean only that the company subjected the wine to cellar treatment (holding it for a while, for example).

On labels of wine sold in Canada, the dealer whose name and address must be indicated is the person for whom or by whom the wine is produced for sale. The person might or might not be the actual producer of the wine.

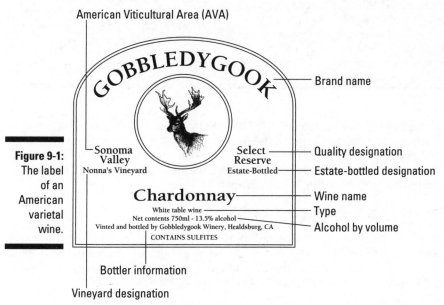

Figure 9-1: The label of an American varietal wine.

American Viticultural Area (AVA)

GOBBLEDYGOOK — Brand name

Sonoma Valley
Nonna's Vineyard

Select Reserve — Quality designation
Estate-Bottled — Estate-bottled designation

Chardonnay — Wine name
White table wine — Type
Net contents 750ml - 13.5% alcohol — Alcohol by volume
Vinted and bottled by Gobbledygook Winery, Healdsburg, CA
CONTAINS SULFITES

Bottler information

Vineyard designation

© Akira Chiwaki

Labels on wines that are made outside the U.S. but sold within the U.S. must also carry the phrase *imported by* as well as the name and business location of the importer.

The EU hierarchy of wine

Although each country within the European Union makes its own laws regarding the naming of wine, these laws must fit within the framework of the European Union law. This framework provides two levels into which every single EU-produced wine must fit:

✔ **Quality wine:** Wines with official appellations of origin. (Each appellation law defines the geographic area, the grapes that may be used, grape-growing practices, wine-making and aging techniques, and so on.) This category is abbreviated as QWPSR in English (Quality Wine Produced in a Specific Region) or VQPRD in several other European languages. All AOC, DOC, DO, and QbA wines — to use the abbreviations mentioned in this chapter — fall into this category.

✔ **Table wine:** All other wines produced within the EU. The table wine category has two subcategories: Table wines that carry a precise geographic indication on their labels, such as French *vin de pays* or Spanish *vino de la tierra* wines; and table wines with no geographic indication except the country of origin. These latter wines may not carry a vintage or a grape name.

All other wines sold in the EU fall into a third category:

✔ **Wine:** Wines produced by countries outside the EU, such as the U.S., Canada, or Australia. If a wine has a geographic indication smaller than the country of origin, it enjoys higher status than otherwise.

Canadian regulations are similar. Those regulations require wine labels to indicate the *common name* of the product (that is, *wine*), the net contents, the percentage of alcohol by volume, the name and address of the producer, the wine's country of origin, and the container size. Many of these items must be indicated in both English and French.

The European mandate

Some of the mandatory information on American and Canadian wine labels is also required by the European Union's wine authorities to appear on labels of wines produced or sold in the EU. But additional label items are prescribed by the EU for wines produced in its member countries.

The most important of these additional items is an indication of a wine's so-called quality level — which really means the wine's status in the EU's hierarchy of place-names. In short, every wine made in an EU member country *must* carry one of the following items on the label:

> ✔ A registered place-name, along with an official phrase that confirms that the name is in fact a registered place-name (see the following section for a listing of those official phrases)
>
> ✔ A phrase indicating that the wine is a *table wine,* a status lower than that of a wine with a registered place-name

For U.S. wines, the *table wine* category encompasses all non-sparkling wines that contain up to 14 percent alcohol. This is a distinctly different use of the term *table wine.*

Appellations of origin

A registered place-name is called an *appellation of origin.* In fact, each EU place-name defines far more than just the name of the place that the grapes come from: The place-name connotes the wine's grape varieties, grape-growing methods, and winemaking methods. Each appellation is, therefore, a definition of the wine as well as the wine's name.

European wines with official place-names fall into a European category called QWPSR (Quality Wine Produced in a Specific Region). The following phrases on European labels confirm that a wine is a QWPSR wine and that its name is therefore a registered place-name:

> ✔ **France:** *Appellation Contrôlée* or *Appellation d'Origine Contrôlée* (AC or AOC, in short), translated as *regulated name* or *regulated place-name.* Also, on labels of wines from places of slightly lower status, the initials AO VDQS, standing for *Appellation d'Origine — Vins Délimités de Qualité Supérieure;* translated as *place-name, demarcated wine of superior quality.*
>
> ✔ **Italy:** *Denominazione di Origine Controllata* (DOC), translated as *regulated place-name;* or for certain wines of an even higher status, *Denominazione di Origine Controllata e Garantita* (DOCG), translated as *regulated and guaranteed place-name.*
>
> ✔ **Spain:** *Denominación de Origen* (DO), translated as *place-name;* and *Denominación de Origen Calificada* (DOC), translated as *qualified-origin place-name* for regions with the highest status (of which there are only two, Rioja and Priorat).
>
> ✔ **Portugal:** *Denominação de Origem* (DO), translated as *place-name.*
>
> ✔ **Germany:** *Qualitätswein bestimmter Anbaugebiete* (QbA), translated as *quality wine from a specific region;* or *Qualitätswein mit Prädikat* (QmP), translated as *quality wine with special attributes,* for the best wines. (Read more about Germany's complex appellation system in Chapter 12.)

Phrases on European labels that indicate that a wine is a table wine vary according to country. Each country has two such phrases, one for table wines with a geographic indication (actually Italy has two phrases in this category), and one for table wines with no geographic indication smaller than the country of production. These phrases are

- **France:** *Vin de pays* (country wine) followed by the name of an approved area; *vin de table*

- **Italy:** *Indicazione Geografica Tipica* (translated as *typical geographic indication* and abbreviated as IGT) and the name of an approved area, or *vino da tavola* (table wine) followed by a the name of a geographic area; *vino da tavola*

- **Spain:** *Vino de la tierra* (country wine) followed by the name of an approved area; *vino de mesa*

- **Portugal:** *Vinho Regional* (regional wine) and the name of an approved area; *vinho de mesa*

- **Germany:** *Landwein* (country wine) and the name of an approved area; *Deutscher tafelwein*

Table 9-1 lists the European wine designations for easy reference.

Table 9-1		European Wine Designations at a Glance	
Country	*QWPSR Designation(s)*	*Table Wine Designation with Geographic Indication*	*Table Wine Designation without Geographic Indication*
France	AOC	Vin de pays	Vin de table
	VDQS		
Italy	DOCG	IGT; Vino da tavola (and geographic name)	Vino da tavola
	DOC		
Spain	DOC	Vino de la tierra	Vino de mesa
	DO		
Portugal	DO	Vinho regional	Vinho de mesa
Germany	QmP	Landwein	Deutscher tafelwein
	QbA		

Figure 9-2 shows a European wine label as it would appear in the U.S.

The phrase for a registered place-name in the U.S. is *American Viticultural Area* (AVA). But the phrase does *not* appear on wine labels (refer to Figure 9-1). Nor does any such phrase appear on labels of Australian or South American wines.

Some optional label terms

Besides the mandatory information required by government authorities, all sorts of other words can appear on wine labels. These words can be meaningless phrases designed to make you think that you're getting a special quality wine, or words that provide useful information about what's in the bottle. Sometimes the same word can fall into either category, depending on the label. This ambiguity occurs because some words that are strictly regulated in some producing countries are not at all regulated in others.

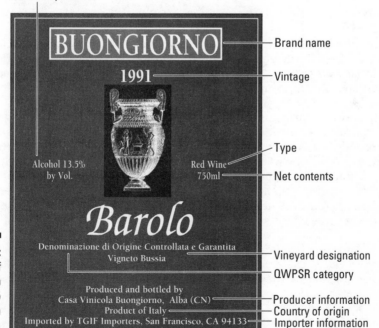

Figure 9-2: The label of a European wine to be sold in the U.S.

Alcohol by volume

BUONGIORNO — Brand name

1991 — Vintage

Alcohol 13.5% by Vol.

Red Wine — Type

750ml — Net contents

Barolo

Denominazione di Origine Controllata e Garantita — Vineyard designation
Vigneto Bussia — QWPSR category

Produced and bottled by
Casa Vinicola Buongiorno, Alba (CN) — Producer information
Product of Italy — Country of origin
Imported by TGIF Importers, San Francisco, CA 94133 — Importer information

© Akira Chiwaki

Vintage

The word *vintage* followed by a year, or the year listed alone without the word *vintage,* is the most common optional item on a wine label (refer to Figure 9-2). Sometimes the vintage appears on the front label, and sometimes it has its own small label above the front label.

The *vintage year* is nothing more than the year in which the grapes for a particular wine were harvested. (*Nonvintage* wines are blends of wines whose grapes were harvested in different years.) But there is an aura surrounding vintage-dated wine that causes many people to believe that any wine with a vintage date is by definition better than a wine without a vintage date. *In fact, there is no correlation between the presence of a vintage date and the wine's quality.*

Generally speaking, *what* vintage a wine is — that is, whether the grapes grew in a year with perfect weather or whether the grapes were meteorologically challenged — is an issue you need to consider a) only when you buy top quality wines, and b) mainly when those wines come from parts of the world that experience significant variations in weather from year to year — in a nutshell, Europe.

Reserve

Reserve is our favorite meaningless word on American wine labels. The term is used to convince you that the wine inside the bottle is special. This trick usually works because the word *does* have specific meaning and *does* carry a certain amount of prestige on labels of wines from many other countries.

In Italy and Spain, for example, the word *reserve* (or its foreign language equivalent, which looks something like *reserve*) indicates a wine that has received extra aging at the winery before release. Implicit in the extra aging is the idea that the wine was better than normal and, therefore, worthy of the extra aging. So a Chianti Classico Riserva is considered a better and more expensive wine than the same producer's basic Chianti Classico. A Rioja Gran Reserva (Spain even has *degrees* of reserve) is better than the same producer's Rioja Reserva, which is better than that producer's regular Rioja.

In some other countries, like France, the use of *reserve* is not regulated. However, its use is generally consistent with the notion that the wine is better in quality than a given producer's norm.

In the U.S., the word *reserve* has historically been used in the same sense — as in Beaulieu Vineyards Georges de Latour Private Reserve, the best Cabernet that Beaulieu Vineyards makes. But these days, the word is bandied about so much that it no longer has meaning. For example, some California wines labeled *Proprietor's Reserve* sell for $6 a bottle. Those wines are not only the *least* expensive wines in a particular producer's lineup, but also some of the least expensive wines, period. Other wines are labeled Special Reserve, Vintage Reserve, Vintner's Reserve, or Reserve Selection — all utterly meaningless phrases.

Estate-bottled

Estate is a genteel word for a wine farm, a combined grape-growing and wine-making operation. The words *estate-bottled* on a wine label indicate that the company that bottled the wine also grew the grapes and made the wine. In other words, *estate-bottled* suggests accountability from the vineyard to the winemaking through to the bottling. The winery does not necessarily have to own the vineyards, but it has to control the vineyards and perform the vineyard operations.

Estate-bottling is an important concept to those of us who believe that you can't make good wine unless the grapes are as good as they can possibly be. If *we* made wine, we'd sure want to control our own vineyards.

We wouldn't go so far as to say that great wines *must* be estate-bottled, though. Ravenswood Winery — to name just one example — makes some terrific wines from the grapes of small vineyards owned and operated by private landowners. And some large California landowners, such as the Sangiacomo brothers, are quite serious about their vineyards but do not make wine themselves; they sell their grapes to various wineries. None of those wines would be considered estate-bottled.

Sometimes French wine labels carry the words *domaine-bottled* or *château-bottled* (or the phrase *mis en bouteille au château/au domaine*). The concept is the same as estate-bottled, with *domaine* and *château* being equivalent to the American term *estate*.

Vineyard name

Wines in the medium-to-expensive price category — those that cost about $25 or more — might carry on the label the name of the specific vineyard where the grapes for that wine grew. Sometimes one winery will make two or three different wines that are distinguishable only by the vineyard name on the label. Each wine is unique because the *terroir* of each vineyard is unique. (For an explanation of *terroir,* see Chapter 5.) These single vineyards might or might not be identified by the word *vineyard* next to the name of the vineyard.

Italian wines, which are really into the single-vineyard game, will have *vigneto* or *vigna* on their labels next to the name of the single vineyard. Or they won't. It's optional.

Other optional words on the label

You'll be pleased to know that we have just about exhausted our list of terms that you might find on a wine label.

One additional expression on some French labels is *Vieilles Vignes (vee yay veen),* which translates as *old vines.* Because old vines produce a very small quantity of fruit compared to younger vines, the quality of their grapes and of the resulting wine is considered to be very good. The problem is, the phrase is unregulated. Anyone can claim that his vines are old.

The word *superior* can appear in French *(Supérieure)* or Italian *(Superiore)* as part of an AOC or DOC place-name (refer to the section "The mandatory sentence," earlier in this chapter, for a refresher on these acronyms). It means the wine attained a higher alcohol level than the nonsuperior version of the same wine. Frankly, it's a distinction not worth losing sleep over.

The word *Classico* appears on the labels of some Italian DOC and DOCG wines when the grapes come from the heartland of the named place.

Part III
Around the World of Wine

The 5th Wave — By Rich Tennant

@RICHTENNANT

"Well, I'm enough of a wine expert to know that if the boat were sinking, there'd be several cases of this Bordeaux that would go into a lifeboat before you would."

In this part . . .

We're flattered if you've gotten to this point by reading every word we've written so far. But we realize that you might have landed here by skipping lots of stuff earlier in the book. That's okay with us — the meat and potatoes of the book are right here.

The seven chapters in this part are chock full of information about the major wines of the world, including our recommendations on specific wines to buy. We devote one entire chapter each to the wines of France, Italy, and the U.S., because these are such important wine countries. We also give a whole chapter to Champagne and other sparkling wines, and end with dessert — a chapter on fortified and dessert wines. Happy drinking!

Chapter 10

Doing France

· ·

In This Chapter

▶ *Crus,* classified growths, *chateaux,* and *domaines*

▶ Why Bordeaux wines are legendary

▶ The scarcity issue in fine Burgundy

▶ Robust red Rhônes

▶ White gems of the Loire and Alsace

▶ The South rises again!

· ·

France. What comes to mind when you hear that word? Strolling along Paris's grand boulevard, the Champs Elysées? Romance? Beautiful, blue water and golden sun on the French Riviera?

When we think of France, we think of wine. Bordeaux, Burgundy, Beaujolais, Chablis, Champagne, and Sauternes are not only famous wines — they are also places in France where people live, work, eat, and drink (wine, of course!). France has the highest per capita wine consumption of any major country in the world. They've set the standard for the rest of us.

The French Model

Why has France become the most famous place in the world for wine? For one thing, the French have been doing it for a long time — making wine, that is. Centuries before the Romans conquered Gaul and planted vineyards, the Greeks arrived with their vines.

Equally important is French *terroir,* the magical combination of climate and soil that, when it clicks, can yield grapes that make breathtaking wines. And what grapes! France is the home of almost all the renowned varieties in the world — Cabernet Sauvignon, Chardonnay, Merlot, Pinot Noir, Syrah, and Sauvignon Blanc, just to name a few. (See Chapter 3 for more information on these grape varieties.)

France is the model, the standard setter, for all the world's wines: Most wine-producing countries now make their own versions of Cabernet Sauvignon, Chardonnay, Merlot, Pinot Noir, and so on, thanks to the success of these grapes in France. If imitation is the sincerest form of flattery, French wine-makers have had good reason to blush for a long time now.

Understanding French wine law

French lawmakers have reason to blush, too. France's system of defining and regulating wine regions — the *Appellation d'Origine Contrôlée,* or AOC (translated as *regulated place name* or *regulated origin name*) system, established in 1935 — has been the legislative model for most other European countries. The European Union's (EU's) framework of wine laws, within which the AOC system now operates, is also modeled on the French system.

To understand French wines and wine laws, you need to know five things:

- Most French wines are named after places. (These are not arbitrary places; they are places registered and defined in French wine regulations.) When we talk about French wines and the regions they come from, most of the time the region and the wine have the same name (as in Burgundy, from Burgundy).

- The French wine system is hierarchical. Some wines (that is, the wines of some places) officially have higher rank than other wines.

- Generally, the smaller and more specific the place for which a wine is named, the higher its rank.

- Just because a wine carries a high rank doesn't necessarily mean that it's better than the next wine; it just means that it *should* be better. The laws rank the potential of the place where the wine comes from, and are not infallible indications of a wine's actual quality.

- The wine's rank or grade is always stated on the label, usually in small letters underneath the name of the wine.

There are four possible ranks of French wine, according to French wine law. You can determine the rank of a French wine at a glance by seeing which of the following French phrases appears on the label. (Wines of higher rank generally cost more.) From highest to lowest, the rankings are

- **Appellation Contrôlée,** or AOC (or AC), the highest grade. On the label, the place-name of the wine usually appears between the two French words, as in Appellation Bordeaux Contrôlée.

✔ **Vin Délimité de Qualité Supérieure,** or VDQS wine (translated as *demarcated wine of superior quality*). These words appear on the label immediately below the name of the wine.

✔ **Vin de pays,** meaning *country wine.* On the label, the phrase is always followed by a place-name, such as *Vin de Pays de l'Hérault,* which indicates the area where the grapes grew; the places or regions are generally much larger than the places or regions referred to in the two higher rankings.

✔ **Vin de table,** ordinary French table wine that carries no geographic indication other than "France." By law, these wines may not indicate a grape variety or vintage. (See Chapter 9 for more about table wines.)

Here's how these four categories of French wines fit within the European Union's two-tier system described in Chapter 9:

✔ All AOC and VDQS wines fall into the EU's higher tier, QWPSR (Quality Wine Produced in a Specific Region, or simply *quality wine*).

✔ All *vins de pays* and *vins de table* fall into the EU's lower tier, table wines.

Fine distinctions in the ranks

But France's system of place-naming its wines is actually a bit more complex than the four neat categories described in the preceding section might imply. Although all AOC wines/places hold exactly the same legal status — they're all generals in the French wine army, let's say — the market accords some AOCs higher regard (and higher prices) than others, based on the specificity of their terroir.

Some large AOC territories have smaller AOC zones nestled within them. Imagine three concentric circles. Any wines produced from grapes grown within the entire area of the three circles may carry a particular AOC place-name, such as Bordeaux (assuming that the proper grape varieties are used and the wine conforms to the regulations for Bordeaux in all other respects). But wines whose grapes come from the territory of the two smaller circles are entitled to a different, more specific AOC name, such as the district, Haut-Médoc. And wines whose area of production is limited to the smallest circle can use yet another AOC name, such as Pauillac, a village. (They're all generals, but some of them have silver stars.)

The more specific the place described in the wine name, the finer the wine is generally considered to be in the eyes of the market, and the higher the price the winemaker can ask. Naturally, a winemaker will use the most specific name to which his wine is entitled.

In increasing order of specificity, an AOC name can be the name of

- A region (Bordeaux or Burgundy, for example)
- A district (Haut-Médoc or Côte de Beaune)
- A subdistrict (Côte de Beaune-Villages)
- A village or commune (Pauillac or Meursault)
- A specific vineyard (Le Montrachet)

Unfortunately, unless you're an expert at French geography and place-names, you won't know which type of place an AOC name refers to just by looking at the label.

France's Wine Regions

France has five wine regions that are extremely important for the quality and renown of the wines they produce, and several other regions that make interesting wines worth knowing about. The three major regions for red wine are Bordeaux, Burgundy, and the Rhône; for white wines, Burgundy is again a major region, along with the Loire and Alsace. Each region specializes in certain grape varieties for its wines, based on climate, soil, and local tradition. Table 10-1 provides a quick reference to the grapes and wines of these five regions.

Table 10-1	Major Wine Regions of France and Their Wines	
Region/ Red Wines	*White Wines*	*Grape Varieties*
Bordeaux		
Bordeaux		Cabernet Sauvignon, Merlot, Cabernet Franc, Petite Verdot, Malbec*
	Bordeaux Blanc	Sauvignon Blanc, Sémillon, Muscadelle*
Burgundy		
Burgundy		Pinot Noir
	White Burgundy	Chardonnay
Beaujolais		Gamay
	Chablis	Chardonnay

Region/ Red Wines	White Wines	Grape Varieties
Rhône		
Hermitage		Syrah
Côte-Rôtie		Syrah, Viognier*
Châteauneuf-du-Pape		Grenache, Mourvèdre, Syrah, (and many others)*
Côtes du Rhône		Grenache, Mourvèdre, Carignan, Syrah, (and many others)*
	Condrieu	Viognier
Loire		
	Sancerre; Pouilly-Fumé	Sauvignon Blanc
	Vouvray	Chenin Blanc
	Muscadet	Melon de Bourgogne, alias Muscadet
Alsace		
	Riesling	Riesling
	Gewürztraminer	Gewürztraminer
	Tokay-Pinot Gris	Pinot Gris
	Pinot Blanc	Pinot Blanc

* Wines are blended from several grape varieties

Two other significant French wine regions are Provence and Languedoc-Roussillon, both in the South of France. And wine districts in Southwest France, such as Cahors, produce good-value wines that are now of better quality than ever.

We cover all these regions in this chapter, in more or less detail according to the importance of the region. For more specific information on French wines, see our book *French Wine For Dummies* (John Wiley Publishing, Inc.).

Bordeaux: The Incomparable

You must know French wine to know wine — French wines are that important in the wine world. Likewise, you must know Bordeaux to know French wine.

Bordeaux is a wine region in western France named after the fourth-largest French city (see Figure 10-1). It produces 10 percent of all French wine and 26 percent of all AOC wine. Most Bordeaux wines are dry reds; 15 percent of the region's production is dry white, and 2 percent is sweet white wine, such as Sauternes.

Because the Bordeaux region is situated on the Atlantic coast, it has a maritime climate, with warm summers and fairly mild winters. The maritime weather brings rain, often during harvest time. The weather is variable from year to year, and the character and quality of the vintages therefore also vary; when all goes well, such as in 1996 and 2000, great wines are produced.

Bordeaux makes wines at many levels of price and quality. Prices, for example, range from $6 a bottle for simple Bordeaux to well over $500 a bottle for Château Pétrus, one of the most expensive red Bordeaux wines. (*Old* vintages of Pétrus cost even *more!*) Most fine Bordeaux wines, both red and white, start at about $25 a bottle when they are first released for sale, two or three years after the vintage.

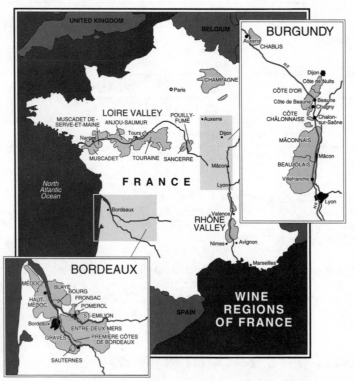

Figure 10-1: The wine regions of France.

© Akira Chiwaki

The taste of really great Bordeaux

When young, the finest red Bordeaux wines have a deep cranberry hue and aromas of blackcurrants, plums, spice, cedar, and cassis. For the first ten years or so, these wines can be very dry in texture, almost austere, with tannin masking the fruity flavors. Eventually, the wines turn garnet, develop an extraordinarily complex bouquet and flavor, and soften in tannin. The very finest red Bordeaux wines will frequently take 20 years or more before reaching their maturity; some have lasted well over 100 years (see Chapter 21).

Bordeaux's reputation as one of the greatest wine regions in the world revolves around the legendary red wines of Bordeaux — *grands vins* (great wines) made by historic *châteaux* (wine estates) and capable of improving for many decades (see Chapter 21). But these wines sit at the top of a red Bordeaux pyramid; quantitatively, they are only a small part of the region's red wine production. Middle-level Bordeaux reds are ready to drink within 10 to 15 years of the harvest, and other Bordeaux reds are enjoyable young, within two to five years of the vintage date.

The subregions of red Bordeaux

Two distinct red wine production zones exist within the Bordeaux region; these two areas have come to be called the Left Bank and the Right Bank — just as in Paris. While many of the least expensive Bordeaux reds are blended from grapes grown all through the Bordeaux region — and thus they carry the region-wide AOC designation, Bordeaux — the better wines come from specific AOC *districts* or AOC *communes* that are located in either the Right Bank or the Left Bank.

The Left Bank vineyards lie west of the Garonne River (the more southerly of the two rivers depicted in the Bordeaux inset of Figure 10-1) and the Gironde Estuary into which the Garonne empties. The Right Bank vineyards lie east and north of the Dordogne River (the more northerly of the two rivers depicted in the inset), and east of the Gironde Estuary. (The middle ground in between the two rivers is more important for white wine than for red.)

Of the various wine districts on the Left Bank and the Right Bank, four (two on each bank) are the most important:

Left Bank (the western area)	*Right Bank (the eastern area)*
Haut-Médoc	St-Emilion
Pessac-Léognan	Pomerol

The Left Bank and the Right Bank differ mainly in soil composition: Gravel predominates on the Left Bank, and clay prevails on the Right Bank. As a result, Cabernet Sauvignon, which has an affinity for gravel, is the principal grape variety in the Haut-Médoc *(oh meh doc)* and Pessac-Léognan *(pay sac lay oh nyahn)*. Merlot, which does well in clay, dominates the St-Emilion *(sant em eel yon)* and Pomerol *(pohm eh roll)* wines. (Both areas grow Cabernet Sauvignon *and* Merlot, as well as Cabernet Franc and two less significant grapes. See Chapter 3 for more information on grape varieties.)

You can therefore conclude correctly that Left Bank and Right Bank Bordeaux wines are markedly different from one another. But wines from the Haut-Médoc and Pessac-Léognan are quite similar; likewise, it can be difficult to tell the difference among wines from Pomerol and St-Emilion (on the Right Bank).

Each bank — in fact, each of the four districts — has its avid fans. The older, better-established Left Bank generally produces austere, tannic wines with more pronounced blackcurrant flavor. Left Bank wines usually need many years to develop and will age for a long time, often for decades — typical of a Cabernet Sauvignon-based wine.

Bordeaux wines from the Right Bank are better introductory wines for the novice Bordeaux drinker. Because they are mainly Merlot, they are more approachable; you can enjoy them long before their Left Bank cousins, often as soon as five to eight years after the vintage. They are less tannic, richer in texture, and plummier in flavor, and they generally contain a bit more alcohol than Left Bank reds.

The Médoc mosaic

Historically, the Haut-Médoc has always been Bordeaux's most important district, and it deserves special attention. The Haut-Médoc is actually part of the Médoc peninsula. The name *Médoc* has two meanings. It refers to the entire area west of the wide Gironde Estuary (see Figure 10-1), and it is also the name for the northernmost district of the Left Bank. In other words (in the same word, actually), Médoc is frequently used as an umbrella term for the combined districts of Médoc and Haut-Médoc (the two districts which occupy the Médoc peninsula).

Of the two districts, the Haut-Médoc, in the south, is by far the more important for wine. The Haut-Médoc itself encompasses four famous wine communes: St. Estèphe *(sant eh steff)*, Pauillac *(poy yac)*, St-Julien *(san jhoo lee ehn)*, and Margaux *(mahr go)*. Table 10-2 gives a general description of each commune's wines.

Table 10-2	The Four Principal Communes in the Haut-Médoc
Commune	*Wine Characteristics*
St-Estèphe	Firm, tannic, earthy, chunky, and slow to mature; typical wine — Château Montrose
Pauillac	Rich, powerful, firm, and tannic, with blackcurrant and cedar aromas and flavors; very long-lived; home of three of Bordeaux's most famous wines — Lafite-Rothschild, Mouton-Rothschild, and Latour
St-Julien	Rich, flavorful, elegant and finesseful, with cedary bouquet; typical wine — Château Ducru-Beaucaillou
Margaux	Fragrant, supple, harmonious, with complex aromas and flavors; typical wine — Château Palmer

Two other communes in the Haut-Médoc — Listrac *(lee strahk)* and Moulis *(moo lees)* — make less well-known wines. Any vineyards in the Haut-Médoc that are not located in the vicinity of these six communes carry the district-wide appellation, *Haut-Médoc,* rather than that of a specific commune.

The names of these districts and communes are part of the official name of wines made there, and appear on the label.

Classified information

Have you ever wondered what a wine expert was talking about when he smugly pronounced that a particular Bordeaux was a *second growth?* Wonder no more. He's talking about a château (as wine estates are called in Bordeaux) that got lucky about 150 years ago.

Back in 1855, when an Exposition (akin to a World's Fair) took place in Paris, the organizers asked the Bordeaux Chamber of Commerce to develop a classification of Bordeaux wines. The Chamber of Commerce delegated the task to the Bordeaux wine brokers, the people who buy and re-sell the wines of Bordeaux. These merchants named 61 top red wines — 60 from the Médoc and one from what was then called Graves (and today is known as Péssac-Leognan). They divided these 61 wines into five categories, known as *crus* or *growths.* (In Bordeaux, a *cru* refers to a wine estate.) Their listing is known as the classification of 1855; to this day, these *classified growths* enjoy special prestige among wine lovers. The following list shows the five categories and names the first growths:

- ✔ **First Growths (5 châteaux)**

    Château Lafite-Rothschild
    Château Latour
    Château Margaux
    Château Haut-Brion
    Château Mouton-Rothschild (elevated from a Second Growth in 1973)

- ✔ **Second Growths (14 châteaux)**

- ✔ **Third Growths (14 châteaux)**

- ✔ **Fourth Growths (10 châteaux)**

- ✔ **Fifth Growths (18 châteaux)**

The 61 ranked wine estates are sometimes referred to as Great Growths or *Grands Crus Classés*. To appreciate the honor attached to being one of the Great Growths, bear in mind that there are about 8,000 châteaux (and over 13,000 wine producers) in Bordeaux!

The 1855 classification has held up remarkably well over time. Sure, a few of the 61 properties are not performing up to their classification today, while other unclassified châteaux now probably deserve to be included. But because of the politics involved, no changes in classification ranking have been made, with one dramatic exception (see "The Mouton exception" sidebar), nor are any foreseen in the near future. (See Appendix B in our book *French Wine For Dummies* for a complete listing of the 61 wines in the 1855 classification.)

The Mouton exception

The one dramatic exception to the "no changes in the 1855 classification" rule occurred in 1973. That year, the late Baron Philippe de Rothschild, finally (and rightfully) triumphed in his 50-year battle with the French government to have his beloved Château Mouton-Rothschild upgraded from a second growth to a first growth. The Minister of Agriculture (at that time, Jacques Chirac!) decreed that Château Mouton-Rothschild was indeed a first growth (which Bordeaux wine lovers considered it to be all along, in quality if not in official status). The Baron's motto, written in French on his family crest, had to change. Before 1973, it read

> First, I cannot be; second, I do not deign to be; Mouton, I am.

The Baron changed the motto on his 1973 Château Mouton-Rothschild to read

> First, I am; second, I was; Mouton does not change.

A postscript to this wonderful story: We adopted an adorable little kitten, a Blue Point Siamese, in 1973. Since Mouton-Rothschild is one of our favorite wines, and since our little kitten demonstrated the same firm, tenacious qualities as the wine, we named him Mouton. He was with us for 20 years, proving that he had the same quality of longevity as the wine for which he was named. He is buried in our backyard, in an old wooden crate of 1973 Mouton-Rothschild.

Just to confuse things even more: Although the 1855 classification completely ignored the wines of St-Emilion, the AOC commission classified those wines a century later, in 1955. The wines fall into three quality categories:

✔ Currently, 13 chateaux have the highest ranking, *Premier Grand Cru Classé*. Two of the 13, Château Ausone and Château Cheval Blanc, are on their own pedestal as "Category A"; the other 11 are "Category B" *Premier Grand Cru Classé* wines.

✔ A middle category, *Grand Cru Classé*, consists of 55 chateaux.

✔ The third category, simply "*Grand Cru*," encompasses some 200 properties.

Look for these three designations on bottles of St-Emilion. The wines of Pessac-Léognan were classified in 1953, and again in 1959. (For more info on St-Emilion's and Pessac-Léognan's classified Bordeaux, see Chapter 4 of *French Wine For Dummies*; also, in the same book, Appendix B lists the entire classification of *Premier Grand Cru Classé* and *Grand Cru Classé* St-Emilion wines and the 1959 classification of Pessac-Léognan wines.)

The wines of Pomerol have never been officially classified.

Bordeaux to try when you're feeling flush

If you're curious to try a prestigious red Bordeaux, let this list guide you. In addition to all five first growths listed in the previous section, we recommend the following classified growths from the Médoc, as well as some wines from the three other principal subregions: Pessac-Léognan, St-Emilion, and Pomerol. Consult the "Practical advice on drinking red Bordeaux" section just ahead, before you drink the wine.

Médoc wines

Château Léoville-Las-Cases	Château Clerc-Milon	Château Lynch-Bages
Château Léoville-Barton	Château Gruaud-Larose	Château Montrose
Château Rauzan-Ségla	Château Pichon-Lalande	Château Ducru-Beaucaillou
Château Palmer	Château Lagrange	Château Grand-Puy-Lacoste
Château Cos D'Estournel	Château Pichon-Baron	Château La Lagune
Château Léoville-Poyferré	Château d'Armailhac	Château Branaire-Ducru
Château Pontet-Canet	Château Prieuré-Lichine	Château Batailley
Château Haut-Batailley	Château Malescot	Château Talbot
Château Duhart-Milon-Rothschild	St.-Exupéry	
	Château Calon-Ségur	

Pessac-Léognan wines

Château La Mission-Haut-Brion	Château Haut-Bailly	Château de Fieuzal
Château Pape-Clément	Domaine de Chevalier	Château La Louvière
Château La Tour-Haut-Brion	Château Smith-Haut-Lafitte	

Pomerol wines

Château Pétrus*
Château Lafleur*
Château Latour à Pomerol
Château Certan de May

Château Trotanoy
Château Clinet
Vieux-Château-Certan
Château Gazin
Château Lafleur-Pétrus

Château L'Evangile
Château La Fleur de Gay
Château La Conseillante
Château l'Eglise Clinet

* Very expensive

St-Emilion wines

Château Cheval Blanc
Château Figeac
Château Troplong Mondot
Château Clos Fourtet

Château La Dominique
Château Grand Mayne
Château Ausone
Château Magdelaine

Château Canon-La-Gaffelière
Château L'Arrosée
Château Pavie-Macquin
Château Pavie

The value end of the Bordeaux spectrum

As you might have suspected, the best buys in Bordeaux wines are not the illustrious classified growths. For really good values (and wines that you can drink within a few years of the vintage), look for Bordeaux wines that were not included in the 1855 classification. In the Médoc, nearly 300 red wines are now grouped under the category *cru bourgeois*. These wines generally sell in the $15 to $30 range; some of them are even as good as the lesser-quality classified growths. We recommend the following cru bourgeois wines:

Château Monbrison
Château Sociando Mallet
Château Poujeaux
Château de Pez
Château Les Ormes-de-Pez
Château Haut-Beauséjour
Château Labegorce-Zédé

Château Phélan-Ségur
Château Meyney
Château Chasse-Spleen
Château Gloria
Château Haut-Marbuzet
Château Bel Air
Château Monbousquet

Château d'Angludet
Château Coufran
Château Fourcas-Hosten
Château Lanessan
Château Loudenne
Château Greysac
Château Poujeaux

Reverse chic: Drinking inexpensive Bordeaux

Some wine snobs wouldn't think of ordering anything but Classified Growth Bordeaux in restaurants. But if you're just getting acquainted with these wines, starting with an expensive, top-rated Bordeaux doesn't make any sense. Begin with inexpensive, easier-drinking Bordeaux wines first, so that you can develop a context for evaluating and appreciating the finer Bordeaux. The contrast of simpler Bordeaux really helps you understand the majesty of the great Bordeaux wines. Besides, every dinner doesn't call for a great Bordeaux. A modest Bordeaux is perfectly suitable for simpler fare, such as stew or meat loaf.

Other inexpensive Bordeaux wines carry such appellations as Côtes de Bourg, Premières Côtes de Blaye, Premières Côtes de Bordeaux, Côtes de Castillon, Lalande de Pomerol, Lussac-St-Emilion, Montagne-St-Emilion, St.-Georges-St-Emilion, Puisseguin-St-Emilion (all mainly in the $10 to $18 range), Fronsac, and Canon-Fronsac (the last two in the $18 to $25 range).

A vast group of Bordeaux producers have never received any classification; their wines are informally referred to as *petits châteaux*. At $6 to $12, these relatively light-bodied reds (and whites) are real bargains — and they're drinkable upon release. Many of these wines carry the general "Bordeaux" or "Bordeaux Supérieur" appellations. *Petits châteaux* are the Bordeaux wines of choice when you're looking for a young, inexpensive, approachable Bordeaux with dinner. Of course, these wines don't say *petits châteaux* on their labels. (We never said Bordeaux would be easy!) You'll know them by their price. (For a listing of inexpensive red and white Bordeaux wines, see Chapters 5 and 6 in *French Wine For Dummies*.)

Practical advice on drinking red Bordeaux

Because the finest red Bordeaux wines take many years to develop, they are often not good choices in restaurants, where the vintages available tend to be fairly recent. And when mature Bordeaux wines are available in restaurants, they are usually extremely expensive. Order a lesser Bordeaux when you're dining out, and save the best ones for drinking at home.

Red Bordeaux wines go well with lamb, venison, simple cuts of meat, and hard cheeses, such as Comte or Cheddar. If you plan to serve a fine red Bordeaux from a good but recent vintage (see Appendix C), you should decant it at least an hour before dinner and let it aerate (see Chapter 8); serve it at about 62° to 66°F (17° to 19°C). Better yet, if you have good storage conditions (see Chapter 21), save your young Bordeaux for a few years — it will only get better.

Fine recent Bordeaux vintages have been 2000 (which shows promise of being truly great), 1998, 1996, 1995, 1990, 1986, and 1982.

Bordeaux also comes in white

White Bordeaux wine comes in two styles, dry and sweet. The dry wines themselves fall into two groups: inexpensive wines for enjoying young, and wines so distinguished and ageworthy that they rank among the great dry white wines of the world.

Two areas of the Bordeaux region are important for white wine production:

- ✔ The large district south of the city of Bordeaux is known as the Graves (*grahv*; see the Bordeaux inset in Fig. 10-1). The Graves district and the Pessac-Léognan district (directly north, around the city of Bordeaux) are home to the finest white wines of Bordeaux, both dry and sweet. (We cover the great dessert wine from the southern Graves, Sauternes, in Chapter 16.)

- ✔ In the middle ground between the Garonne and Dordogne Rivers, east of Graves and Pessac-Léognan, a district called Entre-Deux-Mers *(ahn treh-douh-mare)* is also known for its dry, semi-dry, and sweet white Bordeaux wines.

A few white wines also come from the predominantly red-wine Haut-Médoc district, such as the superb Pavillon Blanc du Château Margaux.

Sauvignon Blanc and Sémillon, in various combinations, are the two main grape varieties for white Bordeaux. It's a fortunate blend: The Sauvignon Blanc component offers immediate charm in the wine, while the slower-developing Sémillon gives the wine a viscous quality and depth, enabling it to age well. In general, the higher the percentage of Sémillon in the wine, the more ageworthy the wine is.

The top dry white Bordeaux wines are crisp and lively when they are young, but they develop richness, complexity, and a honeyed bouquet with age. In good vintages (see Appendix C), the best whites need at least ten years to develop and can live many years more. (See Chapter 21 for more information on older Bordeaux.)

Table 10-3 lists the top 12 white wines of Pessac-Léognan and Graves, in our rough order of preference, and shows their grape blends. We've separated the wines into an A and B group because the three wines in the first group literally are in a class by themselves, quality-wise; they possess not only more depth and complexity but also more longevity than other white Bordeaux. Their prices reflect that fact — the A group wines range from $85 to $250 per bottle, whereas the B group wines cost between $25 and $65. (For more info about white Bordeaux, see Chapter 6 in *French Wine For Dummies*.)

Table 10-3	Top 12 Dry White Bordeaux
Wine	*Grape Varieties*
Group A	
Château Haut-Brion Blanc	Sémillon, 50 to 55%; Sauvignon Blanc, 45 to 50%
Château Laville-Haut-Brion	Sémillon, 60%; Sauvignon Blanc, 40%
Domaine de Chevalier	Sauvignon Blanc, 70%; Sémillon, 30%

Wine	Grape Varieties
Group B	
Château de Fieuzal	Sauvignon Blanc, 50 to 60%; Sémillon, 40 to 50%
Château Pape-Clément	Sémillon, 45%; Muscadelle, 10%; Sauvignon Blanc, 45%
Château Smith-Haut-Lafitte	Sauvignon Blanc, 100%
Château Couhins-Lurton	Sauvignon Blanc, 100%
Château La Louvière	Sauvignon Blanc, 70%; Sémillon, 30%
Clos Floridene	Sémillon, 70%; Sauvignon Blanc, 30%
Château La Tour-Martillac	Sémillon, 60%; Sauvignon Blanc, 30%; other, 10%
Château Malartic-Lagravière	Sauvignon Blanc, 100%
Château Carbonnieux	Sauvignon Blanc, 65%; Sémillon, 35%

Burgundy: The Other Great French Wine

Burgundy, a wine region in eastern France, southeast of Paris (refer to Figure 10-1), stands shoulder-to-shoulder with Bordeaux as one of France's two greatest regions for dry, non-sparkling wines. Unlike Bordeaux, however, Burgundy's fame is split nearly equally between its white and red wines — and the best white Burgundies, in general, are even more expensive than their red counterparts.

Also unlike Bordeaux, good Burgundy is often scarce. The reason is simple: Not counting Beaujolais (which is technically Burgundy, but really a separate type of wine), Burgundy produces only 25 percent as much wine as Bordeaux!

Burgundy's vineyards are more fragmented than Bordeaux's. The French Revolution in 1789 is partly to blame. French nobility and the Catholic Church were once the major vineyard owners in Burgundy, but after the Revolution, vineyard land was distributed to the populace. (Bordeaux, once owned by the English, and more distant from Paris, was considered somehow less French and was not really that affected by the Revolution.) France's Napoleonic Code, which requires all land to be equally divided among one's heirs, over time, further fragmented each family's property in Burgundy.

As the result of these occurrences, Burgundy (or, as the French call it, *Bourgogne,* pronounced *bor guh nyeh*) today is a region of small vineyard holdings. The few large vineyards that do exist have multiple owners, with some families owning only two or three rows of vines in a particular vineyard. (One famous Burgundy vineyard, Clos de Vougeot, has about 82 owners!) The typical Burgundy winemaker's production varies from 50 cases to 1,000 cases of wine a year, per type — far from enough to satisfy wine lovers all over the world. Compare that to Bordeaux, where the average château owner makes 15,000 to 20,000 cases of his principal wine annually.

In Burgundy, the winemaker calls his property a *domaine,* certainly a more modest name than *château,* and a proper reflection of the size of his winery.

Chardonnay, Pinot Noir, Gamay

Burgundy has a *continental* climate (warm summers and cold winters) and is subject to localized summer hailstorms that can damage the grapes and cause rot. The soil is mainly limestone and clay.

Burgundy's *terroir* is particularly suited to the two main grape varieties of the region, Pinot Noir (for red Burgundy) and Chardonnay (for white Burgundy). In fact, nowhere else in the entire world does the very fickle, difficult Pinot Noir grape perform better than in Burgundy.

In the southerly Beaujolais district of Burgundy, the soil becomes primarily granitic but also rich in clay and sand, which is very suitable for the Gamay grape of this area.

Districts, districts everywhere

Burgundy has five districts, all of which make quite distinct wines. The districts are the following (to see where in Burgundy each of these districts is situated, refer to the Burgundy inset in Figure 10-1):

- The Côte d'Or *(coat dor)*
- The Côte Chalonnaise *(coat shal oh naze)*
- Chablis *(shah blee)*
- The Mâconnais *(mack coh nay)*
- Beaujolais *(boh jhoe lay)*

The heart of Burgundy, the *Côte d'Or* (which literally means *golden slope*), itself has two parts: Côte de Nuits *(coat deh nwee)* in the north and the Côte de Beaune *(coat deh bone)* in the south.

The Chablis district makes only white wines, and the Mâconnais makes mainly white wines. Beaujolais makes almost totally red wines, but — even though Beaujolais is part of Burgundy — Beaujolais is an entirely different wine, because it is made with the Gamay grape rather than Pinot Noir. The same is true of Mâcon Rouge (from the Mâconnais district) — even the small amount that's made from Pinot Noir rather than from Gamay does not resemble true red Burgundy. (Actually, very little red Mâcon is exported; the world sees mainly white Mâcon.)

Thus, the term *red Burgundy* refers primarily to the red wines of the Côte d'Or and also to the less well-known — and less expensive — red wines of the Côte Chalonnaise. Likewise, when wine lovers talk about *white Burgundy,* they are usually referring just to the white wines of the Côte d'Or and the Côte Chalonnaise. They'll use the more precise names, Chablis and Mâcon, to refer to the white wines of those parts of Burgundy. On the other hand, when wine lovers talk about the region, Burgundy, they could very well be referring to the whole shebang, including Beaujolais, or all of Burgundy *except* Beaujolais. It's an imprecise language.

Don't ever mistake the inexpensive red California wine that calls itself *burgundy* — or the inexpensive California wine that calls itself *chablis* — for the real McCoys from France. The imposter, generic burgundy and chablis are the products of various ordinary grapes grown in industrial-scale vineyards 6,000 miles away from the Côte d'Or. We'd be surprised if either one had even a drop of the true grapes of Burgundy — Pinot Noir or Chardonnay — in them.

From the regional to the sublime

The soils of the Burgundy region vary from hillside to hillside and even from the middle of each hill to the bottom. You can find two different vineyards growing the same grape but making distinctly different wines, only two meters apart from each other across a dirt road!

In a region with such varied terroir, specificity of site becomes extremely relevant. A wine made from a tiny vineyard with its own particular characteristics is more unique, precious, and rare than a wine blended from several vineyards or a wine from a less-favored site.

The AOC structure for Burgundy wines recognizes the importance of site. While there are region-wide AOCs, district-wide AOCs, and commune AOCs — just as in Bordeaux — *there are also AOC names that refer to individual vineyards.* In fact, some of these vineyards are recognized as better than others: Some of them are *premier cru (prem yay crew),* meaning first growth, while the very best are *grand cru,* meaning great growth.

The terms *premier cru* and *grand cru* are used in Bordeaux, too. However, in Bordeaux, the terms sometimes represent status bestowed on a winery by a classification outside the AOC law (as when a First Growth calls itself a *Premier Grand Cru Classé* on its label). In Burgundy, *premier cru* and *grand cru* are official distinctions within the AOC law. Their meaning is extremely precise.

Table 10-4 gives examples of AOC names in Burgundy, listed in order of increasing specificity.

Table 10-4	The Structure of Burgundy AOC Names
Specificity of Site	*Examples*
Region-wide	Bourgogne Rouge
District-wide	Côte de Beaune-Villages; Mâcon-Villages
Village or commune	Pommard; Gevrey-Chambertin; Volnay
Premier cru*	Nuits-St. Georges Les Vaucrains; Beaune Grèves; Vosne-Romanée Les Suchots
Grand cru*	Musigny; La Tâche; Montrachet

* Refers to specific vineyard sites.

When considering the price and availability of each category of wines, keep the following in mind:

✔ The two broadest categories — regional and district place-names — account for 65 percent of all Burgundy wines. Such wines retail for $10 to $25 a bottle. (You *can* buy affordable Burgundies at this level.)

✔ Commune (also referred to as *village*) wines, such as Nuits-St. Georges or Chambolle-Musigny, make up 23 percent of Burgundy and are in the $25 to $40 per bottle price range. Fifty-three communes in Burgundy are official appellations.

✔ Premier crus, such as Meursault Les Perrières or Chambolle-Musigny Les Chaumes, account for 11 percent of Burgundy wines; 561 vineyards are entitled to a premier cru appellation. The wines can range from $30 to $90 per bottle.

✔ The 30 grand crus, such as Chambertin, represent only *1 percent* of Burgundy's wines. Prices for grand cru Burgundies — both red and white — start in the $75 price range and can go up to well over $500 a bottle for Romanée-Conti, normally Burgundy's most expensive red wine.

Burgundy AOCs (once again, with feeling)

Burgundies with regional, or region-wide, AOCs are easy to recognize — they always start with the word *Bourgogne (boor guh nyeh).* In the following list, read the AOC names down each column to see how the names change, becoming more specific from district to grand cru.

	Red Burgundy	*White Burgundy*
Region:	Bourgogne Rouge	Bourgogne Blanc
District:	Côte de Nuits-Villages	Côte de Beaune (also red)
Commune:	Chambolle-Musigny	Puligny-Montrachet
Premier cru:	Chambolle-Musigny Les Amoureuses	Puligny-Montrachet Les Pucelles
Grand cru:	Musigny	Bâtard-Montrachet; Montrachet

Thankfully, you can actually tell the difference between a premier cru and a grand cru Burgundy by looking at the label. Premier cru wines usually carry the name of their commune plus the vineyard name — usually in the same-sized lettering — on the label and, often, the words *Premier Cru* (or *1er Cru).* If a vineyard name is in smaller lettering than the commune name, often the wine is not a premier cru but a wine from a single-vineyard site in that commune. (Not all single vineyards have premier cru status.) Grand cru Burgundies carry only the name of the vineyard on the label. (For a complete listing of all grand cru Burgundies, see Appendix B in *French Wine For Dummies.*)

If a wine is made from the grapes of two or more premier crus in the same commune, it can be called a premier cru but it won't carry the name of a specific premier cru vineyard. The label will carry a commune name and the words *premier cru.*

The Côte d'Or: The heart of Burgundy

The Côte d'Or, a narrow 40-mile stretch of land with some of the most expensive real estate in the world, is the region where all the famous red and white Burgundies originate.

The northern part of the Côte d'Or is named the Côte de Nuits, after its most important (commercial) city, Nuits-Saint-Georges. This area makes red Burgundies almost exclusively (although one superb white Burgundy, Musigny Blanc, and a couple of other white Burgundies do exist on the Côte de Nuits). The following wine communes, from north to south, are in the Côte de Nuits:

- **Marsannay** *(mahr sah nay):* Known mainly for rosés

- **Fixin** *(fee san):* Sturdy, earthy, firm red wines

- **Gevrey-Chambertin** *(jehv ray sham ber tan):* Full-bodied, rich red wines; eight grand crus, such as Chambertin, Chambertin Clos de Bèze

- **Morey-Saint Denis** *(maw ree san d'nee):* Full, sturdy red wines; grand crus are Bonnes Mares (part), Clos de la Roche, Clos Saint-Denis, Clos de Tart, Clos des Lambrays

- **Chambolle-Musigny** *(shom bowl moo sih nyee):* Soft, elegant red wines; grand crus include Musigny and Bonnes Mares (part)

- **Vougeot** *(voo joe):* Medium-bodied red wines; grand cru is Clos de Vougeot

- **Vosne-Romanée** *(vone roh mah nay):* Elegant, rich, velvety red wines; grand crus include Romanée-Conti, La Tache, Richebourg, Romanée-Saint-Vivant, La Romanée, and La Grand Rue

- **Flagey-Échézeaux** *(flah jhay eh sheh zoe):* Hamlet of Vosne-Romanée; grand crus are Grands-Échézeaux and Échézeaux

- **Nuits-Saint-Georges** *(nwee san johrjes):* Sturdy, earthy, red wines; no grand crus; fine premier crus

The names of these communes are also the names of their wines.

The taste of fine red Burgundy

Red Burgundy is paler than Bordeaux, ranging in color from garnet to cherry or ruby, because the Pinot Noir grape does not have nearly as much color as Cabernet Sauvignon or Merlot grapes. It's rather full-bodied in terms of its alcohol and is relatively low in tannin. The characteristic aroma is small red fruits — cherries and berries — and woodsy, damp-earth, or mushroomy scents. When a red Burgundy ages,

it often develops a silky texture, richness, and a natural sweetness of fruit flavors; sometimes a bouquet of leather, coffee, and well-hung game emerges.

With some exceptions (for example, a powerful wine from a great vintage, such as 1995 or 1996), red Burgundy should be consumed within ten years of the vintage — and even sooner in a weaker vintage (see Appendix C).

Practical advice on buying Burgundy

Nice of the Burgundians to make everything so stratified and clear, isn't it? Premier cru Burgundies are always better than commune wines, and grand crus are the best of all, right? Well, it ain't necessarily so! In order of importance, these are the criteria to follow when you are buying Burgundy:

✔ **The producer's reputation:** Based on wines he has made in recent years

✔ **The vintage year:** Quality fluctuates greatly from year to year

✔ **The appellation:** The name of the commune or vineyard and its specificity

The producer and the vintage are *considerably* more important than the appellation in Burgundy. Good vintages for red Burgundy are 1999, 1997, 1996, 1995, and 1990. For white Burgundy, 1999, 1997, 1996, 1995, 1992, and 1989 are quite good.

The southern part of the Côte d'Or, the Côte de Beaune, is named after its most important city, Beaune (the commercial and tourist center of the Côte d'Or). Both white and red Burgundies are made in the Côte de Beaune, but the white Burgundies are more renowned. The following communes, from north to south, make up the Côte de Beaune:

✔ **Ladoix *(lah dwah):*** Seldom-seen, inexpensive red and white wines; part of the grand cru vineyards, Corton (red) and Corton-Charlemagne (white) are in this commune

✔ **Pernand-Vergelesses *(per nahn ver jeh less):*** Little-known red and white wines; good buys

✔ **Aloxe-Corton *(ah luss cortohn):*** Full, sturdy wines; several red grand crus that all include the name Corton and one magnificent white grand cru (Corton-Charlemagne) are here

✔ **Chorey-lès-Beaune *(shor ay lay bone):*** Mainly good-value red wine and a little white wine

✔ **Savigny-lès-Beaune *(sah vee nyee lay bone):*** Mostly red wines; fine values here, too

✔ **Beaune *(bone):*** Soft, medium-bodied reds; some whites; fine premier crus here

✔ **Pommard *(pohm mahr):*** Sturdy, full red wines; some good premier crus (Rugiens and Epénots)

✔ **Volnay *(vohl nay):*** Soft, elegant red wines; good premier crus (Caillerets and Clos des Ducs)

- ✔ **Auxey-Duresses** *(awe see duh ress)*, **Monthélie** *(mon tel lee)*, **Saint-Romain** *(san roh man)*, **Saint-Aubin** *(sant oh ban):* Four little-known villages producing mainly red wines, but some white wines; excellent values

- ✔ **Meursault** *(muhr so):* The northernmost important white Burgundy commune; full-bodied, nutty wines; some excellent premier crus (Les Perrières and Les Genevrières)

- ✔ **Puligny-Montrachet** *(poo lee nyee mon rah shay):* Home of elegant white Burgundies; grand crus include Montrachet (part), Chevalier-Montrachet, Bâtard-Montrachet (part), and Bienvenues-Bâtard Montrachet, plus very fine premier crus

- ✔ **Chassagne-Montrachet** *(shah sahn nyah mon rah shay):* A bit sturdier than Puligny; the rest of the Montrachet and Bâtard-Montrachet grand crus are situated here, along with Criots-Bâtard Montrachet grand cru; also, some earthy, rustic reds

- ✔ **Santenay** *(sant nay):* Light-bodied, inexpensive red wines here

- ✔ **Maranges** *(ma rahnj):* Little-known, mainly red, inexpensive wines

All of these red wines are made entirely with the Pinot Noir grape and the whites are made entirely from Chardonnay. The different characteristics of the wines are due to their individual terroirs.

Tips on drinking Burgundy

Red Burgundy is a particularly good wine to choose in restaurants. Unlike Bordeaux and other Cabernet Sauvignon-based wines, red Burgundy is usually approachable when young because of its softness and its enticing aromas and flavors of red fruits. Moreover, red Burgundy, like all Pinot Noirs, is a versatile companion to food. It's the one red wine that can complement fish or seafood; it is ideal with salmon, for example. Chicken, turkey, and ham are also good matches for Burgundy. With richer red Burgundies, beef and game (such as duck, pheasant, rabbit, or venison) all go well.

Red Burgundy is at its best when served at cool temperatures — about 60° to 62°F (17°C). It should *not* be decanted. Even older Burgundies seldom develop much sediment, and too much aeration would cause you to lose the wonderful Burgundy aroma, which is one of the greatest features of this wine.

On the other hand, white Burgundy often benefits from decanting, especially grand cru and premier cru white Burgundies from younger vintages (five years old or younger). Great young white Burgundies, such as Corton Charlemagne, really have not evolved completely in their first few years; the extra aeration will help bring out their aromas and flavors. And remember, don't serve them too cold! The ideal temperature range for serving the better white Burgundies is 58° to 62°F (15° to 17°C).

Tables 10-5 and 10-6 list the best Burgundy producers and their greatest wines, in rough order of quality. For a more complete listing of Burgundy producers, see Chapter 7 in *French Wine For Dummies*.

Table 10-5	Best Red Burgundy Producers and Their Greatest Wines
Producer	*Recommended Wines*
Domaine Leroy*	Musigny, Richebourg, Chambertin (*all* of Leroy's grand crus and premier crus)
Domaine de la Romanée-Conti*	Romanée-Conti; La Tâche; Richebourg; Grands Echézeaux
Domaine Comte de Vogüé	Musigny (Vieilles Vignes); Bonnes Mares
Anne Gros	Richebourg; Clos de Vougeot
Georges et Christophe Roumier	Musigny; Bonnes Mares; Chambolle-Musigny Les Amoureuses
Ponsot	Clos de la Roche (Vieilles Vignes); Chambertin; Clos St-Denis (Vieilles Vignes); Griotte-Chambertin
Armand Rousseau	Chambertin (*all* of his grand crus); Gevrey-Chambertin Clos St-Jacques
Méo-Camuzet	Vosne-Romanée premier crus (any of his three); Clos de Vougeot; Richebourg; Corton
Hubert Lignier	Clos de la Roche; Charmes-Chambertin
Domaine Dujac	Clos de la Roche; Bonnes Mares
Joseph Roty	Any of his grand cru Chambertins
Nicolas Potel	Beaune and Volnay premier crus
Jayer-Gilles	Échézeaux; Nuits-St.-Georges Les Damodes
Louis Jadot	Romanée-St-Vivant; Chambertin Clos de Beze; Musigny
Domaine Jean et J.L. Trapet	Grand cru, premier cru Chambertins
Domaine Jean Grivot	Échézeaux; Nuits-St.-Georges premier crus
Michel Lafarge	Volnay premier crus; Beaune Les Grèves

(continued)

Table 10-5 *(continued)*

Producer	Recommended Wines
Domaine Robert Chevillon	Nuits-St.-Georges Les St.-Georges; Nuits-Georges Les Vaucrains
Domaine /Maison J. Faiveley	Nuits-St.-Georges and Mercurey premier crus
Jacques-Fréderick Mugnier	Musigny; Bonnes Mares
Domaine Bruno Clair	Gevrey-Chambertin, Marsannay premier crus
Bouchard Pere & Fils	All grand cru and premier crus
Domaine Henri Gouges	Nuits-St.-Georges and Mercurey premier crus

These wines are very expensive.

Table 10-6   Best White Burgundy Producers and Their Greatest Wines

Producer	Recommended Wines
Domaine Ramonet*	Montrachet; Bâtard-Montrachet; Bienvenue-Bâtard-Montrachet; any of his Chassagne-Montrachet premier crus
Coche-Dury*	Corton-Charlemagne; Meursault premier cru (any)
Domaine des Comtes Lafon	Meursault premier crus (any); Le Montrachet
Domaine Leflaive	Chevalier-Montrachet; Bâtard-Montrachet; Puligny-Montrachet premier crus (any)
Domaine Étienne Sauzet	Bâtard-Montrachet; Bienvenue-Bâtard-Montrachet; Puligny-Montrachet Les Combettes
Louis Carillon	Bienvenue-Bâtard-Montrachet; Puligny-Montrachet premier crus (any)
Michel Niellon	Bâtard-Montrachet; Chevalier-Montrachet; Chassagne-Montrachet Les Vergers
Verget	Bâtard-Montrachet; Chevalier-Montrachet; Meursault premier crus (any)
Guy Amiot	Chassagne-Montrachet premier crus (any)
Louis Latour	Corton-Charlemagne; Puligny-Montrachet premier crus (any)

Producer	Recommended Wines
Colin-Deléger	Chassagne-Montrachet premier crus (any); Puligny-Montrachet premier crus (any)
Jean-Noël Gagnard	Chassagne-Montrachet premier crus (any)
Louis Jadot	Corton-Charlemagne; Chassagne-Montrachet Les Caillerets; Beaune Grèves; Puligny-Montrachet premier crus (any)
Domaine François Jobard	Meursault premier crus (any)
Domaine Bernard Morey	Chassagne-Montrachet Les Caillerets; Puligny-Montrachet La Truffierè
Domaine Marc Morey	Chassagne-Montrachet premier crus (any)

* These wines are very expensive and rare.

The Côte Chalonnaise: Bargain Burgundies

The sad fact about Burgundy is that many of the best wines are costly. But one of Burgundy's best-kept secrets is the wines of the Côte Chalonnaise (the district that lies directly south of the Côte d'Or). Five villages here are home to some very decent Burgundies. True, Côte Chalonnaise Burgundies are not so fine as Côte d'Or Burgundies (they're a bit earthier and coarser), but we're talking $15 to $30 retail per bottle here. Four villages or communes whose names appear as appellations on wine labels are the following:

✔ **Mercurey *(mer cure ay):*** Mostly red wine, and a small amount of white; the best wines of the Chalonnaise come from here, and also the most expensive ($22 to $30); two of the better producers of Mercurey are J.Faiveley and Antonin Rodet

✔ **Rully *(rue yee):*** Approximately equal amounts of red and white wine; the whites, although a bit earthy, are significantly better than the reds; look for the wines of the producer Antonin Rodet

✔ **Givry *(gee vree):*** Mostly red wine, and a small amount of white; reds are better than the whites (but quite earthy); Domaine Joblot's Givry is especially worth seeking out

✔ **Montagny *(mon tah nyee):*** All white wine; look for Antonin Rodet's and Louis Latour's Montagny

The taste of fine white Burgundy

White Burgundy combines a richness of flavor — peaches, hazelnuts, and honey in Meursault; floweriness and butterscotch in a Puligny or Chassagne-Montrachet — with lively acidity and a touch of oak. With age, even more flavor complexity develops. The wine leaves your mouth with a lingering reminder of all its flavors. Chardonnay wines from other regions and countries can be good, but there's nothing else quite like a great white Burgundy.

Another village specializes in the Aligoté grape (a second white grape permitted in Burgundy) that makes a particularly crisp and lively wine:

✔ **Bouzeron** *(boo zer ohn)***:** Aubert de Villaine is the quality producer here; try his Bourgogne Rouge, Bourgogne Blanc (made from Pinot Noir and Chardonnay respectively), or Bourgogne Aligoté de Bouzeron

Chablis: Unique white wines

The village of Chablis, northwest of the Côte d'Or, is the closest Burgundian commune to Paris (about a two-hour drive). Although Chablis' wines are 100 percent Chardonnay — just like the white Burgundies of the Côte d'Or — they are quite a different style from Côte d'Or whites. Almost all Côte d'Or white Burgundies are fermented and aged in oak, for example, but many Chablis producers use only stainless steel. Also, Chablis' climate is cooler, producing wines that are intrinsically lighter-bodied, somewhat austere, and more acidic. Chablis wine is very dry and sometimes flinty, without quite the rich, ripe style of Côte d'Or white Burgundies. (Recent Chablis vintages — from 1997 through 2000 — have been so warm, however, that the wines have been tasting riper than usual.) For a classic, cool-climate Chablis, try to find a bottle from the 1995 or 1996 vintage.

Chablis is an ideal companion to seafood, especially oysters. Like all other white Burgundies, Chablis should be served cool (58° to 60°F, or 15°C), not cold.

The Chablis worth trying

Chablis is at its best at the premier cru and grand cru level. Simple village Chablis costs about $15 to $25 and, frankly, you can often find better white wines from Mâcon, the Chalonnaise, or the Côte d'Or (Bourgogne Blanc) at that price.

The seven grand cru Chablis are Les Clos, Valmur, Les Preuses, Vaudésir, Grenouilles, Bougros, and Blanchot. (Another vineyard that's actually — but not technically — grand cru is La Moutonne; this vineyard is a part of the Vaudésir and Les Preuses grand cru acreage but does not have a grand cru appellation in its own right.) Grand cru Chablis wines range in price from $35 to $85, depending on the producer. Grand cru Chablis from good vintages (see Appendix C) can age and improve for 15 years.

There are 22 premier cru Chablis appellations, but the six most well-known are Fourchaume, Montée de Tonnerre, Vaillons, Mont de Milieu, Montmains, and Les Forêts (also known as Forest). Premier cru Chablis wines range in price from $20 to $50, depending on the producer, and can age up to ten years in good vintages.

Seven outstanding producers of Chablis

Seven producers really stand out in Chablis. For a true understanding of this underrated wine, you should try to buy their grand or premier cru Chablis. *Try* is the operative word here; these are small producers whose wines are available only in better stores:

- ✔ **Francois Raveneau** and **René et Vincent Dauvissat:** Both still use oak for fermenting and aging their wine.

- ✔ **Louis Michel:** Uses stainless steel exclusively.

- ✔ **Jean Dauvissat:** Uses mainly stainless steel.

- ✔ **Jean Collet**, **Jean-Paul Droin**, and **Verget:** Other consistently fine producers of Chablis.

Mâcon: Affordable whites

If you're thinking that $20 or more sounds like too much to spend for a bottle of white Burgundy or Chablis for everyday drinking, we have an alternative wine for you: white Mâcon. Many of the best white wine buys — not only in France, but in the world — come from the Mâconnais district.

The Mâconnais lies directly south of the Chalonnaise and north of Beaujolais. It has a milder, sunnier climate than the Côte d'Or to the north. Wine production centers around the city of Mâcon, a gateway city to Provence and the Riviera. The hills in the Mâconnais contain the same chalky limestone beloved by Chardonnay that can be found in Burgundy districts to the north. In northern Mâcon, you can even find a village called Chardonnay, for which the famous grape was perhaps named.

Mâcon's white wines, in fact, are 100 percent Chardonnay. Most of them are simply called *Mâcon* or *Mâcon-Villages* (a slightly better wine than Mâcon, because it comes from specific villages), and they retail for $10 to $15 a bottle. Often better are Mâcons that come from just one village. The name of the village is appended to the name Mâcon (as in Mâcon-Lugny or Mâcon-Viré).

Mâcon whites are medium-bodied, crisp, fresh, and lively yet substantial wines that are usually unoaked. You should enjoy them while they are young, generally within three years of the vintage.

The best Mâcon whites come from the southernmost part of the district and carry their own appellations — Pouilly-Fuissé *(pwee fwee say)* and Saint-Véran *(san ver ahn)*.

- Pouilly-Fuissé is a richer, fuller-bodied wine than a simple Mâcon, is often oaked, and is a bit more expensive (around $18 to $24; up to $40 for the best examples). To try an outstanding example of Pouilly-Fuissé, buy Château Fuissé, which, in good vintages, compares favorably with more expensive Cote d'Or white Burgundies.

- Saint-Véran is very possibly the best-value wine in all of Mâcon ($12 to $18). Especially fine is the Saint-Véran of Verget, who is one of the best producers of Mâconnais wines.

Beaujolais: As delightful as it is affordable

Are you surprised that Beaujolais is in the Burgundy region? Beaujolais is so famous that it stands alone. It even has its own red grape, Gamay. Actually, the fact that Beaujolais is part of Burgundy is merely a technicality. It's really a different wine.

The Beaujolais district is situated south of the Mâconnais, in the heart of one of the greatest gastronomic centers of the world; good restaurants abound in the area, as well as in the nearby city of Lyon.

The easiest-drinking Beaujolais

If you're a white wine, white Zinfandel, or rosé wine drinker (or even a non-wine drinker!), Beaujolais might be the *ideal* first red wine to drink — a bridge, so to speak, to more serious red wines. It's delicious, has lots of fruity character (although it's a dry wine), and doesn't require serious contemplation. Beaujolais is truly a fun wine.

Beaujolais and *Beaujolais Supérieur* (one percent higher in alcohol) are the easiest Beaujolais wines. Their AOCs are district-wide (meaning their grapes can come from anywhere in the Beaujolais district), but actually these wines come from the southern part of Beaujolais where the soil is mainly clay and sand. They are fresh, fruity, uncomplicated, light-bodied wines that sell for $8 to $10 and are best a year or two after the vintage. They are fine wines for warm weather, when a heavier red wine would be inappropriate.

The serious versions

Beaujolais has its serious side, too. The best Beaujolais are made in the northern part of the Beaujolais district where the soil is granite-based. *Beaujolais-Villages* is a wine blended from the grapes of (some of) 39 designated villages that produce fuller, more substantial wine than simple Beaujolais. It costs a dollar or two more, but it's well worth the difference.

Beaujolais that's even higher quality comes from ten specific areas in the north. The wines of these areas are known as *cru* Beaujolais, and only the name of the cru appears in large letters on the label. (The wines are not actually named Beaujolais.) Cru Beaujolais have more depth and, in fact, need a little time to develop; some of the crus can age and improve for four or five years or more. They range in price from about $9 to $18. Table 10-7 lists the ten cru Beaujolais as they are geographically situated, from south to north, along with a brief description of each cru.

Table 10-7	The Ten Cru Beaujolais
Cru	*Description*
Brouilly *(broo yee)*	The largest cru in terms of production and the most variable in quality; light and fruity; drink within three years
Côte de Brouilly	Distinctly better than Brouilly, fuller and more concentrated; vineyards are higher in altitude; drink within three years
Regnié *(ray nyay)*	The newest village to be recognized as a cru; very similar to Brouilly; not quite so good as Côte de Brouilly
Morgon *(mor gohn)*	At its best, full and earthy; can age for five to seven years; look for Duboeuf's Morgon, *Domaine Jean Descombes*

(continued)

Table 10-7 (continued)

Cru	Description
Chiroubles (sheh roob leh)	One of our favorites; the quintessential, delicate, delicious, perfumed Beaujolais; tastes of young red fruits; very pretty; drink it within two years of the vintage
Fleurie (flehr ee)	Medium-bodied, rich, with a velvety fruitiness; the most popular cru (and, along with Moulin-á-Vent, the most expensive, at $13 to $18); quite reliable; can age for four years
Moulin-à-Vent (moo lahn ah vahn)	Clearly the most powerful, concentrated cru, and the one that can age the longest (ten years or more); this is one Beaujolais that really needs three or four years to develop
Chénas (shay nahs)	Bordering Moulin-à-Vent (in fact, much of it can be legally sold as the more famous Moulin-à-Vent); what is sold as Chénas is usually well priced; drink within four years
Juliénas (jhool yay nahs)	The insider's Beaujolais; often the most consistent and the best of the crus; full-bodied and rich, can last five years or more; seldom disappoints
Saint-Amour (sant ah more)	The most northerly cru in Beaujolais; perfectly named for lovers on Valentine's Day (or any other day); soft, light to medium-bodied, delicious berry fruit; drink within two or three years

SNOB ALERT

Celebration time: Beaujolais Nouveau

Each year on the third Thursday in November, the new vintage of Beaujolais — called Beaujolais Nouveau — is released all over the world with great fanfare. This youngster — only six weeks old! — is a very grapey, easy-to-drink, delicious wine with practically no tannin but lots of fruitiness. Beaujolais Nouveau is particularly popular in the U.S., where it is served at many a Thanksgiving dinner because of the timing of its annual debut. It sells for $6 to $9 and is at its best within the first year of the vintage.

Beaujolais in action

To really get a feeling for being in France, visit a bistro in Paris or Lyon and order a carafe of young Beaujolais with your charcuterie, pâte, or chicken. No wine slides down the throat as easily!

Young, uncomplicated Beaujolais wines should *definitely* be served chilled, at about 55°F (13°C), to capture their fruity exuberance. The fuller cru Beaujolais, on the other hand, are best at about the same temperature as red Burgundy (58° to 60°F; 14°C).

Most Beaujolais is sold by large *négociants* — firms that buy grapes and wine from growers and blend, bottle, and sell the wine under their own labels. Two of the largest and most reliable Beaujolais négociants are Georges Duboeuf and Louis Jadot; Jadot also owns two very fine domaines, in Moulin-a-Vent and in Morgon. (For a list of other Beaujolais producers, see Chapter 8 in *French Wine For Dummies*.)

The Hearty Rhônes of the Valley

The Rhône *(rone)* Valley is in southeastern France, south of Beaujolais, between the city of Lyon and the region of Provence. The growing season in the Rhône Valley is sunny and hot. The wines reflect the weather: The red wines are full, robust, and high in alcohol. Even some of the white wines tend to be full and powerful. But the wines from the southern part of the Rhône are distinctly different from those in the northern Rhône Valley. (For a detailed explanation of how the Northern and Southern Rhône differ as wine districts, read Chapter 9 of *French Wine For Dummies*.)

For a good, reliable dry red wine that costs about $8 to $12, look no farther than the Rhône Valley's everyday red wine, Côtes du Rhône. The Rhône Valley makes more serious wines — mostly red — but Côtes du Rhône is one of the best inexpensive red wines in the world.

Generous wines of the south

Most (in fact, over 90 percent of) Rhône wines come from the Southern Rhône. They are generally inexpensive and uncomplicated. The dominant grape variety in the southern Rhône is the prolific Grenache, which makes easy-going wines that are high in alcohol and low in tannin.

Besides Côtes du Rhône, other southern Rhône wines to look for are

- Côtes du Ventoux *(vahn too),* which is similar to, but a bit lighter than, Côtes du Rhône

- Côtes du Rhône-Villages, from 50 villages making fuller and a bit more expensive wines than Côtes du Rhône, 16 of which are entitled to use their names on the label, such as "Cairanne — Côtes du Rhône-Villages"

- The single-village wines Gigondas *(jhee gon dahs)* and Vacqueyras *(vah keh rahs)*

The last two wines are former Côtes du Rhône-Villages wines that graduated and are now entitled to their own appellations. Gigondas ($20 to $30) is particularly rich and robust and can live for ten years or more in good vintages. Vacqueyras is less powerful and robust than Gigondas but also less expensive (mainly $12 to $18); Vacqueyras is a particularly good buy.

Two interesting dry rosé wines of the southern Rhône are Tavel *(tah vel)* and Lirac *(lee rahk);* Lirac is less well known and therefore less expensive. (Tavel ranges from $13 to $23, Lirac a little less; Lirac can also be red.) Both are made from the Grenache and Cinsault grapes. They can be delightful on hot, summer days or at picnics. As with most rosé wines, they are best when they are very young.

But **Châteauneuf-du-Pape** *(shah toe nuf doo pahp)* is the king in the Southern Rhône. Its name recalls the fourteenth century, when nearby Avignon (not Rome) was the home of the Popes. Almost all Châteauneuf-du-Pape is a blended red wine: As many as 13 grape varieties can be used, but Grenache, Mourvèdre, and Syrah predominate. At its best, Châteauneuf-du-Pape is full-bodied, rich, round, and ripe. In good vintages, it will age well for 15 to 20 years. Most red Châteauneuf-du-Pape wines (a little, very earthy, white Châteauneuf-du-Pape is also made) retail in the $25 to $35 price range, but the very best ones can cost up to $60. Two of the finest Châteauneuf-du-Papes are *Château Rayas* (nearly 100 percent Grenache from very old vines) and *Château de Beaucastel* (which can age 20 years or more).

Noble wines of the north

The two best red wines of the entire Rhône — **Côte-Rôtie** *(coat roe tee)* and **Hermitage** *(er mee tahj)* — are produced in the Northern Rhône Valley. Both are made from the noble Syrah grape (but a bit of white Viognier wine is sometimes used in Côte Rôtie).

Although both are rich, full-bodied wines, **Côte-Rôtie** is the more finesseful of the two. It has a wonderfully fragrant aroma — which always reminds us of green olives and raspberries — and soft, fruity flavors. In good vintages, Côte Rôtie can age for 20 years or more (see Appendix C). Most Côte-Rôties are in the $40 to $75 price range.

The most famous producer of Côte-Rôtie is Guigal; his single-vineyard Côte-Rôties — La Mouline, La Landonne, and La Turque — are legendary but rare and particularly expensive (over $200 a bottle!).

Red Hermitage is clearly the most full-bodied, longest-lived Rhône wine. It is a complex, rich, tannic wine that needs several years before it begins to develop, and it will age easily for 30 years or more in good vintages (1999, 1998, 1995, 1991, 1990, 1989, and 1988 were all excellent vintages in the Northern Rhône). The best red Hermitages sell today for $50 to $75, and a few are even over $100, although lesser Hermitages are as low as $35 to $40.

The three best producers of Hermitage are Jean-Louis Chave, Chapoutier, and Paul Jaboulet Aîné (for his top Hermitage, La Chapelle).

Jaboulet also makes a less expensive little brother to Hermitage, a **Crozes-Hermitage** (a separate appellation) called Domaine de Thalabert. It's as good as — if not better than — many Hermitages, can age and improve for 10 to 15 years in good vintages, and is reasonably priced at $21 to $23. It's a wine to buy.

Cornas, also made entirely from Syrah, is another fine Northern Rhône red wine. Cornas resembles Hermitage in that it is a huge, tannic wine that needs 10 to 20 years of aging. It ranges in price from $30 to $75. Two Cornas producers to look for are Domaine August Clape and Jean-Luc Colombo.

A small amount of white Hermitage is produced from the Marsanne and Roussanne grape varieties. White Hermitage is traditionally a full, heavy, earthy wine that needs eight to ten years to fully develop. Chapoutier's fine Hermitage Blanc, Chante-Alouette, however, is all Marsanne (about $75) and made in a more approachable style. The other great white Hermitage is Chave's; about $80, it is complex, rich, and almost as long-lived as his red Hermitage.

Condrieu *(cohn dree oo),* made entirely from Viognier, is the other white wine to try in the Northern Rhône. It's one of the most fragrant, floral dry wines in existence. Its flavors are delicate but rich, with delicious fresh apricot and peach notes; it makes a wonderful accompaniment to fresh fish. Condrieu (which sells for $40 to $60) is best young, however. And, because Condrieu is a small wine zone, the best Condrieu wines are hard to find. Look for them in finer wine shops and better French restaurants. (For more info on Rhône wines and producers, see Chapter 9 in *French Wine For Dummies*.)

The Loire Valley: White Wine Heaven

Have you been Chardonnay-ed out yet? If you're looking for white-wine alternatives to Chardonnay, discover the Loire *(l'wahr)* Valley wine region. Lots of white wines come from there, but none of them are Chardonnay! For the record, you can find red wines and some dry rosés, too, in the Loire, but the region is really known for its white wines.

The Loire Valley stretches across northwest France, following the path of the Loire River from central France in the east to the Atlantic Ocean in the west. The rather cool climate, especially in the west, produces relatively light-bodied white wines.

In the eastern end of the Valley, just south of Paris, are the towns of Sancerre and Pouilly-sur-Loire, located on opposite banks of the Loire River. Here, the Sauvignon Blanc grape thrives, making lively, dry wines that have spicy, green-grass flavors. The two principal wines in this area are **Sancerre** *(sahn sehr)* and **Pouilly-Fumé** *(pwee foo may)*.

✔ Sancerre is the lighter, drier, and livelier of the two. It's perfect for summer drinking, especially with shellfish or light, freshwater fish, such as trout. Look for the Sancerres of Domaines Henri Bourgeois or Lucien Crochet.

✔ Pouilly-Fumé is slightly fuller and less spicy than Sancerre and can have attractive gun-flint and mineral flavors. Pouilly-Fumé can be quite a fine wine when made by a good producer such as Didier Dagueneau or Ladoucette. Because it is fuller, Pouilly-Fumé goes well with rich fish, such as salmon, or with chicken or veal.

Most Sancerre and Pouilly-Fumé wines sell in the $15 to $25 price range, but a few of the better Pouilly-Fumés can cost up to $50. These wines are at their best when they're young; drink them within four years of the vintage.

In the central Loire Valley, near the city of Tours (where beautiful châteaux of former French royalty can be found), lies the town of Vouvray *(voo vray)*. The Chenin Blanc grape makes better wine in the central Loire than it does anywhere else in the world. The wines of **Vouvray** come in three styles: dry (sec), medium-dry (demi-sec), or sweet (called *moelleux*, pronounced *m'wah leuh*). The sweet wines can be made only in vintages of unusual ripeness, which occur infrequently. There is also a sparkling Vouvray.

REMEMBER

Here a Pouilly, there a Pouilly

You might get the two *Pouilly* wines — Pouilly-Fuissé and Pouilly-Fumé — confused, but they are very different wines. The Chardonnay-based Pouilly-Fuissé, from the Mâcon in Burgundy, is a fuller-bodied wine and usually oaky. Pouilly-Fumé, made from Sauvignon Blanc, is lighter and crisper.

The best wines of Vouvray, the sweet *(moelleux)*, need several years to develop and can last almost forever, thanks to their remarkable acidity; their prices begin at about $20. Three renowned Vouvray producers are Philippe Foreau of Clos Naudain, Gaston Huet-Pinguet, and Didier Champalou.

TIP

Less expensive Vouvrays, priced at $10 to $15, are pleasant to drink young. Even the drier versions are not truly bone dry and are a good choice if you cannot tolerate very dry wines. They go well with chicken or veal in cream sauce, or with fruit and soft cheese after dinner.

The Loire Valley's best red wines come from the Central Loire. Made mainly from Cabernet Franc, they carry the place-names of the villages the grapes come from: Chinon *(shee nohn)*, Bourgueil *(boorguh'y)*, Saint-Nicolas-de-Bourgueil *(san nee co lah deh boor guh'y)*, and Saumur-Champigny *(saw muhr shahm pee n'yee)*. They're all delightful, inexpensive ($10 to $20), medium-bodied reds that can be enjoyed with white meat dishes or fish.

The third wine district of the Loire Valley is the Pays Nantais *(pay ee nahn tay)*, named after the city of Nantes, right where the Loire River empties into the Atlantic Ocean. The vineyards around Nantes are home of the Muscadet grape (also known as the Melon). The wine, also called **Muscadet** *(moos cah day)*, is light and very dry, with apple and mineral flavors — perfect with clams, oysters, and river fish (and, naturally, ideal for summer drinking).

TECHNICAL STUFF

Most Muscadets comes from the Sèvre-et-Maine AOC zone, and those words appear on the label. Frequently you will also see the term *sur lie,* which means that the wine was aged on its *lees* (fermentation yeasts) and bottled straight from the tank. This procedure gives the wine liveliness, freshness, and sometimes a slight prickle of carbon dioxide on the tongue.

REAL DEAL

The best news about Muscadet is the price. You can buy a really good Muscadet for $6 to $12. Buy the youngest one you can find because Muscadet is best within two years of the vintage. It is not an ager. (See Chapter 12 in *French Wine For Dummies* for more info on Loire Valley wines and producers.)

Alsace Wines: French, Not German

It's understandable that some wine drinkers confuse the wines of Alsace *(ahl zas)* with German wines. Alsace, in northeastern France, is just across the Rhine River from Germany. Originally a part of Germany, Alsace became French in the seventeenth century. Germany took the region back in 1871 only to lose it to France again in 1919 as a result of World War I. To complicate things further, both Alsace and Germany grow some of the same grapes (Riesling and Gewürztraminer, for example). But most Alsace wines are dry, while most German wines are medium-dry or sweet.

Alsace wines are unique among French wines in two ways. All Alsace wines come in a long-necked bottle called a *flûte*. And almost all Alsace wines carry a grape variety name as well as a place-name (that is, Alsace). The wines of Alsace also happen to represent very good value.

Considering Alsace's northerly latitude, you'd expect the region's climate to be cool. But thanks to the protection of the Vosges Mountains to the west, Alsace's climate is quite sunny and temperate, and one of the driest in France — in short, perfect weather for grape growing.

Although some Pinot Noir exists, 91 percent of Alsace's wines are white. Four are particularly important: Riesling, Pinot Blanc, Pinot Gris, and Gewürztraminer. Each reflects the characteristics of its grape, but they all share a certain aroma and flavor, sometimes called a spiciness, that can only be described as the flavor of Alsace.

Riesling is the king of Alsace wines (remember that it's a *dry* wine here). Alsace Riesling has a fruity aroma but a firm, dry, almost steely taste. Although, like most Alsace wines, it can be consumed young, a Riesling from a good vintage can easily age and improve for ten years or more. Rieslings are in the $15 to $35 price range.

Alsace **Pinot Blanc** is the lightest of the four wines. In a slight reinterpretation of traditional Alsace style, some producers make their Pinot Blanc medium-dry to appeal to wine drinkers who are unfamiliar with the region's wines. Other producers make it bone dry. Either way, it's best in its youth. Pinot Blanc is quite inexpensive, selling for $10 to $15.

Tokay-Pinot Gris is an Alsace wine whose name resembles a famous Hungarian dessert wine, Tokaji — but there is no relationship. Tokay-Pinot Gris is made from Pinot Gris, the same variety that you find in Italy as Pinot Grigio. Here in Alsace, it makes a rich, spicy, full-bodied, characterful wine. Alsace's Pinot Gris retails in the $15 to $20 range; it goes well with spicy meat dishes and can work with slightly sweet or sour flavors.

The **Gewürztraminer** grape has such intense, exotic, spicy aromas and flavors that it's a love-it-or-leave-it wine (one of us loves it — the other leaves it!). But it certainly has its followers. And this grape is clearly at its best in Alsace. If you haven't tried an Alsace Gewürztraminer yet, you haven't tasted one of the most unique wines in the world. It's quite low in acidity and high in alcohol, a combination that gives an impression of fullness and softness. It goes best with *foie gras* and strong cheeses, and some people like it with spicy Asian cuisine. Gewürztraminer sells for about the same price as Riesling but doesn't age quite as well.

For more info on Alsace wines and producers, see Chapter 11 in *French Wine For Dummies.*

The South and Southwest

The most dynamic wine regions in France are all located in the southern part of the country. Not that winemaking is new in the South; in fact, it's the oldest wine-producing area in France. The Greeks made wine in Provence in the sixth century B.C. The South is also the part of France that makes the most wine. Languedoc-Roussillon, a dual wine region, produces over 40 percent of France's wine!

Most southern French wines didn't get much international attention until the 1980s. Nowadays, wines from the South of France are very "in." The world has discovered that these wines are now vastly improved in quality, as well as very affordable.

Southwest France, the huge area between Bordeaux and the Spanish border, also makes wine (well, it's French, isn't it?), and many wine regions here are also experiencing a renaissance. Like the South, it's mainly red wine country, but you can find some interesting whites, rosés, sparkling wines, and dessert wines, as well. You might say that the South and Southwestern France are the country's "new" frontiers.

The Midi: France's bargain basement

The sunny, dry Languedoc-Roussillon *(lahn guh doc roo see yohn)* region, also known as the Midi *(mee dee),* has long been the country's largest wine-producing area. The region produces mainly red wines; in fact, more than half of France's red wines come from here. Traditionally, these robust red wines were made from typical grape varieties of the South, such as Carignan, Cinsault, and Grenache. But in the last two decades, better varieties such as Syrah, Cabernet Sauvignon, and Merlot have become popular with growers. Winemakers use these grapes both for varietal wines and in blends.

In this region, look especially for the red wines from the AOC zones of Corbières, Minervois, St-Chinian, Fitou, and Costières de Nîmes. In addition, many varietal wines carrying the designation *Vin de Pays d'Oc* are often good values. They're made from grapes that can come from anywhere in the Languedoc-Roussillon region, rather than from a specific AOC zone.

The best news is that most of these wines are under $15, and many are under $10! Two of the better-known brands of varietal wines (with the Vin de Pays d'Oc appellation) are Fortant de France and Réserve St. Martin.

Timeless Provence

Provence *(pro vahns)* — southeast of the Rhône Valley, east of Languedoc-Roussillon, and west of Northern Italy — may be France's most beautiful region. Home of the Riviera, Nice, and Cannes, it's certainly the country's most fashionable and touristy region. But it's also an ancient land, with a thriving old capital, Aix-en-Provence. The excellent light and climate have always attracted great artists, such as Vincent Van Gogh, who painted many of their best works here.

Wine has always been part of Provence's culture and economy. Provence is best known for its rosés, which so many tourists enjoy on the Riviera, but Provence's red wines are now winning the most critical acclaim. Rosé wines still dominate in the region's largest AOC wine zone, Côtes de Provence, but in three other important AOC zones — Coteaux d'Aix-en-Provence, Les Baux-de-Provence, and Bandol — red wines rule. Bandol, and its foremost producer, Domaine Tempier, enjoy Provence's greatest reputation for reds. Cassis (no relation to the blackcurrant liqueur of the same name), a small AOC zone on the Mediterranean coast near Marseilles, makes distinctive, aromatic white wines.

Provence's reds and rosés derive from the same grape varieties used in Languedoc-Roussillon — Grenache, Cinsault, Mourvèdre, Carignan, Syrah, and Cabernet Sauvignon. The main varieties in white Cassis are Clairette and Marsanne.

For more info on the wines and producers of Languedoc-Roussillon and Provence, see Chapter 13 in *French Wine For Dummies.*

Southwest France

The large area that borders the Atlantic Ocean south of the Bordeaux region is known as Southwest France — but it's actually composed of many individual wine districts. Three of the most significant are situated near Bordeaux.

- ✔ **Bergerac** *(ber jhe rak)* is known for its Bordeaux-like red and white wines, without the Bordeaux prices. Merlot dominates Bergerac's red wines, while Sémillon and Sauvignon Blanc are the main varieties for its whites, some of which cost as little as $7 a bottle.

- ✔ **Monbazillac** *(mon bah zee yak)* specializes in sweet dessert wines similar to the Sauternes of the Bordeaux region (see Chapter 16 for more on Sauternes), but Monbazillac's wines are considerably less expensive — and less complex — than Sauternes.

- ✔ **Cahors** *(cah or)*, which makes red wines only, is Southwest France's most prestigious red wine district. The main grape variety is Malbec. Nowhere else in the world, except Argentina, does this variety play such an important role. The best wines of the traditional Cahors producers, such as Château Lagrezette, are dark, tannic reds that need about ten years of aging before they mature. Prices for Château Lagrezette Cahors wines begin at $18 to $20.

Two other districts in Southwest France, **Gaillac** *(gah yack)* and **Juraçon** *(joo rahn sohn)*, specialize in white dessert wines — quite good in quality. Gaillac also makes fruity, lightly sparkling wines. The last French AOC district before you cross the Pyrénées Mountains into Spain is **Irouléguy** *(ee roo leh gee)*; spicy, tannic red wines are made here by natives who speak not French, but Basque. (Chapter 14 of *French Wine For Dummies* provides much more information on the wines and producers of Southwest France.)

Other French Wine Regions

Two of France's three least-known wine regions have something in common: They are located in the foothills and slopes of the Alps in eastern France, next to Switzerland. In fact, skiers are probably the most familiar with their wines. They are the **Jura** *(joo rah)* and **Savoie** *(sah v'wah)* — sometimes anglicized as *Savoy*.

Jura makes two interesting wines: "Yellow Wine" *(Vin Jaune)* — made nowhere else in France — and "Straw Wine" *(Vin de Paille)*, a little of which is also made in the Northern Rhône. The Yellow Wine, from the Savagnin grape variety, is comparable to a light Spanish fino Sherry, but it's not fortified. Château-Chalon is the most famous example of Vins Jaunes *(van joh'n)*. Vin de Paille *(van deh pah'ee)* is known as Straw Wine because of the traditional way in which it's made: The grapes (Savagnin or Chardonnay) are harvested late, arranged on straw mats or in baskets, and then placed in attics to dry — similar to Tuscany's dessert wine, Vin Santo (see Chapter 16). The resulting wine is rich, concentrated, nutty, and raisiny.

Savoie's wines, mainly white, are typically dry and light-bodied. Seyssel *(say sell)*, Savoie's best-known appellation, is known for its slightly sparkling wines as well as its still whites.

Corsica, renowned historically as the birthplace of Napoleon, is a large, mountainous island 100 miles southeast of Provence. It's best known for its medium-bodied, well-priced red and rosé wines. (For more info on the wines and producers of France's minor wine regions, see Chapter 14 in *French Wine For Dummies*.)

Chapter 11

Italy, the Heartland of Vino

- -

In This Chapter

▶ Italy's Big "B" wines

▶ Chianti: Still famous after all these years

▶ A trio from Verona

▶ The *vino bianco* quality revival

- -

More than 2,000 years after Julius Caesar conquered Gaul, the Italians continue to take the world by storm. With passion, artistic flair, impeccable taste, and flawless workmanship as their weapons, the Italians have infiltrated the arenas of fashion, film, food, and of course, wine.

Thanks to the popularity of Italian restaurants, most of us have frequent opportunities to enjoy the best-selling Italian wines such as Pinot Grigio, Soave, Valpolicella, and Chianti. But Italy makes other wines, too — many of them among the greatest wines on earth. And just about every one of Italy's thousand-something wines is terrific with food, because Italian wines are made specifically to be enjoyed during a meal. That's how the Italians drink it.

We focus on Italy's three most renowned wine areas — Piedmont, Tuscany, and Northeastern Italy — in this chapter. We also look at some of the other Italian regions whose wines you are likely to find in your wine shop or *ristorante*. If you're looking for more detailed information on Italian wines, be sure to get our book *Italian Wine For Dummies* (John Wiley Publishing, Inc.).

The Vineyard of Europe

Tiny, overachieving Italy — 60 percent the size of France, three-quarters the size of California — makes (just like France) almost 30 percent of the world's wines! Wine is the lifeblood of the Italian people. Vines grow all over, and no meal could possibly occur without a bottle of wine on the table.

The downside of wine's omnipresence in Italy is that Italians often take wine for granted. Italy took 28 years longer than France to develop a wine classification system, for example; and still today, 40 years after creating that system, Italy has yet to incorporate official recognition of her best vineyard sites *(crus)* into her wine laws, as the French have done in Burgundy. Italy's casual attitude toward wine has slowed the acceptance of even the top Italian wines by many serious wine lovers around the world — although recognition of Italian wines has grown considerably over the last decade.

Another handicap of Italian wines, for wine drinkers in other countries who want to learn about them, is that most Italian wines are made from native grape varieties that don't exist elsewhere (and when transplanted, don't perform nearly as well as in Italy). Grapes such as Nebbiolo, Sangiovese, Aglianico, and Barbera, to name just a few, can make outstanding wine in Italy, but their names are unfamiliar. Table 11-1 lists the grape varieties behind some wines of Italy's most important wine regions.

Table 11-1   Grape Varieties of Some Major Italian Wine Regions

Region/ Red Wine	White Wine	Grape Varieties
Piedmont		
Barolo		Nebbiolo
Barbaresco		Nebbiolo
Gattinara		Nebbiolo, Bonarda*
	Gavi	Cortese
Tuscany		
Chianti, Chianti Classico		Sangiovese, Canaiolo, and others*
Brunello di Montalcino		Sangiovese Grosso
Vino Nobile di Montepulciano		Sangiovese, Canaiolo, and others*
Carmignano		Sangiovese, Cabernet Sauvignon*
Super-Tuscans**		Cabernet Sauvignon, Sangiovese, and others*

Region/ Red Wine	White Wine	Grape Varieties
Veneto		
	Soave	Garganega, Trebbiano, and others*
Valpolicella		Corvina, Rondinella, Molinara*
Amarone		(Same grapes as Valpolicella; semi-dried)
Bardolino		Corvina, Rondinella, Molinara*
	Bianco di Custoza	Trebbiano, Garganega, Tocai*
	Lugana***	Trebbiano

* Blended wines, made from two or more grapes.
** Untraditional wines produced mainly in the Chianti district; see the discussion under Tuscany.
*** Much of the Lugana wine zone is actually in Lombardy

On the upside, Italy is blessed with such a variety of soils and climates —
from Alpine foothills in the north to Mediterranean coastlines in the south —
that the range of her wines is almost endless. (A curious wine lover could
keep busy for a lifetime exploring the hundreds of wines in Italy!) Italy's hilly
landscape provides plenty of high-altitude relief for grapevines even in the
warm south.

The ordinary and the elite

Italy's wines, as we outside of Italy know them, fall into two distinct groups:

✓ Inexpensive red and white wines often sold in large value-priced bottles
for everyday drinking with meals in the casual Italian fashion

✓ The better wines, which range from good to great in quality

One of the best-known Italian wines in the first category is Lambrusco, a
frothy, slightly sweet (and delicious) red wine that has been a first wine for
many wine drinkers outside Italy. In the second category is Barolo, one of the
world's finest red wines, along with many other fine Italian wines.

Categories of Italian wine, legally speaking

Because Italy is a member of the European Union (EU), her official system of categorizing wines (her *appellation* system) must conform to the two-tier EU system. (See "The EU hierarchy of wine" in Chapter 9 for more information.) In the upper tier — Quality Wines Produced in a Specific Region (QWPSR) — Italy has two categories of wine:

- ✔ DOCG wines *(Denominazione di Origine Controllata e Garantita)*, translated as *regulated and guaranteed place-name,* a small group of elite wines. The long Italian phrase corresponding to the initials DOCG appears on the labels of these wines.

- ✔ DOC wines *(Denominazione di Origine Controllata)*, translated as *regulated place-name,* Italy's basic QWPSR wines. The phrase *Denominazione di Origine Controllata* appears on the labels of these wines.

The terms DOC and DOCG refer both to wine zones and the wines of those zones. The DOCG Soave, for example, is both a place (a specific production zone defined and regulated by Italian law, named after a town called Soave) and the wine of that place.

In the lower EU tier — table wine — Italy has another two categories of wine:

- ✔ IGT wines *(Indicazione di Geografica Tipica)*, which are table wines with a geographic indication on the label. Most of these wines were previously labeled as *vino da tavola* followed by a geographic designation, and you still find this wording on some labels.

- ✔ Ordinary table wines that carry no geographical indication except "Italy."

Italy's wine regions

Italy is said to have 20 wine regions, which correspond exactly to her political regions (see Figure 11-1). (In other words, wine is produced everywhere in Italy.) What we would call a wine region in France, such as Burgundy or Alsace, we refer to as a wine *zone* in Italy to avoid confusion with the political region.

Many of the finest wines come from the north: the Piedmont region in the northwest, Tuscany in north-central Italy, and the three regions (informally called the Tre Venezie) of Northeastern Italy.

© Akira Chiwaki

Figure 11-1:
The wine
regions
of Italy.

Reds Reign in Piedmont

Piedmont's claim to wine fame is the Nebbiolo *(neb bee OH lo)* grape, a noble red variety that produces great wine only in northwestern Italy. The proof of Nebbiolo's nobility is its wines: Barolo *(bah RO lo)* and Barbaresco *(bar bah RES co)* are two of the world's great red wines. Both are DOCG wines made entirely from the Nebbiolo grape in the Langhe hills around Alba, and each is named after a village within its production zone.

Both Barolo and Barbaresco are robust reds — very dry, full-bodied, and high in tannin, acidity, and alcohol. Their aromas suggest tar, violets, roses, ripe strawberries, and (sometimes) truffles — the kind that grow in the ground, not the chocolate! Barolo is more full-bodied than Barbaresco and usually requires a bit more aging; otherwise, the two wines are very similar. Like most Italian wines, they show at their best with food. Good Barolo and Barbaresco wines usually start at about $40 and run to over $100 per bottle.

Most Barolos and Barbarescos are not wines to drink young. Production rules stipulate that Barolo is not Barolo until it has aged for three years at the winery, or for five years if it is called *Riserva*. (Barbaresco's minimum aging is two years, or four for Riserva.) But both wines benefit from additional aging. When traditionally made, Barolo and Barbaresco often require 10 to 15 years' total aging, from the year of the vintage — and they usually benefit from a few hours of aeration before drinking to soften their somewhat tough tannins. (See Chapter 8 for instructions on aerating wine.)

Both Barbaresco and especially Barolo have something in common with Burgundy in France: *You must find a good producer to really experience the wine at its best.* To guide you in that endeavor, we list whom we consider the best producers of Barolo and of Barbaresco, in our rough order of preference. Some producers — including Giacomo Conterno, both Mascarellos, Giuseppe Rinaldi, and Bruno Giacosa — clearly make traditionally styled wines; others — such as Gaja, Sandrone, and Voerzio — make modern-style wines; and some, such as Ceretto and Vietti, combine aspects of both winemaking styles. (We prefer the traditionally made wines, but all three styles have some excellent producers.)

Barolo
Giacomo Conterno
Giuseppe Mascarello
Giuseppe Rinaldi
Bartolo Mascarello
Bruno Giacosa
Vietti
Gaja
Aldo Conterno
Marcarini
Ceretto
Luciano Sandrone
Paolo Scavino
E. Pira & Figli
Roberto Voerzio
Podere Colla
Marchesi di Barolo
Prunotto
Pio Cesare
Elio Altare
Luigi Pira
Conterno-Fantino

Renato Ratti
Elvio Cogno
Cordero di Montezemolo
Clerico
Manzone
Giacomo Borgogno
Michele Chiarlo
Fontanafredda
Parusso

Barbaresco
Bruno Giacosa
Gaja
Ceretto (*aka* Bricco Asili)
Marchesi di Gresy
Albino Rocca
Bruno Rocca
La Spinetta
Produttori del Barbaresco
Fratelli Cigliuti
Moccagatta
Paitin

Tradition versus "new-style"

One Barolo can differ from another (and one Barbaresco from another) quite a lot according to the wineries' production methods. Traditionally made wines are more tannic and need more time to develop but typically have greater longevity than new-style wines do. The new-style wines are fruitier in flavor but often oaky-tasting, and are ready to drink sooner — as soon as two to five years after they are released. Many producers are in one winemaking camp or the other, while some producers make their wines in a middle-ground style.

Two other good Nebbiolo-based wines, the DOCGs Gattinara *(gah tee NAH rah)* and Ghemme *(GAE mae)*, come from northern Piedmont, where the Nebbiolo grape is called Spanna. Although Gattinara and Ghemme seldom get the praise that the two Big B's (Barolo and Barbaresco) enjoy, they offer the same enticing Nebbiolo aromas and flavors — especially Gattinara — in a less full-bodied style. Priced at $30 to $40 a bottle, Gattinara from a good producer may be one of the world's most underrated wines. Look for Antoniolo's, Nervi's, and Travaglini's Gattinaras; Antichi Vigneti di Cantalupo (about $40) is the leading Ghemme producer.

Weekday reds

The Piedmontese reserve serious wines like Barolo and Barbaresco for Sunday dinner or special occasions. What they drink on an everyday basis are the red wines Dolcetto *(dohl CHET to)*, Barbera *(bar BEAR ah)*, and Nebbiolo (grown outside of prestigious DOCG zones, such as Barolo and Barbaresco). Of the three, Dolcetto is the lightest-bodied and is usually the first red wine served in a Piedmontese meal.

Dolcetto

If you know enough Italian to translate the phrase *la dolce vita,* you might think that the name Dolcetto indicates a sweet wine. Actually, the Dolcetto grape tastes sweet but the *wine* is distinctly dry and somewhat grapey with noticeable tannin. Dolcetto is often compared to Beaujolais (France's easy-drinking red wine; see Chapter 10), but it is drier and more tannic than most Beaujolais wines and goes better with food (at least in our opinion).

Dolcetto sells for $11 to $20. The best Dolcetto wines are from the zones of Dogliani, Diano d'Alba, and Alba; the labels of these wines carry the grape name, Dolcetto, along with the name of the area. Just about all of our recommended Barolo producers make a Dolcetto, usually Dolcetto d'Alba. A favorite producer of ours who happens to make only Dolcetto di Dogliani is Quinto Chionetti.

Barbera

While Dolcetto is unique to Piedmont, the Barbera grape is the second most widely planted red grape variety in all of Italy. (Sangiovese is *the* most widely planted red variety.) But it's in Piedmont — specifically the Asti and Alba wine zones — that Barbera excels. It's a rich, red wine with high acidity and generous black-cherry fruit character.

Barbera d'Alba is generally a bit fuller, riper, and richer than the leaner Barbera d'Asti — but Barbera d'Asti from certain old vineyards rivals Barbera d'Alba in richness and in power. (Link the d' with the word following it when pronouncing these names: *DAL ba, DAHS tee.*) Barbera happens to be our favorite everyday wine, especially with pasta or pizza — or anything tomatoey.

Barbera is more popular in the United States than it has ever been, and we couldn't be more delighted, as it's now easier to find. Two different styles of Barbera are available:

- ✔ The traditional style, aged in *casks* (large oak containers that impart little, if any, oak flavor to the wine), which sells for about $10 to $25.

- ✔ The newer, oak-influenced, Barbera aged in *barriques* (small, new barrels of French oak), which sells in the $25 to $45 range (somebody has to pay for those expensive barriques!)

Although both types of Barbera are very good, with few exceptions we prefer the simpler, less expensive, traditional style. (Frankly, we're getting tired of all the oak flavor in wines these days.)

Two particularly good producers of Barbera d'Alba are Vietti and Giacomo Conterno. Vietti also makes a terrific Barbera d'Asti called "La Crena."

Nebbiolo

A third weekday red from Piedmont is Nebbiolo d'Alba, a wine made from Nebbiolo grapes grown in vineyards outside the prized Barolo or Barbaresco zones. The wine is lighter in body and easier to drink than either Barolo or Barbaresco, and it sells for about $15 to $18 a bottle. Other variations are Roero Rosso, made almost entirely from Nebbiolo, and Nebbiolo Langhe. (For more specific information on Piedmontese wines, see Chapter 4 of *Italian Wine For Dummies.)*

Whites in a supporting role

Almost all of Piedmont's wines are red, but the region does boast two interesting dry whites. Gavi, named for a town in southern Piedmont, is a very dry wine with pronounced acidity. Most Gavis sell for $13 to $20, while a premium Gavi, La Scolca's Black Label, costs around $40.

Arneis *(ahr NASE)* is a white wine produced in the Roero zone near Alba from a long-forgotten grape called Arneis, which was rescued by Alfredo Currado, owner of Vietti winery, 35 years ago. Arneis is a dry to medium-dry wine with rich texture. It's best when it is consumed within two years of the vintage; a bottle sells for $18 to $24. Besides Vietti's, look for Bruno Giacosa's and Ceretto's Arneis.

Tuscany the Beautiful

Florence, Siena, Michelangelo's David, the leaning tower of Pisa . . . the beautiful region of Tuscany has more than her share of attractions. Only one wine could possibly compare in fame — and that, too, comes from Tuscany: Chianti.

Chianti: Italy's great, underrated red

Chianti is a large wine zone extending through much of Tuscany. The zone — all of it DOCG status, deservedly or not — has seven districts. Chianti wines may use the name of the district where their grapes grow or the simpler appellation, Chianti, if their production does not qualify for a district name (if grapes from two districts are blended, for example).

The district known as *Chianti Classico* is the heartland of the zone, the best area, and — lucky for us — the one district whose wines are widely available. The only other Chianti district that can rival Chianti Classico in quality is *Chianti Rufina (ROO fee nah;* not to be confused with the renowned Chianti producer Ruffino), whose wines are fairly available, especially from the well-known producer Frescobaldi.

Besides varying according to their district of production, Chianti wines vary in style according to their aging: *Riserva* wines are quite often aged in French oak, may be released only after two years or more at the winery, and have potential for long life. Chianti wines can also vary according to their grape blend — although, in practice, most Chiantis are made almost entirely from the Sangiovese grape.

Chianti is a very dry red wine (there's no such animal as *white* Chianti) that, like most Italian wines, tastes best with food. It ranges from light-bodied to almost full-bodied, often has an aroma of cherries and sometimes violets, and has a flavor reminiscent of tart cherries. The best Chianti wines have very concentrated fruit character and usually taste best from five to eight years after the vintage — although in good vintages they have no problem aging for ten or more years.

Brunello with American roots

The largest producer of Brunello di Montalcino is actually an American family — the Marianis of New York. In 1978, they established Castello Banfi in the southern part of the Montalcino zone, and today they are leaders in research into the grapes and terroirs of Montalcino.

These days, Chianti is better than ever. From simple $10 to $12 Chianti to the more substantial Chianti Classico (generally between $15 and $20), Chianti remains one of the wine world's great values. Even Chianti Classico Riservas are good values, with most of them priced in the $23 to $35 range.

Chianti is more consistent in quality than Barolo, especially in the Classico district, but it's still smart to know the good producers. Here is an alphabetical list of some of our favorites. (If 39 favorite producers seems excessive, remember that Chianti is a fairly large area with many thousands of growers and winemakers; for more info on Chianti wines, see Chapter 8 in *Italian Wine For Dummies*.)

Great Chianti Producers

Badia a Coltibuono	Cecchi-Villa Cerna	Podere Il Palazzino
Barone Ricasoli (aka Castello di Brolio)	Le Corti	Poggio al Sole
La Brancaia	Fattoria di Felsina	Querciabella
Carpineto	Fattoria Nittardi	Riecine
Castellare di Castellina	Fontodi	Rocca di Castagnoli
Castell'in Villa	Frescobaldi	Ruffino
Castello d'Albola	Isole e Olena	San Fabiano Calcinaia
Castello dei Rampolla	Marchesi Antinori	San Felice
Castello di Ama	La Massa	San Giusto a Rentennano
Castello di Fonterutoli	Melini	Selvapiana
Castello di Gabbiano	Monsanto-Il Poggio	Tenute Folonari
Castello di Verrazzano	Montevertine	Villa Cafaggio
Castello di Volpaia	Nozzole	Viticcio

Brunello di Montalcino, overnight celebrity

While Chianti has been famous for centuries, another great Tuscan wine, Brunello di Montalcino, exploded on the scene only some 30 years ago — and became an overnight success with staying power.

South of the Chianti zone sits the fortress town of Montalcino. The local wine, Brunello di Montalcino *(brew NEL lo dee mon tahl CHEE no)*, originated in the nineteenth century but was pretty much unheard of outside Tuscany until 1970 when the Biondi-Santi family, a leading producer in Montalcino, presented some of its oldest wines to writers. Their 1888 and 1891 vintages were still drinking well. (In fact, they were in excellent shape!) The rest is history, as they say. Today, Brunello di Montalcino, a DOCG wine, is considered one of the greatest, long-lived red wines in existence, with a price-tag to match ($45 to over $100).

Brunello di Montalcino comes from a particular *clone,* or strain, of the Sangiovese grape, which is the grape of Chianti. It's an intense, concentrated, tannic wine that demands aging (up to 20 years) when traditionally made, and benefits from several hours of aeration before serving. Lately, some producers in Montalcino have been making a more approachable style of Brunello.

Rosso di Montalcino is a less expensive ($23 to $30), ready-to-drink wine made from the same grape and grown in the same production area as Brunello di Montalcino. Rosso di Montalcino from a good Brunello producer is a great value, offering you a glimpse of Brunello without breaking the bank.

To really appreciate Brunello di Montalcino, seek out one of the producers recommended in the following list (in our rough order of preference). Brunellos from traditional winemakers, such as Biondi-Santi, Costanti, and Pertimali, need at least 15 to 20 years of aging in good vintages (1999, 1997, 1995, 1990, 1988, 1985, and 1975 are recent great vintages for Brunello). Brunellos from modern-style producers, such as Caparzo, Altesino, and Col d'Orcia, can be enjoyed within ten years. Younger than ten years — drink Rosso di Montalcino. (For a more complete listing of Brunello di Montalcino producers, see Chapter 8 in *Italian Wine For Dummies.*)

Great Brunello di Montalcino Producers

Case Basse of Soldera (very expensive)	Castello Banfi
Biondi-Santi (very expensive)	Il Poggione
Altesino (especially Montosoli vineyard)	Ciacci Piccolomini
Costanti	Poggio Antico
Pertimali di Livio Sassetti	Tenuta Caparzo (especially its "La Casa")

Vino Nobile, Carmignano, and Vernaccia

Three more Tuscan wines of note include two reds — Vino Nobile di Montepulciano *(NO be lay dee mon tay pul chee AH no)* and Carmignano *(car mee NYAH no)* — and Tuscany's most renowned white wine, Vernaccia di San Gimignano *(ver NAH cha dee san gee mee NYAH no)*. All three are DOCG wines.

The Montepulciano wine zone, named after the town of Montepulciano, is located southeast of the Chianti zone. Vino Nobile's principal grape is the Prugnolo Gentile (a.k.a. Sangiovese). From a good producer, Vino Nobile di Montepulciano can rival the better Chianti Classicos. Eight producers we recommend are Poderi Boscarelli, Fattoria del Cerro, Avignonesi, Lodola Nuova, La Braccesca, Dei, Fassati, and Poliziano. Vino Nobile producers now also make a lighter, readier-to-drink wine, called Rosso di Montepulciano.

The Carmignano wine region is directly west of Florence. Although Sangiovese is the main grape of Carmignano — just as it is for Chianti — Cabernet Sauvignon is also one of this wine zone's traditional grapes. As a result, Carmignano's taste is rather akin to a Chianti with the finesseful touch of a Bordeaux. Two outstanding producers of Carmignano are Villa di Capezzana and Ambra.

Vernaccia di San Gimignano is named for the medieval walled town of San Gimignano, west of the Chianti Classico zone. Vernaccia is generally a fresh white wine with a slightly oily texture and an almondy flavor, and it is meant to be drunk young. For an unusual interpretation, try Teruzzi & Puthod's oak-aged riserva, Terre di Tufo, a pricey but very good Vernaccia (about $21). Most Vernaccias are in the $11 to $13 range. In addition to Teruzzi & Puthod, producers to look for are Montenidoli (especially the wine called Fiore), Cecchi, and Casale-Falchini.

Super-Tuscans

When Chianti sales lost momentum in the 1970s, progressive producers caught the attention of the world by creating new red wines that are today collectively known as super-Tuscans. The pioneering examples include Sassicaia *(sas ee KYE ah)*, from Marchese Incisa della Rocchetta, and Tignanello *(tee nyah NEL loh)* and Solaia *(so LYE ah)* from Piero Antinori. These and similar wines could not be called Chianti — either because they were produced outside the Chianti zone or because their grape blend (generally Cabernet Sauvignon, Cabernet Franc, and/or Sangiovese) did not conform to DOC requirements for Chianti.

Today, dozens of super-Tuscan wines exist. Their actual grape blends vary from wine to wine; besides Cabernet, some producers use Merlot or even Syrah with their Sangiovese, while others use only native Tuscan grapes. What these wines have in common is that they are expensive, ranging from $30 on up to $75, with a few well over $100 per bottle. The most famous super-Tuscan wines, Sassicaia, Ornellaia, and Solaia, prized by wine collectors, can cost $200 in good vintages (see "Tuscany" in the vintage chart, Appendix C).

Super-Tuscan wines vary greatly in style because of differing grape varieties and microclimates. They can range from very good Chianti-like wines to Bordeaux-type or California Cabernet-type wines, depending on the varying amounts of Sangiovese, Cabernet Sauvignon, Merlot, and so on, and their specific vineyard areas.

Now that Chianti has reestablished itself in the world market, these relatively new wines have become less prominent — but most major Chianti producers still make a super-Tuscan wine.

A dozen of our favorite super-Tuscan wines are the following (listed alphabetically, with their grape blend; producer's name in parentheses):

- ✔ Cepparello — all Sangiovese (Isole e Elena)
- ✔ Grattamacco — Sangiovese, Malvasia Nera, Cabernet Sauvignon (Grattamacco)
- ✔ Masseto — all Merlot (Tenuta dell'Ornellaia)
- ✔ Ornellaia — mainly Cabernet Sauvignon; some Merlot, Cabernet Franc (Tenuta dell'Ornellaia)
- ✔ Percarlo — 100 percent Sangiovese (San Giusto a Rentennano)
- ✔ Le Pergole Torte — entirely Sangiovese (Montevertine)
- ✔ Prunaio — mainly Sangiovese (Viticcio)
- ✔ Sammarco — 80 percent Cabernet Sauvignon, 20 percent Sangiovese (Castello dei Rampolla)
- ✔ Sassicaia — 75 percent Cabernet Sauvignon, 25 percent Cabernet Franc (Tenuta San Guido)
- ✔ I Sodi di San Niccolò — mostly Sangiovese (Castellare di Castellina)
- ✔ Solaia — 80 percent Cabernet Sauvignon, 20 percent Sangiovese (Antinori)
- ✔ Tignanello — 80 percent Sangiovese, 20 percent Cabernet Sauvignon (Antinori)

Sangiovese at the table

Lighter Chianti wines go well with pasta, prosciutto, and roast chicken or squab. With Chianti Classicos and riservas, lamb, roast turkey, veal, steak, and roast beef are fine accompaniments. For the robust Brunello di Montalcino and super-Tuscan wines, try pheasant, steak, game, or chunks of fresh Parmesan cheese. Serve these wines at cool room temperature, 62° to 66° F (16° to19° C).

Decant young (less than ten years old) super-Tuscan wines two or three hours before serving. (For a more complete listing of super-Tuscan wines, see Chapter 8 in *Italian Wine For Dummies*.)

A Cornucopia of Northeastern Wines

The three regions in the northeastern corner of Italy (refer to Figure 11-1) are often referred to as the *Tre Venezie* — the Three Venices — because they were once part of the Venetian Empire. Colorful historical associations aside, each of these regions produces red and white wines that are among the most popular Italian wines outside of Italy — as well as at home.

Three gentlewines from Verona

Chances are that if your first dry Italian wine wasn't Chianti or Pinot Grigio, it was one of Verona's big three: the white Soave *(so AH vay)* or the reds, Valpolicella *(val po lee CHEL lah)* or Bardolino *(bar do LEE noh)*. These enormously popular wines hail from Northeast Italy, around the picturesque city of Verona — Romeo and Juliet's hometown — and the beautiful Lake Garda.

Of Verona's two reds, Valpolicella is the fuller. The lighter Bardolino is a pleasant summer wine when served slightly cool. (Bolla and Masi are two of the largest producers of both.) Most Valpolicella, Bardolino, and Soave wines are priced in the $9 to $12 range, as are two other white wines of the region, Bianco di Custoza and Lugana. Some of the better Veronese wines, from the following recommended producers, have slightly higher prices:

- ✔ **Soave:** Pieropan, Gini, Anselmi, Santa Sofia
- ✔ **Valpolicella:** Allegrini, Quintarelli, Dal Forno, Le Ragose, Bertani, Alighieri, Tommasi, Masi
- ✔ **Bardolino:** Guerrieri-Rizzardi, Cavalchina, Fratelli Zeni

Amarone della Valpolicella (also simply known as Amarone), one of Italy's most full-bodied red wines, is a variant of Valpolicella. It's made from the same grape varieties (refer to Table 11-1), but the ripe grapes are dried on mats for several months before fermentation, thus concentrating their sugar and flavors. The resulting wine is a rich, potent (14 to 16 percent alcohol), long-lasting wine, perfect for a cold winter night and a plate of mature, hard cheeses. Some of the best producers of Amarone are Quintarelli, Bertani, Masi, Tommasi, Le Ragose, Allegrini, and Dal Forno.

The Austrian-Italian alliance

If you have traveled much in Italy, you probably realize that in spirit Italy is not one unified country but 20 or more different countries linked together politically. Consider Trentino-Alto Adige. Not only is this mountainous region (the northernmost in Italy; refer to Figure 11-1) dramatically different from the rest of Italy, but also the mainly German-speaking Alto Adige (or South Tyrol) in the north is completely different from the Italian-speaking Trentino in the south. (Before World War I, the South Tyrol was part of the Austro-Hungarian Empire.) The wines of the two areas are different, too — yet the area is considered a single region!

Alto Adige produces red wine, but most of it goes to Germany, Austria, and Switzerland. The rest of the world sees Alto Adige's white wines — Pinot Grigio, Chardonnay, Pinot Bianco, Sauvignon, and Gewürztraminer — which are priced mainly in the $12 to $16 range.

One local red wine to seek out is Alto Adige's Lagrein, from a native grape variety of the same name. It's a robust, hearty wine, somewhat rustic in style, but it offers a completely unique taste experience. Hofstätter is a producer who makes a particularly good Lagrein.

Alto Adige produces Italy's best white wines, along with nearby Friuli. Four producers to look for are Alois Lageder, Hofstätter, Tiefenbrunner, and Peter Zemmer. Here are some highlights of each brand:

- Lageder's Pinot Bianco from the Haberlehof vineyard and his Sauvignon from the Lehenhof vineyard are exceptional examples of their grape varieties and are among the best wines from these two varieties that we've tasted.

- Hofstätter's Gewürztraminer, from the Kolbenhof vineyard, is as fine a wine as you can find from this tricky grape variety. Hofstätter also makes Italy's best Pinot Nero (Pinot Noir), called Villa Barthenau.

- Tiefenbrunner's Müller Thurgau (*MULE lair TOOR gow*) from his Feldmarschall Vineyard (the region's highest altitude vineyard) could well be the wine world's best wine from this otherwise lackluster variety.

- Peter Zemmer produces reliable Chardonnay and Pinot Grigio wines in the $11 to $12 price range.

Trentino, the southern part of the Trentino-Alto Adige region, is not without its own notable wines. Some excellent Chardonnays come from Trentino, for example; two of the best are made by Pojer & Sandri and Roberto Zeni.

(In fact, we recommend any of the wines from these two producers.) Elisabetta Foradori is a Trentino producer who specializes in red wines made from the local variety, Teroldego *(teh ROLL day go)* Rotaliano. Her best red wines, Granato and Sgarzon, are based on Teroldego and always get rave reviews from wine critics. Also, one of Italy's leading sparkling wine producers, Ferrari, is in Trentino. (See Chapter 15 for more information on sparkling wine producers.)

The far side: Friuli-Venezia Giulia

Italy has been justifiably known in the wine world for its red wines. But in the last 20 years, the region of Friuli-Venezia Giulia (refer to Figure 11-1), led by the pioneering winemaker the late Mario Schiopetto, has made the world conscious of Italy's white wines as well.

Near the region's eastern border with Slovenia, the districts of Collio and Colli Orientali del Friuli produce Friuli's best wines. Red wines exist here, but the white wines have given these zones their renown. In addition to Pinot Grigio, Pinot Bianco, Chardonnay, and Sauvignon, two local favorites are Tocai Friulano and Ribolla Gialla (both fairly rich, full, and viscous).

A truly great white wine made here is Silvio Jermann's Vintage Tunina, a blend of five varieties, including Pinot Bianco, Sauvignon, and Chardonnay. Vintage Tunina is a rich, full-bodied, long-lived white of world-class status. It sells in the $35 to $40 range and, frankly, it's worth the money. Give the wine about ten years to age and then try it with rich poultry dishes or pasta.

We list our recommended producers in Friuli alphabetically:

Great Producers in Friuli

Abbazia di Rosazzo/Walter Filiputti
Girolamo Dorigo
Livio Felluga
Gravner
Jermann
Miani
Lis Neris-Pecorari
Plozner
Doro Princic
Ronco del Gelso

Ronco del Gnemiz
Ronco dei Rosetti, of Zamò
Ronco dei Tassi
Russiz Superiore, of Marco Felluga
Mario Schiopetto
Venica & Venica
Vie di Romans
Villa Russiz
Volpe Pasini

For more info on the wines of Northeastern Italy, see Chapter 7 in *Italian Wine For Dummies.*

Snapshots from the Rest of Italy

Italy's wines are by no means confined to the five regions that we discuss individually. A quick tour of some of Italy's other regions will prove the point. (For more complete info on the wines of Italy's other regions, see *Italian Wine For Dummies*.) Refer to Figure 11-1 for the location of each of the following regions:

- ✔ **Lombardy:** In the northern part of this region, near the Swiss border, the Valtellina wine district produces four fairly light-bodied red wines from the Nebbiolo grape: Sassella, Inferno, Grumello, and Valgella. Most of these wines are inexpensive (about $9 to $18) and, unlike Barolo or Barbaresco, can be enjoyed young. Lombardy is also the home of Italy's best sparkling wine district, Franciacorta. (See Chapter 15 for more on Franciacorta and Italy's other sparkling wines.)

- ✔ **Emilia-Romagna:** This is the home of Lambrusco, one of Italy's most successful wines on the export market. For a different Lambrusco experience, try a dry one if you can find it. (You might have to go to Emilia-Romagna for that — but, hey, that's not so bad. Bologna and Parma, two gastronomic meccas, are in this region.)

- ✔ **Liguria:** This narrow region south of Piedmont, along the Italian Riviera, is also the home of Cinque Terre, one of Italy's most picturesque areas. The region's two fine white wines, Vermentino and Pigato, are just made for Liguria's pasta with pesto, its signature dish.

- ✔ **Marches** (also known as **Marche**): Verdicchio is a dry, inexpensive white wine that goes well with fish, is widely available, and improves in quality with every vintage. Try the Verdicchio dei Castelli di Jesi from Fazi-Battaglia or Umani Ronchi, great values at $8 to $10. Marche's best red wine, Rosso Cònero, at $15 to $20, is one of Italy's fine red wine buys.

- ✔ **Umbria:** The region of Perugia and Assisi makes some good red and white wines. Orvieto, a white, is widely available for around $10 from Tuscan producers such as Antinori and Ruffino. Two interesting red wines are Torgiano, a Chianti-like blend (try Lungarotti's Rubesco Riserva DOCG), and Sagrantino di Montefalco DOCG, a medium-bodied, characterful wine made from the local Sagrantino grape.

- ✔ **Latium:** This region around Rome makes the ubiquitous, inexpensive Frascati, a light, neutral wine from the Trebbiano grape; Fontana Candida is a popular brand.

- ✔ **Abruzzo:** Montepulciano d'Abruzzo, an inexpensive, easy-drinking, low tannin, low-acid red wine, comes from here; it's a terrific everyday red, especially from a quality producer such as Masciarelli. Abruzzo is also home to two other fine producers, Cataldi Madonna and the great Eduardo Valentini, whose sought-after Trebbiano d'Abruzzo is perhaps the world's greatest white wine from the otherwise ordinary Trebbiano.

✔ **Campania:** Some of the best wines in Southern Italy are produced here, around Naples. The full-bodied, tannic Taurasi, a DOCG wine from the Aglianico grape, is one of the great, long-lived red wines in Italy. Premium producers are Mastroberardino (look for his single-vineyard Taurasi, called Radici), Feudi di San Gregorio, and Terredora. The same producers also make two unique whites, Greco di Tufo and Fiano di Avellino. They're full-flavored, viscous wines with great aging capacity that sell in the $18 to $24 range. Falanghina ($12 to $15) is another exciting, light-bodied white Campania wine.

✔ **Basilicata:** The instep of the Italian boot, Basilicata has one important red wine, Aglianico del Vulture. It's similar to Taurasi, but not quite so intense and full-bodied. D'Angelo and Paternoster are leading producers.

✔ **Apulia:** This region makes more wine than any other in Italy. Generally, it is inexpensive, full-bodied red wine, such as Salice Salentino (from the native variety, Negroamaro) and Primitivo.

✔ **Sicily:** Once known only for its Marsala, a sweet, fortified wine, Sicily is now making quality reds and whites. Established wineries such as Corvo (a.k.a. Duca di Salaparuta) and Regaleali have been joined by exciting, new wineries such as Planeta, Morgante, Donnafugata, and Benanti to produce some of Italy's more intriguing wines — especially reds, many made from Sicily's superb variety, Nero d'Avola.

✔ **Sardinia:** This large island off the eastern coast of Italy makes delicate white wines and characterful reds from native grape varieties and from international varieties such as Cabernet Sauvignon. Sella & Mosca, Argiolas, and Santadi are three leading producers. Two of the more popular Sardinian wines are the white Vermentino and the red Cannonau, both of which sell in the $10 to $15 range.

Chapter 12

Elsewhere in Europe

. . . .

. . . .

*F*ifteen years ago, we never used the phrase *European wine* in talking generally about the wines of France, Italy, Spain, Portugal, and Germany. The wines had nothing in common.

But today, two factors have changed the way we look at the wines of these countries. First, Europe has unified, and the wines of the European Union member countries now share a common legislative umbrella. Second, non-European wines — from California, Australia, Chile, and South America — have inundated the U.S. market, popularizing a nomenclature (varietal names, such as Chardonnay) and flavors (fruity, fruitier, fruitiest) foreign to the European, or *Old World,* model.

When we compare Europe's wines to non-European, or *New World,* wines, we notice that the diverse wines of Europe have many things in common after all. Most European wines are usually named for their place of production instead of their grape (see Chapter 4); European winemaking is tethered to tradition; the wines reflect local tastes more than international trends (although, sadly, we are now seeing an emerging "internationalization" of wine styles); and the wines are relatively low in fruitiness. European wines embody the traditions of the people who make them and the flavors of the earth from which they grow, compared to New World wines, which embody grape variety.

Despite these similarities among European wines, the countries of Europe each make distinctly different wines. The importance of France and Italy has earned each of these countries a whole chapter, while the rest of Europe shares the spotlight here.

Intriguing Wines from Old Spain

Spain is a hot, dry, mountainous country with more vineyard land than any other country on earth. It ranks third in the world in wine production, after France and Italy.

Spanish wine has awakened from a long period of dormancy and under-achievement. Spain is now one of the wine world's most vibrant arenas. For decades, only Spain's most famous red wine region, Rioja *(ree OH ha)*, and the classic fortified wine region, Sherry, had any international presence for fine wines. (For more on Sherry, see Chapter 16.) Now, at least six other wine regions in Spain are making seriously good wines. Besides Rioja, the following regions are an important part of the wine quality picture in Spain today (see Figure 12-1):

- Ribera del Duero *(ree BEAR ah dell DWAIR oh)*, now famous for its red wines, has helped to ignite world interest in Spanish wines.

- Priorato *(pree or AH toe)*, mountainous and inaccessible, and one of the world's hot new red wine regions, is north of the city of Tarragona, in northeast Spain.

- Penedés *(pen eh DAIS)* is important for both its red and white wines, as well as its sparkling wines (known as *Cava;* see Chapter 15).

- The Rías Baixas *(REE ahse BYCE ahse)* region of Galicia *(gah LEETH ee ah)* is gaining acclaim for its exciting white wine, Albariño.

- Navarra *(nah VAR rah)*, an area long known for its dry rosé wines, is now an emerging red wine region.

- Rueda *(ru AE dah)* is known for well-made, inexpensive white wines.

Like Italy's, Spain's wine laws provide for a bilevel QWPSR category: *Denominaciónes de Origen* (DO) and a higher classification, *Denominaciónes de Origen Calificada* (DOC), the latter created in 1991. So far, Rioja and Priorato are the only two regions that have been awarded the DOC (also known as DOCa). Wines that do not qualify as DO fall into the table wine category *Vino de la Tierra* (equivalent to the French *Vins de Pays*). See Chapter 9 for more about wine classifications.

Rioja rules the roost

Rioja, in north-central Spain (see Figure 12-1), has historically been the country's major red wine region (even if today Ribera del Duero and Priorato are catching up — fast!). Three-quarters of Rioja's wine is red, 15 percent *rosado* (rosé), and 10 percent white.

Figure 12-1:
The wine
regions
of Spain.

The principal grape in Rioja is Tempranillo *(tem prah NEE yoh),* clearly Spain's greatest red variety. But another three varieties are permitted for red Rioja wine — Garnacha (Grenache), Graciano, and Mazuelo — and the wine is typically a blend of two or more varieties.

The Rioja region has three districts, the cooler, Atlantic-influenced Rioja Alavesa and Rioja Alta and the warmer Rioja Baja. Most of the best Riojas are made from grapes in the two cooler districts, but some Riojas are blended from grapes of all three districts.

Traditional production for red Rioja involved many years of aging in small barrels of American oak before release, which created pale, gentle, some-times tired and oaky-tasting wines that lacked fruitiness. The trend has been to replace some of the oak aging with bottle aging, resulting in wines that are now much fresher-tasting. In the cellars of the more progressive winemakers, barrels made of French oak now join the traditional barrels of American oak — which has always given Rioja its characteristic vanilla aroma. (See Chapter 5 for a discussion of oak barrels.)

Red Riojas have several faces. Sometimes the wine receives no oak aging at all and is released young. Sometimes the wine ages (in oak and in bottle) for two years at the winery and is labeled *crianza;* these wines are still fresh and fruity in style. Some wines age for three years and carry the designation *reserva.* The finest wines age for five years or even longer, earning the status of *gran reserva.* These terms appear on the labels — if not on the front label itself, then on a rear label which is the seal of authenticity for Rioja wines.

Prices start at around $10 for crianza reds and go up to about $40 for some of the gran reservas. The best recent vintages for Rioja are 2001, 1995, 1994, 1989, 1982, and 1981.

The following Rioja producers have been particularly consistent in quality for their red wines:

- CVNE (Compañía Vinícola del Norte de España), commonly referred to as CUNE *(coo nay)*
- Bodegas Muga
- R. Lopez de Heredia
- La Rioja Alta
- Marqués de Murrieta Ygay
- Marqués de Riscal
- Bodegas Montecillo

Most white Riojas these days are merely fresh, neutral, inoffensive wines, but Marqués de Murrieta and R. Lopez de Heredia still make a traditional white Rioja, golden-colored and oak-aged, from a blend of local white grape varieties, predominantly Viura. We find both of these traditional whites fascinating: lots of flavor, voluptuous, with attractive traces of oxidation, and capable of aging. They're not everybody's cup of tea, true, but the wines sure have character! They have so much presence that they can accompany foods normally associated with red wine, as well as traditional Spanish food, such as paella or seafood. The Murrieta white sells for about $16, and the Lopez de Heredia is about $20.

Ribera del Duero challenges

Ribera del Duero, two hours north of Madrid by auto, is one of Spain's most dynamic wine regions. Perhaps nowhere else in the world does the Tempranillo grape variety reach such heights, making wines with body, deep color, and finesse. For many years, Ribera del Duero was dominated by one producer, the legendary Vega Sicilia. In fact, Spain's single most famous great wine is Vega Sicilia's Unico (Tempranillo, with 20 percent Cabernet Sauvignon) — an intense, concentrated, tannic red wine with enormous longevity; it ages for ten years in casks and then sometimes ages further in the bottle. Unico is available mainly in the top Spanish restaurants; if you're lucky enough to find it in a retail shop, it could cost about $300 — a bottle, that is. Even Unico's younger, less intense, and more available brother, the Vega Sicilia Valdubuena, retails for about $100.

But Vega Sicilia is no longer the only renowned red wine in Ribera del Duero. Alejandro Fernández's Pesquera, entirely Tempranillo, has gained high praise over the last 15 years. Pesquera is a big, rich, oaky, tannic wine with intense fruit character. The Reserva sells for about $28, while the younger Pesquera is $20. Three other fine producers of Ribera del Duero are Bodegas Mauro, Viña Pedrosa, and Bodegas Téofilo Reyes, who are all making red wines that rival Pesquera.

Priorato: Emerging from the past

Back in the twelfth century, monks founded a monastery (or "priory") in the harsh, inaccessible Sierra de Montsant Mountains, about 100 miles southwest of Barcelona in the Catalonia region, and planted vines on the steep hillsides. As time passed, the monastery closed, and the vineyards were abandoned — because life was simply too difficult in this area (which in time became known as Priorat, or Priorato).

Cut to the twentieth century — in fact less than 25 short years ago. Some enterprising winemakers, among them Alvaro Palacios, rediscovered the area and decided that conditions were ideal for making powerful red wines. Fortunately, some old vines — mainly Garnacha and Carignan, two of Spain's native varieties — existed there, planted by locals early in the twentieth century.

No Spanish wine region has been more in the spotlight lately than Priorato. And yet Priorato has not become a tourist destination, because it's so inaccessible. The region's volcanic soil, composed mainly of slate and schist, is so infertile that not much other than grapes can grow there. The climate is harshly continental: very hot, dry summers, very cold winters. The steep slopes must be terraced; many vineyards can be worked only by hand. And grape yields are very low.

Amazingly rich, powerful red wines, made primarily from Garnacha and Carignan, have emerged from this harsh landscape. Many are as rugged as the land, with high tannin and alcohol; some wines are so high in alcohol that they have an almost Port-like sweetness. Because winemaking in Priorato is not cost-effective, to say the least, and the quantities are so small, the wines are necessarily quite expensive; prices begin at about $40.

Priorat reds to look for include Clos Mogador, Clos Erasmus, Alvaro Palacios, Clos Martinet, l'Hermita, Morlanda, Mas d'En Gil, and Pasanau.

Four other Spanish regions to watch

The action in Spanish wines — especially when value is your concern — definitely doesn't end with Rioja, Ribera del Duero, and Priorato.

Penedés

The Penedés wine region is in Catalonia, south of Barcelona (refer to Figure 12-1). It's the home of most Spanish sparkling wines, known as *Cava*, which we discuss in Chapter 15.

Any discussion of Penedés' still wines must begin with Torres, one of the world's great family-owned wineries. Around 1970, Miguel Torres pioneered the making of wines in Spain from French varieties, such as Cabernet Sauvignon and Chardonnay, along with local grapes, such as Tempranillo and Garnacha.

All the Torres wines are clean, well made, reasonably priced, and widely available. They start in the $10 range for the red Sangre de Toro (Garnacha–Carignan) and Coronas (Tempranillo–Cabernet Sauvignon) and the white Viña Sol. The top-of-the-line Gran Coronas Mas La Plana Black Label, a powerful yet elegant Cabernet Sauvignon, costs about $40 to $45.

Freixenet, the leading Cava producer, is now also in the still wine business. Its wines include the inexpensive René Barbier varietals and two fascinating Segura Viudas wines (a Cava brand owned by Freixenet), both $15 to $16. Creu de Lavit is a subtle but complex white that's all Xarel-lo (pronounced *sha REL lo*), a native grape used mainly for Cava production. The red Mas d'Aranyo is mainly Tempranillo. We particularly recommend Creu de Lavit.

The white wine from Galicia

Galicia, in northwest Spain next to the Atlantic Ocean and Portugal (refer to Figure 12-1), was not a province known for its wine. But from a small area called Rías Baixas *(REE ahse BYCE ahse)*, tucked away in the southern part of Galicia, an exciting, new white wine has emerged — Albariño. Rías Baixas is, in fact, one of the world's hottest white wine regions. We use "hot" to mean "in demand," not to describe the climate, because Rías Baixas is cool and damp a good part of the year, and verdant year-round.

Some Spanish wine terms

You will see some of the following terms on a Spanish wine label:

Blanco: White

Bodega: Winery

Cosecha *(coh SAY cha)* or **Vendimia** *(ven DEE me yah):* The vintage year

Crianza *(cree AHN zah):* For red wines, this means that the wine has aged for at least six months in oak; for white and rosé wines, crianza means that the wines aged at least three months in oak. (Some regions have stricter standards.)

Gran reserva: Wines produced only in exceptional vintages; red wines must age at least five years, including a minimum of two years in oak; white gran reservas must age at least four years before release, including six months in oak.

Reserva: Wines produced in the better vintages; red reservas must age a minimum of three years, including one year in oak; white reservas must age for two years, including six months in oak.

Tinto *(TEEN toe):* Red

This region now boasts 190 wineries, compared to only 30 to 40 just a decade ago. Modern winemaking, the cool climate, and low-yielding vines have combined to make Albariño wines a huge success, especially in the U.S., its leading market. We love this lively unoaked white, with its vivid, floral aromas and flavors reminiscent of apricots, white peaches, pears, and green apples. It's a perfect match with seafood and fish. But the Albariño grape — known as Alvariñho in northern Portugal (south of Rías Baixas) — makes wines that are very high in acidity and, therefore, not to everyone's taste.

Albariños to look for include Bodega Morgadío, Lusco, Bodegas Martin Codax, Fillaboa, Pazo de Señorans, Pazo de Barrantes, and Vionta; all are in the $16 to $18 range.

Navarra

Once upon a time, the word *Navarra* conjured up images of inexpensive, easy-drinking dry rosé wines (or, to the more adventurous, memories of running the bulls in Pamplona, Navarra's capital city). Today, Navarra, just northeast of Rioja, is rapidly becoming known for red wines that are similar to, but somewhat less expensive than, the more famous wines of Rioja.

Many Navarra reds rely on Tempranillo, along with Garnacha, but you can also find Cabernet Sauvignon, Merlot, and various blends of all four varieties in the innovative Navarra region. Look for the wines of the following three Navarra producers: Bodegas Julian Chivite *(HOO lee ahn cha VEE tay)*, Bodegas Guelbenzu *(gwel BEN zoo)*, and Bodegas Magana.

The Verdejo from Rueda

The Rueda region, west of Ribera del Duero, produces one of Spain's best white wines from the Verdejo grape. The wine is clean and fresh, has good fruit character, and sells for an affordable $9. The Rioja producer Marquis de Riscal makes one of the leading and most available examples.

Portugal: More Than Just Port

Portugal is justifiably famous for its great dessert wine, Port (discussed in Chapter 16). But lately, wine lovers are discovering the other dimensions of Portuguese wine. Thanks to serious modernizing of its vineyards and wine-making practices, Portugal is now making very good dry wines, especially reds. Most of these wines come from native Portuguese grape varieties, of which the country has hundreds. We expect Portugal's well-priced wines to play a larger role in world wine markets in the twenty-first century.

Portugal's highest rank for wines is *Denominação de Origen* (DO), which has been awarded to the wines of 32 regions. The table wine category includes eight *Vinho Regional* (VR) regions, equivalent to France's *Vin de Pays,* and the simple *Vinho de Mesa* (table wines).

Portugal's "green" white

On hot summer evenings, the most appropriate wine can be a bottle of bracing, slightly effervescent, white Vinho Verde *(VEEN yo VAIRD)*. The high acidity of Vinho Verde refreshes your mouth and makes the wine especially good with grilled fish or seafood.

Portuguese wine terms

The following terms might appear on Portuguese wine labels:

Colheita *(col YAY tah):* Vintage year

Garrafeira *(gar rah FAY rah):* A reserva that has aged at least two years in a cask and one in a bottle if it's red; six months in a cask, six months in a bottle if it's white

Quinta *(KEEN ta):* Estate or vineyard

Reserva: A wine of superior quality from one vintage

Tinto *(TEEN toe):* Red

The Minho region, Vinho Verde's home, is in the northwest corner of Portugal, directly across the border from the Rías Baixas wine region of Spain. (The region is particularly verdant because of the rain from the Atlantic Ocean — one theory behind the wine's name.)

Two styles of white Vinho Verde exist on the market. The most commonly found brands (Aveleda and Casal Garcia), which sell for $6 or $7, are medium-dry wines of average quality that are best served cold.

The more expensive Vinho Verdes ($15 to $20) are varietal wines made from either the Alvariñho grape (Rías Baixas's Albariño), Loureiro, or Trajadura. They are more complex, dryer, and have more concentration than basic Vinho Verde, and they are Portugal's best whites. Unfortunately, these finer Vinho Verdes are more difficult to find than the inexpensive ones; look for them in better wine shops or in Portuguese neighborhoods (or on your next trip to Portugal!).

There is also a red Vinho Verde — in fact, the majority of wines from this DO region are red. It is a *highly* acidic wine — you definitely need to acquire a taste for it (which we haven't acquired yet!).

Noteworthy Portuguese red wines

Possibly the best dry red wine in Portugal, Barca Velha, comes from the Douro region, where the grapes for Port (officially known as *Porto*) grow. Made by the Ferreira Port house, Barca Velha is a full-bodied, intense, concentrated wine that needs years to age — Portugal's version of Vega Sicilia's Unico, but at a considerably lower price (about $65). Like Unico, not much is made, and it's produced only in the best vintages.

Fortunately, the Port house of Ramos Pinto (now owned by Roederer Champagne) makes inexpensive, top-quality, dry red Douro wines that are readily available. Duas Quintas (about $11) has ripe, plummy flavors and a velvety texture; it's surprisingly rich but supple, and it's a great value.

The Douro region boasts other terrific dry red wines, most of them fairly new and based on the grapes traditionally used for Port. Brands to look for include Quinta do Vale D. Maria, Quinta do Vallado, Quinta do Crasto, and Quinta de la Rosa.

Other good red Portuguese wines to try include

✔ **Quinta do Carmo:** The majority owner of this estate in the dynamic Alentejo region in southern Portugal is Château Lafite-Rothschild. A rich, full-bodied wine, it sells for $25. Don Martinho, a second-label wine from the estate, is about half the price of Quinta do Carmo.

- **Quinta de Pancas:** One of the few Cabernet Sauvignons in Portugal, Quinta de Pancas comes from the Alenquer region, north of Lisbon; it sells for about $15.

- **Quinta de Parrotes:** Made from the local Castelão Frances grape variety, Quinta de Parrotes, from the same estate in Alenquer as the Quinta de Pancas, is a steal at $11.

- **Quinta da Bacalhôa:** An estate-bottled Cabernet Sauvignon made by the esteemed Portuguese winemaker Joào Pires in Azeitao (south of Lisbon), Bacalhôa has the elegance of a Bordeaux; it sells for $18.

- **The red wines of J.M. da Fonseca Successores** (no relation to the Fonseca Port house): This firm is producing some of the best red wines in Portugal. Look for Quinta da Camarate, Morgado do Reguengo, Tinto Velho Rosado Fernandes, and all of da Fonseca's Garrafeiras.

- **The wines of Joao Portugal Ramos:** A tireless winemaker who consults for various wineries and also owns three properties, Ramos has a golden touch and yet maintains the typicity of his wines. Some wines sell under his own name; others are Marquês de Borba and Vila Santa.

Germany: Europe's Individualist

German wines march to the beat of a different drum. They come in mainly one color: white. They're fruity in style, often off-dry or sweet, low in alcohol, and rarely oaked. Their labels carry grape names, which is an anomaly in Europe. And their classification system is not based on the French AOC system, as most other European wines are.

Germany is the northernmost major wine-producing country in Europe — which means that its climate is cool. Except in warmer pockets of southern Germany, red grapes don't ripen adequately, which is the reason most German wines are white. The climate is also erratic from year to year, meaning that vintages do matter for fine German wines. Germany's finest vineyards are situated along rivers such as the Rhine and the Mosel, which temper the extremes of the weather and help the grapes ripen.

Riesling and its cohorts

In Germany's cool climate, the noble Riesling (*REESE ling*) grape finds true happiness. But Riesling represents only 21 or 22 percent of Germany's vine-yard plantings.

Another major, but less distinguished, German variety is Müller-Thurgau (pronounced *MULE lair TOOR gow*), a crossing between the Riesling and Silvaner (or possibly Chasselas) grapes. Its wines are softer than Riesling's with less character and little potential for greatness.

After Müller-Thurgau and Riesling, the most planted grapes in Germany are Silvaner, Kerner, Scheurebe *(SHOY reb beh),* and Ruländer (Pinot Gris). Among Germany's red grapes, Spätburgunder (Pinot Noir) is the most widely planted, mainly in the warmer parts of the country.

Germany's wine laws and wine styles

Like most European wines, German wines are named after the places they come from — usually a combination of a village name and a vineyard name, such as Piesporter (town) Goldtröpfchen (vineyard).

Unlike most European wines, however, the grape name is also usually part of German wine names (as in Piesporter Goldtröpfchen *Riesling*). And the finest German wines have yet another element in their name — a *Prädikat (PRAY di cat),* which is an indication of the ripeness of the grapes at harvest (as in Piesporter Goldtröpfchen Riesling *Spätlese*). Wines with a Prädikat hold the highest rank in the German wine system.

Germany's system of assigning the highest rank to the ripest grapes is completely different from the concept behind most other European appellation systems, which is to bestow the highest status on the best vineyards or districts. Germany's system underscores the country's grape-growing priorities: Ripeness — never guaranteed in a cool climate — is the highest goal.

German wine law divides wines with a Prädikat into six levels. From the least ripe to the ripest (that is, from the lowest to the highest), they are

- ✔ Kabinett *(KAB ee net)*
- ✔ Spätlese *(SHPATE lay seh)*
- ✔ Auslese *(OUSE lay seh)*
- ✔ Beerenauslese *(BEER en OUSE lay seh),* abbreviated as *BA*
- ✔ Eiswein *(ICE vine)*
- ✔ Trockenbeerenauslese *(TROH ken BEER en OUSE lay seh),* abbreviated as *TBA*

At the three highest Prädikat levels, the amount of sugar in the grapes is so high that the wines are inevitably sweet. Many people, therefore, mistakenly believe that the Prädikat level of a German wine is an indication of the wine's sweetness. In fact, the Prädikat is an indication of the amount of sugar in the *grapes at harvest,* not the amount of sugar in the wine. At lower Prädikat levels, the sugar in the grapes can ferment fully, to dryness, and for those wines there is *no direct correlation between Prädikat level and sweetness of the wine.*

Wines whose (grape) ripeness earns them a Prädikat are categorized as QmP wines *(Qualitätswein mit Prädikat),* translated as *quality wines with special attributes* (their ripeness). They are QWPSR wines in the eyes of the EU (see Chapter 9). When the ripeness of the grapes in a particular vineyard is insufficient to earn the wine a Prädikat name, the wine can still qualify as a "quality wine" in Germany's second QWPSR tier, called QbA *(Qualitätswein bestimmter Anbaugebiet),* translated as *quality wine from a special region.* Often the term *Qualitätswein* alone will appear on labels of QbA wines.

Less than 10 percent of Germany's wine production falls into the lower, table wine categories *Landwein* (table wines with geographic indication) or *Deutscher Tafelwein.*

Dry, half-dry, or gentle

The common perception of German wines is that they are all sweet. Yet many German wines taste dry, or fairly dry. As wine drinkers' tastes have changed over the years, both in Germany itself and abroad, the sweetness of German wines has changed as well. Today, you can find German wines at just about any sweetness or dryness level you like.

Most inexpensive German wines, such as Liebfraumilch, are light-bodied, fruity wines with pleasant sweetness — wines that are easy to enjoy without food. The German term for this style of wine is *lieblich,* which translates as "gentle" — a poetic but apt descriptor. The very driest German wines are called *trocken* (dry). Wines that are sweeter than trocken but dryer than lieblich are called *halbtrocken* (half-dry). The words *trocken* and *halbtrocken* sometimes appear on the label, but not always.

You can make a good stab at determining how sweet a German wine is by reading the alcohol level on the label. If the alcohol is low — about nine percent, or less — the wine probably contains grape sugar that didn't ferment into alcohol and is therefore sweet. Higher alcohol levels suggest that the grapes fermented completely, to dryness.

Although we generally prefer dry white wines, we find that a bit of sweetness in German wines can be appealing — and in fact can improve the quality of the wine. That's because sweetness undercuts the wines' natural high acidity and gives the wines better balance. In truth, most off-dry German wines don't really taste as sweet as they are, thanks to their acidity.

One way that German winemakers keep some sweetness in their wines is called the *süssreserve* (sweet reserve) method. In this method, a winemaker ferments his wine fully dry. Before fermentation, however, he holds back as much as 25 percent of his grape juice. Later, he blends this grape juice with his dry wine. The unfermented grape juice (the süssreserve) contributes a natural, juicy sweetness to the wine.

What's noble about rot?

Wine connoisseurs all over the world recognize Germany's sweet, dessert-style wines as among the greatest wines on the face of the earth. Most of these legendary sweet wines owe their sweetness to an ugly but magical fungus known as *botrytis cinerea,* pronounced *bo TRY tis sin eh RAY ah,* commonly called *noble rot.*

Noble rot infects ripe grapes in late autumn if a certain combination of humidity and sun is present. This fungus dehydrates the berries and concentrates their sugar and their flavors. The wine from these infected berries is sweet, amazingly rich, and complex beyond description. It can also be expensive: $100 a bottle or more.

Wines at the BA and TBA Prädikat levels are usually made entirely from grapes infected with noble rot (called *botrytised* grapes) and are generally richly textured and sweet. *Auslese* level wines often come from some partially botrytised grapes, and when they do, they are likely to be sweet, although never to the extent of a BA or TBA.

Another way that Nature can contribute exotic sweetness to German wines is by freezing the grapes on the vine in early winter. When the grape grower harvests the frozen grapes and presses them, most of the water in the berries separates out as ice. The sweet, concentrated juice that's left to ferment makes a luscious sweet Prädikat-level wine called *Eiswein* (literally, ice wine). Eisweins differ from BAs and TBAs because they lack a certain flavor that derives from botrytis, sometimes described as a honeyed character.

Both botrytised wines and Eisweins are referred to as *late-harvest wines,* not only in Germany but all over the world, because the special character of these wines comes from conditions that normally occur only when the grapes are left on the vine beyond the usual point of harvest.

Germany's wine regions

Germany has 13 wine regions — 11 in the west and 2 in the eastern part of the country (see Figure 12-2).

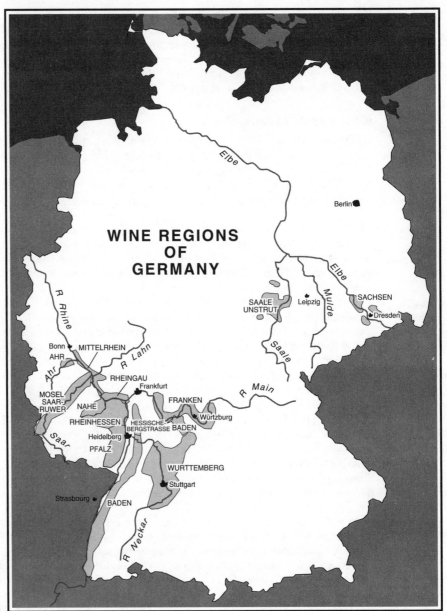

WINE REGIONS
OF
GERMANY

© Akira Chiwaki

Figure 12-2:
The wine
regions of
Germany.

The most famous of these 13 are the Mosel-Saar-Ruwer region, named for the Mosel River and two of its tributaries, along which the region's vineyards lie; and the Rheingau region, along the Rhine River.

A secret code of German place-names

If you don't speak German and you don't know German geography intimately, you'll find deciphering German wine names tricky, to say the least. But here's a bit of information that can help. In German, the possessive is formed by adding the suffix *-er* to a noun. When you see names like Zeller or Hochheimer — names that end in *-er* — on a wine label, the next word is usually a vineyard area that "belongs" to the commune or district with the *-er* on its name (Zell's Swartze Katz, Hochheim's Kirchenstück). The name of the region itself always appears on labels of QbA and Prädikat wines.

Mosel-Saar-Ruwer: The Mosel-Saar-Ruwer *(MO zel zar ROO ver)* is a dramatically beautiful region, its vineyards rising steeply on the slopes of the twisting and turning Mosel River. The wines of the region are among the lightest in Germany (usually containing less than 10 percent alcohol); they are generally delicate, fresh, and charming. Riesling dominates the Mosel-Saar-Ruwer with 55 percent of the plantings. Wines from this region are instantly recognizable because they come in green bottles rather than the brown bottles that other German regions use.

The Mosel boasts dozens of excellent winemakers who produce really exciting Riesling wines. Some of our favorites include, in alphabetical order:

Egon Müller	Meulenhof
Dr. Fischer	J.J. Prüm
Friedrich Wilhelm Gymnasium	Reichsgraf Von Kesselstatt
Karlsmühle	Willi Schaefer
Dr. Loosen	Selbach-Oster
Maximin Grünhauser	Zilliken
Merkelbach	

Rheingau: The Rheingau *(RYNE gow)* is among Germany's smaller wine regions. It, too, has dramatically steep vineyards bordering a river, but here the river is Germany's greatest wine river, the Rhine. The Riesling grape occupies more than 80 percent of the Rheingau's vineyards, many of which are south-facing slopes that give the Riesling an extra edge of ripeness. Rheingau wine styles tend toward two extremes: trocken wines on the one hand and sweet late-harvest and Eisweins on the other. Recommended Rheingau producers include Georg Breuer, Knyphausen, Franz Küntsler, Schloss Schönborn, Leitz, and Robert Weil.

Rheinhessen: The Rhine River lends its name to three other German wine regions, Rheinhessen *(RYNE hess ehn)*, the Pfalz (formerly called the Rheinpfalz), and the tiny Mittelrhein region. Rheinhessen is Germany's largest wine region, producing huge quantities of simple wines for everyday enjoyment. Liebfraumilch originated here, and it's still one of the most important wines of the region, commercially speaking. The Rheinhessen's highest quality wines come from the Rheinterrasse, a vineyard area along the river. Particularly good producers include Gunderloch, Heyl Zu Herrnsheim, and Strub.

Pfalz: Almost as big as the Rheinhessen, the Pfalz *(fallz)* has earned somewhat more respect from wine lovers for its fairly rich and full-bodied white wines and its very good reds — all of which owe their style to the region's relatively warm climate. Müller-Thurgau, Riesling, Silvaner, and Kerner are among the most planted grape varieties of the Pfalz, but qualitatively Scheurebe and Blauburgunder (Pinot Noir) are important. To experience the best of the Pfalz, look for wines from Dr. Bürklin-Wolf, Rainer Lingenfelder, Müller-Catoir, and Basserman-Jordan.

Nahe: One other German region of importance for the quality of its wines is Nahe *(NAH heh)*, named for the Nahe River and situated west of Rheinhessen. The Riesling wines here are relatively full and intense. Favorite producers include Diel, Kruger-Rumpf, Prinz zu Salm-Dahlberg, and Dönnhoff.

Switzerland: Stay-at-Home Wines

Nestled between Germany, France, and Italy, Switzerland is in a perfectly logical location for growing grapes and making fine wine. Vineyards grace the country's three faces — French-speaking, German-speaking, and Italian-speaking. But few wine lovers outside of Switzerland have much opportunity to taste Swiss wines because the production is tiny and because the wines are so popular within Switzerland itself.

About half of Switzerland's wines are white; most are made from Chasselas — a grape cultivated with much less distinction in Germany, eastern France, and the Loire Valley. In Switzerland, Chasselas wines tend to be dry, fairly full-bodied, and unoaked, with mineral and earthy flavors. Other white grapes include Pinot Gris, Sylvaner, Marsanne, Petit Arvine, and Amigne — the latter two indigenous to Switzerland. Merlot is an important red grape (especially in the Italian-speaking Ticino region), along with Pinot Noir and Gamay.

Because of Switzerland's varied terrain (hills of varying altitudes, large lakes, sheltered valleys), numerous microclimates exist. Wine styles therefore vary, from relatively full-bodied reds and whites to delicate, crisp white wines.

Switzerland's major wine regions include the Vaud, along Lake Geneva; Valais, to the east, along the Rhône River; Neuchâtel, in western Switzerland, north of the Vaud; Ticino, in the south, bordering Italy; and Thurgau in the north, bordering Germany.

When you do find a bottle of Swiss wine, you might be surprised to discover how costly it is — $18 to $30 in the U.S., reflecting high production costs. (But quality is generally also high.) If you buy a bottle of white Swiss wine in Switzerland, you might also be surprised to find a screw-cap closure — one of Switzerland's more courageous contributions to the art of wine enjoyment, considering the historically poor image of screw-cap wines.

Austria's Exciting Whites (and Reds)

Austria makes more than twice as much wine as Switzerland — which is still a tiny amount! All of it comes from the eastern part of the country, where the Alps recede into hills. Dedicated young winemakers, small family wineries, and high quality dry wines typify Austria's wine industry today, making Austria one of the world's most exciting countries for wine.

The ratio of white to red wines in Austria is 72/28. The reds hail mainly from the region of Burgenland, bordering Hungary, one of the warmest parts of the country. They're medium- to full-bodied, often engagingly spicy, with vivid fruity flavor — and often the international touch of significant oaky character. Many of them are based on unusual, native grape varieties such as the spicy Blaufrankish (Lemberger), the gentler St. Laurent, or Blauer Zweigelt (a crossing of the other two).

Austria's best white wines occupy two camps:

- ✔ Dry, firm, and generally unoaked, ranging from light- to full-bodied
- ✔ Luscious late-harvest whites, made from either botrytised, extremely ripe, or dried grapes

While the excellence of Austria's sweet whites has long been recognized, her dry whites and reds have gained recognition only since the late 1980s.

The country's single most important grape variety is the native white Grüner Veltliner. Its wines are full-bodied yet crisp, with rich texture and herbal or sometimes spicy-vegetal flavors (especially green pepper). They're extremely food-friendly, and usually high quality. Some people in the wine trade have nicknamed Grüner Veltliner "GruVe"; we agree with that characterization!

Müller-Thurgau ties for second in plantings with Welschriesling, a grape popular in Eastern Europe for inexpensive wines that achieves high quality only in Austria. But Riesling, grown mainly in the region of Lower Austria, is more important than these two for its quality. In fact, some experts believe that Austria's finest wines are its Rieslings (while others prefer Grüner Veltliner).

In some parts of Austria, for example in the Wachau district, wines are named in the German system — a town name ending in *-er* followed by a vineyard name and a grape variety. In other parts of Austria, such as Burgenland, the wine names are generally a grape name (or, increasingly, a proprietary name) followed by the name of the region.

Austria's wine laws draw from the German model, with QWPSR wine divided into *Qualitätswein* and *Prädikatswein* categories. (One difference is that *Kabinett* falls into the *Qualitätswein* category.) But some people believe that an appellation system based on terroir (rather than ripeness levels) would better express the diversity of Austria's vineyard regions. Authorities introduced a new system called *Districtus Austria Controllatus* (DAC) on a limited basis in early 2003.

The Re-emergence of Hungary

Of all the wine-producing countries in Eastern Europe that broke free from Communism in the late 1980s and early 1990s and have resumed wine production under private winery ownership, Hungary seems to have the greatest potential as a wine superpower. In addition to a winemaking tradition that dates back to pre-Roman times, Hungary has a wealth of native and international grape varieties and plenty of land suited to vineyards, with a wide range of climates, soils, and altitudes.

The Hungarians are a proud and creative people — or so we concluded from our guide on our recent trip there, who mentioned (more than once) that Hungarians invented the hologram, the carburetor, contact lenses, and the ballpoint pen, among other essentials of modern life. Their wine consumption has increased significantly since the country gained independence, fueling an improvement in wine quality. International investment in vineyards and wineries has also made a huge contribution.

Hungary produces the equivalent of about 38 million cases of wine a year, 82 percent of which is white. Although the country is northerly — its capital, Budapest, sits at the same latitude as Quebec City — its climate is relatively warm because the country is landlocked and somewhat surrounded by mountains. Three large bodies of water do affect the microclimate of certain wine regions: Lake Neusiedel, between Hungary and Austria in the northwest; Lake Balaton, Europe's largest lake, in the center of Hungary's western half (which is called Transdanubia); and the Danube River, which runs north to south right through the middle of the country. Hungary has 22 official wine regions, but their names are not yet particularly important outside Hungary.

The one Hungarian wine region that does have international fame is Tokaj-Hegyalja *(toe KYE heh JAH yah),* which takes its name from the town of Tokaj and owes its reputation to its world-class dessert wine, Tokaji Azsu *(toe KYE as ZOO).* The word *Aszu* refers to botrytised grapes (described earlier in this chapter in the section "What's noble about rot?"). The wine takes its character from Furmint and Harslevelu grapes, both native white varieties, and sometimes Muscat grapes, that have been infected by botrytis.

Tokaji Azsu wines are labeled as three, four, five, or six Puttonyos, according to their sweetness, with six Puttonyos wines being the sweetest. (*Puttonyos* are baskets used to harvest the botrytised grapes, as well as a measure of sweetness.) All Tokaji Azsu wines sell in 500 ml bottles, and they range in price from about $30 to $135 per bottle, depending on their sweetness level.

Tokaji Azsu wines vary not only according to their sweetness, but also according to their style. Some wines have fresher, more vibrant fruity character, for example; some have aromas and flavors that suggest dried fruits; some have the smoky character and tannin of new oak barrels; and some have complex non-fruity notes such as tea leaves or chocolate. This range of styles is due mainly to different winemaking techniques among producers.

Tokaji Azsu has a complicated production method that leaves plenty of room for individual interpretation. Some of the issues that winemakers differ on — besides the normal issues of grape blend — include

- ✔ Whether the botrytised grapes (which are compressed into a paste of sorts) soak in wine (made from non-moldy grapes), partially-fermented wine, or simply juice, to create the liquid that is then fermented into the final wine

- ✔ Whether the wine should mature in new or old oak barrels

- ✔ Whether the wine should be exposed to oxygen during aging (by leaving airspace in the barrels)

Apart from Tokaji Azsu, Hungary produces a range of dry and semi-dry wines, both white and red, including table wines from the Tokaj-Hegyalja region, such as the varietal Tokaji Furmint. Most of these wines are named for their grape variety and are quite inexpensive. Kadarka is Hungary's most prestigious native red grape variety.

Hungary is in line to become a member of the European Union, and its categories of wine therefore resemble those of EU countries (see Chapter 9). Wines at the highest level are classified as *Minosegi Bor (mih no SHAY ghee BOR)*, followed by *Tájbor* (country wine) and *Asztali Bor* (table wine).

Greece's Ancient (and Modern) Treasures

We find it hard to comprehend that a country which practically invented wine, way back in the seventh century BC, could be an emerging wine region today. But that's the way it is. Greece never stopped making wine for all those centuries, but her wine industry took the slow track, inhibited by Turkish rule, political turmoil, and other real life issues. The modern era of Greek winemaking began only in the 1960s, and it has made particularly strong strides only in the last decade.

Today, Greece ranks 13th in the world in wine production — just ahead of Hungary and behind Chile. But quantity isn't the real news: quality is. Many Greek wines today are top-quality, especially the wines of small, independent wineries, and they make it worth your effort to discover them.

Although Greece is a southern country and famous for its sunshine, its grape-growing climate is actually quite varied, because many vineyards are situated at high altitudes where the weather is cooler. (Most of Greece is mountainous, in fact.) Its wines are mainly (60 percent) white; some of those whites are sweet dessert wines, but many are dry.

One of Greece's greatest wine assets — and handicaps, at the same time — is its abundance of native grape varieties, a few hundred of them. These native grapes make Greek wines particularly exciting for curious wine lovers to explore, but their unfamiliar names make the wines difficult to sell. Fortunately for the marketers, Greece also produces wines from internationally-famous grape varieties such as Chardonnay and Cabernet Sauvignon, which can be very good.

Some of the vineyard regions of Greece whose names you are likely to see on wine labels (and the names of some of their place-name wines) include

✔ **Macedonia:** The northernmost part of Greece, with mountainous terrain and cool climates. Naoussa, a medium-bodied red wine with spicy, floral, and fruity flavors, is one of the most famous wines.

- ✔ **The Peloponnese:** A large peninsula in the southern part of Greece with varied climate and soil, and many noteworthy wines, such as the soft, red Nemea; the dry whites Patras and Mantinia; and the sweet wines Mavrodaphne de Patras (red) and Muscat de Patras (white).

- ✔ **Crete:** The largest Greek island, which makes both white and red wines, many of which are varietally-named along with the place-name of Crete.

In addition, Greece has numerous small islands that make wine. One of the most famous is Santorini, which is also the name of the island's delicate white wine.

Greece's most important native grape varieties for white wine are Assyrtiko *(ahs SEER tee koh),* which makes Santorini; Rhoditis (actually a pink grape), which makes Patras white; and Savatiano, the most widely planted white grape. Retsina, a traditional Greek wine made by adding pine resin to the fermenting grape juice (resulting in a flavor not unlike some oaky Chardonnays), is mainly from Savatiano.

The most important grape varieties for red wine are Aghiorghitiko *(aye your YEE tee koh),* which makes Nemea, and Xynomavro *(zee NO mah vro),* which is the grape used in Naoussa.

Greece is a member of the European union, and its appellation system for wine therefore conforms to the EU's two-tiered structure. At the top (QWPSR) level Greece has two categories:

- ✔ AOQS, *Appellation d'Origine de Qualité Supérieure* (yes, that's French!) for dry and off-dry wines

- ✔ AOC, *Appellation d'Origine Contrôlée,* for dessert and fortified wines

Table wines with a geographic name are called *vins de pays* (regional wines). Other terms that have formal definitions under Greek wine regulations include *reserve* (QWPSR wines with a minimum two or three years aging, for whites and reds respectively), *grande reserve* (one additional year of aging), and *cava* (a table wine — in the EU sense of being at the lower appellation tier — with the same aging requirements as reserve).

Chapter 13

The Brave New World of Wine

*W*hat do the wines of North and South America, South Africa, Australia, and New Zealand have in common? For one thing, none of them are produced in Europe. In fact, you could say that they are the wines of "Not Europe."

The name most often used in wine circles for Not Europe is the *New World.* Undoubtedly this phrase, with its ring of colonialism, was coined by a European. Europe, home of all the classic wine regions of the world, producer of more than two-thirds of the wines in the world, is the Old World. Everything else is nouveau riche.

When we first heard the expression *New World* applied to wines, we thought it was absurd. How can you lump together wine regions as remote as Napa Valley, the Finger Lakes, Coonawarra, and Santiago? But then we started thinking about it. In Europe, they've been making wines for thousands of years. Which hillsides to plant, which grapes should grow where, how dry or sweet a particular wine should be — these decisions were all made long ago, by the grandparents and great-great-grandparents of today's winemakers. But in Not Europe, the grape-growing and winemaking game is wide open; every winery owner gets to decide for himself where to grow his grapes, what grape variety to plant, and what style of wine to make. The wines of the New World do have that in common.

The more we thought about it, the more similarities we found among New World wine regions as compared to Europe. Finally, we concluded that the New World is an actual winemaking entity whose legislative reality, spirit, and winemaking style are unique from those of the Old World — as generalizations go.

We could easily fill 400 pages on the wines of the U.S., Canada, Chile, Argentina, Australia, New Zealand, and South Africa alone, if only we had the space. Fortunately, New World wines are easy for you to explore without a detailed road map: In the New World, there's very little encoded tradition to decipher and very little historical backdrop against which the wines need to be appreciated.

In this chapter, we explore the wines of Australia, New Zealand, Chile, Argentina, and South Africa. We devote the next chapter to the wines of the United States, with a short look at Canada, too.

The old and the new

In wine terms, the New World is not just geography but also an attitude and approach to wine. Some winemakers in Europe approach wine the liberated New World way, and some winemakers in California are dedicated Old World traditionalists. Keep that in mind as you look over the following comparison between the Old and the New. And remember, we're talking generalizations here — and generalizations are never always true.

New World	Old World
Innovation	Tradition
Wines named after grape varieties	Wines named after region of production
Expression of the fruit is the winemaking goal	Expression of *terroir* (the particular place where the grapes grow, with its unique growing conditions) is the winemaking goal
Technology is revered	Old-fashioned methods are favored
Wines are flavorful and fruity	Wines are subtle and less fruity
Grape-growing regions are broad and flexible	Grape-growing regions are relatively small and fixed
Winemaking resembles science	Winemaking resembles art
Winemaking processes are controlled	Intervention in winemaking is avoided as much as possible
The winemaker gets credit for the wine	The vineyard gets the credit

Australian Wine Power

Make no mistake about it: Australia is one of the world powers of wine. In the course of just a few decades, the wine industry of Australia has transformed itself into perhaps the most technologically advanced, forward-thinking wine nation on earth.

Vinifera grapevines came to Australia from South Africa and from Europe in the late eighteenth and early nineteenth centuries (the country has no native vines). As recently as 1960, most Australian wines were rich and sweet, many of them fortified — a far cry from the fresh red and white table wines of today. In 1980, Chardonnay production was negligible; now Chardonnay is Australia's top white grape for fine wine. Australia's fruity, well-priced, well-made wines of the past two decades have rapidly earned fans worldwide. Today, Australia ranks seventh in the world in wine production.

Approximately the same size as the continental U.S., Australia has about 1,300 wineries but still produces less than half as much wine as California. Australia's wine regions are mainly in the southern, cooler part of the country, with many of them clustered in the state of Victoria, the southern part of South Australia, and the cooler parts of New South Wales.

Winemaking, grapes, and terroir

Australia's number one grape for fine wine is Syrah, locally called *Shiraz,* followed by Cabernet Sauvignon, Chardonnay, Riesling, and Semillon. The wines are generally labeled with the name of their grape variety, which must constitute at least 85 percent of the wine.

Shiraz wines are particularly interesting because they come in numerous styles, from very light, quaffable wines brimming with fresh strawberry fruit (delicious but simple) to serious, complex wines that need time to evolve. Another very interesting varietal wine is Semillon (pronounced *SEM eh lon* in Australia, as opposed to the French *sem ee yon* elsewhere in the world), especially from the Hunter Valley. Some are aged in oak, similar to Chardonnay, while a few unoaked Semillons, simple when young, take on a fascinating nutty, honey, orange marmalade flavor with age.

The success of Australia's wines stems from a generally warm, dry climate (which provides winemakers with excellent raw material for their work) and from the winemakers' embrace of technology to achieve wines that preserve the intense flavors of their grapes and are soft and pleasant to drink from an early age. Australian wines epitomize user-friendliness.

Those who know a lot about Australian wine can describe the country's wine regions in great detail, differentiating stylistic nuances from one area to the next the way that Francophiles distinguish the villages of the Côte de Nuits. But for drinkers of inexpensive Australian wines, the whole discussion of Australian wine regions is academic. Most Australian wine in export markets is labeled simply as coming from *South Eastern Australia,* meaning that the grapes could have come from any of three states, a huge territory. It's the taste that you drink, mate, not the place.

We mention some of the more famous regions of Australia, state by state, in the following section. If you're interested in learning about these regions — and the many others that we don't mention — in more detail, read James Halliday's excellent *Wines of Australia* (Mitchell Beazley, 2003), or Halliday's even more comprehensive *The Wine Atlas of Australia and New Zealand,* 2nd Edition (Angus & Robertson, 1998).

Australia's wine regions

Australia's most important state for wine production is **South Australia,** whose capital is Adelaide (see Figure 13-1). South Australia makes about 50 percent of Australia's wine. While many vineyards in South Australia produce inexpensive wines for the thirsty home market, vineyards closer to Adelaide make wines that are considered among the country's finest. Among these fine wine regions are

- **Barossa Valley:** North of Adelaide, this is one of Australia's oldest areas for fine wine; it's a relatively warm area famous especially for its robust Shiraz and Cabernet Sauvignon, as well as rich Semillon and Riesling (grown in the cooler hills). Most of Australia's largest wineries, including Penfolds, are based here.

- **Clare Valley:** North of the Barossa Valley, this climatically diverse area makes the country's best Rieslings in a dry, crisp style, as well as fine Shiraz, Cabernet Sauvignon, and Malbec.

- **McLaren Vale:** South of Adelaide, with a mild climate influenced by the sea, this region is particularly admired for its Sauvignon Blanc, Chardonnay, Riesling, and Semillon; Grenache and Shiraz are its best reds.

- **Adelaide Hills:** Situated partially within the Adelaide city limits, this fairly cool region sits between the Barossa and McLaren Vale areas and is the home to rather good Pinot Noir, Chardonnay, and Riesling.

✔ **Limestone Coast:** This zone, along the southern coast of South Australia, has become one of the most important areas for fine wine, both red and white. Of the five regions within the Limestone Coast zone, the most renowned are Coonawarra and Padthaway.

✔ **Coonawarra:** About 200 miles southeast of Adelaide, this cool region is famous for its red soil and perhaps Australia's best Cabernet Sauvignon.

✔ **Padthaway:** Just north of Coonawarra is this cool area, known for its white wines, particularly Chardonnay, Sauvignon Blanc, and Riesling.

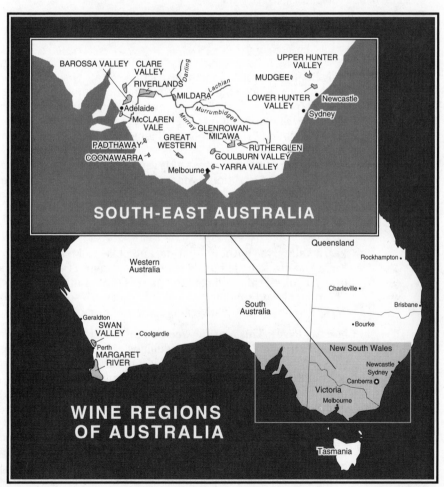

Figure 13-1:
The wine regions of Australia.

© Akira Chiwaki

Odd couples

Although winemakers all over the world make blended wines — wines from more than one grape variety — generally the grape combinations follow the classic French models: Cabernet Sauvignon with Merlot and Cabernet Franc, for example, or Sémillon with Sauvignon Blanc. Australia has invented two completely original formulas:

✔ Shiraz with Cabernet Sauvignon

✔ Semillon with Chardonnay

The grape in the majority is listed first on the wine label, and the percentages of each grape are indicated.

Adjoining South Australia is **Victoria,** a smaller state that makes 15 percent of Australia's wines. While South Australia is home to most of Australia's largest wineries, Victoria has *more* wineries (over 250); most of them are small. Victoria's fine wine production ranges from rich, fortified dessert wines to delicate Pinot Noirs. Principal regions include

✔ **Rutherglen:** In the northeast, this long-established, warm climate zone is an outpost of traditional winemaking and home of an Australian specialty, fortified Muscats and Tokays.

✔ **Goulburn Valley:** In the center of the state, Goulburn Valley is known especially for its full-bodied reds, especially Shiraz.

✔ **Yarra Valley:** In southern Victoria, and close to Melbourne (the capital), Yarra Valley and neighboring regions Mornington Peninsula and Geelong have a cool, maritime climate that makes them suitable for fine Pinot Noir, Chardonnay, and sparkling wine. Yarra Valley is also noted for its Bordeaux varieties — Cabernet Sauvignon, Cabernet Franc, and Merlot.

✔ **Murray River:** This area between Victoria and New South Wales includes the Mildura region. Lindemans, one of Australia's largest wineries — renowned for its Bin 65 Chardonnay, one of the largest-selling Chardonnays in the world — is situated here.

New South Wales, with its capital, Sydney, is Australia's most populous state, and the first to grow vines; today it makes 31 percent of Australia's wine. Grape growing is exploding here, especially in the interior, in regions called the Central Ranges and Southern New South Wales. High-volume production of everyday wines comes from an interior area called the Riverina. (We get a kick trying to pronounce its alternate name, the Murrumbidgee Irrigation Area.) Fine wine, for now, comes from three other areas:

- **Lower Hunter Valley:** An historic grape-growing area 80 miles north of Sydney, with a very warm, damp climate and heavy soils. Long-lived Semillon is its best wine, but Chardonnay, Shiraz, and Cabernet Sauvignon are also important.

- **Upper Hunter Valley:** A drier area north of the Hunter River and farther from the coast, and the home of Rosemount Estate. The Upper Hunter makes particularly good Chardonnay.

- **Mudgee:** An interior area near the mountains. Mudgee specializes in reds such as Merlot and Cabernet Sauvignon but also makes Chardonnay.

Western Australia, the country's largest state, with its most isolated wine area — in the southwest corner — makes little wine compared to the preceding three states, but quality is high. The warm, dry Swan Valley is the state's historic center of wine production, but two cooler climate regions have become more important:

- **Margaret River:** This relatively temperate region near the Indian Ocean makes excellent Cabernet Sauvignons, Chardonnays, and Semillons, especially from such fine wineries as Leeuwin Estate and Cape Mentelle.

- **Great Southern:** Cooler than Margaret River, Great Southern's specialty is crisp, age-worthy Riesling. This huge, diverse region produces intense, aromatic Cabernet Sauvignon as well as fine Shiraz and Chardonnay; on the southern coast, Pinot Noir is successful.

Tasmania, an island south of Victoria, has some cool microclimates where producers such as Pipers Brook are proving what potential exists for delicate Pinot Noirs, Chardonnays, and sparkling wines.

The Rise of New Zealand

The history of fine winemaking in New Zealand is relatively short, having been hampered by conservative attitudes towards alcohol. In the 1980s, New Zealand finally began capitalizing on its maritime climate, ideal for producing high-quality wines, and started planting grapes in earnest. Today, it makes less than one-tenth of the wine of its nearest neighbor, Australia, but its production is increasing every year.

Situated farther south than Australia, New Zealand is, in general, cooler. Of the country's two large islands, the North Island is the warmer. Red grapes grow around Auckland and Hawkes Bay (especially known for its Cabernet Sauvignon), and Müller-Thurgau, Chardonnay, and Sauvignon Blanc are that island's main white varieties. Martinborough, a cooler district at the southern end of North Island, makes very good Pinot Noir.

On the South Island, Marlborough — the country's largest and commercially most important wine region — is the country's top production zone for Chardonnay and, especially, Sauvignon Blanc.

Increasingly, however, Pinot Noir is significant in Marlborough and throughout the South Island; it has now surpassed Cabernet Sauvignon as New Zealand's most planted red variety. In the central part of the South Island, Central Otago, home of the world's most southerly grapevines, has emerged as one of the world's great new regions for Pinot Noir. Vines are planted on hillsides for more sunshine and less risk of frost. The low-yielding vines here produce stunning Pinot Noir wines, with lots of concentration.

Four large producers dominate New Zealand's wine production: Montana (sold in the U.S. under the Brancott label, to avoid confusion with the state of Montana), Corbans, Villa Maria, and Nobilo. But in the last 20 years, a number of small, boutique wineries have sprung up, especially on the South Island, and are making excellent wine.

New Zealand whites are generally unoaked wines with pronounced flavor, rich texture, and high acidity. New Zealand Sauvignon Blanc is so distinctive — pungent and intense, with a flavor that could be compared to asparagus, limes, cut green grass, or passion fruit — that it became recognized almost overnight in the late 1980s as a new prototype of Sauvignon Blanc.

The Old and the New of Chile

Chile's wine industry wears the designation *New World* somewhat uncomfortably. The Spanish first established vineyards in Chile in the mid-sixteenth century, and the country has maintained a thriving wine industry for its home market for several centuries. Nothing new about that. What *is* new about Chile, however, is the growth of her wine industry since the mid-1980s. And what's "worldly" is her rapid development of a strong export market, and her shift toward French grape varieties such as Cabernet Sauvignon, Merlot, and Chardonnay — with an almost-forgotten red Bordeaux variety called Carmenère definitely in the running, on the outside post position.

Blessed isolation

With the Pacific Ocean to the west and the Andes Mountains to the east, Chile is an isolated country. This isolation has its advantages in terms of grape growing: Phylloxera hasn't yet taken hold in Chile — as it's done in just about every other winemaking country — and vinifera vines can therefore grow on their own roots. (For an explanation of phylloxera, see Chapter 3.) Chile's other viticultural blessings include a range of mountains along the coast, which blocks the ocean dampness from most vineyards, and the ocean's general tempering influence on a relatively hot climate.

Most of Chile's vineyards are in the Central Valley, which lies between the coastal range and the Andes. Growing conditions in the Central Valley's three main wine regions — Maipo, Rapel, and Maule — vary from east to west: The eastern area near the Andes is sunnier and drier, and the western area is damper. Another major wine region is Aconcagua, to the north of the Central Valley. From north to south, Chile's wine regions are

- ✔ **Aconcagua:** North of Santiago, this is the warmest area for fine grapes, but Aconcagua also includes many high-altitude zones, as well as the cool, coastal Casablanca region, which is producing exciting Chardonnays and Sauvignon Blancs.

- ✔ **Maipo:** Just south of Santiago, Maipo is Chile's most famous region, where many of the major wineries are based. Santiago and Pirque are important subregions; Cabernet Sauvignon, Merlot, and Chardonnay do well here.

- ✔ **Rapel:** A region that includes the renowned Colchagua as well as the Cachapoal subregions, Rapel is slightly cooler than Maipo. Cabernet Sauvignon and Sauvignon Blanc are its most planted grape varieties.

- ✔ **Maule:** The Curicó subregion (which includes the Lontué district) is located in Maule, which is cooler and less dry than Rapel. Cabernet Sauvignon, Merlot, and Sauvignon Blanc are important varieties here.

Foreign flavor

Wineries and winemakers from France, Spain, and the U.S. now play a major role in the Chilean wine industry. Château Lafite-Rothschild, for example, is an owner of the Los Vascos winery. Château Mouton-Rothschild has partnered with Chile's Concha y Toro to create Almaviva, a superpremium Bordeaux-type blend. France's renowned enologist, Michel Rolland, is a consultant at Casa Lapostolle, a Chilean winery owned by the French family that makes Grand Marnier liqueur. The Miguel Torres winery in Curicó is Spanish-owned. Augustin Huneeus of Franciscan Vineyards in California has a property called Veramonte in Chile's Casablanca region. Also, the Robert Mondavi Winery has partnered with Chile's Caliterra winery and co-produces a superpremium wine called Seña with Chile's Errazuriz Winery.

The face and taste of the wines

Like most New World wines, Chile's wines are generally named for their grape varieties; they carry a regional (or sometimes a district) indication, too. The reasonable prices of the basic wines — mainly from $6 to $10 in the U.S. — make these wines excellent values.

Stylistically, Chile's wines generally lack the exuberant fruitiness of Californian and Australian wines. And yet they are not quite so subtle and understated as European wines. The whites once lagged behind the reds in quality but have now caught up, thanks partly to the Casablanca region.

The most exciting news on the Chilean wine front recently is the emergence of super-premium reds. These elite Chilean red wines, in the $40 to $80 price range, are frequently blends of grape varieties. Established favorites — such as Concha y Toro's Don Melchor Cabernet Sauvignon and Cousiño Macul's Finis Terrae, a Cabernet–Merlot blend (both about $40) — now enjoy the company of Errázuriz's Don Maximiano Founder's Reserve (mainly Cabernet Sauvignon, about $60); Montes Alpha M (a "Bordeaux blend," about $72); Seña (mainly Cabernet Sauvignon with Merlot and Carménère, about $70); Almaviva (mainly Cabernet Sauvignon with Carménère and Cabernet Franc, about $80); Carmen Vineyards' Gold Reserve Cabernet Sauvignon (about $70); and Casa Lapostolle's new Clos Apalta (mainly Merlot with some Cabernet Sauvignon and Carménère, about $70).

But inexpensive varietals remain a strong suit for Chile. The most important wineries for the export market include Caliterra, Carmen, Casa Lapostolle, Concha y Toro, Cousiño Macul, Errazuriz, Los Vascos, Montes, Mont Gras, Santa Carolina, Santa Rita, and Undurraga.

Argentina, a Major Player

Argentina produces about four times as much wine as Chile does, or approximately as much as the entire U.S. It boasts the largest wine production in South America and the fifth-largest wine production in the world. But until the 1990s, Argentina's wine industry was quite old-fashioned and catered mainly to local tastes. That has changed. You can now say that Argentina is a major player in the world wine market.

Wine grapes have grown in Argentina since the mid-sixteenth century, as they have in Chile. But Argentina's source of vines was more diverse; for example, many vines were brought over by the vast numbers of Italian immigrants.

Argentina's wine regions are situated mainly in the western part of the country, where the Andes Mountains divide Argentina from Chile. High altitude tempers the climate, but the vineyards are still very warm by day, cool by night, and desert dry. Rivers flow through the area from the Andes and provide water for irrigation.

The vast majority of Argentina's vineyards are in the state of Mendoza, Argentina's largest wine region, roughly at the same latitude as Santiago, Chile. Within the Mendoza region are various wine districts (the names of which sometimes appear on wine labels) such as Maipú, Luján, San Martín, and Luján de Cuyo. San Juan, just north of Mendoza and considerably hotter, is Argentina's second-largest wine region. La Rioja, east of San Juan and Argentina's oldest wine-producing region, is known for a subvariety of Torrontés known as Torrontés Riojano.

The Torrontés variety, probably indigenous to Galicia, Spain, produces an inexpensive ($6 to $10), light-bodied, high-acid, aromatic white wine that is becoming Argentina's signature white. It's especially fine with appetizers, seafood, and fish.

Argentina's red wines are generally higher in quality than its whites. The little-known Malbec grape variety, now seldom used in its ancestral home, Bordeaux, has emerged as Argentina's flagship variety. Malbec has adapted extremely well to Argentina's Mendoza region, and winemakers are now learning how it varies in Mendoza's subzones. Arguments continue as to which is Argentina's greatest red variety, Cabernet Sauvignon or Malbec (we lean towards Cabernet Sauvignon). But the fact remains that good Cabernet wines come from almost every wine-producing country; only Argentina and Cahors, a small region in Southwest France, have had success with Malbec.

Foreign investment has brought not only capital but also winemaking know-how to complement Argentina's natural resources. Bodega Norton, purchased by an Austrian crystal producer in 1989, is now making some of the best wines in Argentina, such as its 1999 Privada Estate Reserve ($20), a blend of Merlot, Malbec, and Cabernet Sauvignon. Moët & Chandon, another immigrant, is already Argentina's largest sparkling wine producer; it also makes the Terrazas varietal wines. Kendall Jackson is here as well, with its Mariposa Winery, as are several Bordeaux producers, such as Bordeaux's Lurton family, with Château Lurton. French enologist Michel Rolland has worked wonders at Trapiche; try Trapiche's great-value Oak Cask Cabernet Sauvignon or Oak Cask Malbec, both about $10. Rolland, who knows the world's vineyards as well as anyone on the planet, has personally invested in Argentine vineyards; *that* says something about Argentina's potential!

Catena Estate has emerged as one of Argentina's top wine producers. Try its Cabernet Sauvignon or Malbec (both around $21), or the super-premium Malbec Alta or Cabernet Sauvignon Alta, both about $54. They are some of the finest wines being made in South America today.

Other Argentine wines we recommend include Bodega Weinert, Trapiche, Etchart, Bodega Norton, Michel Torino, Terrazas, Navarro Correas, Santa Julia, Bodegas Salentein, and Valentín Bianchi. Argentina's basic wines are generally priced the same as Chile's, in the $6 to $10 range. Great values!

New Hope in South Africa

Vines came to South Africa in the 1650s with the Dutch, the first European settlers. At the end of the eighteenth century, South Africa was producing a luscious fortified wine called Constantia, which became sought after in European royal courts. The country began focusing seriously on table wine production only in the 1980s. Today, South Africa ranks eighth in the world in wine production.

Just about all of South Africa's table wines come from an area known as the Coastal Region, around the Cape of Good Hope. Traditionally, large firms dominated South Africa's wine industry, and they continue to do so. KWV, formerly a wine growers' cooperative, is one of the country's largest wineries. The gigantic Distell firm, which now includes the Stellenbosch Farmers' Winery Group and the Bergkelder Group, is South Africa's largest winery.

South Africa's principal wine regions

Although South Africa has some cooler microclimates, especially around the southern coast (near the Cape of Good Hope) and in higher altitudes, the climate in most of its wine regions is warm and dry.

South African style: Old World meets New World

Although we technically place South Africa's wines in the New World, we must admit that they are rather reminiscent of European wines. The taste of a South African Cabernet Sauvignon, for example, might remind you of a French wine — but not quite. On the other hand, it doesn't really resemble a New World red from California or Australia, either. South African wines manage to combine the subtlety and finesse of French wines along with a touch of the voluptuous ripeness of California wines. In short, they are somewhat between both worlds.

South Africa's Wine of Origin legislation in 1973 created ten wine districts (and a number of subdistricts). Almost all the vineyards are near the southwestern coast, in Cape Province (within 90 miles of Cape Town, the country's most fascinating and picturesque city).

The five major districts — mainly in the Coastal Region area — are

- **Constantia:** The oldest wine-producing area in the country (located south of Cape Town)

- **Stellenbosch:** East of Cape Town; the most important wine district in quantity and quality

- **Paarl:** North of Stellenbosch; home of the KWV and the famous, beautiful Nederburg Estate; the second-most important wine district

- **Franschhoek Valley:** A subdistrict of Paarl; many innovative winemakers here

- **Robertson:** East of Franschhoek, the only major district not in the Coastal Region; a hot, dry area, known mainly for its Chardonnays

The small, cool Hermanus/Walker Bay area, bordering the Indian Ocean, is also showing promise with Pinot Noir and Chardonnay, led by the innovative Hamilton Russell Winery. A newly added (11th) wine district, Elgin, is on the coast between Stellenbosch and Walker Bay. A cool area, Elgin shows promise for its intensely flavored Sauvignon Blancs and for Pinot Noirs. The latest area to show promise is Darling Hills, north of Cape Town, led by an up-and-coming winery, Groote Post.

About 35 percent of South Africa's wines qualify as Wine of Origin (WO). Wine of Origin regulations are based on the French *Appellation Contrôlée* laws (see Chapter 10), and they strictly designate vineyards, allowable grape varieties, vintage-dating, and so on. Varietal wines must contain at least 75 percent of the named variety; exported wines (complying with the stricter European Union regulations) must contain 85 percent of the named variety.

Steen, Pinotage, and company

The most common wine grape variety in South Africa is Chenin Blanc, often locally called *Steen.* This versatile grape primarily makes medium-dry to semi-sweet wines, but also dry wines, sparkling wines, late harvest botrytis wines, and rosés.

Cabernet Sauvignon and Merlot (and, to a lesser extent, Shiraz and Pinot Noir) have become increasingly important red varieties, while Sauvignon Blanc and

Chardonnay are becoming popular white varieties. Cabernet Sauvignon and Sauvignon Blanc do particularly well in South Africa's climate. (A very assertive version of Sauvignon Blanc is produced here.)

And then you have Pinotage. Uniquely South African, Pinotage is a grape born as a crossing between Pinot Noir and Cinsaut (the same as Cinsault, the Rhône variety) back in 1925. However, Pinotage didn't appear as a wine until 1959. Pinotage wine combines the cherry fruit of Pinot Noir with the earthiness of a Rhône wine. It can be a truly delicious, light- to medium-bodied red wine that makes for easy drinking, or a more powerful red. Although some good Pinotage wines sell for $12 to $16, the best Pinotages cost more. Kanonkop Estate, a specialist in this variety, makes a $25 Pinotage.

While Pinotage is a pleasant wine, certainly worth trying, we believe South Africa's future is with Cabernet Sauvignon and Merlot (and blends of these grapes) for its red wines and Sauvignon Blanc and Chardonnay for its whites.

Chapter 14

America, America

*W*hen the *conquistadors* came to the New World of America in search of gold, Spanish missionaries accompanied them and planted the first wine grapevines in what is now southern California. These "Mission" grapes, as they were called, still exist, but the noble grape varieties — Cabernet Sauvignon, Chardonnay, and the rest of the gang — have supplanted them to produce today's fine wines. One thing that hasn't changed is that California is still the focus of the American wine scene, although most of the wine business has moved north; southern California is now mainly filled with cars and people!

In this chapter, we cover American wines, paying particular attention to California's special wine regions, Napa Valley and Sonoma, but also discussing California's other wine regions, as well as Oregon, Washington State, and New York. We end with a quick look at Canada's up-and-coming wines.

The New World of American Wine

Even though the United States produced some wine commercially in the nineteenth century, the U.S. wine industry made it big only beginning in the 1970s. Prohibition from 1920 to 1933, the Great Depression, and WWII were serious blows to the wine business — and recovery was slow.

Before 1970, only a few dozen operating wineries existed in California; today, the state has well over 800 bonded wineries (about a dozen or so "giants," but mainly small, family-owned operations).

California's growth has stimulated interest in wine all across the country. Today, wineries exist in all of the 50 United States. But wine production is an important industry in only four states: California (the largest wine producing state, by far), Washington, Oregon, and New York. The U.S. currently is fourth in world wine production — although well behind the two leaders, Italy and France (Spain is a distant third).

Homegrown ways

The wines of the U.S. — especially California — are the essence of New World wine-think. Winemakers operate freely, planting whatever grape variety they wish, wherever they wish to plant it. They blend wines from different regions together as they wish. (Blending among states is trickier, because of federal rules.)

TECHNICAL STUFF

A smorgasbord of AVAs

In naming their wines, winemakers often choose to use a less specific AVA designation rather than a smaller, more specific one, in order to widen their options in buying grapes and wine. A winery in Alexander Valley, within Sonoma County, for example, might use the broader *Sonoma County* AVA instead of Alexander Valley if it buys grapes from (or owns vineyards in) other areas of the county and wishes to use those grapes in its wine. It could use the larger *North Coast* AVA if it blends in grapes or wine from neighboring counties, like Napa. And if low price is a goal, the winery will use the even broader *California* AVA in order to buy cheaper grapes from the industrial vineyards of the Central Valley (the San Joaquin Valley) or other parts of the state where grapes and wine are less expensive than in Sonoma

County. Sometimes wineries use the *California* appellation even for their better wines, to give themselves complete freedom in sourcing their grapes. (This practice doesn't occur in smaller viticultural areas, such as southern Pennsylvania, where there are few alternative sources of grapes.) While specificity of place is admired, on the one hand, making a good wine at a good price through geographical blending is also admired. The relative merits depend on who's doing the admiring.

Traditional or not, America's way of making and naming wine sits just right with wine drinkers in the U.S.: American wines now account for about 75 percent of all wine sales in the United States.

U.S. wines have elevated grape varieties to star status. Until California began naming wines after grapes, Chardonnay, Merlot, Pinot Noir, and Cabernet Sauvignon were just behind-the-scenes ingredients of wine — but now they *are* the wine. Lest anyone think that all wines from a particular grape are the same, however, winemakers have emerged as celebrities who put their personal spin on the best wines. In the California scenario especially, the land — the terroir — has been secondary, at least until recently.

American winemakers have embraced technology in their efforts to create wines that taste like fruit. California's two important universities for winemaking — California State University at Fresno and, especially, the University of California at Davis — have become world leaders in the scientific study of wine. Even European winemakers now make pilgrimages to California to study at U.C. Davis.

Playing by their own rules

An appellation system for wines does exist in the U.S., and like the classic French model, it defines various vineyard regions. But the U.S. system of American Viticultural Areas (AVAs) establishes only the geographical boundaries of wine zones; it does not stipulate which grape varieties can be planted, the maximum yield of grapes per acre (see "Vine-growing vernacular" in Chapter 5), or anything else that would link the geography to a particular type of wine. AVA names, the names of the regions of production, therefore have secondary importance on wine labels after the name of the grape.

Wines labeled with the name of a grape variety in the U.S. must contain at least 75 percent of that grape variety, according to federal law. Wines with an AVA indication must have at least 85 percent of grapes from that AVA. Wines with vintage years must derive at least 95 percent from the named vintage.

California, USA

When most wine drinkers think about American wine, they think of California. That's not surprising — the wines of California make up about 88 percent of U.S. wine production.

California's Gallo winery is the largest winery by far in the state — in fact, until recently, it was the largest winery in the world — producing one out of every four bottles of wine sold in the U.S. (Recently, a large New York-based conglomerate, Constellation Brands, through a series of acquisitions became the country's largest wine firm.)

Signifying nothing

The words *reserve, special selection, private reserve, barrel select, vintners reserve, classic,* and so on have no legal definition in the U.S. Although many premium wineries use these terms to indicate their special or better wines, most of the larger wineries use the same terms on their inexpensive bottlings as marketing tools (see the "Reserve" section in Chapter 9).

It was the Robert Mondavi Winery, however, that stimulated fine wine production in the United States. Robert Mondavi left his family's winery (Charles Krug Winery) to start his own operation in 1966, a winery dedicated to making premium wines. These finer wines — his own, and those of the many producers who would follow in his steps — would be varietally named Cabernet Sauvignon, Chardonnay, and so on. Identifying the wines by their grape varieties was a reaction against the nondescript jug wines that were then popular, wines labeled with names borrowed from Europe's wine regions, such as Burgundy and Chablis. Today, even Gallo is very much in the varietal wine business.

Where California wines grow

In sunny California, there's no lack of warm climate for growing grapes. For fine wine production, the challenge is to find areas cool enough, with poor enough soil, so that grapes don't ripen too quickly, too easily, without full flavor development (see "Vine-growing vernacular" in Chapter 5). Nearness to the Pacific Coast and higher altitudes both assure cooler climates more so than latitude does. Fine wines therefore come from vineyards up and down almost the whole length of the state.

Chardonnay rules the roost — for now

Chardonnay, the sales leader among varietal wines in the U.S. for the last 15 years or so, still rules the market. But two red wines are beginning to catch up: Cabernet Sauvignon and Merlot. In fact, Merlot became so popular for a while that American producers could hardly grow the grapes fast enough. Softer, less tannic, and more approachable than Cabernet Sauvignon, Merlot became the hot, new red wine in the U.S., especially with consumers just getting into red wine. Cabernet Sauvignon is still the red wine leader in the U.S., however.

The most important fine wine areas and districts include the following (see Figure 14-1):

✔ **North Coast:**
Napa Valley
Sonoma County
Mendocino and Lake Counties

✔ **North-Central Coast:**
Livermore and Santa Clara Valleys (San Francisco Bay area)
Santa Cruz Mountains
Monterey County

✔ **Sierra Foothills**

✔ **South-Central Coast:**
San Luis Obispo County
Santa Barbara County

Figure 14-1:
The wine regions of California.

© Akira Chiwaki

When the wines are good

Weather variations from year to year are far less dramatic in California than they are in most European wine regions. One major reason is that rain doesn't fall during the growing season in much of California. (Rain at the wrong time is the usual cause of Europe's poorer vintages.) Using irrigation, winemakers in effect control the water to the vines. Ironically, one factor that can cause vintage variation in California is lack of water for irrigation due to drought.

Napa Valley: As Tiny as It Is Famous

Napa Valley is about a 90-minute drive northeast of the beautiful bay city of San Francisco. Many of California's most prestigious wineries — and certainly its most expensive vineyard land — are in the small Napa Valley, where 232 wineries have managed to find space. (In 1960, Napa Valley had only 25 wineries.) The region's size is actually much tinier than its reputation: Napa produces less than five percent of California's wine grapes.

The southern part of the Valley, especially the Carneros district, is the coolest area, thanks to ocean breezes and mists from the San Pablo Bay. Carneros — which extends westward into Sonoma County — has become the vineyard area of choice for grape varieties that enjoy the cool climate: Chardonnays, Pinot Noirs, and grapes for sparkling wines. North towards Calistoga — away from the bay influence — the climate gets quite hot (but always with cool nights).

Wineries and vineyards occupy almost every part of Napa Valley. Many vineyards are on the valley floor, some are in the hills and mountains to the west (the Mayacamas Mountains), and some are in the mountains to the east (especially Howell Mountain). Napa winemakers and grape growers have established 13 AVAs besides the broad Napa Valley AVA itself and the even broader (six-county) North Coast AVA. These other 13 are the following:

- ✔ Spring Mountain, Diamond Mountain, and Mt. Veeder (all in the western mountains)
- ✔ Howell Mountain, Stags Leap District, Atlas Peak (all hilly or mountainous areas in eastern Napa Valley)
- ✔ Chiles Valley (in the easternmost part of Napa Valley)
- ✔ Rutherford, Oakville, Yountville, and St. Helena (on the valley floor)
- ✔ Wild Horse Valley (in southeastern Napa Valley)
- ✔ Los Carneros (part in Napa Valley, part in Sonoma)

The grapes of Napa

Almost everyone in Napa who makes table wine makes a Cabernet Sauvignon and a Chardonnay, and many Napa producers now also make Merlot.

The six most important wines in Napa are the two whites, Chardonnay and Sauvignon Blanc (often labeled Fumé Blanc), and the four red wines, Cabernet Sauvignon, Merlot, Pinot Noir (mainly from cool Carneros), and Zinfandel. But blended wines have become increasingly important in the last 15 years. If red, these blends are usually made from red Bordeaux varieties (Cabernet Sauvignon, Cabernet Franc, Merlot, and sometimes even Malbec and Petit Verdot). If white, they're usually made from the white Bordeaux grapes (Sauvignon Blanc and Sémillon). Some of these blends are referred to as Meritage wines — not just in Napa but across the U.S. — although few carry the word *Meritage* on their labels.

Who's who in Napa (and for what)

If just about every winery in Napa makes a Chardonnay and a Cabernet Sauvignon, how can you distinguish the wineries from one another? Good question — with no easy answer. The following alphabetical list indicates some of the better wine producers in Napa Valley, as well as their best wines, and could help steer you in the right direction. We know the list looks overwhelming, but . . . that's Napa!

Our list includes Napa classics as well as some personal favorites. Sparkling wine producers are covered under "California" in Chapter 15.

From $6 to $100-plus

You can find Chardonnays, Cabernets, Pinot Noirs, and Merlots from California at prices as low as $6 a bottle. Better wines can be quite expensive, however. Most mid-range varietal wines are in the $25 to $50 range. *Reserves, single-vineyard wines,* and *special selection wines* generally cost from $50 to $100 and up.

Sauvignon Blancs — somewhat less in demand than Chardonnay, Cabernet, Pinot Noir, and Merlot — are the best values among California's premium wines. You can find many good ones for around $14, although a few are priced as high as $35. Red Zinfandels are also still a bargain, but their prices are climbing as they become more popular. You can still find many red Zins from $12 to $18, although a few premium Zinfandels are well over $20. If you like White Zinfandels, which are distinctly sweeter than the reds, you can save yourself a bundle; they're in the $5 to $8 range.

Although all the wineries in the following list are situated in Napa Valley, their wines are not necessarily made with Napa-grown grapes; the geographic name on the label tells you where the grapes came from.

- **Acacia Winery:** Pinot Noir, Chardonnay
- **Anderson's Conn Valley:** Cabernet Sauvignon, Chardonnay
- **Araujo Estate:** Cabernet Sauvignon (Eisele Vineyard), Syrah
- **Beaulieu Vineyard:** Cabernet Sauvignon Private Reserve (Georges de Latour), Cabernet Sauvignon (Rutherford)
- **Beringer Vineyards:** Cabernet Sauvignon (single-vineyard wines), Chardonnay Private Reserve, Merlot (Bancroft Ranch)
- **Bryant Family Vineyard:** Cabernet Sauvignon (small winery; scarce)
- **Burgess Cellars:** Zinfandel, Cabernet Sauvignon
- **Cafaro Cellars:** Cabernet Sauvignon, Merlot, Syrah
- **Cain Cellars:** Cain Five (five Bordeaux varieties), Cain Cuvée
- **Cakebread Cellars:** Cabernet Sauvignon, Sauvignon Blanc, Chardonnay
- **Caymus Vineyard:** Cabernet Sauvignon (especially *Special Selection*)
- **Chappellet:** Chenin Blanc, Cabernet Sauvignon
- **Chateau Montelena:** Cabernet Sauvignon, Calistoga Cuvée Red, Chardonnay
- **Chateau Potelle:** Cabernet Sauvignon, Chardonnay, Zinfandel
- **Clos du Val:** Cabernet Sauvignon, Sémillon, Chardonnay
- **Corison:** Cabernet Sauvignon
- **Cuvaison:** Chardonnay, Cabernet Sauvignon
- **Dalla Valle:** Cabernet Sauvignon, Maya (blend of Cabernet Franc/Cabernet Sauvignon)
- **Diamond Creek:** Cabernet Sauvignon
- **Dominus Estate:** Dominus (mainly Cabernet Sauvignon), Napanook
- **Duckhorn:** Merlot, Cabernet Sauvignon, Sauvignon Blanc
- **Dunn Vineyards:** Cabernet Sauvignon (especially Howell Mountain)
- **El Molino:** Chardonnay, Pinot Noir
- **Étude:** Pinot Noir, Cabernet Sauvignon
- **Elyse Vineyards:** Zinfandel
- **Far Niente:** Cabernet Sauvignon, Chardonnay
- **Fife Vineyards:** Zinfandel, Cabernet Sauvignon, Petite Sirah

- **Flora Springs:** Trilogy (blend of Cabernet Sauvignon, Merlot, Cabernet Franc), Cabernet Sauvignon Reserve, Chardonnay Reserve

- **Forman Vineyard:** Chardonnay, Cabernet Sauvignon

- **Franciscan Estate:** Chardonnay, Magnificat Red, Cabernet Sauvignon

- **Franus Winery:** Zinfandel, Cabernet Sauvignon

- **Freemark Abbey:** Cabernet Sauvignon (Bosché and Sycamore Vineyards)

- **Frog's Leap Winery:** Cabernet Sauvignon, Zinfandel, Sauvignon Blanc

- **Grace Family Vineyards:** Cabernet Sauvignon (small production; mailing list only)

- **Green and Red Vineyard:** Zinfandel

- **Grgich Hills Cellar:** Chardonnay, Cabernet Sauvignon, Zinfandel, Fumé Blanc

- **Groth Vineyards:** Cabernet Sauvignon (especially Reserve)

- **Harlan Estate:** Cabernet Sauvignon (small winery; very scarce)

- **Hartwell Vineyard:** Cabernet Sauvignon

- **Havens Wine Cellars:** Merlot

- **Heitz Wine Cellars:** Cabernet Sauvignon (Martha's Vineyard)

- **Hendry Ranch:** Zinfandel (all single-vineyard wines)

- **Hess Collection Winery:** Cabernet Sauvignon, Chardonnay

- **Jarvis Estate:** Cabernet Sauvignon, Chardonnay

- **Charles Krug:** Cabernet Sauvignon, Chardonnay (Family Reserves)

- **La Jota:** Cabernet Sauvignon, Cabernet Franc, Petite Sirah, Viognier

- **Lang & Reed:** Cabernet Franc

- **Lewis Cellars:** Cabernet Sauvignon, Chardonnay

- **Livingston-Moffett:** Cabernet Sauvignon (Moffett Vineyard)

- **Long Vineyards:** Chardonnay, Riesling, Pinot Grigio, Sangiovese

- **Markham Vineyards:** Chardonnay, Merlot, Cabernet Sauvignon

- **Mayacamas Vineyards:** Cabernet Sauvignon, Sauvignon Blanc

- **Robert Mondavi:** Cabernet Sauvignon (especially Reserve), Pinot Noir Reserve, Barbera (La Famiglia di Robert Mondavi)

- **Newton Vineyard:** Chardonnay, Merlot, Cabernet Sauvignon

- **Neyers Vineyards:** Chardonnay, Merlot, Syrah

- **Nickel & Nickel:** Cabernet Sauvignon (all single-vineyard wines)

- **Niebaum-Coppola Estate:** Rubicon (mainly Cabernet Sauvignon), all Estate wines, including Edizone Pennino Zinfandel
- **Oakville Ranch Vineyards:** Cabernet Sauvignon
- **Opus One:** Opus One (mainly Cabernet Sauvignon)
- **Pahlmeyer Winery:** Red (Cabernet blend), Merlot, Chardonnay
- **Paradigm:** Cabernet Sauvignon, Merlot
- **Patz & Hall:** Chardonnay
- **Joseph Phelps Vineyards:** Insignia (Cabernet blend), Cabernet Sauvignon
- **Pine Ridge Winery:** Cabernet Sauvignon, Chardonnay
- **Pride Mountain:** Cabernet Sauvignon
- **Quintessa Estate:** Quintessa (Bordeaux blend)
- **Kent Rasmussen Winery:** Pinot Noir, Chardonnay
- **Rudd Estate:** Chardonnay, Sauvignon Blanc, Cabernet Sauvignon
- **Saddleback Cellars:** Cabernet Sauvignon
- **Saintsbury:** Pinot Noir (all), Chardonnay
- **Selene:** Merlot, Sauvignon Blanc
- **Shafer Vineyards:** Cabernet Sauvignon (especially Hillside Select)
- **Signorello Vineyards:** Chardonnay, Cabernet Sauvignon, Sémillon
- **Silver Oak Cellars:** Cabernet Sauvignon
- **Silverado Vineyards:** Cabernet Sauvignon, Chardonnay (Carneros)
- **Sky Vineyards:** Zinfandel
- **Smith-Madrone:** Riesling, Chardonnay, Cabernet Sauvignon
- **Spottswoode Winery:** Cabernet Sauvignon, Sauvignon Blanc
- **Staglin Family Vineyard:** Cabernet Sauvignon
- **Stag's Leap Wine Cellars:** Cask 23 (Cabernet blend), Cabernet Sauvignon (Fay Vineyard and SLV), Chardonnay
- **Stony Hill Vineyard:** Chardonnay, Riesling
- **Storybook Mountain:** Zinfandel
- **Swanson Vineyards:** Cabernet Sauvignon, Sangiovese, Merlot, Syrah
- **The Terraces:** Zinfandel, Cabernet Sauvignon
- **Trefethen Vineyards:** Cabernet Sauvignon, Chardonnay, Riesling (dry)
- **Truchard Vineyards:** Syrah, Chardonnay, Merlot, Pinot Noir

- ✔ **Turley Wine Cellars:** Zinfandel (all single-vineyard Zinfandels)
- ✔ **Turnbull Cellars:** Cabernet Sauvignon, Turnbull Red "Black Label"
- ✔ **Viader Vineyards:** Viader Red (Cabernet Sauvignon/Cabernet Franc)
- ✔ **Vine Cliff Cellars:** Cabernet Sauvignon, Chardonnay
- ✔ **Whitehall Lane Winery:** Cabernet Sauvignon, Merlot
- ✔ **ZD Wines:** Cabernet Sauvignon, Chardonnay

Down-to-Earth in Sonoma

If you leave San Francisco over the beautiful Golden Gate Bridge, you'll be in Sonoma in an hour. The differences between Napa and Sonoma are remarkable. Many of Napa's wineries are showy (and downright luxurious), but most of Sonoma's are rustic, country-like, and laid-back. The millionaires bought into Napa; Sonoma is just folks (with some exceptions, of course).

On the other hand, Sonoma *is* the home of the famously successful Gallo of Sonoma, Sebastiani, Glen Ellen, Korbel, Kendall-Jackson, Simi, and Jordan wineries — not exactly small time operations! E. & J. Gallo, one of the world's largest wineries, has moved into Sonoma in a *big* way. We have the sneaking impression that if we visit Sonoma in 15 or 20 years, it will bear a striking resemblance to Napa. But we hope not; we like it just the way it is.

Sonoma's AVAs

Sonoma is larger and more spread out than Napa. Its climate is similar to Napa's, except that some areas near the coast are definitely cooler. Although there's plenty of Chardonnay, Cabernet Sauvignon, and Merlot in Sonoma, the region's varied microclimates and terrain have allowed three other varieties to excel — Pinot Noir, Zinfandel, and Sauvignon Blanc.

The viticultural areas (AVAs) of Sonoma County (roughly from south to north) and their principal grape varieties (and wines) are the following:

- ✔ **Sonoma Valley:** Chardonnay (to a lesser extent, Pinot Noir, Cabernet Sauvignon, Zinfandel)
- ✔ **Sonoma Mountain:** Cabernet Sauvignon
- ✔ **Russian River Valley:** Pinot Noir, Chardonnay, sparkling wine, Zinfandel
- ✔ **Sonoma-Green Valley** (within Russian River Valley): Sparkling wine, Chardonnay, Pinot Noir

- **Chalk Hill** (within Russian River Valley): Chardonnay, Sauvignon Blanc
- **Dry Creek Valley:** Zinfandel, Cabernet Sauvignon
- **Alexander Valley:** Cabernet Sauvignon, Chardonnay, Sauvignon Blanc
- **Knight's Valley:** Cabernet Sauvignon, Sauvignon Blanc
- **Rockpile:** Sonoma's newest AVA (2002), in the northwestern part of the county; Zinfandel, Cabernet Sauvignon, Syrah, Petite Sirah

Sonoma County has two more AVAs: Northern Sonoma, a patchwork area encompassing Russian River Valley, Alexander Valley, Dry Creek Valley, and Knight's Valley; and Sonoma Coast, a hodgepodge of land in western Sonoma, along the coast. Also, the North Coast AVA takes in Sonoma County.

The Carneros AVA is shared with Napa Valley; that area is important for Pinot Noir, Chardonnay, sparkling wine, and Merlot.

Pinot Noir lovers should look for wines from Russian River Valley producers, such as Williams & Selyem, Rochioli, Gary Farrell, and Dehlinger. We agree with those who say that the Russian River Valley is the source of some of the best Pinot Noir in the entire New World.

Recommended Sonoma producers and wines

The following list includes some of Sonoma's better producers, listed alphabetically, along with their best wines. It's *slightly* less staggering than the Napa list.

Although these wineries are all based in Sonoma County, their wines might be made from grapes grown elsewhere. Cline Cellars, for example, uses grapes mainly from Contra Costa County east of San Francisco. Check the labels to find out.

- **Arrowood Vineyards:** Chardonnay, Cabernet Sauvignon, Syrah
- **Benziger Family Winery:** Cabernet Sauvignon, Chardonnay (Carneros)
- **Davis Bynum Winery:** Pinot Noir, Zinfandel
- **Chalk Hill Winery:** Chardonnay, Sauvignon Blanc
- **Chateau St. Jean:** Chardonnay (Robert Young, Belle Terre, Durell Ranch), Cabernet Sauvignon (Cinq Cépages)
- **Chateau Souverain:** Cabernet Sauvignon, Chardonnay, Sauvignon Blanc
- **Cline Cellars:** Mourvèdre, Zinfandel

- **B. R. Cohn:** Cabernet Sauvignon (Olive Hill Vineyard)
- **H. Coturri:** Zinfandel
- **Dehlinger Winery:** Pinot Noir, Chardonnay, Syrah
- **De Loach Vineyards:** Chardonnay, Zinfandel
- **Gary Farrell Wines:** Pinot Noir, Chardonnay, Zinfandel
- **Ferrari-Carano:** Chardonnay, Fumé Blanc, Cabernet Sauvignon
- **Fisher Vineyards:** Chardonnay (Whitney's Vineyard), Cabernet Sauvignon
- **Flowers:** Pinot Noir, Chardonnay
- **Foppiano Vineyards:** Petite Sirah, Cabernet Sauvignon, Merlot
- **Gallo of Sonoma:** Chardonnay (Laguna Ranch), Zinfandel (Frei Ranch)
- **Geyser Peak Winery:** Cabernet Sauvignon, Merlot
- **Hanna Winery:** Sauvignon Blanc, Zinfandel, Cabernet Sauvignon
- **Hanzell Vineyards:** Chardonnay
- **Hartford Court:** Pinot Noir (all), Zinfandel
- **Paul Hobbs:** Cabernet Sauvignon, Chardonnay, Pinot Noir
- **Jordan Vineyard:** Cabernet Sauvignon, Chardonnay
- **Kendall-Jackson:** Cabernet Sauvignon, Chardonnay, Zinfandel
- **Kenwood Vineyards:** Cabernet Sauvignon (Artist Series), Zinfandel
- **Kistler Vineyards:** Chardonnay (all vineyards and selections), Pinot Noir (all vineyards)
- **Kunde Estate:** Chardonnay, Zinfandel, Viognier
- **La Crema:** Chardonnay, Pinot Noir
- **Landmark Vineyards:** Chardonnay
- **Laurel Glen Vineyard:** Cabernet Sauvignon, Reds, Terra Rosa
- **Limerick Lane Cellars:** Zinfandel
- **MacRostie Wines:** Chardonnay (Carneros)
- **Marcassin:** Chardonnay (all vineyards; very scarce; by mailing list)
- **Marietta Cellars:** Cabernet Sauvignon, Petite Sirah, Zinfandel, Old Vine Red (Zin blend)
- **Marimar Torres Estate:** Chardonnay, Pinot Noir
- **Martinelli Vineyard:** Zinfandel, Chardonnay (Russian River Valley)
- **Matanzas Creek Winery:** Chardonnay, Sauvignon Blanc, Merlot

- **Peter Michael Winery:** Chardonnay (all selections), Les Pavots (Cabernet Sauvignon-based blend)

- **Pezzi King:** Cabernet Sauvignon, Chardonnay, Zinfandel

- **Preston Vineyards:** Zinfandel, Syrah, Viognier

- **Quivira Vineyards:** Zinfandel

- **Rabbit Ridge Vineyards:** Zinfandel, Barbera, Chardonnay

- **A. Rafanelli Winery:** Zinfandel, Cabernet Sauvignon (mailing list)

- **Ravenswood:** Zinfandel (especially single-vineyards), Merlot (especially Sangiacomo Vineyard), Pickberry (Cabernet Sauvignon/Merlot blend)

- **J. Rochioli Vineyard:** Pinot Noir (all), Sauvignon Blanc, Zinfandel

- **St. Francis Winery:** Zinfandel, Merlot, Cabernet Sauvignon

- **Sausal Winery:** Zinfandel (all), Sangiovese

- **Seghesio Family Estates:** Zinfandel (all), Sangiovese, Barbera

- **Sonoma-Cutrer Vineyards:** Chardonnay (all selections)

- **Stonestreet:** Cabernet Sauvignon (all), Chardonnay, Merlot

- **Joseph Swan Vineyards:** Pinot Noir, Zinfandel

- **Trentadue Winery:** Petite Sirah, Old Patch Red

- **Williams & Selyem Winery:** Pinot Noir (all), Zinfandel, Chardonnay (all wines very scarce; by mailing list)

Mendocino and Lake Counties

Lake County, dominated by Clear Lake, is Napa's neighbor to the north, while Mendocino County is directly north of Sonoma.

If you have the chance, it's worth your while to drive up the beautiful California coastline from San Francisco on Route 1 to the quaint, old town of Mendocino — perhaps with a side trip to view the magnificent, giant redwoods of the Pacific Coast. Tourists are scarcer up here than in Napa or Sonoma, and that makes it all the nicer: You'll be genuinely welcomed at the wineries.

The cool Anderson Valley in Mendocino County is ideal for growing Chardonnay, Pinot Noir, Gewürztraminer, and Riesling, and for the production of sparkling wine. The wily Roederer Champagne house bypassed Napa and Sonoma to start its sparkling wine operation here and has done extremely well in a short time — as have Pacific Echo and Handley, two other successful sparkling wine producers in Anderson Valley (see Chapter 15 for sparkling wine producers).

The following list includes recommended producers and their best wines. Producers are listed alphabetically, by county.

Mendocino County

- ✔ **Edmeades:** Zinfandel (especially single-vineyards), Chardonnay
- ✔ **Fetzer Vineyards:** Pinot Noir Reserve, Cabernet Sauvignon Reserve
- ✔ **Greenwood Ridge Vineyards:** Riesling, Pinot Noir, Zinfandel
- ✔ **Handley Cellars:** Chardonnay, Gewürztraminer, Sauvignon Blanc
- ✔ **Jepson Vineyards:** Chardonnay, Sauvignon Blanc
- ✔ **Lolonis Winery:** Cabernet Sauvignon (all), Zinfandel (Private Reserve)
- ✔ **McDowell Valley Vineyards:** Syrah Reserve, Viognier
- ✔ **Navarro Vineyards:** Gewürztraminer, Chardonnay (Reserve)

Lake County

- ✔ **Guenoc Winery:** Cabernet Sauvignon, Chardonnay, Langtry Meritage Red (Cabernet blend), Petite Sirah Reserve
- ✔ **Steele Wines:** Chardonnay, Zinfandel, Pinot Noir, Pinot Blanc

San Francisco Bay Area

The San Francisco Bay area includes wine regions north, east, and south of the city: Marin County to the north; Alameda and Livermore to the east; and Santa Clara Valley and San Mateo to the south.

The urban spread, from Palo Alto to San Jose (Silicon Valley) and eastward, has taken its toll on vineyards in both the Livermore and Santa Clara Valleys. These two growing regions, both cooled by breezes from the San Francisco Bay, are therefore relatively small.

In Livermore, directly east of San Francisco, Sauvignon Blanc and Sémillon have always done well. In Santa Clara Valley, south of San Francisco with the Santa Cruz Mountains on its western side, Chardonnay, Cabernet Sauvignon, and Merlot are the three big grape varieties (and wines).

We list our recommended wineries alphabetically, by locality.

Marin County

- ✔ **Kalin Cellars:** Sauvignon Blanc, Sémillon, Chardonnay, Pinot Noir; wine-maker Terry Leighton gets his grapes from diverse areas, including Livermore
- ✔ **Sean H. Thackrey:** Orion Old Vines Red (Syrah blend), Pleiades; grapes come from several different areas, including Napa

Alameda County

- ✔ **Edmunds St. John:** Syrah, Rocks and Gravel (Rhône blend); grapes are sourced from throughout the state
- ✔ **Rosenblum Cellars:** Zinfandel (especially single-vineyards); uses mainly Sonoma Valley and Napa Valley fruit

Livermore Valley

- ✔ **Concannon Vineyard:** Sauvignon Blanc, Petite Sirah
- ✔ **Murrietta's Well:** Zinfandel
- ✔ **Wente Vineyards:** Chardonnay, Sauvignon Blanc

Santa Clara Valley

- ✔ **J. Lohr Winery:** Chardonnay, Cabernet Sauvignon (Paso Robles)

San Mateo County

- ✔ **Cronin Vineyards:** Chardonnay (all selections)
- ✔ **Thomas Fogarty Winery:** Gewürztraminer, Chardonnay, Pinot Noir

Santa Cruz Mountains

Standing atop one of the isolated Santa Cruz Mountains, you can quickly forget that you're only an hour's drive south of San Francisco. The rugged, wild beauty of this area has attracted quite a few winemakers, including some of the best in the state. (Paul Draper of Ridge Vineyards and Randall Grahm of Bonny Doon are but two.) The climate is cool on the ocean side, where Pinot Noir thrives. On the San Francisco Bay side, Cabernet Sauvignon is the important red variety. But Chardonnay is the dominant grape on both sides.

The following is a list of recommended producers in the Santa Cruz Mountains, listed alphabetically along with their best wines:

- ✔ **Bargetto:** Chardonnay, Cabernet Sauvignon, Gewürztraminer, fruit wine
- ✔ **Bonny Doon Vineyard:** Le Cigare Volant Red (Rhône blend), Old Telegram (Mourvèdre)
- ✔ **David Bruce Winery:** Pinot Noir (Santa Cruz), Zinfandel (Paso Robles)
- ✔ **Cinnabar Vineyards:** Chardonnay, Cabernet Sauvignon
- ✔ **Kathryn Kennedy Winery:** Cabernet Sauvignon
- ✔ **Mount Eden Vineyards:** Chardonnay Estate, Cabernet Sauvignon, Pinot Noir
- ✔ **Ridge Vineyards:** Cabernet Sauvignon Monte Bello, Geyserville (Zin blend), Zinfandel (all)
- ✔ **Santa Cruz Mountain Vineyard:** Pinot Noir, Cabernet Sauvignon

Down in Old Monterey

Monterey County has a little bit of everything — a beautiful coastline, the chic town of Carmel, some very cool (as in temperature, not chicness) vineyard districts and some very warm areas, mountain wineries and Salinas Valley wineries, a few gigantic wine firms and lots of small ones. The wineries have had their growing pains, such as learning how to avoid vegetal flavors in their wines (lesson learned), determining the best areas for various grape varieties, and figuring out how to cope with the phylloxera louse (see Chapter 3 for more information on phylloxera).

Chardonnay leads the way here — as it does in most of the state. But the cooler parts of Monterey are also principal sources of Riesling and Gewürztraminer. Cabernet Sauvignon and Pinot Noir are the leading red varieties in the mountain areas.

The following are our recommended producers in Monterey County, and one producer from neighboring San Benito County (listed alphabetically):

- ✔ **Bernardus Winery:** Chardonnay, Sauvignon Blanc, Marinus (mainly Cabernet Sauvignon), Pinot Noir
- ✔ **Calera** (San Benito County): Pinot Noir (especially single-vineyard selections), Viognier, Chardonnay
- ✔ **Chalone Vineyard:** Chardonnay, Pinot Blanc, Chenin Blanc

- ✔ **Chateau Julien:** Chardonnay, Merlot, Cabernet Sauvignon
- ✔ **Durney Vineyard:** Cabernet Sauvignon
- ✔ **Estancia Estates:** Chardonnay, Cabernet Sauvignon, Merlot, Pinot Noir, Sauvignon Blanc
- ✔ **Morgan Winery:** Chardonnay, Pinot Noir (Monterey Reserve), Sauvignon Blanc, Syrah
- ✔ **Paraiso Springs Vineyard:** Pinot Blanc, Chardonnay, Riesling
- ✔ **Talbott Vineyards:** Chardonnay

Thar's Wine in Them There Foothills

No wine region in America has a more romantic past than the Sierra Foothills. The Gold Rush of 1849 carved a place in history for the Foothills. It also brought vineyards to the area to provide wine for the thirsty miners. One of the vines planted at that time was certainly Zinfandel — still the region's most famous wine. Indeed, many of the oldest grapevines in the U.S., some over 100 years old — mainly Zinfandel — are here in the Sierra Foothills.

In fact, very little has changed in the Sierra Foothills over the years. This is clearly the West Coast's most rustic wine region — perhaps the country's. Therein lies its charm. A visit to the Foothills is like a trip into the past, when life was simple.

The Sierra Foothills is a sprawling wine region east of Sacramento, centered in Amador and El Dorado Counties, but spreading north and south of both. Two of its best-known viticultural areas are Shenandoah Valley and Fiddletown. Summers can be hot, but many vineyards are situated in high altitudes, such as around Placerville in El Dorado. Soil throughout the region is mainly volcanic in origin.

The following are our recommended producers in the Sierra Foothills (listed alphabetically), along with their best wines:

- ✔ **Amador Foothill Winery:** Zinfandel
- ✔ **Boeger Winery:** Zinfandel, Barbera, Sauvignon Blanc
- ✔ **Karly:** Zinfandel, Syrah, Sauvignon Blanc, Marsanne
- ✔ **Monteviña:** Barbera, Zinfandel, Sangiovese
- ✔ **Renaissance Vineyard:** Riesling (Late Harvest), Sauvignon Blanc
- ✔ **Renwood Winery:** Barbera, Zinfandel (especially Grandpère Vineyard)

> ✔ **Shenandoah Vineyards:** Zinfandel, Sauvignon Blanc
>
> ✔ **Sierra Vista Winery:** Zinfandel, Syrah
>
> ✔ **Sobon Estate:** Zinfandel, Viognier
>
> ✔ **Stevenot Winery:** Cabernet Sauvignon, Zinfandel

San Luis Obispo: Mountain Meets Maritime

San Luis Obispo County is another region of vastly diverse viticultural areas. These include, for example, the warm, hilly Paso Robles region (north of the town of San Luis Obispo) where Zinfandel and Cabernet Sauvignon reign, and the cool, maritime Edna Valley and Arroyo Grande (south of the town), home of some very good Pinot Noirs and Chardonnays. The areas are so different climatically that we group the producers separately.

We recommend the following producers in San Luis Obispo (listed alphabetically), along with their best wines:

Paso Robles

> ✔ **Adelaida Cellars:** Cabernet Sauvignon
>
> ✔ **Claiborne & Churchill:** Chardonnay, Gewürztraminer, Riesling
>
> ✔ **Eberle Winery:** Zinfandel, Syrah, Cabernet Sauvignon
>
> ✔ **Justin Vineyards:** Isosceles (Cabernet blend), Cabernet Sauvignon, Cabernet Franc, Chardonnay
>
> ✔ **Meridian Vineyards:** Chardonnay (especially Reserve), Syrah
>
> ✔ **Peachy Canyon Winery:** Zinfandel
>
> ✔ **Treana Winery:** Red (Cabernet, Syrah, Merlot, others)
>
> ✔ **Wild Horse Vineyards:** Pinot Noir, Chardonnay, Malvasia Bianca, Pinot Grigio, Pinot Blanc

Edna Valley and Arroyo Grande

> ✔ **Alban Vineyards:** Viognier (Estate), Syrah, Grenache
>
> ✔ **Edna Valley Vineyard:** Chardonnay, Pinot Noir

- **Laetitia Vineyard:** Chardonnay, Pinot Noir
- **Saucelito Canyon Vineyard:** Zinfandel
- **Talley Vineyards:** Chardonnay, Pinot Noir

Santa Barbara, California Paradise

The most exciting viticultural areas in California — if not in the entire country — are in Santa Barbara County. Even though Spanish missionaries had vineyards planted there 200 years ago, it was as late as 1975 before the first major winery (Firestone Vineyards) opened for business. In light of what we now know — that is, how well-suited Santa Barbara is to grape growing — 1975 was a late start.

The cool Santa Maria, Santa Ynez, and Los Alamos Valleys — which lie north of the city of Santa Barbara — run east to west, opening towards the Pacific Ocean and channeling in the ocean air. The cool climate is ideal for Pinot Noir and Chardonnay. In the Santa Maria Valley, one of the main sources of these varieties, the average temperature during the growing season is a mere 74°F. Further south, in the Santa Ynez Valley, Riesling also does well.

Pinot Noir has earned Santa Barbara much of its acclaim as a wine region. Santa Barbara is now generally recognized as one of the five great American wine regions for this variety — the other four being Carneros, the Russian River Valley, Anderson Valley (in Mendocino County), and the Willamette Valley (in Oregon). In Santa Barbara, Pinot Noir wines seem to burst with luscious strawberry fruit, laced with herbal tones. These wines tend to be precocious; they're delicious in their first four or five years — not the *keepers* that the sturdier, wilder-tasting Russian River Pinot Noirs seem to be. But why keep them when they taste so good?

The following are some recommended producers in Santa Barbara (listed alphabetically), along with their best wines:

- **Au Bon Climat:** Pinot Noir, Chardonnay (especially single-vineyard bottlings of both), Pinot Blanc
- **Babcock Vineyards:** Sauvignon Blanc, Chardonnay, Pinot Noir
- **The Brander Vineyard:** Sauvignon Blanc
- **Byron Vineyard:** Chardonnay (especially Reserve), Pinot Noir
- **Cambria Winery:** Chardonnay, Pinot Noir (Julia's Vineyard), Syrah
- **Cottonwood Canyon:** Pinot Noir

- **Fiddlehead Cellars:** Pinot Noir, Sauvignon Blanc
- **Firestone Vineyard:** Chardonnay, Sauvignon Blanc
- **Foxen Vineyard:** Pinot Noir, Syrah, Viognier, Chenin Blanc
- **The Gainey Vineyard:** Chardonnay, Pinot Noir, Sauvignon Blanc
- **Daniel Gehrs:** Chenin Blanc, Sauvignon Blanc, Syrah, Viognier
- **Richard Longoria:** Chardonnay, Pinot Noir, Merlot
- **The Ojai Vineyard:** Chardonnay, Syrah, Pinot Noir
- **Fess Parker Winery:** Chardonnay, Syrah, Viognier
- **Qupé Cellars:** Syrah, Chardonnay, Roussanne, Marsanne, Viognier
- **Sanford Winery:** Pinot Noir (especially Sanford & Benedict Vineyard), Chardonnay, Sauvignon Blanc
- **Santa Barbara Winery:** Pinot Noir, Chardonnay, Syrah
- **Lane Tanner:** Pinot Noir, Syrah
- **Zaca Mesa Winery:** Chardonnay, Syrah

Elsewhere in California

One interesting winery in California's Central Valley, one in the Dunnigan Hills (north of the Central Valley), and one in southern California complete our portrait of recommended California wineries. Although these locations are normally too warm to grow grapes for fine wine, variables such as altitude — or, in the case of southern California, cool ocean breezes — often create microclimates conducive to the production of fine wine.

Central Valley

- **Bogle Vineyards:** Petite Sirah, Sauvignon Blanc, Zinfandel, Merlot

Dunnigan Hills (Yolo County)

- **R. H. Phillips Vineyard:** Syrah (EXP), Viognier (EXP), Sauvignon Blanc, Tempranillo (EXP), Chardonnay Estate (Toasted Head)

Southern California

- **Moraga:** Red (Cabernet Sauvignon, Merlot)

Mini-trends in California wine

Experimentation is a constant in California. Although Chardonnay, Cabernet Sauvignon, and Merlot are the anointed grape varieties at the moment, winemakers can never know whether they're missing the boat on some other important grape — unless they try growing it.

Some producers have become enchanted with the grape varieties from France's Rhône Valley — the red grapes Syrah, Grenache, Mourvèdre, and Cinsault and the white Viognier. These producers are collectively referred to as the Rhône Rangers. Other producers are riding the wave called Cal-Ital, growing Italian grapes such as Sangiovese, Dolcetto, and Pinot Grigio. (Some Italian grapes, like Barbera, have been grown in California since the days of the Italian immigrants, about 100 years ago.) And next year — who knows? — the new grape could be Spain's Tempranillo. Stay tuned.

Oregon, A Tale of Two Pinots

Because Oregon is north of California, most people assume that Oregon's wine regions are cool. And they're right. But the main reason for Oregon's cool climate is that no high mountains separate the vineyards from the Pacific Ocean. The ocean influence brings cool temperatures and rain. Grape growing and winemaking are really completely different in Oregon than in California.

Winemaking is a fairly new industry in Oregon, but it is growing rapidly. From a handful of wineries in the early 1970s, the state now has well over 100, and that number increases every year.

Oregon first gained respect in wine circles for its Pinot Noir, a grape that needs cool climates to perform at its best (see "A Primer on Red Grape Varieties" in Chapter 3). The Eyrie Vineyards released the state's first Pinot Noir in 1970, but national recognition for the state's Pinots came only after the excellent 1983 and 1985 vintages. Today Pinot Noir is still Oregon's flagship wine; a vast majority of the state's wineries make a Pinot Noir.

Oregon's other Pinot

Because Chardonnay is the companion grape to Pinot Noir in France's Burgundy region (see Chapter 10), and because Chardonnay wine is hugely popular in America, Chardonnay is a fairly important variety in Oregon. However, a second white grape variety has emerged to challenge Chardonnay's domination: Pinot Gris.

David Lett, founder and winemaker of The Eyrie Vineyards and Oregon's Pinot Noir pioneer, is also the man who made Oregon's first Pinot Gris in the early 1970s, followed by Ponzi Vineyards and Adelsheim Vineyards. Today, over 50 wineries in Oregon make Pinot Gris. Now, more and more California wineries are also making Pinot Gris — but in California, wineries are producing a lighter, Italian-style wine, which they in fact usually call Pinot Grigio. Oregon's Pinot Gris resembles the more flavorful Alsace Pinot Gris wine.

Pinot Gris has many things going for it. Because it doesn't particularly need oak aging to give it complexity (but it takes to oak well when that's the wine-maker's preference), Pinot Gris can be ready to drink six months after the vintage.

Oregon Pinot Gris is medium-bodied; its color ranges from light golden yellow to copper-pink, its aromas are reminiscent of pears and apples, sometimes of melon, and it has surprising depth and complexity. It's an excellent food wine, even when it's slightly sweet; it works well especially with seafood and salmon, just the kind of food that it's paired with in Oregon. And the best news is the price. Many of Oregon's Pinot Gris cost around $15 in retail stores.

Who's who in Willamette Valley

The main home of Pinot Noir and Pinot Gris in Oregon is the Willamette (*will AM ett*) Valley, directly south of the city of Portland in northwest Oregon. The cool Willamette Valley has established itself in the last 30 years as the most important wine region in Oregon; in fact, 70 percent of the state's wineries are situated here.

Willamette Valley is a convenient wine destination to visit because the city of Portland, with all its fine restaurants, hotels, and shops, is 30 minutes north of this wine region.

Willamette Valley is huge and encompasses several counties. Yamhill County, directly southwest of Portland, has the greatest concentration of wineries, all of which produce Pinot Noir. But quite a few wineries are located in Washington County, west of Portland, and in Polk County, south of Yamhill.

Here are some of the better producers in the Willamette Valley, primarily for Pinot Noir and Pinot Gris (but sometimes also Chardonnay or Riesling), listed alphabetically:

Adelsheim Vineyard

Amity Vineyards

Archery Summit

Argyle (for sparkling wines)

Beaux Frères

Benton Lane Winery

Bethel Heights

Brick House

Broadley Vineyards

Cameron Winery

Chateau Benoit

Chehalem

Cooper Mountain

Cristom Vineyards

Domaine Drouhin Oregon

Domaine Serene

Duck Pond

Edgefield Winery

Elk Cove Vineyards

Eola Hills

Erath Vineyards

Evesham Wood

The Eyrie Vineyards

Firesteed Cellars

Hinman Vineyards (a.k.a. Silvan Ridge)

Ken Wright Cellars

King Estate (located just south of Willamette Valley)

Kramer Vineyards

Lange Winery

Montinore Vineyards

Oak Knoll Winery

Panther Creek Cellars

Patricia Green Cellars

Ponzi Vineyards

Redhawk Vineyard

Rex Hill Vineyards

Shafer Vineyard

Sokol Blosser Winery

St. Innocent Winery

Stangeland Vineyards

Torii Mor Winery

Tualatin Vineyards

Van Duzer Vineyards

Willakenzie Estates

Willamette Valley Vineyards

Witness Tree Vineyard

Yamhill Valley Vineyards

Two other Oregon wine regions

Two other wine regions of note in Oregon are both in the southwest part of the state: the Umpqua Valley (around the town of Roseburg) and farther south, next to California's northern border, the Rogue River Valley.

Considerably warmer than Willamette, the Umpqua Valley is the site of Oregon's first winery, Hillcrest Vineyard, founded in 1962. The main grape varieties in Umpqua are Pinot Noir, Chardonnay, Riesling, and Cabernet Sauvignon. Major wineries are Henry Estate and Girardet Wine Cellars, known for their Pinot Noir and Chardonnay.

The Rogue River Valley is warmer still; therefore, Cabernet Sauvignon and Merlot often perform better than Pinot Noir there. Chardonnay is the leading white wine, but Pinot Gris is becoming popular. Bridgeview Vineyards, the region's largest winery, is doing an admirable job with Pinot Gris as well as

Pinot Noir. Three other vineyards to watch are Ashland Vineyards, Valley View Winery, and Foris Vineyards — the latter a specialist in Merlot and Cabernet Sauvignon.

Wine on the Desert: Washington State

Although Washington and Oregon are neighboring states, their wine regions have vastly different climates due to the location of the vineyards relative to the Cascade Mountains, which cut through both states from north to south.

On Washington's western, or coastal, side, the climate is maritime — cool, plenty of rain, and lots of vegetation. (In Oregon, almost all the vineyards are located on the coastal side.) East of the mountains, Washington's climate is continental, with hot, very dry summers and cold winters. Most of Washington's vineyards are situated in this area, in the vast, sprawling Columbia and Yakima Valleys.

Washington's winemakers have found that with irrigation, many grapes can flourish in the Washington "desert." The Bordeaux varieties — Merlot, Cabernet Sauvignon, Cabernet Franc, Sauvignon Blanc, and Sémillon — are the name of the game, along with Syrah and the ever-present Chardonnay. Washington first became well-known for the quality of its Merlots. (One winery, Columbia Crest, makes the largest-selling Merlot in the United States in the over-$10 price category.) But lately, Washington's Syrah wines are gaining many of the accolades. In fact, Washington might be the single best region in the U.S. for this exciting varietal wine. Cabernet Sauvignon and Cabernet Franc are also excellent varietal wines in Washington.

Washington does have a few vineyards west of the Cascades, around Puget Sound, where Riesling grows well. In fact, many of the larger wineries, such as Chateau Ste. Michelle and Columbia Winery, are located in the Puget Sound area, near the thriving city of Seattle (but they obtain almost all of their grapes from the Columbia and Yakima Valleys). Selling wine in Seattle is a bit easier than in the desert! Chateau Ste. Michelle, along with the even larger Columbia Crest (both under the same corporate ownership — Stimson Lane), are the giants in the state; they account for over 50 percent of all of Washington's wines at present. Two other large Washington wineries are The Hogue Cellars and Washington Hills Cellars.

Like Oregon, Washington got off to a late start in the wine business. With the exception of Chateau Ste. Michelle and Columbia Winery, both founded in the 1960s, practically none of the current wineries existed as late as 1980. Remarkably, within the past two decades, more than 200 wineries have opened in Washington, making it the U.S.'s second-largest wine producer!

Washington's wine regions

Washington has five major vineyard areas, two very large regions and three small. The five regions, listed according to size, are

✔ **Columbia Valley:** The largest in terms of acreage, this region accounts for over half of Washington's vinifera varieties (see Chapter 4). A large percentage of the state's wineries, even those located in the Puget Sound/Seattle area, use grapes from this region.

✔ **Yakima Valley:** This region is the second largest in acreage; more wineries are actually located here than in the huge Columbia Valley.

✔ **Walla Walla Valley:** Although only 5 percent of the state's *vinifera* grapes grow here, this fast-growing region in the southeast corner of Washington is home to some of the state's top wineries, such as Leonetti Cellar, Woodward Canyon, Waterbrook Winery, Canoe Ridge Vineyard, and L'Ecole # 41.

✔ **Puget Sound:** About 35 wineries are located here, around Seattle. In this cool, moist climate, Pinot Gris and Pinot Noir are the leading varieties.

✔ **Red Mountain:** Washington's newest (2001) and smallest AVA is actually within the Yakima Valley AVA, but its red clay soil and high altitude earned it a separate appellation. About 12 wineries here concentrate on Cabernet Sauvignon, Merlot, and Syrah.

Who's who in Washington

No, we're not talking about cabinet members and senators here! The following are our recommended wine producers in Washington, grouped alphabetically, along with some of their best wines:

✔ **Andrew Will Cellars:** Cabernet Sauvignon, Merlot

✔ **Arbor Crest Wine Cellars:** Sauvignon Blanc, Chardonnay, Riesling

- **Badger Mountain Winery:** Chardonnay, Cabernet Franc
- **Barnard Griffin Winery:** Sémillon, Chardonnay, Fumé Blanc, Merlot
- **Bookwalter Winery:** Cabernet Sauvignon, Merlot
- **Canoe Ridge Vineyard:** Merlot, Chardonnay, Cabernet Sauvignon
- **Chateau Ste. Michelle:** Merlot, Cabernet Sauvignon, Chardonnay (especially Cold Creek Vineyard of all three), "Eroica" Riesling (with Dr. Loosen), Col Solare Meritage (with Antinori)
- **Chinook Wines:** Sauvignon Blanc, Sémillon, Chardonnay
- **Columbia Crest Winery:** Reserve Red (Cabernet-Merlot blend), Sémillon, Syrah, Merlot, Cabernet Sauvignon, Sémillon-Chardonnay
- **Columbia Winery:** Cabernet Sauvignon, Cabernet Franc, Syrah, Merlot (especially Red Willow Vineyard of all four)
- **Covey Run Winery:** Chardonnay, Lemberger
- **DeLille Cellars:** Chaleur Estate (Bordeaux-style blend), Chaleur Estate Blanc (Sauvignon Blanc-Sémillon blend), D2 (second label of Chaleur Estate), Harrison Hill (Cabernet Sauvignon), Syrah
- **DiStefano Winery:** Cabernet Sauvignon
- **L'Ecole #41:** Merlot (Seven Hills), Cabernet Sauvignon, Sémillon
- **Glen Fiona:** Syrah
- **Gordon Brothers Cellars:** Chardonnay, Merlot, Cabernet Sauvignon
- **Hedges Cellars:** Red Mountain Reserve (Bordeaux-style blend), Cabernet/Merlot, Fumé/Chardonnay, Three Vineyard Red
- **The Hogue Cellars:** Merlot, Cabernet Sauvignon (Reserve), Blue Franc (Lemberger), Chenin Blanc, Sémillon-Chardonnay, Sémillon
- **Hoodsport Winery:** Lemberger, Sémillon
- **Hyatt Vineyards:** Merlot, Cabernet Sauvignon
- **Januik Winery:** Merlot, Cabernet Sauvignon
- **Kiona Vineyards:** Lemberger, Cabernet Sauvignon, Merlot
- **Leonetti Cellar:** Cabernet Sauvignon (especially Seven Hills Vineyard), Merlot, Sangiovese
- **Matthews Cellars:** Merlot, Yakima Valley Red (Bordeaux-style blend)
- **McCrea Cellars:** Chardonnay, Syrah
- **Northstar:** Merlot
- **Owen-Sullivan Winery:** Syrah, Cabernet Franc, Merlot
- **Paul Thomas:** Cabernet Sauvignon, Merlot, Chardonnay
- **Pepper Bridge Winery:** Cabernet Sauvignon, Merlot

✓ **Powers Winery:** Cabernet Sauvignon, Merlot, Chardonnay

✓ **Preston Wine Cellars:** Cabernet Sauvignon, Merlot (Reserves)

✓ **Quilceda Creek Vintners:** Cabernet Sauvignon

✓ **Sagelands Vineyard:** Cabernet Sauvignon, Merlot

✓ **Sandhill Winery:** Cabernet Sauvignon, Merlot

✓ **Seven Hills**:** Merlot, Cabernet Sauvignon

✓ **Snoqualmie Vineyards:** Cabernet Sauvignon, Merlot, Syrah

✓ **Tamarack Cellars:** Merlot, Cabernet Sauvignon, Firehouse Red

✓ **Tefft Cellars:** Sangiovese, Cabernet Sauvignon

✓ **Thurston Wolfe Winery:** Syrah

✓ **Washington Hills Cellars:** Cabernet Sauvignon, Merlot, Chardonnay, Sémillon, Cabernet Franc ("Apex" is this winery's premium label; it also uses the "W. B. Bridgman" label)

✓ **Waterbrook Winery:** Cabernet Sauvignon, Merlot, Chardonnay Cabernet Franc, Sauvignon Blanc

✓ **Wineglass Cellars:** Cabernet Sauvignon, Merlot

✓ **Woodward Canyon Winery:** Chardonnay, Cabernet Sauvignon, Merlot

**Seven Hills Winery is actually just across the border in Oregon, but the vineyard is in Walla Walla Valley, Washington.

The Empire State

New York City may be the capital of the world in many ways, but its state's wines do not get the recognition they deserve, perhaps because of California's overwhelming presence in the U.S. market. The oldest continuously operating winery in the United States, Brotherhood Winery, opened its doors in New York's Hudson Valley in 1839. And the largest wine company in the United States, Canandaigua Wine Company (now known as Constellation Brands), has its headquarters in the Finger Lakes. New York is the third largest wine producing state in the U.S.

New York's most important region is the Finger Lakes in western New York, where four large lakes temper the otherwise cool climate. This AVA produces about 80 percent of New York's wines. The other two important regions are the Hudson Valley, along the Hudson River north of New York City, and Long Island, which has three AVAs: North Fork of Long Island (the most important); the Hamptons, on the island's South Fork; and Long Island itself, using grapes from all over Long Island.

In the early days (prior to 1960), most of New York's wines were made from native American varieties, such as Concord, Catawba, Delaware, and Niagara, as well French-American hybrid grapes such as Seyval Blanc, Baco Noir, and Maréchal Foch.

Common wisdom held that the relatively cold New York winters could not support *Vitis vinifera* varieties. But a Russian immigrant, the late, great Dr. Konstantin Frank, proved all the naysayers wrong when he succeeded in growing Riesling (followed by many other vinifera varieties) in 1953 in Hammondsport, in the Finger Lakes region. (The first wines from vinifera grapes were actually made in 1961 at his winery, Dr. Frank's Vinifera Wine Cellars.) Today, his son Willy Frank runs one of the most successful wineries in the state, with an entire line of fine vinifera wines and an excellent sparkling wine.

The Long Island story

This generation's success story in New York wine has taken place on Long Island. In 1973, Alec and Louisa Hargrave got the idea that Long Island's North Fork (about a two-hour drive east of New York City) had the ideal climate and soil for vinifera grapes. Today, Long Island has 28 wineries and is still growing! Like Washington state, Long Island seems particularly suited to Merlot, but Chardonnay, Riesling, Cabernet Sauvignon, Cabernet Franc, and Sauvignon Blanc are also grown, plus some Gewürztraminer and Pinot Noir.

Who's who in New York

The New York wine industry has grown from 19 wineries in 1976 to 169 today — about half of them in the Finger Lakes region, and most of them small, family-run operations. The following are lists of recommended producers in New York's three major wine regions, listed alphabetically.

The Finger Lakes Region

Anthony Road Wine Company	Lakewood Vineyards
Casa Larga Vineyards	Lamoreaux Landing Wine Cellars
Dr. Frank's Vinifera Wine Cellars	Lucas Vineyards
(and its affiliate, Chateau Frank, for sparkling wines)	McGregor Vineyard
Fox Run Vineyards	Prejean Winery
Glenora Wine Cellars (especially for sparkling wines)	Standing Stone
Hazlitt 1852 Vineyards	Swedish Hill Vineyard
Heron Hill Vineyards	Wagner Vineyards
Hunt Country Vineyards	Widmer's Wine Cellars
King Ferry Winery	Hermann J. Wiemer Vineyard
Knapp Vineyards	

Hudson River Valley Region

Adair Vineyards

Baldwin Vineyards

Benmarl Vineyard

Brotherhood America's Oldest Winery, Ltd.

Cascade Mountain Vineyards

Clinton Vineyards

Magnanini Winery

Millbrook Vineyards

Rivendell Winery

Long Island Region

Bedell Cellars

Castello di Borghese/Hargrave Vineyard

Channing Daughters Winery (South Fork)

Corey Creek Vineyards

Duck Walk (South Fork)

Gallucio Estate/Gristina Winery

Jamesport Vineyards

Laurel Lake Vineyards

Lenz Winery

Lieb Family Cellars

Loughlin Vineyards

Manor Hill Vineyards

Martha Clara Vineyards

Macari Vineyards

Old Field Vineyards

Old Brookville-Banfi (Nassau County)

Osprey's Dominion

Palmer Vineyards

Paumanok Vineyards, Ltd.

Peconic Bay Vineyards

Pelligrini Vineyards

Pindar Vineyards

Pugliese Vineyards

Raphael

Schneider Vineyards

Sherwood House Vineyards

Ternhaven Cellars

Wolffer Estate

Oh, Canada

Ask many wine lovers in the U.S. about Canadian wines, and you'll probably get a blank stare in response. Canada's wines are known mainly to Canadians, who consume the bulk of their country's production.

The 1990s brought incredible growth to the Canadian wine industry: The number of wineries grew from 30 to well over 100. Wine is made in four of Canada's provinces, but Ontario has bragging rights as the largest producer, with about 50 percent of the national production. British Columbia ranks second. Quebec and Nova Scotia also produce wine.

To identify and promote wines made entirely from local grapes (some Canadian wineries import wines from other countries to blend with local production), the provinces of Ontario and British Columbia have established an appellation system called VQA, Vintners' Quality Alliance. This system regulates the use of provincial names on wine labels, establishes which grape varieties can be used (vinifera varieties and certain hybrids), regulates the use of the terms *icewine, late harvest,* and *botrytised* (see the "Germany: Europe's Individualist" section in Chapter 12 for an explanation of these terms), and requires wines to pass a taste test.

Ontario

Ontario's vineyards are cool-climate wine zones, despite the fact that they lie on the same parallel as Chianti Classico and Rioja, warmer European wine regions discussed in Chapters 11 and 12. Sixty percent of the production is white wine, from Chardonnay, Riesling, Gewürztraminer, Pinot Blanc, Auxerrois, and the hybrids Seyval Blanc and Vidal. Red wines come from Pinot Noir, Gamay, Cabernet Sauvignon, Cabernet Franc, Merlot, and the hybrids Maréchal Foch and Baco Noir.

Ontario's VQA rules permit the use of the appellation Ontario and also recognize three *Designated Viticultural Areas* (DVAs), listed in order of importance:

- ✔ **Niagara Peninsula:** Along the south shore of Lake Ontario
- ✔ **Pelee Island:** Eleven miles south of the Canadian mainland, in Lake Erie, Canada's most southerly vineyards
- ✔ **Lake Erie North Shore:** The sunniest of Canada's viticultural areas

Because winter temperatures regularly drop well below freezing, icewine is a specialty of Ontario. It is gradually earning the Canadian wine industry international attention, particularly for the wines of Inniskillin Winery.

British Columbia

The rapidly growing wine industry of British Columbia now boasts more than 50 wineries. Production is mainly white wine — from Auxerrois, Bacchus, Chardonnay, Ehrenfelser, Gewürztraminer, Pinot Gris, and Riesling — but red wine production is increasing, mainly from Pinot Noir and Merlot. Bacchus and Ehrenfelser are vinifera crossings developed in Germany.

The Okanagan Valley in southeast British Columbia, where the climate is influenced by Lake Okanagan, is the center of wine production. VQA rules recognize four Designated Viticultural Areas, listed in order of importance:

- ✔ **Okanagan Valley**
- ✔ **Similkameen Valley**
- ✔ **Fraser Valley**
- ✔ **Vancouver Island**

Chapter 15

Bubbling Beauties

In the universe of wine, sparkling wines are a solar system unto themselves. They are produced in just about every country that makes wine, and they come in a wide range of tastes, quality levels, and prices. Champagne, the sparkling wine from the Champagne region of France, is the brightest star in the sky, but by no means the only one.

Sparkling wines are distinguished (and distinguishable) from other wines by the presence of bubbles — *carbon dioxide* — in the wine. In the eyes of most governments, these bubbles must be a natural by-product of fermentation in order for a wine to be officially considered a sparkling wine.

In many wine regions, sparkling wines are just a sideline to complement the region's table wine production, but in some places, sparkling wines are serious business. At the top of that list is France's Champagne region (where sparkling wine was — if not invented — made famous). Italy's Asti wine zone is another important region, as is France's Loire Valley, northeastern Spain, and parts of California. Even Australia, New Zealand, and South Africa are now making some interesting sparklers.

The cool rule

Many sparkling wine regions are very cool areas, where grapes don't ripen sufficiently for *still* (non-sparkling) wine production. Vinified normally, the wines of these regions would be extremely high in acid, disagreeably tart, and very thin; the reds would lack color. But the elaborate process of sparkling wine production (the *traditional method* of production as practiced in the Champagne region, and described later in this chapter) turns the climate's deficits into virtues, and transforms the ugly duckling grapes into graceful swans.

All That Glitters Is Not Champagne

Champagne, the sparkling wine of Champagne, France, is the gold standard of sparkling wines for a number of reasons:

- ✔ Champagne is the most famous sparkling wine in the world; the name has immediate recognition with everyone, not just wine drinkers.
- ✔ A particular technique for making sparkling wine was perfected in the Champagne region.
- ✔ Champagne is not only the finest sparkling wine in the world, but also among the finest wines in the world of any type.

Because of Champagne's fame, the name *champagne* appears on labels of all sorts of sparkling wines that don't come from the Champagne region and that don't taste like Champagne. Wine producers use the name "champagne" to make their sparkling wines more saleable; many wine drinkers themselves use the word "champagne" indiscriminately to refer to all wines that have bubbles.

Ironically, much of the sparkling wine sold in the U.S. that's called "champagne" is not even made with the same techniques as true Champagne. Most imitation champagnes are made by a technique that takes only a few months from beginning to end (compared to a few years to make Champagne), costs less to the winery, and works more effectively on an industrial scale.

Within the European Union, only the wines of the Champagne region in France can use the name Champagne.

Whenever we use the word Champagne, we'll be referring to true Champagne, from the region of the same name; we use the generic term *sparkling wine* to refer to bubbly wines collectively, and sparkling wines other than Champagne.

Sparkling Wine Styles

All sparkling wines have bubbles, and nearly all of them are either white or pink (which is far less common than white). That's about as far as broad generalizations will take us in describing sparkling wines.

Some sparkling wines are downright sweet, some are bone dry, and many fall somewhere in the middle, from medium-dry to medium-sweet. Some have toasty, nutty flavors and some are fruity; among those that are fruity, some are just nondescriptly grapey, while others have delicate nuances of lemons, apples, cherries, berries, peaches, and other fruits.

The sparkling wines of the world fall into two broad types, according to how they're made:

- ✔ Wines that express the character of their grapes; these wines tend to be fruity and straightforward, without layers of complexity.

- ✔ Wines that express complexity and flavors (yeasty, biscuity, caramel-like, honeyed) that derive from winemaking and aging, rather than expressing overt fruitiness.

How sweet is it?

Nearly all sparkling wines are not technically dry, because they contain measurable amounts of residual sugar, usually as the result of sweetening added at the last stage of production. But all sparkling wines don't necessarily taste sweet. The perception of sweetness depends on two factors: the actual amount of sweetness in the wine (which varies according to the wine's style) and the wine's balance between acidity and sweetness.

Here's how the balance factor operates. Sparkling wines are usually very high in acidity, because the grapes weren't particularly ripe at harvest (having grown in a cool climate). The wine's carbon dioxide also gives an acidic impression in the mouth. But the wine's sweetness counterbalances its acidity and vice versa. Depending on the particular acid/sugar balance a sparkling wine strikes, the wine might taste dry, very slightly sweet, medium sweet, or quite sweet.

Champagne itself is made in a range of sweetness levels, the most common of which is a dry style called *brut* (see "Sweetness categories" later in this chapter). Sparkling wines made by the *traditional method* used in Champagne (see "How Sparkling Wine Happens" later in this chapter) are made in the same range of styles as Champagne.

Inexpensive sparkling wines tend to be medium sweet in order to appeal to a mass market that enjoys sweetness. Wines labeled with the Italian word *spumante* tend to be overtly sweet. (See the section "Italian spumante: Sweet or dry," later in this chapter.)

How good is it?

When you taste a sparkling wine, the most important consideration is whether you like it — just as for a still wine. If you want to evaluate a sparkling wine the way professionals do, however, you have to apply a few criteria that don't apply to still wines (or are less critical in still wines than in sparkling wines). Some of those criteria are

✔ **The appearance of the bubbles.** In the best sparkling wines, the bubbles are tiny and float upward in a continuous stream from the bottom of your glass. If the bubbles are large and random, you have a clue that the wine is a lesser-quality sparkler. If you don't see many bubbles at all, you could have a bad bottle, a poor or smudged glass, or a wine that may be too old.

Tiny variations in glassware can drastically affect the flow of bubbles — even if two glasses appear identical. If the wine in your glass looks almost flat, but another glass of wine from the same bottle is lively with bubbles, blame the glass and not the wine. (In this case, you should be able to *taste* the bubbles, even if you can't *see* many of them.) See Chapter 8 for our recommendations about glasses for Champagne and other sparkling wines.

✔ **The feel of the bubbles in your mouth.** The finer the wine, the less aggressive the bubbles feel in your mouth. (If the bubbles remind you of a soft drink, we hope you didn't pay more than $5 for the wine.)

✔ **The balance between sweetness and acidity.** Even if a bubbly wine is too sweet or too dry for your taste, to evaluate its quality you should consider its sweetness/acid ratio and decide whether these two elements seem reasonably balanced.

✔ **The texture.** Traditional-method sparkling wines should be somewhat creamy in texture as a result of their extended lees aging. (See the next section for an explanation of *traditional method* and *lees*.)

✔ **The finish.** Any impression of bitterness on the finish of a sparkling wine is a sign of low quality.

How Sparkling Wine Happens

When yeasts convert sugar into alcohol, carbon dioxide is a natural by-product. If fermentation takes place in a closed container that prevents this carbon dioxide from escaping into the air, the wine becomes sparkling. With nowhere else to go, the carbon dioxide (CO_2) becomes trapped in the wine in the form of bubbles.

Most sparkling wines actually go through *two* fermentations: one to turn the grape juice into still wine without bubbles (that's called a *base wine*) and a subsequent one to turn the still wine into bubbly wine (conveniently called the *second fermentation*). The winemaker has to instigate the second fermentation by adding yeasts and sugar to the base wine. The added yeasts convert the added sugar into alcohol and CO_2 bubbles.

Beginning with the second fermentation, the longer and slower the wine-making process, the more complex and expensive the sparkling wine will be. Some sparkling wines are ten years in the making; others are produced in only a few months. The slow-route wines can cost more than $100 a bottle, while bubblies at the opposite end of the spectrum can sell for as little as $4.

Although many variations exist, most sparkling wines are produced in one of two ways: through *second fermentation in a tank,* or through *second fermentation in a bottle.*

Economy of scale

The quickest, most efficient way of making a sparkling wine involves conducting the second fermentation in large, closed, pressurized tanks. This method is called the *bulk method, tank method, cuve close* (meaning *closed tank* in French), or *charmat method* (after a Frenchman named Eugene Charmat, who championed this process).

Sparkling wines made in the charmat (pronounced *shar mah*) method are usually the least expensive. That's because they're ready for sale soon after harvest and they're usually made in large quantities. Also, the grapes used in making sparkling wine by the charmat method (Chenin Blanc, for example) are usually *far* less expensive than the Pinot Noir and Chardonnay typically used in the *traditional* or *champagne method* described in the next section.

The following occurs in the charmat method:

✔ A base wine is *seeded* with sugar and yeast, and it ferments. The carbon dioxide created by the fermentation becomes trapped in the wine, thanks to the closed tank, the pressure within the tank, and the cold temperature.

✔ The wine — now a dry sparkling wine with higher alcohol than the base wine had — is filtered (under pressure) to remove the solid deposits (the *lees*) from the second fermentation.

✔ Before bottling, some sweetness is added to adjust the wine's flavor, according to the desired style of the final wine.

The whole process can take just a few weeks. In some exceptional cases, it might be extended to a few months, allowing the wine to rest between the fermentation and the filtration.

Small is beautiful

The charmat method is a fairly new way of producing sparkling wines, dating back barely 100 years. The more traditional method is to conduct the second fermentation in the individual bottles in which the wine is later sold.

Champagne has been made in this way for over 300 years and, according to French law, can be made in no other way. Many other French sparkling wines use the same process, as do the best sparkling wines from Spain, California, and elsewhere.

The technique of conducting the second fermentation in the bottle is called the *classic* or *traditional method* in Europe; in the U.S., it's called the *champagne method* or *méthode champenoise*.

Bottle fermentation (or, more correctly, second fermentation in the bottle) is an elaborate process in which every single bottle becomes an individual fermentation tank, so to speak. Including the aging time at the winery before the wine is sold, this process requires a minimum of fifteen months and usually takes three years or more. Invariably, bottle-fermented sparkling wines are more expensive than tank-fermented bubblies.

The elements of bottle fermentation are as follows:

✔ Each bottle is filled with a mixture of base wine and a sugar-and-yeast solution, closed securely, and laid to rest in a cool, dark cellar.

✔ The second fermentation slowly occurs inside each bottle, producing carbon dioxide and fermentation lees.

✔ As the bottles lie in the cellar, the interaction of the lees and the wine gradually changes the wine's texture and flavor.

✔ Eventually — 12 months to several years after the second fermentation — the bottles undergo a process of shaking and turning so that the lees fall to the neck of each upside-down bottle.

- ✔ The lees are flash-frozen in the neck of each bottle and expelled from the bottle as a frozen plug, leaving clear sparkling wine behind.

- ✔ A sweetening solution (called a *dosage*) is added to adjust the flavor of the wine, and the bottles are corked and labeled for sale.

Actually, the classic method as practiced in Champagne involves several processes that occur way before the second fermentation. For example, the pressing to extract the juice from the grapes must be gentle and meticulous to prevent the grapeskins' bitter flavors — and their color, in the case of black grapes — from passing into the juice. Another step crucially important to the quality of the sparkling wine is blending various wines after the first fermentation to create the best composite base wine for the second fermentation.

After the first fermentation, each Champagne house has hundreds of different still wines, because the winemaker keeps the wines of different grape varieties and different vineyards separate. To create his base wine, or *cuvée,* he blends these wines in varying proportions, often adding some *reserve wine* (older wine purposely held back from previous vintages). More than 100 different wines could go into a single base wine, each bringing its own special character to the blend. What's particularly tricky about blending the base wine — besides the sheer volume of components in the blend — is that the winemaker has to see into the future and create a blend *not* for its flavor today but for how it will taste in several years, after it has been transformed into a sparkling wine. The men and women who blend sparkling wines are true artists of the wine world.

Taste: The proof of the pudding

Tank-fermented sparklers tend to be fruitier than traditional-method sparkling wines. This difference occurs because in tank fermentation, the route from grape to wine is shorter and more direct than in bottle fermentation. Some winemakers use the *charmat,* or tank, method because their goal is a fresh and fruity sparkling wine. Asti, Italy's most famous sparkling wine, is a perfect example. You should drink charmat-method sparklers young, when their fruitiness is at its max.

Second fermentation in the bottle makes wines that tend to be less overtly fruity than charmat-method wines. Chemical changes that take place as the wine develops on its fermentation lees diminish the fruitiness of the wine and contribute aromas and flavors such as toastiness, nuttiness, caramel, and yeastiness. The texture of the wine can also change, becoming smooth and creamy. The bubbles themselves tend to be tinier, and they feel less aggressive in your mouth than the bubbles of tank-fermented wines.

Champagne and Its Magic Wines

Champagne. Does any other word convey such a sense of celebration? Think of it: Whenever people, in any part of the world, want to celebrate, you might hear them say, "This calls for Champagne!" ("This calls for iced tea!" just isn't quite the same.)

Champagne, the real thing, comes only from the region of Champagne (*sham pahn yah*) in northeast France. Dom Pérignon, the famous monk who was cellar master at the Abbey of Hautvillers, didn't invent Champagne, but he did achieve a number of breakthroughs that are key to making Champagne as we now know it. He perfected the method of making white wine from black grapes, for example, and, most importantly, he mastered the art of blending wines from different grapes and different villages to achieve a complex base wine. (See the previous section to find out what "base" wine is.)

Champagne is the most northerly vineyard area in France. Most of the important Champagne *houses* (as Champagne producers are called) are located in the cathedral city of Rheims (French spelling, *Reims*) — where 17-year-old Joan of Arc had Prince Charles crowned King of France in 1429 — and in the town of Epernay, south of Rheims. Around Rheims and Epernay are the main vineyard areas, where three permitted grape varieties (two black and one white) for Champagne flourish. These areas are

- ✔ The Montagne de Reims (south of Rheims), where the best Pinot Noir grows
- ✔ The Côte des Blancs (south of Epernay), home of the best Chardonnay
- ✔ The Valleé de la Marne (west of Epernay), most favorable to Pinot Meunier (a black grape) although all three grape varieties grow there

Most Champagne is made from all three grape varieties. Pinot Noir contributes body, structure, and longevity to the blend; Chardonnay offers delicacy, freshness, and elegance; and Pinot Meunier provides precocity, floral aromas, and fruitiness.

What makes Champagne special

The cool climate in Champagne is marginal for grape growing, and the grapes struggle to ripen sufficiently in some years. Even in warmer years, the climate dictates that the grapes will always be high in acidity — a sorry state for table wine but perfect for sparkling wine.

The cool climate and the region's chalky, limestone soil are the leading factors contributing to Champagne's excellence.

Three other elements help distinguish Champagne from all other sparkling wines:

- The number and diversity of vineyards (over 300 *crus,* or individual vineyards), which provide a huge range of unique wines for blending

- The cold, deep, chalky cellars (many built during Roman times) in which Champagnes age for many years

- The 300 years of experience the *Champenois* (as the good citizens of Champagne are called) have in making sparkling wine

The result is an elegant sparkling wine with myriad tiny, gentle bubbles, complexity of flavors, and a lengthy finish. Voilá! Champagne!

Non-vintage Champagne

Non-vintage (NV) Champagne — any Champagne without a vintage year on the label — accounts for 85 percent of all Champagne. Its typical blend is two-thirds black grapes (Pinot Noir and Pinot Meunier) and one-third white (Chardonnay). Wine from three or more harvests usually goes into the blend. And remember, the wines from as many as 30 or 40 different villages (or more) from each year can also be part of the blend. The Champagne winemaker is by necessity a master blender.

Each Champagne house blends to suit its own house style for its non-vintage Champagne. (For example, one house may seek elegance and finesse in its wine, another might opt for fruitiness, and a third might value body, power, and longevity.) Maintaining a consistent house style is vital because wine drinkers get accustomed to their favorite Champagne's taste and expect to find it year after year.

Most major Champagne houses age their non-vintage Champagne for two and one-half to three years before selling it, even though the legal minimum for non-vintage is just 15 months. The extra aging prolongs the marrying time for the blend and enhances the wine's flavor and complexity. If you have good storage conditions (see Chapter 21), aging your non-vintage Champagne for one to three years after you purchase it will usually improve the flavor, in our opinion.

Most non-vintage Champagnes sell for $25 to $45 a bottle. Often, a large retailer will buy huge quantities of a few major brands, obtaining a good discount that he passes on to his customers. Seeking out stores that do a large-volume business with Champagne is worth your while.

Vintage Champagne

In about five of every ten years, the weather in Champagne is good enough to make a Vintage Champagne — that is, the grapes are ripe enough that some wine can be made entirely from the grapes of that year without being blended with reserve wines from previous years.

Champagne had exceptionally good weather in the 1980s; many houses made Vintage Champagne every year from 1981 to 1990, with the exception of 1984 and 1987. The decade of the '90s was more typical; four years — 1991, 1992, 1993 and 1994 — are of unremarkable quality, while 1995 and especially 1996 are of vintage quality. Just about all Champagne houses have made both 1995 and 1996 Vintage Champagnes. It's too early to be certain of the ultimate quality of the vintages from 1997 through 2000, but 1998 looks remarkable, on the level of 1996 or even better; the other three vintages appear to be average to good.

Champagne houses decide for themselves each year whether to make a Vintage Champagne. Factors that a house might take into consideration — besides the quality of the vintage — include the need to save some wine to use as reserve wines for their non-vintage Champagnes (85 percent of their business, after all), and/or whether a particular vintage's style suits the "house style." For example, although 1989 was a rather good vintage, a few houses decided that Champagnes made from this vintage would be too soft (low in acidity) and/or too precocious (lacking longevity) for them, and did not choose to make a Vintage Champagne in 1989.

The minimum aging requirement for Vintage Champagne is three years, but many houses age their Vintage Champagnes four to six years in order to enhance the wines' flavor and complexity. Vintage Champagnes fall into two categories:

- ✔ Regular vintage, with a price range of $35 to $60 a bottle; these wines simply carry a vintage date in addition to the name of the house.

- ✔ Premium vintage (also known as a *prestige cuvée* or *tête de cuvée*), such as Moët & Chandon's Dom Pérignon, Roederer's Cristal, or Veuve Clicquot's La Grande Dame; the typical price for prestige cuvées ranges from $60 to well over $100 per bottle.

Vintage Champagne is invariably superior to non-vintage for the following reasons:

- ✔ The best grapes from the choicest vineyards are put into Vintage Champagne (this is *especially* so for prestige cuvées).

- ✔ Usually, only the two finest varieties (Pinot Noir and Chardonnay) are used in Vintage Champagne. Pinot Meunier is saved mainly for non-vintage Champagne.

✔ Most Champagne houses age Vintage Champagnes at least two years more than their non-vintage wines. The extra aging assures more complexity.

✔ The grapes all come from a year that's above average, at least — or superb, at best.

Vintage Champagne is more intense in flavor than non-vintage Champagne. It is fuller-bodied and more complex, and its flavors last longer in your mouth. Being fuller and richer, these Champagnes are best with food. Non-vintage Champagnes — being lighter, fresher, and less complicated — are suitable as apéritifs, and they are good values. Whether a Vintage Champagne is worth its extra cost or not is a judgment you have to make for yourself.

Blanc de blancs and blanc de noirs

A small number of Champagnes derive only from Chardonnay; that type of Champagne is called *blanc de blancs* — literally, "white (wine) from white (grapes)." A blanc de blancs can be a Vintage Champagne or a non-vintage. It usually costs a few dollars more than other Champagnes in its category. Because they are generally lighter and more delicate than other Champagnes, blanc de blancs make ideal apéritifs. Not every Champagne house makes a blanc de blancs. Four of the best, all Vintage Champagnes, are Taittinger Comte de Champagne, Billecart-Salmon Blanc de Blancs, Deutz Blanc de Blancs, and Pol Roger Blanc de Chardonnay.

Blanc de noirs Champagne (made entirely from black grapes, often just Pinot Noir) is rare but does exist. Bollinger's Blanc de Noirs *Vieilles Vignes Francaises* ("old vines") is absolutely the best, but it is very expensive (about $300) and hard to find. The 1985 Bollinger Blanc de Noirs is one of the two best Champagnes we've ever had; the other is the 1928 Krug.

Rosé Champagne

Rosé Champagnes — pink Champagnes — can also be vintage or non-vintage. Usually, Pinot Noir and Chardonnay are the only grapes used, in proportions that vary from one house to the next.

Winemakers create a rosé Champagne usually by including some red Pinot Noir wine in the blend for the base wine. A few actually vinify some of their red grapes into pink wines, the way that you would make a rosé still wine, and use that as the base wine. Colors vary quite a lot, from pale onion-skin to salmon to rosy pink. (The lighter-colored ones are usually better quality.)

Rosés are fuller and rounder than other Champagnes and are best enjoyed with dinner. (Because they have become associated with romance, they're popular choices for wedding anniversaries and Valentine's Day.)

Refrigerator blues

Don't leave your Champagne — or any other good sparkling wine — in your refrigerator for more than a few days! Its flavor will become flat from the excessively cold temperature. Also, long-term vibrations caused by the cycling on and off of the refrigerator motor are not good for any wine — especially sparkling wine. (See Chapter 21 for more on storing your wine properly.)

Like blanc de blancs Champagnes, rosés usually cost a few dollars more than regular Champagnes, and not every Champagne house makes one. Some of the best rosés are those of Roederer, Billecart-Salmon, Gosset, and Moët & Chandon (especially its Dom Pérignon Rosé).

For some people, rosé Champagne has a bad connotation because of the tons of sweet, insipid, cheap pink wines — sparkling and otherwise — on the market. But rosé Champagne is just as dry and has the same high quality as regular (white) Champagne.

Sweetness categories

Champagnes always carry an indication of their sweetness on the label, but the words used to indicate sweetness are cryptic: extra dry is not really dry, for example. In ascending order of sweetness, Champagnes are labeled

- **Extra brut, brut nature,** or **brut sauvage:** Totally dry
- **Brut:** Dry
- **Extra dry:** Medium dry
- **Sec:** Slightly sweet
- **Demi-sec:** Fairly sweet
- **Doux:** Sweet

The most popular style for Champagne and other serious bubblies is brut. However, the single best-selling Champagne in the U.S., Moët & Chandon's White Star, actually is an extra dry Champagne. Brut, extra dry, and demi-sec are the three types of Champagne you find almost exclusively nowadays.

Who's drinking Champagne

Not surprisingly, France leads the world in Champagne consumption, drinking almost twice as much as the rest of the world put together. The UK is the leading foreign market for Champagne. The U.S. is second, and Germany is third, followed by Belgium, Switzerland, and Italy. But the U.S. buys the most prestige cuvée Champagne, especially Dom Pérignon.

Recommended Champagne producers

The Champagne business — especially the export end of it — is dominated by about 25 or 30 large houses, most of whom purchase from independent growers the majority of grapes they need to make their Champagne. Of the major houses, only Roederer and Bollinger own most of the vineyards from which they get their grapes — a definite economic and quality-control advantage for them.

Moët & Chandon is by far the largest Champagne house. In terms of worldwide sales, the next-largest houses are Veuve Clicquot, Mumm, Vranken, Laurent-Perrier, Pommery, and Lanson. The following lists name some of our favorite producers, grouped according to the style of their Champagne: light-bodied, medium-bodied, or full-bodied. (For an understanding of the term *body* as it applies to wine, see Chapter 2.)

Light, elegant styles

Laurent-Perrier
Taittinger
Ruinart
Jacquesson*
Pommery
Piper-Heidsieck

G.H. Mumm
Bruno Paillard*
Perrier-Jouët
J. Lassalle*
Billecart-Salmon

Medium-bodied styles

Charles Heidsieck
Pol Roger
Moët & Chandon

Deutz
Cattier*
Philipponnat

Full-bodied styles

Krug
Louis Roederer
Bollinger
Gosset
Veuve Clicquot

Alfred Gratien*
Delamotte
Salon*
Paul Bara*

* Small producer; may be difficult to find.

Madame Lily Bollinger's advice on drinking Champagne

When Jacques Bollinger died in 1941, his widow, Lily Bollinger, carried her famous Champagne house through the difficult years of the German occupation of France. She ran the company until her death in 1977. Bollinger prospered under her leadership, doubling in size. She was a beloved figure in Champagne, where she could be seen bicycling through the vineyards every day. In 1961, when a London reporter asked her when she drank Champagne, Madame Bollinger replied:

"I only drink Champagne when I'm happy, and when I'm sad. Sometimes I drink it when I'm alone. When I have company I consider it obligatory. I trifle with it if I am not hungry and drink it when I am. Otherwise I never touch it — unless I'm thirsty."

The redoubtable Madame Lily Bollinger died at the age of 78, apparently none the worse for all that Champagne.

The following list names, in rough order of preference, Champagne houses whose vintage and prestige cuvées have been in top form lately. (For more info on Champagne, see Ed McCarthy's *Champagne For Dummies,* John Wiley Publishing, Inc.).

- **Krug:** Grande Cuvée; Vintage; NV Rosé; Clos du Mesnil
- **Louis Roederer:** Cristal
- **Bollinger:** Grande Année; Blanc de Noirs Vieilles Vignes
- **Moët & Chandon:** Dom Pérignon
- **Veuve Clicquot:** Vintage; La Grande Dame
- **Pommery:** Cuvée Louise; Cuvée Louise Rosé
- **Gosset:** Celebris; Celebris Rosé; NV Grande Réserve
- **Philipponnat:** Clos des Goisses
- **Pol Roger:** Cuvée Sir Winston Churchill
- **Salon:** Vintage Blanc de Blancs
- **Taittinger:** Comtes de Champagne; Comtes de Champagne Rosé
- **Billecart-Salmon:** Blanc de Blancs; Cuvée Elisabeth Salmon Rosé
- **Alfred Gratien:** Cuvée Paradis (NV)
- **Laurent-Perrier:** Grand Siècle
- **Cattier:** Clos du Moulin (NV)

> ✔ **Jacquesson:** Signature; Signature Rosé
>
> ✔ **Deutz:** Cuvée William Deutz; Cuvée William Deutz Rosé
>
> ✔ **Perrier-Jouët:** Fleur de Champagne; Fleur de Champagne Rosé
>
> ✔ **Ruinart:** Dom Ruinart Blanc de Blancs
>
> ✔ **Lanson:** Noble Cuvée
>
> ✔ **Charles Heidsieck:** Blanc des Millenaires
>
> ✔ **Piper-Heidsieck:** Champagne Rare

Other Sparkling Wines

Wineries all over the world have adopted the techniques used in the Champagne region to make sparkling wines that emulate Champagne. These wines differ from Champagne, however, because their grapes are not grown in the terroir of the Champagne region and because, in some cases, their grapes are not even the same varieties as those used in Champagne. Other sparkling wines are made using the tank fermentation rather than the bottle fermentation method specifically to attain a certain style, or to reduce production costs.

French sparkling wine

France makes many other sparkling wines besides Champagne, especially in the Loire Valley, around Saumur, and in the regions of Alsace and Burgundy. Sparkling wine made by the traditional method (second fermentation in the bottle) often carries the name *Crémant,* as in Crémant d'Alsace, Crémant de Loire, Crémant de Bourgogne, and so on. Grape varieties are those typical of each region (see Chapter 10).

Some of the leading brands of French sparkling wines are Langlois-Château, Bouvet Ladubay, Gratien & Meyer (all from the Loire Valley), Brut d'Argent, Kriter, and Saint Hilaire. These wines sell for $10 to $15 and are decent. They're perfect for parties and other large gatherings, when you might want to serve a French bubbly without paying a Champagne price. (For more info on French sparkling wines, see *French Wine For Dummies.*)

American sparkling wine

Sparkling wine is made in almost as many states as still wine is, but California and New York are the most famous for it. Two fine producers of New York

State sparkling wines in the traditional method are Chateau Frank and Lamoreaux Landing, both under $20.

A sparkling wine deserving special mention — which hails, improbably, from New Mexico — is Gruet. Owned by France's little-known Champagne Gruet, the New Mexican winery makes three excellent bubblies, a NV Brut and NV Blanc de Noirs, both about $18, and a Vintage Blanc de Blancs, $24.

California bubbly is definitely a different wine from Champagne, even when made by a Champagne house using the same methods and the same grape varieties as in Champagne. (It tastes fruitier.) Good California sparkling wines, the ones made in the traditional Champagne method, cost as little as $15 on up to $30 or more.

Most of California's finest sparkling wines do not call themselves Champagne, but the less-expensive, best-selling ones do. In that second category, Korbel, at about $15, is the only brand that is actually fermented in the bottle.

We recommend the following California sparkling wine producers, listed in our rough order of preference within each category:

U.S.-owned

- ✔ **Iron Horse:** In Green Valley, the coolest part of Sonoma (temperature-wise, that is), Iron Horse is clearly making some of California's finest sparkling wine. Look for its better cuvées, such as the Wedding Cuvée, Russian Cuvée, and Vrai Amis, for about $25. Iron Horse's top-of-the-line sparklers, the Late Disgorged Blanc de Blancs and Late Disgorged Brut, are truly superb, comparable in quality to fine Champagne; they are about $45.

- ✔ **J:** Not content with making some of America's most popular Cabernet Sauvignons and Chardonnays, the Jordan winery in Sonoma now also makes one of the best sparkling wines in the country. And the wine keeps getting better. Now, almost all of its grapes come from the cool Russian River Valley. Quite fruity and fairly delicate, the wine comes in a knockout bottle and sells for $25 to $30.

- ✔ **S. Anderson:** In Napa Valley, S. Anderson continues to produce one of the finest lines of sparkling wines in the U.S. for about $25; look especially for its Blanc de Noirs.

- ✔ **Handley Cellars:** Up in Anderson Valley in Mendocino County, Milla Handley makes some excellent, quite dry sparkling wines; her Rosé Brut is a beauty, at about $25.

French- or Spanish-owned

- **Roederer Estate:** Louis Roederer is such a fine Champagne house that we're not surprised at the smashing success its Anderson Valley winery, near the town of Mendocino, has achieved. Some critics think it's California's best. Wines include a good-value Brut ($24), a delicate rosé ($30) that's worth seeking out, and an outstanding premium cuvée, L'Ermitage ($45).

- **Mumm Cuvée Napa:** Mumm has established itself as one of California's best sparkling wine houses. Much of its production comes from the cool Carneros District; look especially for the Winery Lake Brut and the cherry-like Blanc de Noirs. The price range is $23 to $25.

- **Domaine Carneros:** Taittinger's California winery makes an elegant, high-quality brut ($24 to $26) in cool Carneros. Its premium cuvée, Le Rêve, a $50 blanc de blancs, is stunning.

- **Domaine Chandon:** This Napa Valley winery is part of the Moët & Chandon empire. A must-stop for its restaurant alone, Chandon continues to make solid, consistent sparkling wines at reasonable prices ($15 to $18). Look especially for its premium Etoile (about $30), one of the most elegant sparkling wines in the U.S., and the delicious Etoile Rosé ($35).

- **Gloria Ferrer:** Spain's Freixenet company has built a beautiful winery in windswept Carneros. Its wines are priced right ($18 to $25) and are widely available. The winery is definitely worth a visit.

- **Pacific Echo:** From the cool Anderson Valley, Pacific Echo, owned by Veuve Clicquot, makes a Blanc de Blancs and a Private Reserve that are especially fine ($18 to $25).

Italian spumante: Sweet or dry

Spumante is simply the Italian word for "sparkling," but it has come to refer to sweet, fruity spin-offs of Italy's classic Asti Spumante. Actually, Italy is the home of many fine, dry spumante wines and a popular, slightly sparkling wine called *Prosecco,* as well as sweet spumante. (For more info on Italian sparkling wines, see *Italian Wine For Dummies.*)

Asti and Moscato d'Asti

Asti is a delicious, fairly sweet, exuberantly fruity sparkling wine made in the Piedmont region from Moscato grapes, via the tank method. It's one bubbly that you can drink with dessert (fantastic with wedding cake!). Because freshness is essential in Asti, buy a good brand that sells well. (Asti is not vintage-dated, and so there's no other way to determine how old the wine is.) We recommend Fontanafredda (about $14 to $15), Martini & Rossi ($12), Cinzano, and Gancia (the last two $8 to $9).

For Asti flavor with fewer bubbles, try Moscato d'Asti, a delicate and delicious medium-dry vintage-dated *frizzante* (slightly sparkling wine) that makes a refreshing apéritif. It's also good with dessert and is a great brunch wine. And it has less than 7 percent alcohol! Vietti makes a good one, called Cascinetta, for about $12. Other good producers of Moscato d'Asti are Dante Rivetti, Paolo Sarocco, and Ceretto, whose wine is called Santo Stefano; all of these sell for $12 to $15. Again, freshness is essential. With Moscato d'Asti, let the vintage date guide you; buy the youngest one you can find.

Dry spumante

Using the traditional method, Italy produces a good deal of dry sparkling wine in the Oltrepò-Pavese and Franciacorta wine zones of Lombardy, as well as in Trentino. Italy's dry sparkling wines are very dry with little or no sweetening dosage. They come in all price ranges. Affordable wines include Gancia Brut ($10) and Berlucchi Cuvée Imperiale Brut ($15); good medium-priced wines are Ferrari Brut and Banfi Brut (at about $20). Four upscale (and very good) bruts, all $35 to $40 and up, are Bellavista, Cà del Bosco, Giulio Ferrari, and Bruno Giacosa Extra Brut. Giacosa, well-known for his outstanding Barbarescos and Barolos, makes his 100-percent-Pinot Noir Brut in his spare time, for kicks. Like everything else he produces, it's superb.

Prosecco

This quintessential Italian sparkling wine has become all the rage in parts of the U.S., thanks to the fact that so many Italian restaurants serve it by the glass. Prosecco comes from Prosecco grapes grown near Venice and Treviso. It's a straightforward, pleasant apéritif, low in alcohol (about 11 percent), and it comes in dry, off-dry, and sweet styles. Prosecco is available mainly as a frizzante wine, but it also comes as a spumante (fully sparkling), or even as a non-sparkling wine (which we don't recommend; it's better with bubbles). If you want the driest version, look for Prosecco that's labeled "Extra Dry" or "Extra Brut"; in Italy, unlike France, "extra dry" means exactly that.

Prosecco is the perfect wine to have with Italian antipasto, such as pickled vegetables, calamari, anchovies, or spicy salami. Its fresh, fruity flavors cleanse your mouth and get your appetite going for dinner. Most Prosecco bears the DOC appellation of either Valdobbiadene or Conegliano (or, in some cases, both), which are two villages in the Veneto. The best news is that Prosecco is eminently affordable: It retails for $10 to $18 a bottle. Recommended producers (alphabetically) include Astoria, Bisson, Canevel, Carpenè Malvolti, Mionetto, Nino Franco, Valdo, Zardetto, and Zonin.

Spanish sparkling wines (Cava)

What if you want to spend about $10 or less for a decent sparkling wine? The answer is Spain's sparkling wine, Cava, which sells mainly for $8 to $12 a bottle. Almost all of it comes from the Penedés region, near Barcelona.

Cava is made in the traditional method, fermented in the bottle. But most Cavas use local Spanish grapes. As a result, they taste distinctly different (a nicely earthy, mushroomy flavor) from California bubblies and from Champagne. Some of the more expensive blends do contain Chardonnay.

Two gigantic wineries dominate Cava production — Freixenet (pronounced *fresh net*) and Codorniu. Freixenet's frosted black Cordon Negro bottle has to be one of the most recognizable wine bottles in the world. Other Cava brands to look for are Mont Marçal, Paul Cheneau, Cristalino, Marqués de Monistrol, and Segura Viudas. Juve y Camps, a vintage-dated, upscale Cava, is a worthwhile buy at $15.

Southern stars

Australia, New Zealand, and South Africa now make some very fine sparkling wines in the traditional method. Australia boasts a really good $10 sparkler called Seaview Brut; for something completely unusual, try Seaview's deep red sparkling Shiraz, about $12. Among New Zealand bubblies, one of the finest is that of Highfield Estate in Marlborough. The South African sparkling brut that has really impressed us comes from the Boschendal Estate in the Franschhoek Valley and is called Le Grand Pavillion (about $12 to $13). Traditional-method South African sparkling wines carry the words *Cap Classique* on their labels.

Serving Champagne and Sparkling Wines

Sparkling wine is best cold, about 45°F (7° to 8°C), although some people prefer it less cold (52°F; 11°C). We like the colder temperature because it helps the wine hold its effervescence — and the wine warms up so quickly in the glass, anyway. Because older Champagnes and Vintage Champagnes are more complex, you can chill them less than young, non-vintage Champagne or sparkling wine.

Never leave an open bottle of sparkling wine on the table unless it's in an ice bucket (half cold water, half ice) because it will warm up quickly. Use a sparkling wine stopper to keep leftover bubbly fresh for a couple of days (in the fridge, of course).

Baby Champagnes are "in"

Although Champagnes in small bottles — 375 ml half-bottles and 187 ml splits — normally don't stay as fresh as Champagne in larger bottles, when they sell quickly, size becomes less of an issue. A few savvy Champagne houses have thought of a novel idea for selling their bubblies in the U.S.: Attractively package their Champagnes in small bottles, and make them readily available in nightclubs and bars where young people congregate. A few years ago, Pommery introduced its "POP," a bright blue half-bottle that comes with a straw so that you can even drink it right out of the bottle. It's an extra-dry non-vintage Champagne, not quite as dry as a brut, which suits the casual occasions when this wine is drunk. Not to be outdone, Piper-Heidsieck followed with a bright red split of its non-vintage brut, which it calls "Baby Piper." Both Champagnes have been selling very well, even in the slow economy. Perrier-Jouët is now aggressively marketing its half-bottles and splits; ditto Lanson with its half-bottles, and more houses will surely follow.

Although Champagne is a serious wine, it obviously offers plenty of opportunity for fun!

If you're entertaining, you should know that the ideal bottle size for Champagne is the *magnum,* which is equivalent to two bottles. The larger bottle enables the wine to age more gently in the winery's cellar. Magnums (and sometimes double magnums) are usually the largest bottles in which Champagne is fermented; all larger bottles have had finished Champagne poured into them, and the wine is therefore not as fresh as it is in a magnum or a regular bottle.

Be wary of half-bottles (375 ml) and — worse yet — splits (187 ml)! Champagne in these small bottles is often not fresh. (If you're given a small bottle of Champagne or any sparkling wine as a wedding favor, for example, open it at the first excuse; do not keep it around for a year waiting for the right occasion!)

Champagne and other good, dry sparkling wines are extremely versatile with food — and they are the essential wine for certain kinds of foods. For example, no wine goes better with egg dishes than Champagne. Indulge yourself next time that you have brunch. And when you're having spicy Asian cuisine, try sparkling wine. For us, no wine goes better with spicy Chinese or Indian food!

Fish, seafood, pasta (but not with tomato sauce), risotto, and poultry are excellent with Champagne and sparkling wine. If you're having lamb (pink, not well-done) or ham, pair rosé Champagne with it. With aged Champagne, chunks of aged Asiago, aged Gouda, or Parmesan cheese go extremely well.

Don't serve a dry brut (or extra dry) sparkling wine with dessert. These styles are just too dry. With fresh fruit and desserts that are not too sweet, try a demi-sec Champagne. With sweeter desserts (or wedding cake!), we recommend Asti. (For more info on Champagne with food, see Chapter 14 in *Champagne For Dummies*.)

Ten excuses to drink Champagne (or another good sparkling wine)

1. You have a bottle on hand.

2. Your demanding boss just left for vacation, or better yet, changed jobs.

3. The noisy neighbors next door finally moved out.

4. You finished your income taxes.

5. It's Saturday.

6. The kids left for summer camp.

7. You just found $20 in your old coat pocket.

8. You didn't get a single telephone solicitation all day.

9. The wire muzzle over the cork makes a great cat toy.

10. You have just finished revising a wine book!

Chapter 16

Wine Roads Less Traveled: Fortified and Dessert Wines

- -

In This Chapter

▶ The world's most versatile wine

▶ 80 grapes for one wine

▶ A wine that lasts 200 years

▶ Liquid gold from rotted grapes

- -

The wines we lump together as *fortified wines* and *dessert wines* aren't mainstream beverages that you want to drink every day. Some of them are much higher in alcohol than regular wines, and some of them are extremely sweet (and rare and expensive!). They're the wine equivalent of really good candy — delicious enough that you could get carried away if you let yourself indulge daily. So you treat them as treats, a glass before or after dinner, a bottle when company comes, a splurge to celebrate the start of your diet — tomorrow.

Pleasure aside, from a purely academic point of view you owe it to yourself to try these wines. Seriously! Learning about wine is hard work, but somebody's got to do it.

Timing Is Everything

Many wines enjoyed before dinner, as apéritif wines, or after dinner, as dessert wines, fall into the category of *fortified wines* (called *liqueur wines* by the European Union, or EU; see Chapter 9 for an explanation of EU terms). Fortified wines all have alcohol added to them at some point in their production, giving them an alcohol content that ranges from 16 to 24 percent.

The point at which alcohol is added determines whether the wines are naturally sweet or dry.

- ✔ When fortified with alcohol *during* fermentation, the wines are sweet, because the added alcohol stops fermentation, leaving natural, unfermented sugar in the wine. (See Chapter 1 for an explanation of fermentation.) Port is the classic example of this process.

- ✔ When fortified *after* fermentation (after all the grape sugar has been converted to alcohol), the wines are dry (unless they are subsequently sweetened). Sherry is the classic example of this process.

Some of the wines we call dessert wines don't have added alcohol. Their sweetness occurs because the grapes are at the right place at the right time — when noble rot strikes. (See the discussion of German wines in Chapter 12.) Other dessert wines are sweet because winemakers pick very ripe (but not rotten) grapes and dry them before fermentation to concentrate their juice — just another way of turning grape juice into the nectar of the gods.

Sherry: A Misunderstood Wine

The comedian Rodney Dangerfield built a career around the line, "I get no respect!" His wine of choice should be Sherry, because it shares the same plight. We avoided Sherry like the plague until we found out how good it can be. We thought it was just a sweet, cheap wine that our elderly aunts and the British fancied. Now we realize that the British (and all those elderly aunts) were on to something: Sherry is a wine of true quality and diversity, but it remains undiscovered by most of the world. In a way, we're not sorry, because the price of good Sherry is attractively low.

The Jerez triangle

Sherry comes from the Andalucía region of sun-baked, southwestern Spain. The wine is named after Jerez *(her ETH)* de la Frontera, an old town of Moorish and Arab origin where many of the Sherry *bodegas* are located. (*Bodega* can refer to the actual building in which Sherry is matured or to the Sherry firm itself.)

Actually, the town of Jerez is just one corner of a triangle that makes up the Sherry region. Another corner is Puerto de Santa María, a beautiful, old coast town southwest of Jerez, and home to a number of large bodegas. The third point of the triangle, Sanlúcar de Barrameda (also on the coast but north-west of Jerez), is so blessed with sea breezes that the lightest and driest of

Sherries, *manzanilla,* can legally be made only there. Aficionados of Sherry swear that they can detect the salty tang of the ocean in manzanilla *(mahn zah NEE yah).*

Traveling from Sanlúcar to Jerez, you pass vineyards with dazzling white soil. This soil is *albariza,* the region's famous chalky earth, rich in limestone from fossilized shells. Summers are hot and dry, but balmy sea breezes temper the heat.

The Palomino grape — the main variety used in Sherry — thrives only here in the hot Sherry region on albariza soil. Palomino is a complete failure for table wines because it is so neutral in flavor and low in acid, but it's perfect for Sherry production. Two other grape varieties, Pedro Ximénez *(PAY dro he MAIN ehz)* and Moscatel (Muscat), are used for dessert types of Sherry.

The phenomenon of flor

Sherry consists of two basic types: *fino* (light, very dry) and *oloroso* (rich and full, but also dry). Sweet Sherries are made by sweetening either type.

After fermentation, the winemaker decides which Sherries will become finos or oloroso*s (oh loh ROH sohs)* by judging the appearance, aroma, and flavor of the young, unfortified wines. If a wine is to be a fino, the winemaker fortifies it lightly (until its alcohol level reaches about 15.5 percent). He strengthens future olorosos to 18 percent alcohol.

At this point, when the wines are still in casks, the special Sherry magic begins: A yeast called *flor* grows spontaneously on the surface of the wines destined to be finos. The flor eventually covers the whole surface, protecting the wine from oxidation. The flor feeds on oxygen in the air and on alcohol and glycerin in the wine. It changes the wine's character, contributing a distinct aroma and flavor and rendering the wine thinner and more delicate in texture.

Flor doesn't grow on olorosos-to-be, because their higher alcohol content prevents it. Without the protection of the flor (and because the casks are never filled to the brim), these wines are exposed to oxygen as they age. This deliberate oxidation protects olorosos against further oxidation — for example, after you open a bottle.

Communal aging

Both fino and oloroso Sherries age in a special way that is unique to Sherry making.

The young wine is not left to age on its own (as most other wines would) but is added to casks of older wine that are already aging. To make room for the young wine, some of the older wine is emptied out of the casks and is added to casks of even older wine. To make room in those casks, some of the wine is transferred to casks of even older wine, and so on. At the end of this chain, four to nine generations away from the young wine, finished Sherry is taken from the oldest casks and is bottled for sale.

This system of blending wines is called the *solera* system. It takes its name from the word *solera* (floor), the term also used to identify the casks of oldest wine.

As wines are blended — younger into older, into yet older, and eventually into oldest — no more than half the wine is emptied from any cask. In theory, then, each solera contains small (and ever-decreasing) amounts of very old wine. As each younger wine mingles with older wine, it takes on the characteristics of the older wine; within a few months, the wine of each generation is indistinguishable from what it was before being refreshed with younger wine. Thus, the solera system maintains infinite consistency of quality and style in Sherry.

Because the casks of Sherry age in dry, airy bodegas above ground (rather than humid, underground cellars like most other wines), some of the wine's water evaporates, and the wine's alcoholic strength increases. Some olorosos aged for more than ten years can be as much as 24 percent alcohol, compared to their starting point of 18 percent.

Two makes twelve

So far, so good: two types of Sherry — delicate fino aged under its protective flor, and fuller oloroso, aged oxidatively — and no vintages, because the young wines are blended with older wines. But now Sherry begins to get a bit confusing. Those two types are about to branch into at least twelve. New styles occur when the natural course of aging changes the character of a Sherry so that its taste no longer conforms to one of the two categories. Deliberate sweetening of the wine also creates different styles.

Among dry Sherries, these are the main styles:

- **Fino:** Pale, straw-colored Sherry, light in body, dry, and delicate. Fino Sherries are always matured under flor, either in Jerez or Puerto de Santa María. They have 15 to 17 percent alcohol. After they lose their protective flor (by bottling), finos become very vulnerable to oxidation spoilage, and you must therefore store them in a cool place, drink them young, and refrigerate them after opening. They're best when chilled.

- **Manzanilla:** Pale, straw-colored, delicate, light, tangy, and very dry fino-style Sherry made only in Sanlucar de Barrameda. (Although various styles of manzanilla are produced, *manzanilla fina,* the fino style, is by far the most common.) The temperate sea climate causes the flor to grow thicker in this town, and manzanilla is thus the driest and most pungent of all the Sherries. Handle it similarly to a fino Sherry.

- **Manzanilla pasada:** A manzanilla that has been aged in cask about seven years and has lost its flor. It's more amber in color than a manzanilla fina and fuller-bodied. It's close to a dry amontillado (see the next item) in style, but still crisp and pungent. Serve cool.

- **Amontillado:** An aged fino that has lost its flor in the process of cask aging. It is deeper amber in color and richer and nuttier than the previous styles. *Amontillado (ah moan tee YAH doh)* is dry but retains some of the pungent tang from its lost flor. True amontillado is fairly rare; most of the best examples are in the $20 to $35 price range. Cheaper Sherries labeled "amontillado" are common, so be suspicious if it costs less than $12 a bottle. Serve amontillado slightly cool and, for best flavor, finish the bottle within a week.

- **Oloroso:** Dark gold to deep brown in color (depending on its age), full-bodied with rich, raisiny aroma and flavor, but dry. Olorosos lack the sharp pungency of fino (flor) Sherries. They're usually between 18 and 20 percent alcohol and can age for a few weeks after you open the bottle because they have already been oxidized in their aging. Serve them at room temperature.

- **Palo cortado:** The rarest of all Sherries. It starts out as a fino, with a flor, and develops as an amontillado, losing its flor. But then, for some unknown reason, it begins to resemble the richer, more fragrant oloroso style, all the while retaining the elegance of an amontillado. In color and alcohol content, palo cortado *(PAH loe cor TAH doh)* is similar to an oloroso, but its aroma is quite like an amontillado. Like amontillado Sherry, beware of cheap imitations. Serve at room temperature. It keeps as well as olorosos.

Sweet Sherry is dry Sherry that has been sweetened. The sweetening can come in many forms, such as the juice of Pedro Ximénez grapes that have been dried like raisins. All the following sweet styles of Sherry are best served at room temperature:

- **Medium Sherry:** Amontillados and light olorosos that have been slightly sweetened. They are light brown in color.

- **Pale cream:** Made by blending fino and light amontillado Sherries and lightly sweetening the blend. They have a very pale gold color. Pale cream is a fairly new style.

- **Cream Sherry:** Cream and the lighter "milk" Sherries are rich *amorosos* (the term for sweetened olorosos). They vary in quality, depending on the oloroso used, and can improve in the bottle with age. These Sherries are a popular style.

- ✔ **Brown Sherry:** Very dark, rich, sweet, dessert Sherry, usually containing a coarser style of oloroso.

- ✔ **East India Sherry:** A type of Brown Sherry that has been deeply sweetened and colored.

- ✔ **Pedro Ximénez** and **Moscatel:** Extremely sweet, dark brown, syrupy dessert Sherries. Low in alcohol, these Sherries are made from raisined grapes of these two varieties. As varietally labeled Sherries, they are quite rare today. Delicious over vanilla ice cream (really!).

Wines from elsewhere in the world, especially in the U.S. and Australia, also call themselves "Sherry." Many of these are inexpensive wines in large bottles. Occasionally you can find a decent one, but usually they're sweet and not very good. Authentic Sherry is made only in the Jerez region of Spain and carries the official name, *Jerez-Xérès-Sherry* (the Spanish, French, and English names for the town) on the label (either front or back).

Serving and storing Sherry

The light, dry Sherries — fino and manzanilla — must be fresh. Buy them from stores with rapid turnover; a fino or manzanilla that has been languishing on the shelf for several months will not give you the authentic experience of these wines.

Although fino or manzanilla can be an excellent apéritif, be careful when ordering a glass in a restaurant or bar. Never accept a glass from an already-open bottle unless the bottle has been refrigerated. Even then, ask how long it has been open — more than two days is too much. After you open a bottle at home, refrigerate it and finish it within a couple of days.

We like to buy half-bottles of fino and manzanilla so that we don't have left-over wine that oxidizes. These, and all Sherries, can be stored upright. Try not to hold bottles of fino or manzanilla more than three months, however. The higher alcohol and the oxidative aging of other types of Sherry (amontillado, oloroso, palo cortado, all the sweet Sherries) permit you to hold them for several years.

Manzanilla and fino Sherry are ideal with almonds, olives, shrimp or prawns, all kinds of seafood, and those wonderful tapas in Spanish bars and restaurants. Amontillado Sherries can accompany tapas before dinner but are also fine at the table with light soups, cheese, ham, or salami (especially the Spanish type, *chorizo*). Dry olorosos and palo cortados are best with nuts, olives, and hard cheeses (such as the excellent Spanish sheep-milk cheese, Manchego). All the sweet Sherries can be served with desserts after dinner or enjoyed on their own.

Nut'n Sherry

The bouquet, or aroma, of fino Sherry is often compared with almonds. Amontillados are said to smell like hazelnuts, and olorosos smell like walnuts. And, by the way, the named nuts make ideal accompaniments to each particular sherry.

Recommended Sherries

Sherries are among the great values in the wine world: You can buy decent, genuine Sherries for $7 or $8. But if you want to try the best wines, you might have to spend $12 or more. The following are some of our favorite Sherries, according to type.

Fino

All of these fino Sherries are about $14 to $15:

- González Byass's Tío Pepe *(TEE oh PAY pay)*
- Pedro Domecq's La Ina *(EEN ah)*
- Emilio Lustau's Jarana *(har AHN ah)*
- Valdespino's Inocente

Manzanilla

- Hidalgo's La Gitana (a great buy at $11; $6 for the half-bottle); also, Hidalgo's Manzanilla Pasada

Amontillado

You'll find a great number of cheap imitations in this category. For a true amontillado, stick to one of the following brands:

- González Byass's Del Duque (the real thing, at $38; half-bottle, $20)
- Emilio Lustau (any of his amontillados labeled Almacenista, $33)
- Hidalgo's Napoleon (about $18)
- Osborne's La Honda or Solera Primera ($32 to $33); or Solera A.O.S. ($40)

Oloroso

- ✔ González Byass's Matusalem ($38; half-bottle, $20)
- ✔ Emilio Lustau (any of his olorosos labeled Almacenista, $33)
- ✔ Osborne's "Very Old" ($38)
- ✔ Sandeman's Royal Corregidor (rich, but a bit sweet; about $23)

Palo cortado

You'll find many imitations in this category, too. True palo cortados are quite rare.

- ✔ González Byass's Apostoles ($38; half-bottle, $20)
- ✔ Emilio Lustau (any of his palo cortados labeled Almacenista, $33)
- ✔ Hidalgo's Jerez Cortado (about $33)

Cream

- ✔ Sandeman's Armada Cream (about $12)
- ✔ Emilio Lustau's Rare Cream Solera Reserva ($22)

East India, Pedro Ximénez, Moscatel

- ✔ Emilio Lustau (a quality brand for all three Sherries; all about $22)
- ✔ González Byass's Pedro Ximénez "Noe" ($38; half-bottle, $20)

Montilla: A Sherry look-alike

Northeast of the Sherry region is the Montilla-Moriles region (commonly referred to as Montilla), where wines very similar to Sherry are made in fino, amontillado, and oloroso styles. The two big differences between Montilla *(moan TEE yah)* and Sherry are

- ✔ Pedro Ximénez is the predominant grape variety in Montilla.
- ✔ Montillas usually reach their high alcohol levels naturally (without fortification).

Alvear is the leading brand of Montilla. Reasonably priced ($11), these wines are widely available. Alvear's premium Montillas, labeled Abuelo Diego, are in the $18 to $19 price range.

Marsala, Vin Santo, and the Gang

Italy has a number of interesting dessert and fortified wines, of which Marsala (named after a town in western Sicily) is the most famous. Marsala is a fortified wine made from local grape varieties. It comes in numerous styles, all of which are fortified after fermentation, like Sherry, and aged in a form of the solera system. You can find dry, semi-dry, or sweet versions and amber, gold, or red versions, but the best Marsalas have the word *Superiore* or — even better — *Vergine* or *Vergine Soleras* on the label. Marsala Vergine is unsweetened and uncolored, and is aged longer than other styles.

Marco De Bartoli is the most acclaimed producer of dry-style Marsala. His 20-year-old Vecchio Samperi (about $40 for a 500 ml bottle) is an excellent example of a dry, apéritif Marsala. Pellegrino, Rallo, and Florio are larger producers of note. (For more info on Marsala and all other Sicilian fortified or dessert wines, see Chapter 11 in *Italian Wine For Dummies*.)

Two fascinating dessert wines are made on small islands near Sicily, from dried grapes. One is Malvasia delle Lipari, from the estate of the late Carlo Hauner. This wine has a beautiful, orange-amber color and an incredible floral, apricot, and herb aroma (about $24 for a half-bottle). The other is Moscato di Pantelleria, a very delicious sweet wine. De Bartoli is one of the best producers; look for his Bukkuram Passito Pantelleria (about $45 for a 500 ml bottle).

The region of Tuscany is rightfully proud of its Vin Santo (*vin SAHN toh*), a golden amber wine made from dried grapes and barrel-aged for several years. Vin Santo can be dry, medium-dry, or sweet. We prefer the first two — the dry style as an apéritif, and the medium-dry version as an accompaniment to the wonderful Italian almond cookies called *biscotti*.

Many Tuscan producers make a Vin Santo; four outstanding examples of Vin Santo (conveniently available in half-bottles as well as full bottles) are from Avignonesi (very expensive!), Badia a Coltibuono, Castello di Cacchiano, and San Giusto a Rentennano.

Port: The Glory of Portugal

Port is the world's greatest fortified red wine.

The British invented Port, thanks to one of their many wars with the French, when they were forced to buy Portuguese wine as an alternative to French wine. To insure that the Portuguese wines were stable enough for shipment by sea, the British had a small amount of brandy added to finished wine, and early Port was the result. The English established their first Port house, Warre, in the city of Oporto in 1670, and several others followed.

Ironically, the French, who drove the British to Portugal, today drink three times as much Port as the British! But, of course, the French have the highest per capita consumption of wine in the world.

Home, home on the Douro

Port takes its name from the city of Oporto, situated where the northerly Douro River empties into the Atlantic Ocean. But its vineyards are far away, in the hot, mountainous Douro Valley. (In 1756, this wine region became one of the first in the world to be officially recognized by its government.) Some of the most dramatically beautiful vineyards anywhere are on the slopes of the upper Douro — still very much a rugged, unspoiled area.

Port wine is fermented and fortified in the Douro Valley, and then most of it travels downriver to the coast. The wine is finished and matured in the Port lodges of Vila Nova de Gaia, a suburb of Oporto. From Oporto, the wine is shipped all over the world.

To stop your wine-nerd friends in their tracks, ask them to name the authorized grape varieties for Port (there are more than 80!). In truth, most wine lovers — even Port lovers — can't name more than one variety. These grapes are mostly local and unknown outside of Portugal. For the record, the five most important varieties are *Touriga Nacional, Tinta Roriz* (Tempranillo), *Tinta Barroca, Tinto Cão,* and *Touriga Francesca.*

Many Ports for a storm

Think Sherry is complicated? In some ways, Port is even trickier. Although all Port is sweet, and most of it is red, a zillion styles exist. The styles vary according to the quality of the base wine (ranging from ordinary to exceptional), how long the wine is aged in wood before bottling (ranging from 2 to 40-plus years), and whether the wine is from a single year or blended from wines of several years.

Following is a brief description of the main styles, from simplest to most complex:

✔ **White Port:** Made from white grapes, this gold-colored wine can be off-dry or sweet. We couldn't quite figure out why it existed — Sherries and Sercial Madeiras (discussed later in this chapter) are better as apéritifs and red

Ports are far superior as sweet wines — until someone served us white Port with tonic and ice one day. Served this way, white port can be a bracing warm-weather apéritif.

- **Ruby Port:** This young, non-vintage style is aged in wood for about three years before release. Fruity, simple, and inexpensive (around $12), it's the best-selling type of Port. If labeled *Reserve* or *Special Reserve,* the wine has usually aged about six years and costs a few dollars more. Ruby Port provides a good introduction to the Port world.

- **Vintage Character Port:** Despite its name, this wine is not single-vintage Port — it just tries to taste like one. Vintage Character Port is actually premium ruby blended from higher-quality wines of several vintages and matured in wood for about five years. Full-bodied, rich, and ready-to-drink when released, these wines are a good value at about $17 to $19. But the labels don't always say *Vintage Character;* instead, they often bear proprietary names such as Founder's Reserve (from Sandeman); Bin 27 (Fonseca); Boardroom (Dow); Six Grapes (Graham); First Estate (Taylor Fladgate); Warrior (Warre); and Distinction (Croft). As if *Vintage Character* wouldn't have been confusing enough!

- **Tawny Port:** Tawny is the most versatile Port style. The best tawnies are good-quality wines that fade to a pale garnet or brownish red color during long wood aging. Their labels carry an indication of their average age (the average age of the wines from which they were blended) — 10, 20, 30, or 40 years. Ten-year-old tawnies cost about $25, 20-year-olds sell for $40 to $45, and 30- and 40-year-old tawnies cost a lot more ($90 to well over $100). We consider 10- and 20-year tawnies the best buys; the older ones aren't worth the extra bucks. Tawny Ports have more finesse than other styles and are appropriate both as apéritifs and after dinner. Inexpensive tawnies that sell for about the same price as ruby Port are usually weak in flavor and not worth buying.

A serious tawny Port can be enjoyed in warm weather (even with a few ice cubes!) when a Vintage Port would be too heavy and tannic.

- **Colheita Port:** Often confused with Vintage Port because it's vintage-dated, colheita is actually a tawny from a single vintage. In other words, it has aged (and softened and tawnied) in wood for many years. Unlike an aged tawny, though, it's the wine of a single year. Niepoort is one of the few Port houses that specializes in colheita Port. It can be very good but is quite expensive (about $100).

- **Late Bottled Vintage Port (LBV):** This type *is* from a specific vintage, but usually not from a very top year. The wine ages four to six years in wood before bottling and is then ready to drink, unlike Vintage Port. Quite full-bodied, but not so hefty as Vintage Port, it sells for about $21 to $23.

- **Vintage Port:** The pinnacle of Port production, Vintage Port is the wine of a single year blended from several of a house's best vineyards. It's bottled at only two years of age, before the wine has much chance to shed its tough tannins. It therefore requires an enormous amount of bottle aging to accomplish the development that did not occur in wood. Vintage Port is usually not mature (ready to drink) until about 20 years after the vintage.

Because it's very rich and very tannic, this wine throws a heavy sediment and *must* be decanted, preferably several hours before drinking (it needs the aeration). Vintage Port can live 70 or more years in top vintages.

Most good Vintage Ports sell for $80 to $100 when they're first released (and years away from drinkability). Mature Vintage Ports can sell for well over $100. Producing a Vintage Port amounts to a *declaration of that vintage* (a term you hear in Port circles) on the part of an individual Port house.

✔ **Single Quinta Vintage Port:** These are Vintage Ports from a single estate *(quinta)* that is usually a producer's best property (such as Taylor's Vargellas and Graham's Malvedos). They're made in good years, but not in the best vintages, because then their grapes are needed for the Vintage Port blend. They have the advantage of being readier to drink than declared Vintage Ports — at less than half their price. You should decant and aerate them before serving, however. (Some Port houses, incidentally, are themselves single estates, such as Quinta do Noval, Quinta do Infantado, and Quinta do Vesuvio. When such a house makes a vintage-dated Port, it's a Vintage Port, as well as a single quinta Port. But that's splitting hairs.)

Storing and serving Port

Treat Vintage Ports like all other fine red wines: Store the bottles on their sides in a cool place. You can store other Ports either on their sides (if they have a cork rather than a plastic-topped cork stopper) or upright. All Ports, except white and ruby, keep well for a couple of weeks after opening.

Port-O

The term Port has been borrowed even more extensively around the world than "Sherry" has. Many countries outside the EU, such as Australia, South Africa, and the U.S., make sweet, red wine in the Port style and label it as Port. Some of it can be quite good, but it's never as fine as the genuine article that is made only in Portugal. The trick in identifying authentic Portuguese Port is to look for the word *Porto*, which always appears on the label.

It's worth a try!

Don't let all the complicated styles of Port deter you from picking up a bottle and trying it. If you've never had Port before, you're bound to love it — almost no matter which style you try. (Later, you can fine-tune your preference for one style or another.) Port is, simply, delicious!

You can now find Vintage Ports and some Vintage Character Ports, such as Fonseca Bin 27, in half-bottles — a brilliant development for Port lovers. Enjoying a bottle after dinner is far easier to justify when it's just a half-bottle. The wine evolves slightly more quickly in half-bottles, but considering the wine's longevity, that may even be a bonus!

Serve Port at cool room temperature, 64°F (18°C), although tawny Port can be an invigorating pick-me-up when served chilled during warm weather. The classic complements to Port are walnuts and strong cheeses, such as Stilton, Gorgonzola, Roquefort, mature Cheddar, and aged Gouda.

Recommended Port producers

In terms of quality, with the exception of a few clinker producers, Port is one of the most consistent of all wines. We've organized our favorite Port producers into two categories — outstanding and very good — each presented in rough order of preference. As you might expect, wines in the first group tend to be a bit more expensive. Our rating is based mainly on Vintage Port but can be generally applied to all the various Port styles of the house.

Outstanding

Taylor-Fladgate
Fonseca
Graham
Quinta do Noval "Nacional" (made from ungrafted, pre-phylloxera vineyards; see Chapter 3)

Dow
Smith-Woodhouse
Cockburn *(COH burn)*

Another Portuguese classic

One of the great dessert wines made mainly from the white Muscat grape is Setúbal *(SHTOO bahl).* Produced just south of Lisbon, Setúbal is made similarly to Port, with alcohol added to stop fermentation. Like Port, it's a rich, long-lasting wine. The most important producer is J. M. da Fonseca.

Very Good

Ramos Pinto	Ferreira
Warre	Cálem
Quinta do Noval	Churchill
Niepoort	Delaforce
Croft	Gould Campbell
Sandeman	Martinez
Quarles Harris	Osborne
Quinta do Infantado	Offley Boa Vista
Quinta do Vesuvio	Rebello Valente

Madeira, M'dear

The legendary wine called Madeira comes from the island of the same name, which sits in the Atlantic Ocean nearer to Africa than Europe. Madeira is a subtropical island whose precarious hillside vineyards rise straight up from the ocean. The island is a province of Portugal, but the British have always run its wine trade. Historically, Madeira could even be considered an American wine, for this is the wine that American colonists drank.

Although Madeira's fortified wines were quite the rage 200 years ago, the island's vineyards were devastated at the end of the nineteenth century, first by mildew and then by the phylloxera louse. Most vineyards were replanted with lesser grapes. Madeira has spent a long time recovering from these setbacks. The best Madeira wines are still those from the old days, vintage-dated wines from 1920 back to 1795. Surprisingly, you can still find a few Madeiras from the nineteenth century. The prices are not outrageous, either ($300 to $400 a bottle), considering what other wines that old, such as Bordeaux, cost. (Refer to Chapter 17 for sources of old Madeira.)

Timeless, indestructible, and tasty

Madeira comes in four styles, two fairly dry and two sweet. The sweeter Madeiras generally have their fermentation halted somewhat early by the addition of alcohol. Drier Madeiras have alcohol added after fermentation.

A curiosity of Madeira production is a baking process called the *estufagem (es too FAH jem),* which follows fermentation. The fact that Madeira improves by heating was discovered back in the seventeenth century. When trading ships crossed the equator with casks of Madeira as ballast in their holds, the wine actually improved! Today's practice of baking the wine at home on the island is a bit more practical than sending it around the world in a slow boat.

Madeira spends a minimum of three months, often longer, in heated tanks, in *estufas* (heating rooms), or exposed to the sun (the weather stays warm year-round). Any sugars in the wine become caramelized, and the wine becomes thoroughly *maderized* (oxidized through heating) without developing any unpleasant aroma or taste.

Endless finish

Technically, almost all Madeira starts as white wine, but the heating process and years of maturation give it an amber color with pale green reflections. It has a tangy aroma and flavor that is uniquely its own, and as long a finish on the palate as you'll find on the planet. When Madeira is made from any of the island's four noble grapes (listed later in this section), the grape name indicates the style. When Madeira doesn't carry a grape name — and most younger Madeiras don't — the words *dry, medium-dry, medium-sweet,* and *sweet* indicate the style.

Some of the most memorable wines we've ever tasted were old Madeiras, and so we're afraid we might get carried away a bit, beginning any time now. Their aroma alone is divine, and you keep on tasting the wine long after you've swallowed it. (Spitting is out of the question.) Words truly are inadequate to describe this wine.

If you can afford to buy an old bottle of vintage-dated Madeira (the producer's name is relatively unimportant), you'll understand our enthusiasm. And maybe some day when Madeira production gets back on its feet, every wine lover will be able to experience Vintage Madeira. In the meantime, for a less expensive Madeira experience, look for wines labeled *15 years old, 10 years old,* or *5 years old.* Don't bother with any other type, because it will be unremarkable, and then we'll look crazy.

You never have to worry about Madeira getting too old. It's indestructible. The enemies of wine — heat and oxygen — have already had their way with Madeira during the winemaking and maturing process. Nothing you do after it's opened can make it blink.

Vintage Madeira must spend at least 20 years in a cask, but for the old wines, the aging was even longer. If a Madeira is dated with the word *Solera* — for example, "Solera 1890" — it is *not* a Vintage Madeira but a blend of many younger vintages whose first barrel, or solera, dates back to 1890. Solera-dated Madeiras can be very fine and are generally not as expensive — nor as great — as Vintage Madeiras. Vintage and solera-dated Madeiras are made from one of the following four noble grape varieties (once there were six) and are varietally labeled. Each grape variety corresponds to a specific style of wine; they are listed from driest style to sweetest.

✔ **Sercial:** The Sercial grape grows at the highest altitudes. Thus the grapes are the least ripe and make the driest Madeira. The wine is high in acidity and very tangy. Sercial Madeira is an outstanding apéritif wine with almonds, olives, or light cheeses. Unfortunately, true Sercial is quite rare today.

✔ **Verdelho:** The Verdelho grape makes a medium-dry style, with nutty, peachy flavors and a tang of acidity. It's good as an apéritif or with consommé.

✔ **Bual (or Boal):** Darker amber in color, Bual is a rich, medium-sweet Madeira with spicy flavors of almonds and raisins and a long, tangy finish. Bual is best after dinner. Like Sercial, true Bual is rare today.

✔ **Malmsey:** Made from the Malvasia grape, Malmsey is dark amber, sweet, and intensely concentrated with a very long finish. Drink it after dinner.

Two rare varieties, whose names you may see on some very old bottles, are

✔ **Terrantez:** Medium-sweet, between Verdelho and Bual in style, this is a powerful, fragrant Madeira with lots of acidity. Drink it after dinner.

✔ **Bastardo:** This is the only red grape of the noble varieties. Old Bastardos from the last century are mahogany-colored and rich, but not so rich as the Terrantez.

Sauternes and the Nobly Rotten Wines

Warm, misty autumns encourage the growth of a fungus called *botrytis cinerea* in vineyards. Nicknamed *noble rot,* botrytis concentrates the liquid and sugar in the grapes, giving the winemaker amazingly rich juice to ferment. The best wines from botrytis-infected grapes are among the greatest dessert wines in the world, with intensely concentrated flavors and plenty of acidity to prevent the wine from being excessively sweet.

The greatest nobly rotten wines are made in the Sauternes district of Graves (Bordeaux) and in Germany (see Chapter 12), but they are also produced in Austria and California, among other places.

Sauternes: Liquid gold

Sauternes is a very labor-intensive wine. Grapes must be picked by hand; workers pass through the vineyard several times — sometimes over a period of weeks — each time selecting only the botrytis-infected grapes. Yields are low. Harvests sometimes linger until November, but now and then bad weather in October dashes all hopes of making botrytis-infected wine. Often, only two to four vintages per decade yield decent Sauternes (but the 1980s decade was exceptional; see the vintage chart in Appendix C).

Consequently, good Sauternes is expensive. Prices range from $30 a bottle on up to $300 (depending on the vintage) for Château d'Yquem *(d'ee kem)*. The greatest and most labor-intensive Sauternes, d'Yquem has always been prized by collectors (see Chapter 21). It was the only Sauternes given the status of *first great growth* in the 1855 Bordeaux Classification (see Chapter 10).

Sauternes is now widely available in half-bottles, reducing the cost somewhat. A 375 ml bottle is a perfect size for after dinner, and you can buy a decent half-bottle of Sauternes or Barsac like Château Doisy-Védrines *(dwahs ee veh dreen)* or Château Doisy-Daëne *(dwahs ee dah en)* for $16 to $18.

Mining the gold

The Sauternes wine district includes five communes in the southernmost part of Graves (one of them named Sauternes). One of the five, Barsac, makes wines that are slightly lighter and less sweet than Sauternes and are entitled to their own appellation. The Garonne River and the Ciron, an important tributary, produce the mists that encourage *botrytis cinerea* to form on the grapes.

The three authorized grape varieties are Sémillon, Sauvignon Blanc, and Muscadelle — although the latter is used by only a few châteaux, and even then in small quantities. Sémillon is the king of Sauternes. Most producers use at least 80 percent of Sémillon in their blend.

Wine that is called "Sauterne" (no final "s") is produced in California and other places. This semisweet, rather insipid wine is made from inexpensive grapes and usually sold in large bottles. It bears absolutely no resemblance to true, botrytis-infected Sauternes, from Sauternes, France. California does make late-harvest, botrytis-infected wines, mainly Rieslings, and while they are far better than California Sauterne (even worth trying), they are very different wines from the botrytis wines of Sauternes or of Germany.

Recommended Sauternes

All of the Sauternes in the following list range from outstanding to good. (Wines specifically from Barsac are labeled as such.) In Sauternes, vintages are just as important as in the rest of Bordeaux; check our vintage recommendations in Appendix C.

Outstanding

- **Château d'Yquem:** Can last for 100 years or more
- **Château de Fargues:** Owned by d'Yquem; almost as good as d'Yquem, at one-third the price ($100)
- **Château Climens (Barsac):** At $80, a value; near d'Yquem's level
- **Château Coutet (Barsac):** A great buy ($55 to $60)

Excellent

- **Château Suduiraut:** On the brink of greatness ($55 to $60)
- **Château Rieussec:** Rich, lush style ($55 to $60)
- **Château Raymond-Lafon:** Located next to d'Yquem (about $50)

Very Good

- Château Lafaurie-Peyraguey
- Château Latour Blanche
- Château Guiraud
- Château Rabaud-Promis
- Château Sigalas-Rabaud
- Château Nairac (Barsac)
- Château Doisy-Védrines (Barsac)
- Château Doisy-Daëne (Barsac)
- Château Clos Haut-Peyraguey

Good

- Château Bastor-Lamontagne
- Château Rayne Vigneau
- Château d'Arche

- ✔ Château de Malle
- ✔ Château Suau (Barsac)
- ✔ Château Lamothe-Guignard
- ✔ Château Romieu-Lacoste (Barsac)
- ✔ Château Liot (Barsac)
- ✔ Château Doisy-Dubroca (Barsac)
- ✔ Château Filhot

Letting baby grow

Sauternes has such balance of natural sweetness and acidity that it can age well (especially the better Sauternes mentioned here) for an extraordinarily long time. Unfortunately, because Sauternes is so delicious, it's often consumed young, when it is very rich and sweet. But Sauternes is really at its best when it loses its baby fat and matures.

After about ten to fifteen years, Sauternes's color changes from light gold to an old gold-coin color, sometimes with orange or amber tones. At this point, the wine loses some of its sweetness and develops flavors reminiscent of apricots, orange rind, honey, and toffee. This stage is the best time to drink Sauternes. The better the vintage, the longer Sauternes takes to reach this stage, but once there, it stays at this plateau for many years — sometimes decades — and very gradually turns dark amber or light brown in color. Even in these final stages, Sauternes retains some of its complex flavors.

In good vintages, Sauternes can age for 50 to 60 years or more. Château d'Yquem and Château Climens are particularly long-lived. (We recently had a half-bottle of 1893 Château d'Yquem that was glorious!)

Sauternes is best when served cold, but not ice cold, at about 52° to 53°F (11°C). Mature Sauternes can be served a bit warmer. Because the wine is so rich, Sauternes is an ideal companion for *foie gras* although, ordinarily, the wine is far more satisfying after dinner than as an apéritif. As for desserts, Sauternes is excellent with ripe fruits, lemon-flavored cakes, or pound cake.

Sauternes look-alikes

Many sweet, botrytis-infected wines similar to Sauternes exist; they sell for considerably less money than Sauternes or Barsacs. These wines are not as intense or as complex in flavor, but they are fine values at $15 to $25.

Directly north and adjacent to Barsac is the often overlooked Cérons wine region. You can probably convince many of your friends that a Cérons, served blind, is a Sauternes or Barsac. From the Entre-Deux-Mers district of Bordeaux, look for wines with the Cadillac, Loupiac, or Sainte-Croix-du-Mont appellations — all less expensive versions of Sauternes.

Part IV
When You've Caught the Bug

The 5th Wave
By Rich Tennant

"You bring me here to announce you've quit your job, you're moving out, but you want us to remain friends, and then have the nerve to order a crummy year-old Merlot?!"

In this part . . .

The gestation period of the wine bug is unpredictable. Some people no sooner express interest in wine than they become engrossed in the subject. Other people exhibit mild symptoms for many years before succumbing to the passion. (Lots of people never get bitten by the bug at all.)

But once you've been smitten by the wine bug, you know it. You find yourself subscribing to magazines that your friends never heard of, making new friends with whom you have little in common other than an interest in wine, boycotting restaurants with substandard wine lists, and planning vacations to wine regions!

However quickly you got to this stage, the following five chapters provide fuel for your fire.

Chapter 17

Insider's Guide to Wine Buying

- -

- -

*Y*ou read about a wine that sounds terrific. Your curiosity is piqued; you want to try it. But your local wine shop doesn't have the wine. Neither does the best store in the next town. Or maybe you decide to balance your wine collection by buying some mature wines. But the few older wines you can find in wine shops aren't really what you want.

How do other wine lovers manage to get their hands on special bottles of wine when you can't?

Wines That Play Hard to Get

There's a Catch-22 for wine lovers who have really caught the bug: The more desirable a wine is, the harder it is to get. And the harder it is to get, the more desirable it is.

Several forces conspire to frustrate wine buyers who want to get their hands on special bottles. First, some of the best wines are made in ridiculously small quantities. We wouldn't say that quantity and quality are necessarily incompatible in winemaking, but at the very highest echelons of quality, there usually isn't much quantity to go around.

We once bought six bottles of a grand cru red Burgundy produced by a small grower, Hubert Lignier. We learned that Lignier made only 150 cases of that wine, and 50 of those cases came to the U.S. We found it incredible that we could buy half a case of such a rare wine for ourselves, leaving only 49.5 cases to satisfy the whole rest of the country! Right time, right place.

Today, many small-production wines sell *on allocation* — which means that distributors restrict the quantity that any one store can purchase, sometimes limiting stores to as few as six bottles of a particular wine. Most stores, in turn, limit customers to just one or two bottles.

This brings us to the second factor preventing equal opportunity in wine buying: Wine buying is a competitive sport. If you're there first, you get the wine, and the next guy doesn't. (We've been on the short end of that deal plenty of times, too.)

Buying highly rated wines is especially competitive. When a wine receives a very high score from critics, a feeding frenzy results among wine lovers, not leaving much for Johnny-come-latelies. (See Chapter 18 for information on wine critics and Chapters 19 and 23 for more on wine ratings.)

Finally, wineries usually sell each wine just once, when the wine is young. In the case of some fine wines, such as top Bordeaux wines, the wine isn't at its best yet. But most retailers can't afford to store the wine for selling years later. This means that properly aged wines are usually hard to get.

Playing Hardball

When the wine plays hard-to-get, you have to play hardball. You have to look beyond your normal sources of supply. Your allies in this game are wine auction houses, wine shops in other cities, and the wineries themselves.

Pros and cons of buying wines at auctions

The clear advantage of buying wine through auction houses is the availability of older and rarer wines. In fact, auction houses are the principal source of mature wines — their specialty. (In general, you can obtain younger wines at better prices elsewhere.) At auctions, you can buy wines that are practically impossible to obtain any other way. Many of these wines have been off the market for years, sometimes decades!

The main disadvantage of buying wine at auction houses is that you frequently don't know the storage history — or *provenance* — of the wine you're considering buying. The wine may have been stored in somebody's warm apartment for years. And if the wine does come from a reputable wine collector's temperature-controlled cellar, and thus has impeccable credentials, it will sell for a very high price.

Improving your odds of getting a "good, old bottle"

Acquiring and drinking old wines requires you to be a bit of a gambler. But you *can* reduce the odds against coming up with a bottle well past its peak by following a few easy tips:

✔ Buy from reputable wine merchants and auction houses. They often know the history of their older wines, and most likely acquired the wines from sources that they trust.

✔ Trade bottles only with wine-savvy friends who know the storage history of their wines.

✔ Stick to well-known wines with a proven track record of longevity.

✔ Inspect the wine if you can. Look at the *ullage* (the airspace between the wine and the cork). Ullage of an inch or more can be a danger sign indicating that evaporation has occurred, either from excessive heat or lack of humidity — both of which can spoil the wine. (On a very old wine, say 35 or more years old, an inch of ullage is quite acceptable, though.) Another sign of poor storage is leakage or stickiness at the top of the bottle, suggesting that wine has seeped out through the cork.

✔ Inspect the color. A white wine that is excessively dark or dull, or a red wine that has become quite brown, can be oxidized and too old. (Shine a penlight flashlight through the bottle to check the color of red wines.) But some red wines and Sauternes can show quite a bit of brown and still be very much alive. If you're not sure about the color, get advice from someone who knows about older wines before plunking down your money.

✔ If you buy at auction by telephone or fax, ask the seller to inspect the bottle and describe its fill level and color.

✔ Be wary if the price of the bottle seems too low. Often, what appears to be a bargain is a damaged or over-the-hill wine.

✔ Ask wine-knowledgeable friends or merchants about the particular wines that you are considering buying. Frequently, someone will be familiar with them.

✔ Say a prayer, take out your corkscrew, and plunge in. Live dangerously!

Also, almost all auction houses charge you a buyer's premium, a tacked-on charge that's 10 or 15 percent of your bid. In general, prices of wine at auctions range from fair (rarely, you even find bargains) to exorbitant.

If you're personally present at an auction, be careful not to catch auction fever. The desire to win can motivate you to pay more for the wine than it's worth. Carefully thought-out, judicious bidding is in order. To plan your attack, you can obtain a catalog for the auction ahead of time, usually for a small fee. The catalog lists wines for sale by lots (usually groupings of three, six, or twelve bottles) with a suggested minimum bid per lot.

The phone numbers and Web site addresses for many U.S. auction houses are listed in the "Selling Your Wine" section of Chapter 21.

Pros and cons of buying wine by catalog

A real plus of perusing wine shop catalogs and ordering from your armchair is, of course, the convenience (not to mention the time savings). Most major wine retail stores issue a wine catalog two or more times a year to customers on their mailing lists; just give a call to obtain a free catalog.

Other advantages of buying wine long-distance include the availability of scarce wines and (sometimes) lower prices than you might pay in your home market.

Sometimes, the *only* way to buy certain wines is by catalog, because the sought-after wines made in small quantities are not available in every market. If a wine you want is available locally, but you don't live in a market where pricing is competitive, you might decide that you can save money by ordering the wine from a retailer in another city — even after the added shipping costs.

The penalty box

Still today, many states in the U.S. prohibit residents from receiving wine shipments that originate in other states. By permitting consumers to buy wine only from local, licensed retail stores or wineries, a state government can be sure it's getting all the tax revenue it's entitled to on every wine transaction in its jurisdiction. Wine distributors, who sell wine at wholesale to licensed retailers, have a vested interest in preserving this situation, because in a free-trade scenario, some retail wine sales would circumvent their customers, and them.

Interstate shipping of wine, or *direct trade,* has become one of the most contentious areas of the entire wine business. Some states have sued out-of-state wineries and wine shops for shipping wine to individual residents — and some organizations have even set up scam operations with underage buyers to prove that the laws are necessary to prevent underage drinking. To avoid the risk of prosecution, many wine stores and wineries have discontinued wine shipments to individuals.

Most wine shops and wineries remain sympathetic to out-of-state customers, but deliveries to other states are risky for their businesses unless their state governments and the buyer's state happen to have a reciprocal shipping agreement. The risk is all theirs, too; the store or winery can lose its license, while all the buyer loses is any wine that's confiscated by the authorities.

If you want to buy wine out of state, discuss the issue with the shop or winery from which you plan to purchase the wine. If shipping to you isn't legal, you can sometimes find a solution, such as having the merchant hold the wine for you to pick up personally, or shipping to a friend or relative in a legal state. And be aware that the situation is changing rapidly. Many laws against interstate shipping are being challenged in federal court on the grounds that they restrict commercial trade. Recently, Congress passed a law entitling wine drinkers to ship home wines that they purchase during visits to out-of-state wineries.

One minor disadvantage of buying wine by catalog is that an adult usually must be available to receive the wine. Also, because wine is perishable, you have to make certain that it's not delivered to you during hot (above 75°F/24°C) or cold (below 28°F/-2°C) weather. Spring and autumn are usually the best times for wine deliveries.

Some U.S. wine stores worth knowing

We can't possibly list *all* the leading wine stores that sell wine by catalog or newsletter. But the following purveyors are some of the best. Most of them either specialize in catalog sales or in certain kinds of fine wine that can be difficult to obtain elsewhere. The stores' main wine specialties are listed here:

- Acker, Merrall & Condit, New York, NY; ☎ 212-787-1700; www.ackerstore.com — Burgundy, California Cabernets

- Applejack Liquors, Wheat Ridge, CO; ☎ 303-233-3331; www.applejack.com — perhaps the largest store in the U.S.; Bordeaux, Italian, California, Burgundy

- Addy Bassin's MacArthur Liquors, Washington, D.C.; ☎ 202-338-1433; www.bassins.com — California, Burgundy, Bordeaux, Italian, Rhône, Alsace, Australian, German, Vintage Port

- Brookline Liquor Mart, Allston, MA; ☎ 617-734-7700; www.BLMWine.com — Italian, Burgundy, Rhône

- Burgundy Wine Company, New York, NY; ☎ 212-691-9092; www.burgundywinecompany.com — Burgundy, fine California Chardonnay and Pinot Noir, Rhône

- Calvert Woodley, Washington, D.C.; ☎ 202-966-4403; www.calvertwoodley.com — California, Bordeaux, other French, Italian, German

- The Chicago Wine Company, Niles, IL; ☎ 708-647-8789; www.tcwc.com — Bordeaux, Burgundy, California

- D & M Wines & Liquors, San Francisco, CA; ☎ 800-637-0292; www.dandm.com — Champagne (great prices)

- John Hart Fine Wine, Chicago, IL; ☎ 312-482-9996; www.johnhartfinewine.com — Bordeaux, Burgundy

- Kermit Lynch Wine Merchant, Berkeley, CA; ☎ 510-524-1524 — French country wines, Burgundy, Loire, Rhône

- McCarthy & Schiering, Seattle, WA; ☎ 206-524-9500 or 206-282-8500 — Washington, Oregon, Burgundy, Italian

✔ Marin Wine Cellar, San Rafael, CA; ☎ 415-459-3823; www.marinwinecellar.com — Bordeaux (especially fine, rare, old)

✔ Mills Wine & Spirit Mart, Annapolis, MD; ☎ 800-261-WINE; www.millswine.com — Bordeaux, other French, Italian

✔ Morrell & Co., New York, NY; ☎ 212-688-9370; www.morrell.com — California, Italian, French

✔ North Berkeley Wine, Berkeley, CA; ☎ 510-848-8910 or 800-266-6585; www.northberkeleyimports.com — French, half-bottles

✔ PJ's Wine Warehouse, New York, NY; ☎ 212-567-5500; www.pjwine.com — Italian, Spanish

✔ Pop's Wines & Spirits, Island Park, NY; ☎ 516-431-0025; www.popswine.com — California, Italian, Bordeaux, Long Island

✔ The Rare Wine Company, Sonoma, CA; ☎ 800-999-4342; www.rarewineco.com — Italian, French, Port, Madeira

✔ Rosenthal Wine Merchant, New York, NY; ☎ 212-249-6650; www.madrose.com — Burgundy, Rhône, Loire, Italian

✔ Royal Wine Merchants, New York, NY; ☎ 212-689-4855; www.royalwinemerchants.com — French (especially rare Bordeaux), Italian

✔ Carlo Russo's Wine and Spirit World, Fort Lee, NJ; ☎ 800-946-3276; www.CarloRussowine.com — Italian, Rhône, California

✔ Sam's Wine & Spirits, Chicago, IL; ☎ 800-777-9137; www.samswine.com — French, Italian, California

✔ Sherry-Lehmann, New York, NY; ☎ 212-838-7500; www.sherry-lehmann.com — Bordeaux, Burgundy, California, Italian

✔ Twenty-Twenty Wine Co., West Los Angeles, CA; ☎ 310-447-2020; www.2020wines.com — Bordeaux (especially rare, old), California, Burgundy

✔ Vino, New York, NY; ☎ 212-725-6516; www.vinosite.com — Italian

✔ Wally's, Los Angeles, CA; ☎ 888-9-WALLYS; www.wallywine.com — Italian, California, French

✔ The Wine Club, Santa Ana, CA, ☎ 800-966-5432; San Francisco, CA, ☎ 800-966-7835; www.thewineclub.com — Burgundy, Bordeaux, California

✔ The Winesellar & Brasserie, San Diego, CA; ☎ 858-450-9557; www.winesellar.com — California, Bordeaux

✔ Zachy's, Scarsdale, NY; ☎ 914-723-0241 or 800-723-0241; www.zachys.com — Bordeaux, California, Italian, Burgundy; half-bottles

Wine-of-the-month clubs

It seems that a week doesn't go by without our receiving a solicitation from a wine-buying club, trying to sign us up. (They're not really clubs in the true sense of the word; they're just people trying to sell us wine.) Most wine-buying clubs work on the principle of "The Book of the Month" club, except that the merchandise is wine. These clubs are worthwhile if you don't want to take the time and trouble to select your own wines. You know the old advertisement: "Let Greyhound do the driving!"

The one inherent catch with these companies is that you have to like the wine they select for you. But the wines are usually reasonably priced. It's your decision: convenience versus choice.

One of the largest and most successful mail-order "personal wine services" (as they like to call themselves) is the Massachusetts-based Geerlings & Wade, founded in 1987. For more information about them, call ☎ 800-782-WINE (9463). Two other wine clubs are Tri-Wine, c/o Shaefer's Liquors (☎ 847-673-5711) and Taste of California (☎ 773-235-9463).

Buying time

Every so often you might notice ads in the newspaper or in wine catalogs urging you to buy futures of certain wines (usually Bordeaux, but sometimes California wines). The ads suggest that, to ensure getting a particular wine at the lowest price, you should buy it now for future delivery. In other words, "Give us your money now; you'll get the wine in due course, probably sometime next year when the winery releases it."

Generally, we recommend that you don't buy futures. Often the wine will be the same price, or only slightly higher, when it hits the market. To save little or nothing, you will have tied your money up for a year or more, while the store has made interest on it or spent it. Stores have gone bankrupt. And during recessionary economies in the past, some people who bought wine futures actually paid more for their wine than they would have paid if they had waited for the wine to arrive before purchasing it.

Futures are useful only in two situations: For wines that are made in such small quantity that you're pretty sure the wine will sell out before it reaches the stores; and for a wine that receives an extraordinarily high rating in the wine press before its release, assuring that its price could double and even triple by the time the wine reaches the market.

Here's the bottom line: Buy futures only when you must have a particular wine and buying futures might be the only way you can get it. For most wines, though, keep your wallet in your pocket until the wine is actually available.

Wine online

If the sticky legalities relating to shipping wines across state lines (see "The penalty box" sidebar earlier in this chapter) ever become resolved in favor of free trade (or if the issue fades back into the dormant state it occupied until the mid-1990s), the field of online wine sales could blow wide open. In the meantime, most Internet-only wine operations seem more geared toward talking about wine and promoting their brands than toward selling the stuff.

The major Web sites for purchasing wine online are those of actual bricks-and-mortar wine shops, and we list most of them in the section "Some U.S. wine stores worth knowing," earlier in this chapter.

You can also bid for wine online. Winebid.com (`www.winebid.com`) conducts auctions at its Web site. Acker, Merrall & Condit, a wine shop in New York City that conducts live auctions, also conducts an auction online at `www.ackerwines.com` during the first 12 days of each month; these auctions feature odd lots not suitable for the shop's live auctions.

Directly from the source

You can buy directly from wineries in two ways:

- ✔ You can visit the winery in person and carry away, or ship, the wine.
- ✔ You can order wine via telephone or the Internet (assuming that shipment to your home is legal).

Many smaller wineries sell a fairly large percentage of their wine to visitors. In New York state, for instance, some wineries sell as much as half of their annual production at their doorsteps!

Lots of people think that you can save money by buying directly from the winery. But you usually don't. To avoid undercutting local wine shops that also sell their wines, most wineries charge visitors standard retail-store prices. But you get two bonuses: the excitement of buying the wine where it's made and the good feeling of supporting the people behind the wine.

If you live too far away to visit a particular winery, or if the winery's production is small or in high demand, ordering wine from the winery by mail or telephone may be the only way to get a certain wine. A few small wineries in California and Washington State, for example, produce wines that have been so praised by wine critics that they are available only to those people on the winery's mailing list. (In some cases, the availability of the wines is so tight that there's a waiting list to get on the mailing list, or a lottery determines who actually gets the wines from all those on the mailing list.)

Some wineries whose mailing lists we suggest you join (and the wines to get) include the following, in alphabetical order:

- **Chateau Montelena, Calistoga, CA, ☎ 707-942-5105:** One of California's best wineries makes a classic Estate Cabernet Sauvignon that's almost impossible to find.

- **DeLille Cellars, Woodinville, WA, ☎ 425-489-0544:** This small Washington winery makes sensational, Bordeaux-styled red and white wines called Chaleur Estate that are difficult to find outside of the state.

- **Grace Family Vineyards, St. Helena, CA, ☎ 707-963-0808:** Dick Grace's intensely flavored Cabernet Sauvignons are undoubtedly some of the hardest to get, most sought-after wines in North America (if not the world). He makes only 200 cases a year! Put yourself on his mailing list, if you're patient. It may be a while before you get any wine.

- **Kistler Vineyards, Sebastopol (Sonoma), CA, ☎ 707-823-5603:** Some of California's most highly-rated and scarcest Chardonnays and Pinot Noirs are available only by mail order.

- **Leonetti Cellar, Walla Walla, WA, ☎ 509-525-1428, fax 509-525-4006:** It's impossible to obtain these classic, well-balanced wines — Washington's most sought-after Cabernet Sauvignons and Merlots — unless you're on the mailing list.

- **Pahlmeyer, Napa, CA, ☎ 707-255-2321:** Jason Pahlmeyer's great Estate Red (Cabernet blend) and Merlot are available only by mail order.

- **Peter Michael Winery, Sonoma, CA, ☎ 800-354-4459:** Some of California's very best Chardonnays; available mainly by mail.

- **Quilceda Creek Vintners, Snohomish, WA, ☎ 206-568-2389:** Only about 1,000 cases are made of this rich Cabernet Sauvignon. Getting on the mailing list is definitely your best (if not your only) bet!

- **Rafanelli Winery, Healdsburg, CA, ☎ 707-433-1385:** Dave Rafanelli's Dry Creek Valley (Sonoma) red Zinfandels set the standard for this variety. Unfined, unfiltered — and just about unavailable unless you get on the mailing list; worth the search.

- **Ravenswood, Sonoma, CA, ☎ 707-938-1960:** Joel Peterson's talent for making outstanding red Zinfandels from special single-vineyard sites is legendary; it's difficult to get them unless you're on the mailing list.

- ✔ **Ridge Vineyards, Cupertino, CA, ☎ 408-867-3233:** Located in the Santa Cruz Mountains, one hour south of San Francisco, Ridge Vineyards is one of California's veteran wineries. Although you can sometimes find Ridge's Cabernets and Zinfandels in retail stores, they do sell out quickly. And the winery has a "limited-release program" of some wines available only by mail.

- ✔ **Rosenblum Cellars, Alameda, CA, ☎ 510-865-7007:** Veterinarian Kent Rosenblum makes some single-vineyard red Zinfandels that are, you might say, the cat's meow. Although some of his wines are available in stores, you can get Rosenblum's best Zins only via the mailing list or by visiting the winery.

- ✔ **Williams & Selyem Winery, Healdsburg, CA, ☎ 707-433-6425:** In the Russian River Valley (Sonoma), Williams & Selyem produces some of the finest Pinot Noirs in North America, plus a great Chardonnay — practically impossible to get without being on the winery's mailing list.

Chapter 18

You Never Graduate from Wine School

*L*earning about wine is like space travel: Once you get going, there's no end in sight. Fortunately for those who choose to be educated wine drinkers, learning about wine is a fascinating experience, full of new flavors, new places, and new friends.

Although we teach others about wine, we are also avid students of wine. We can't imagine that we'll ever reach the point where we say, "Now we know enough about wine; we can stop here." So off we go to another vineyard, to another wine tasting, or deep into the pages of another wine magazine. Every step brings not only more knowledge but also more appreciation of this amazing beverage.

Back to the Classroom

The best way to learn about wine and to improve your wine-tasting skills is to take a wine course. Wine classes provide the ideal combination of authoritative instruction and immediate feedback on your tasting impressions.

If you live in a medium-sized or large city, you're sure to find several wine courses available — offered by private individuals, by universities, by local school districts as adult-education extension programs, or by local wine shops or restaurants.

What do the initials MW mean?

You might have noticed that one of the co-authors of this book has "Master of Wine" after her name (which is often shortened to "MW"). Wine professionals receive this title after passing a grueling written and tasting exam. The credential is awarded by the Institute of Masters of Wine in London, which offers preparatory programs and exams in Australia, the U.S., the U.K., and continental Europe. A high level of preliminary knowledge and experience are prerequisites.

For more information, visit the Institute online at www.masters-of-wine.org. By the way, as of this writing, there are only 241 Masters of Wine in the world. Most of them are in the U.K.; there are only 19 MWs in the U.S.

Most wine courses are *wine appreciation* courses — they don't teach you how to make wine, they don't usually provide you with professional credentials, and they're not accredited. (Some professional-level courses and courses offered at an actual university can be exceptions.) The purpose of most wine courses is to provide both information about wine and practice in tasting wine. (For information on professional wine credentials, see "One wine school in action" and "What do the initials MW mean?")

Introductory classes deal with wine grape varieties and how to taste wine, while more advanced classes discuss in depth the various wine regions of the world or the wines of a particular region. Instructors are usually experienced professionals who work in the wine trade or who write about wine.

Brand promotion and education often enjoy too cozy a relationship in the wine field. Many wine instructors, such as distributor salespeople or winery reps, have a vested interest in the brands of wine that they offer as tasting samples in class. As long as the instructor has expertise beyond his or her own brands, you can still benefit from the instruction. But you should request disclosure of any commercial affiliations at the first class. And when possible, consider taking classes from independent instructors instead.

One wine school in action

The following announcement is a shameless plug: We run a wine school in New York City called International Wine Center (www.internationalwinecenter.com). We offer the programs of the Wine & Spirit Education Trust in London; they're geared towards people in the wine trade but are open to anyone who is serious about learning. Unlike courses geared only toward wine drinkers — where entertainment is as much a goal as education — courses for wine professionals are more comprehensive, and the information covered is more technical. For example, our courses cover three levels of study (from beginner to very advanced) and range from 8 to 35 sessions in length; each course has a textbook, self-study materials, and an examination. Students who pass the examination corresponding to their level of study earn a certificate that gives them professional credentials.

But whether they target wine lovers or those in the trade, most wine classes have a lot in common. A typical class usually lasts about two hours; students listen to a lecture on a particular topic and taste six to eight wines related to that topic. The instructor encourages questions. References to maps of wine regions or sketches on the blackboard punctuate the discussion.

At most wine classes, each student sits before a place setting of wine glasses — ideally one glass per wine to be tasted. Water and crackers are available to help students clear their palates between tastes of wine. Next to each student should be a large plastic cup for dumping leftover wine. Each student should receive a printed list of the wines being tasted, as well as other material about the subject of that particular class session.

For the name of a wine school or an individual who offers wine programs in your area, contact the Society of Wine Educators, Washington, DC (☎ 202-347-5677), which has members throughout the U.S., Canada, and some other countries. The Society offers wine instructors the opportunity to become Certified Wine Educators, and those who pass that exam are entitled to identify themselves with the initials CWE — a credential to look for when choosing a wine course.

Wine tastings of all shapes and sizes

Wine tastings are events designed to give enthusiasts the opportunity to sample a range of wines. The events can be very much like classes (seated, seminar-like events), or they can be more like parties (tasters milling around informally). Compared to a wine class, the participants at a wine tasting are more likely to have various levels of knowledge. Tastings don't come in beginner, intermediate, and advanced levels — one size fits all.

Wine tastings are popular because they override the limitations of sampling wine alone, at home. How many wines can you taste on your own (unless you don't mind throwing away nine-tenths of every bottle)? How many wines are you willing to buy on your own? And how much can you learn tasting wine in isolation — or with a friend whose expertise is no greater than yours?

At wine tastings, you can learn from your fellow tasters, as well as make new friends who share your interest in wine. Most importantly, you can taste wine in the company of some individuals who are more experienced than you, which is a real boon in training your palate.

We have led or attended literally thousands of wine tastings in our lives — so far. And it is fair to say that we have learned something about wine at almost all of them.

To attend a wine tasting in your area, contact your wine merchant. Your local shop might sponsor wine-tasting events occasionally (apart from the informal sampling opportunities in the store itself) and should also be aware of wine schools or other organizations that conduct wine tastings in your area.

When in Rome . . .

If you've never been to a wine tasting, we should warn you that a few matters of etiquette apply at most tastings. Familiarizing yourself with this etiquette will help you feel more comfortable. Otherwise, you're likely to be appalled by what you see or hear. Why are those people behaving like that?!

To spit or not to spit?

Remember we mentioned a large, plastic cup that each student in a wine class has for dumping out his leftover wine? Well, we lied. (We wanted to ease you into what we realize might be a shocking concept.) The cup is really for students to *spit out the wine* after tasting it.

Professional wine tasters long ago discovered that if they swallow every wine they taste, they're far less thoughtful tasters by the time they reach wine nine or ten. So spitting became acceptable. In wineries, professional tasters sometimes spit right onto the gravel floor or into the drains. In more elegant surroundings, they spit into a *spittoon,* usually a simple container like a large plastic cup (one per taster) or an ice bucket that two or three tasters share.

At first, naturally, some tasters are loath to spit out wine. Not only have they been brought up to believe that spitting is uncouth, but they've also paid good money for the opportunity to taste the wines. Why waste them?

Well, you can drink all of your wine at a wine tasting, if you wish — and some people do. But we don't advise that you do, for the following reasons:

- Evaluating the later wines will be difficult if you swallow the earlier ones. The alcohol you consume will cloud your judgment.

- Swallowing is not really necessary in order to taste the wine fully. If you leave the wine in your mouth for eight to ten seconds (see Chapter 2), you'll be able to taste it thoroughly — without having to worry about the effects of the alcohol.

- If you are driving to the tasting, you're taking a risk driving home afterwards if you drink instead of spit. The stakes are high — your life and health, others' lives, and your driver's license. Why gamble?

Horizontal or vertical?

Two of the goofiest expressions in the world of wine apply to wine tastings. Depending on the nature of the wines featured, wine-tasting events can be categorized as *vertical tastings* or as *horizontal tastings*. These categories have nothing to do with the position of the tasters themselves — they are usually seated, and they're never lying down (that went out of fashion after the Romans).

A vertical tasting is a wine tasting featuring several vintages of the same wine — Château Latour in each vintage from 1988 to 1998, for example. A horizontal tasting examines wines of a single vintage from several different wineries; usually the wines are of a similar type, such as 1997 Napa Valley Cabernet Sauvignons.

There's no particular name for tastings with less disciplined themes, but we'd like to suggest *paisley*.

The simple solution: Spit out the wine. Just about all experienced wine tasters do. Believe it or not, spitting will seem to be a very normal thing to do at wine tastings after a while. (And, in the meantime, it's one sure way to appear more experienced than you are!)

If you know that you can't bring yourself to spit, be sure to have something substantial to eat before going to a wine tasting. You absorb alcohol more slowly on a full stomach — and the simple crackers and bread at most wine tastings are not sufficient to do the trick.

What's with the sound effects?

Do you have to make that loud slurping or gurgling noise that you hear "serious" wine tasters make at tastings?

Of course you don't. But the drawing of air into your mouth does enhance your ability to taste the wine (as explained in Chapter 2). With a little practice, you can gurgle without making loud, attention-getting noises.

More fine points of wine etiquette

Because smell is such an important aspect of wine tasting, courteous tasters try not to interfere with other tasters' ability to smell. This means

- Smoking (anything) is a complete no-no at any wine tasting.
- Using any scent (perfume, after-shave lotion, scented hair spray, and so on) is undesirable. These foreign odors can really interfere with your fellow tasters' ability to detect the wine's aroma.

Courteous wine tasters also do not volunteer their opinions about a wine until other tasters have had a chance to taste the wine. Serious tasters like to form their opinions independently and are sure to throw dirty looks at anyone who interrupts their concentration.

Most of these wine-tasting etiquette guidelines apply to wine classes as well — and are also relevant when you visit wineries around the world.

Dinner with the winemaker

A popular type of wine event is the winemaker dinner, a multicourse dinner at which a winemaker or winery owner is the guest of honor. Wine drinkers pay a fixed price for the meal and taste various wines from the featured winery that are matched to each course.

As far as learning goes, winemaker dinners rank below seminar-style wine tastings but above many informal, reception-style tastings. These dinners offer the chance to taste wines under ideal circumstances — with food — but we find that the speakers disseminate very little information of any value and give you little opportunity to ask questions.

In their potential for fun, however, winemaker dinners are right up there at the top of the list — even if you don't get to sit next to the winemaker.

Junior year abroad

One of the best — and most fun-filled — ways to learn about wine is to actually visit wine regions and, if possible, speak to the winemakers and producers about their wines. You'll be able to immerse yourself in the region you visit — experiencing the climate firsthand, seeing the soil and the hills, touching the grapes, and so on. You can walk through the vineyards if you wish, visit nearby villages, eat the local food, and drink the wine of the region.

You'll discover that there's something special about the people who devote their lives to making wine. Maybe it's their creativity or their commitment to bringing so much pleasure to the world through their labor. Whatever the reason, they are exceptional people. We have found some of our dearest friends in wine regions throughout the world.

Appointments definitely in order

When you do plan to visit a winery, you usually need to call or write ahead for an appointment.

Blind man's bluff

One of the favorite diversions of wine tasters is tasting wines blind. Before you conjure up thoughts of darkened rooms, blindfolded tasters, or other forms of hanky-panky, let us explain that the tasters are not blind, the bottles are. Or anyway, the bottles have their faces covered.

In *blind tastings,* the identities of the wines are not known to the tasters. The theory behind this exercise is that knowing the identities might prejudice the tasters to prefer (or dislike) a particular wine for its reputation rather than for

"what's in the glass," as they say. Sometimes, extremely skilled tasters taste wines blind and try to identify them (if they can!), in an effort to sharpen their tasting skills even further.

If you don't know enough about wine to be prejudiced by the labels, there's little point in tasting blind. Nevertheless, there's something about blind tasting that really helps you focus your concentration on what you're tasting — and that's always good practice.

The major exceptions are the many large wineries in California that offer scheduled tours or self-guided visits. Many wineries in the U.S. do have tasting rooms that are open every day during the busy tourism months and on weekends during the winter. In these tasting rooms, you can sample wines (sometimes for a small fee), buy wine, and buy souvenirs such as T-shirts or sweatshirts with the logo of the winery imprinted on them.

If you visit wineries that are less geared toward tourism — which is the case in most of the rest of the wine world — you can simply sample the wines, talk to the winemaker or proprietor when he's available (you *have* made an appointment, right?), take an informal tour of the winery, and buy some wine if you wish (an especially nice idea if the wine is not available back home).

Don't know the language? No problema

Don't let your limited (or nonexistent) ability to speak the local language prevent you from visiting wine regions. These days, English is the nearly universal language of the wine world. Even if the person you're visiting doesn't speak English, he'll invariably have someone available (his wife, his son, or his dog) who does. Besides, wine itself is a universal language. A smile and a handshake go a long way towards communicating!

Armchair Travel

Traveling around the world takes time and money. Alternatively, you can travel through the wine world from the comfort of your living room, letting the written word carry you to faraway wine regions. Many retail wine stores sell wine magazines, newsletters, and books.

Recommended reading

The following books are some of *the* established tomes; they take you into great depth on particular aspects of wine. A good source for many of these books is the Wine Appreciation Guild (☎ 800-231-9463); it has an extensive catalog devoted to wine books.

General knowledge

Hugh Johnson and Jancis Robinson, MW, *World Atlas of Wine,* Fifth Edition, London, Mitchell Beazley, 2001. Johnson and Robinson, both English, are probably the world's most respected wine writers. Complete with detailed maps of all of the world's wine regions, this book is essential for any serious wine lover's library. (*Modern Encyclopedia of Wine* and *Pocket Encyclopedia of Wine* are two additional worthwhile books by Hugh Johnson.)

Oz Clarke, *Oz Clarke's New Encyclopedia of Wine,* New York, Harcourt, 1999. Oz Clarke is undoubtedly the wine world's most prolific wine writer — the Stephen King of winedom. This comprehensive encyclopedia is well organized and up-to-date. A great wine reference book.

Jancis Robinson, MW (editor), *The Oxford Companion to Wine,* Second Edition, Oxford, Oxford University Press, 1999. An encyclopedic reference book that sets the standard in the wine field. We would expect no less from Jancis Robinson, one of the truly brilliant wine writers. This book is a "must" for all serious students of wine. (Also check out Robinson's *Vines, Grapes, and Wines,* published by Alfred A. Knopf.)

Bordeaux

Robert M. Parker, Jr., *Bordeaux,* Third Edition, New York, Simon & Schuster, 1998. Robert Parker is certainly America's — if not the world's — most famous wine writer. He earned his reputation for his knowledge of Bordeaux; he was also the first writer to use the 100-point wine rating system. This third edition covers all major Bordeaux wines from 1961 to 1997, with info on wines dating back to 1945 — an essential book for any Bordeaux lover. (Anther book by Parker worth having is *The Wines of the Rhône Valley,* Second Edition, 1997.)

Hubrecht Duijker and Michael Broadbent, *The Bordeaux Atlas and Encyclopedia of Châteaux,* New York, St. Martin's Press, 1997. This is the latest great Bordeaux reference book, written primarily by the prolific Dutchman Hubrecht Duijker. Duijker's several atlases on various wine regions have established him as one of most authoritative wine writers of modern times.

David Peppercorn, MW, *Wines of Bordeaux,* Revised Edition, London, Mitchell Beazley, 2002. England's David Peppercorn is rightfully regarded as one of the great Bordeaux experts. In this succinctly written wine guide, Peppercorn offers his own ratings of Bordeaux wines, when to drink them, and which ones are particularly good values.

Burgundy and the Rhône Valley

Clive Coates, MW, *Côte d'Or*, Berkeley, University of California Press, 1997. This may be the prolific Mr. Coates' best book yet on his favorite wine region. Coates, another one of the fine corps of British wine writers, covers all the major districts of the Côte d'Or (which is the home of all the great red and white Burgundy wines; see Chapter 10), reviews all the producers, and provides detailed information on vintages. A thorough reference book on Burgundy. (Also worth reading is Coates' book on Bordeaux, *Grands Vins,* and his *The Wines of France.*)

Remington Norman, MW, *The Great Domaines of Burgundy,* New York, Henry Holt, 1992. Norman has written a succinct, excellent work on this very complicated wine region.

Remington Norman, MW, *Rhône Renaissance,* San Francisco, The Wine Appreciation Guild Ltd., 1996. This is a much-needed book on a region that has gone through major changes in recent years.

Champagne

Ed McCarthy, *Champagne For Dummies,* New York, Wiley Publishing, Inc., 1999. Your *Wine For Dummies* co-author, a Champagne specialist, has written this comprehensive guide to the world of Champagne, including a section on touring Champagne and a directory of Champagne houses.

Tom Stevenson, *Christie's World Encyclopedia of Champagne & Sparkling Wine,* San Francisco, The Wine Appreciation Guild Ltd., 1998. England's Tom Stevenson knows more about Champagne than the Champenois themselves! A thorough look at Champagne and all of the major sparkling wines of the world.

Richard Juhlin, *2000 Champagnes,* Solna, Sweden, Methusalem AB, 1997. Juhlin, an extremely knowledgeable Swedish lover of Champagne, gives his own very personalized views of the Champagne houses, which are organized by the villages where they are located. Producers are indexed in the back of the book.

Old and rare wines

Michael Broadbent, MW, *Michael Broadbent's Vintage Wine,* New York, Harcourt, 2002. No one has tasted more great wines, especially old and rare ones, than England's Michael Broadbent. This guide to vintage wines going back to the nineteenth century concentrates on Bordeaux, Sauternes, and Burgundy. This is a book for the advanced wine buff. Great stuff from one of the world's greatest French wine connoisseurs.

France

Ed McCarthy and Mary Ewing-Mulligan MW, *French Wine For Dummies,* New York, Wiley Publishing, Inc., 2001. Every French wine region is covered, with special emphasis on Bordeaux, Burgundy, and the Rhône Valley. Dare we say, "Eminently readable"?

James Turnbull, *Fine French Wines,* Paris, Flammarion, 2003. Turnbull selects and describes 220 of France's outstanding wines, covering just about every wine region. An excellent survey for the French wine connoisseur.

Italy

Mary Ewing-Mulligan MW and Ed McCarthy, *Italian Wine For Dummies,* New York, Wiley Publishing, Inc., 2001. Every Italian wine region and every major Italian wine is covered, with special emphasis on Piedmont, Tuscany, Northeastern Italy, and Southern Italy.

Daniele Cernilli and Marco Sabellico, *The New Italy,* London, Mitchell Beazley, 2000. This regional approach to Italy's wines has sections on notable producers in each region, many of whom are new or recent.

Burton Anderson, *Burton Anderson's Best Italian Wines,* London, Little Brown, 2001. Anderson, originally from Minnesota but now living in Tuscany, is one of the world's most highly regarded writers on Italian wines. The recommendations in this book carry the ring of authority that only one with Anderson's vast experience can deliver.

Germany

Stuart Pigott, *The Wine Atlas of Germany,* London, Mitchell Beazley, 1995. Although British, Pigott lives in Germany and is regarded as one of the leading experts writing about the intricacies of German wine. The series editor of this atlas is Hugh Johnson, another German wine lover and a man who knows something about putting together wine atlases. An excellent reference for German wines.

Spain

Jeremy Watson, *The New and Classical Wines of Spain,* Barcelona, Montagud Editores, 2002. The first modern, comprehensive book on the wines of Spain. Watson has performed a great service in providing the wine world with an important reference on one of the world's great wine countries.

California

Stephen Brook, *Wines of California,* London, Mitchell Beazley, 2002. A respected British writer gives us a refreshing look at California's wines in this easy-to-read,

200-page guide. The major part of the book is a directory of wineries, listed alphabetically and succinctly described, with each rated on a scale of one to five stars.

Jim Laube, *California Wine,* Second Edition, New York, Wine Spectator Press, 1999. *The Wine Spectator* is a leading consumer wine magazine in the U.S., and Jim Laube is its California wine expert. This easy-to-use, encyclopedic book is an excellent reference source; Laube lists all of California's wine producers alphabetically, with a rating of their wines, plus some useful wine maps.

Australia and New Zealand

John Beeston, *The Wine Regions of Australia,* St. Leonards, NSW, Australia, Allen & Unwin, 1999. A complete, up-to-date guide to the wine regions of one of the world's increasingly important wine countries.

James Halliday, *Wines of Australia,* London, Australia, Mitchell Beazley, 2003. A compact but expert guide to the wine regions of Australia from the prolific James Halliday, wine writer, winemaker, and barrister.

Michael Cooper, *Wine Atlas of New Zealand*, Auckland, Hodder, Moa Beckett, 2002. Cooper is arguably the world's leading authority on New Zealand's wines. This comprehensive tome is required reading for all New Zealand wine lovers.

Wine magazines

Wine magazines can provide more topical information about wine than books can. They keep you up-to-date on the current happenings in the wine world, give you timely tasting notes on newly released wines, profile the currently hot wines and winemakers, and so on. Also, the classified ads in the back of most wine magazines are a good way to hear about wine-related equipment for sale, wine tours, and other useful offers.

Some magazines that we recommend include

- ✔ *Decanter:* One of the oldest and one of the best, this magazine covers the world but is especially strong on French and Italian wines. *Decanter* also occasionally issues supplements on major wine regions as part of your subscription. It's published monthly in London. ☎ 800-875-2997 (U.S.) or 1444-475675 (U.K.); www.decanter.com.

- ✔ *Wine:* England's other major wine magazine provides good coverage of Europe's wine regions, without attitude. It's published monthly in the U.K. ☎ 914-267-3481 (North America) or 01795-414879 (U.K.); e-mail: wine@wilmington.co.uk.

✔ *Wine Spectator:* A lot of current news is in the *Spectator,* including rather extensive coverage of the world's major wine regions, with plenty of tasting notes. This magazine is published twice monthly. ☎ 800-752-7799; `www.winespectator.com`.

✔ *Wine Enthusiast:* An experienced staff of writers covers the wine world in an authentic fashion. The magazine, part of a large wine accessories company, includes an extensive wine-buying guide. It is published monthly in Elmsford, New York. ☎ 800-829-5901; `www.winemag.com`.

✔ *Wine & Spirits:* This high-class magazine offers comprehensive, thoughtful coverage of wine and spirits. Extensive tasting notes are always included. It's published eight times a year in New York, NY. ☎ 888-695-4660; `www.wineandspiritsmagazine.com`.

Wine newsletters

Wine newsletters are an important part of the information pipeline in the wine world. They usually express the personal opinion of one authoritative writer. They contain mainly wine-tasting notes, as opposed to magazines, which contain feature-length articles along with tasting notes.

One nice thing about newsletters is that they accept no advertising; thus, they can maintain (in theory, at least) more impartiality than magazines. Most wine newsletters are intended for the intermediate to advanced wine buff.

✔ *The Wine Advocate:* Robert M. Parker, Jr., is an attorney-turned-wine critic. His approach to wine is methodical and thorough, complete with ratings of wine on a 100-point scale. Clear and easy-to-read with lots of charts and wine-buying tips, *The Wine Advocate* is a must-read for all serious wine lovers (not for the complete beginner); it covers the world's major wine regions but is especially strong on French wines. Published bimonthly. P.O. Box 311, Monkton, Maryland 21111. ☎ 410-329-6477; `www.eRobertParker.com`.

✔ *International Wine Cellar:* Steve Tanzer combines thoughtful articles, interviews with major wine figures, and extensive tasting notes to make an intelligent guide for the advanced wine buff. Published bimonthly in New York. Tanzer Business Communications, Inc., P.O. Box 20021, New York, NY 10021. ☎ 800-WINE-505.

✔ *The Vine:* England's Clive Coates, MW, is an authority on the wines of Burgundy and Bordeaux. So, as you might expect, *The Vine* (more of a booklet than a newsletter in design) focuses mainly on these two major wine regions; in fact, many of his issues provide in-depth coverage of several leading producers of one area — red wines from Burgundy, for example. This newsletter is for the advanced wine lover. Published monthly in London. ☎ 081-995-8962.

Wine on the Internet

If you're thirsty for wine knowledge, you can spend hours learning about wine from Internet sites. Most wineries and some wine importers have their own home pages, as do several wine magazines. Other sites feature groups of wineries. Here are some of our favorite places to read about, search for, or chat about wine online.

- **WineSpectator.com** (www.winespectator.com): Here you can look up descriptions and ratings of just about any wine that *The Wine Spectator* magazine has ever reviewed. Also featured: articles that have appeared in the magazine, menus pairing food and wine, travel and dining articles, and more.

- **Robert Parker Online** (www.erobertparker.com): Features wine reviews and articles from the world's most powerful wine critic and his team. Subscribers to the site ($99/year) can access these reviews, but even non-subscribers can view Parker's vintage chart and a very useful page of links to sites such as institutional wine promotion boards.

- **Jancis Robinson** (www.jancisrobinson.com): This site features articles and commentary from England's leading wine journalist. Subscribers (approximately $79/year) gain access to her purple pages, where they can even search Robinson's authoritative *Oxford Wine Companion.*

- **Robin Garr's Wine Lovers' Page** (www.wine-lovers-page.com): One of the original wine Web sites, founded in 1994. It features online discussion groups, Wine Questionary (a dictionary of questions and answers), tasting notes, and articles. Despite its slightly busy look, it's a great place to learn about wine.

- **Decanter.com** (www.decanter.com): *Decanter* magazine's site is attractive, free, and full of information about wine, including live chats with wine experts — but its wine search leaves something to be desired.

- **Tastings.com** (www.tastings.com): *Tastings* is the journal of the respected Beverage Testing Institute in Chicago. This site is useful mainly for reading wine reviews and ratings.

- **Wine-searcher** (www.wine-searcher.com): When you type the name of a wine you're looking for, this site tells you where in the world you can buy it and at what price, and it provides links to stores or sites selling the wine.

Chapter 19

Describing and Rating Wine

*W*hen we first got excited about wine, we tried to share our enthusiasm with a relative who appeared to have some interest in the subject (well, he drank a glass now and then). Each time we served a wine, we'd talk about it in great detail. But he wasn't interested. "I don't want to talk about wine — I just want to drink it!" he proclaimed.

On some fundamental level where wine is just a generic beverage, it's certainly possible to drink wine without talking about it. But if you're the kind of person who likes to talk about food, or if you've been bitten by the wine bug, you know that it's difficult (if not impossible) to enjoy wine without talking about it at least a little. Wine is a social pleasure that's enhanced by sharing with others.

Ironically, the experience of a wine is highly personal. If you and three other people taste the same wine at the same time, each of you will have your own impression of that wine based on personal likes and dislikes, physiology, and experience. Maybe some day, if humans learn how to link their minds through Ethernet, someone else will be able to experience your experience of a wine — but until then, your taste is singular. The only way you can share your impressions with others is through conversation — talking about it.

Words Cannot Describe . . .

Language is our main vehicle for communicating our entire experience of life. Our vocabulary of taste is undeveloped, however. When we were young, we were taught a visual vocabulary: what is green, yellow, gold, and orange — and for that matter, what is pine green, jungle green, olive green, forest green, and sea green (thanks, Crayola!). No one ever taught us the precise difference in the words *bitter, astringent,* and *tart.* Yet to talk about wine taste, we use these words as if we all agree on what they mean.

Any discussion of wine's taste is particularly complicated, because wine is a complex beverage that gives us multiple taste sensations:

- ✔ Olfactory sensations (all those flavors we perceive by smelling them in our mouths — as we discuss in Chapter 2)
- ✔ Basic taste sensations (sweetness, sourness, and bitterness)
- ✔ Tactile sensations (the bite of astringency, for example, as well as the prickliness, roughness, smoothness, or other textural impressions of a wine in our mouths)
- ✔ Sensations on the holistic level, a synthesis of all the wine's characteristics taken together

For example, say we just tasted an oaked Sauvignon Blanc from California. We might perceive the wine as intense in oaky and herbaceous aroma, with melon-like flavor (olfactory impressions), very slightly sweet, yet with firm acidity (basic taste impressions), smooth and rich (tactile impressions), a vibrant wine with personality to spare (holistic impression). What sounds like some insufferable wine snob showing off is actually just some poor wine lover trying his best to report the taste data the wine is sending him.

You've probably gotten many a laugh from wine descriptions you've read. At face value, they sound preposterous: *Unctuous, with butter and vanilla flavors that coat the sides of your mouth. Supple and smooth, showing some fatness in the mouth, and a long finish.* (Wait! They forgot to say wet and "liquidy.") Imperfect medium that language is, however, it's the only way we have of communicating the taste of wine.

What the words are worth

Once, we engaged in a humbling yet fascinating exercise. Several wine writers were given a wine to taste, along with eight published tasting notes from other writers, only one of which corresponded to that wine. We were asked to identify that tasting note, as well as the note that seemed the most inappropriate. The description we all voted *least* appropriate for the wine turned out to be the description taken from the back label of the wine bottle! Not one of us had correctly matched the description's words to our taste experience. Again, with another wine, we each discovered that *our* taste and *their* words failed to correspond. Our only possible conclusions were either that we can't taste very well, the writers can't write very well (present company included), or that communicating taste is a hopeless exercise.

Reading wine descriptions (or *tasting notes,* as they're often called) in wine newsletters or magazines can be as difficult as writing them. We must admit that our eyes often glaze over when we try to read tasting notes. And we're not alone. Frank Prial, wine columnist of *The New York Times,* once wrote that ". . . a stranger's tasting notes, to me anyway, are about as meaningful as a Beijing bus schedule."

When It's Your Turn to Speak

Describing your experience or impression of a wine involves two steps: First, you have to form the impression; second, you have to communicate it.

When you drink wine with friends purely for enjoyment and appreciation — over dinner, for example — simple impressions and silly comments are perfectly appropriate. If a wine strikes you as unusually full and voluptuous, why *not* say that it's like Marilyn Monroe? If a wine seems tight and unyielding, go ahead and call it Ebenezer Scrooge. Everyone will know exactly what you mean.

In other circumstances, though, such as when you're attending a wine-tasting event, you probably want to form more considered impressions of each wine so that you can participate in the discussion and gain the most from the event. To form a considered impression, you need to taste thoughtfully.

Organizing your thoughts

The language you use to describe a wine starts with your own thoughts as you taste the wine. Thus, the process of tasting a wine and the process of describing it are intertwined.

Although wine tasting involves examining wine visually and smelling it as well as tasting it, those first two steps are a breeze compared to the third. When the wine is in your mouth, the multiple taste sensations — flavors, texture, body, sweetness or dryness, acidity, tannin, balance, length — occur practically all at once. In order to make sense of the information you receive from the wine, you have to impose some order on the impressions. (Turn to Chapter 2 for information on the steps involved in examining, smelling, and tasting wine.)

One way of organizing the impressions a wine sends you is to classify those impressions according to the nature of the "taste":

✔ The wine's *aromatics* (the olfactory data, all the flavors you smell in your mouth)

✔ The wine's *structure* (its alcohol/sweetness/acid/tannin makeup and its basic tastes — the wine's bricks and mortar, so to speak)

✔ The wine's *texture* (the tactile data, how the wine feels in your mouth; texture is a function of the wine's structural components — a high acid, dry, low-alcohol white wine may feel thin or sharp, for example, whereas a high-alcohol red wine with low tannin may feel soft and silky)

Another way of organizing the impressions a wine sends you is by the sequence of your impressions, as we describe in Chapter 2. The words that tasters use to describe the sequence are

✔ **Attack:** The first impression of sweetness, dryness, or viscosity as the wine enters your mouth.

✔ **Evolution:** The development of the wine in your mouth, a stage when the wine's acidity registers — and subsequently, its tannin. During this phase, the wine's flavors also register, and you notice how well the wine persists across the length of your mouth.

✔ The **finish** or **aftertaste:** Flavors or impressions that register after the wine has been spat or swallowed. Both the duration of the aftertaste and its nature are noteworthy. (A long finish is commendable, for example, and a bitter one is not.)

Writing tasting notes

Some people have a special ability to remember tastes. But other people need to take notes in order to remember what they tasted, let alone what they thought of it. If you have the slightest difficulty remembering the names of wines, jot down the names of wines you try and like so that you can enjoy them — or similar wines — again.

To taste, perchance to drink

In wine circles, tasting and drinking are two different activities. Tasting involves thoughtful evaluation of a wine's quality, flavors, texture, aging potential, and so on; if more than a couple of wines are being tasted comparatively, usually tasters spit the wine out (as we mention in Chapter 18) in order to keep their thinking clear. Drinking involves consumption and sheer appreciation, without any particular analysis of the wine other than the judgment that you like it. (If you don't like it, you don't drink it.)

Unless you're a professional in the wine business, you don't ever have to taste a wine seriously; you can just drink it. However, many wine drinkers have discovered that wine tasting can be a fun way to learn more about wine.

It's a good idea to write comments about wines that you taste, too. Even if you're one of those lucky few who can remember everything you taste, we recommend that you write tasting notes now and then because the exercise of taking notes helps discipline your tasting methods.

When we take notes on wines, we automatically write the letters

- ✔ *C* (for color and appearance in general)
- ✔ *N* (for nose)
- ✔ *T* (for taste)

We put one below the other, under the name of each wine on our tasting sheet, leaving space to record our impressions.

When we taste, we take each wine as it comes: If a wine is very aromatic, we write lots of things next to *N,* but if the aroma is understated we could just write *subtle* or even *not much.* When we taste the wine, we approach it sequentially, noting its attack and evolution, but we hold the wine long enough to note its balance and texture, too. Then (having spat), we often taste the wine again to determine what else it might be saying. Sometimes at that point we arrive at a summary description of the wine, like *a huge wine packed with fruitiness that's ready to drink now,* or *a lean, austere wine that will taste better with food than alone.* Our tasting notes are a combination of fragmented observation — *high acid, very tart* — and summary description.

At first, your own notes will be brief. Just a few words, like *soft, fruity* or *tannic, hard* are fine to remind you later what the wine was like. And as an evaluation of overall quality, there's absolutely nothing wrong with *yum!*

Describing wine: Purism versus poetry

Some people have the idea that there's a right way and a wrong way to describe wine. Many *enologists* (people who have earned a degree in the science of winemaking), for example, usually favor a scientific approach to describing wine. This approach relies on descriptors that are objective, quantifiable, and reproducible — such as the level of acidity in a wine (which is measurable) or specific aroma and flavor descriptors (reproducible in laboratory tests). They dislike fanciful or unspecific terms, such as *rich, generous,* or *smooth.*

Other people who aren't scientists (ourselves included) believe that strictly scientific descriptions usually fail to communicate the spirit of a wine. We're all for noting the relative acidity, tannin, and alcohol levels of a wine, but we won't stop there; we like to describe the overall personality of a wine, even if we have to use language that's more personal than universal.

Sometimes, if a wine is really a great wine, tasters stumble into the most controversial realm of wine description: poetry. We never *try* to come up with picturesque metaphorical descriptions for wines, but sometimes a wine just puts the words in our mouths. One memorable wine in our early days of tasting was a 1970 Brunello di Montalcino that we described as a rainbow in the mouth, its flavors so perfectly blended that each one is barely perceptible individually. Recently a friend of ours described a glass of great but young Vintage Port as "like rubbing a cat in the wrong direction."

If a wine inspires you to such fanciful description, by all means go with it; only a cold-blooded scientist would resist. The experience of that wine will become memorable through the personal words you use to name it.

But beware of anyone who is moved to poetry over every wine. The vast majority of wines are prosaic, and their descriptions should be, too.

And when you do lapse into metaphor over a wine, don't necessarily expect others to understand what you mean or even to approve. Literal types will be all over you, demanding to know what a rainbow tastes like and how a wine can possibly resemble a cat.

In the end, the experience of wine is so personal that the best any of us can do is to *try* to describe the experience to others. Your descriptions will be meaningful to people who share your approach and your language, especially if they are tasting the wine along with you. But someone else picking up your notes will find them incomprehensible. Likewise, you'll find some wine descriptions you read incomprehensible. Such is the nature of the exercise.

Rating Wine Quality

When a wine critic writes a tasting note, he usually accompanies it with a point score, a judgment of the wine's quality on a scale of 20 or 100. You'll see these numbers plastered all over the shelves in your wine shop and in wine advertisements.

Because words are such a difficult medium for describing wine, the popularity of number ratings has spread like wildfire. Many wine lovers don't bother to read the descriptions in a critic's wine reviews — they just run out to buy the wines with the highest scores. (Hey, they're the best wines, right?) Wines that receive high scores from the best-known critics sell out almost overnight as the result of the demand generated by their scores.

Numbers do provide a convenient shorthand for communicating a critic's opinion of a wine's quality. But number ratings are problematic, too, for a number of reasons:

✔ The sheer precision of the scores suggests that they are objective, when in fact they represent either the subjective opinion of an individual critic or the combined subjective opinions of a panel of critics.

✔ Different critics can apply the same scale differently. For example, some might assign 95 points only to wines that are truly great compared to all wines of all types, while others could assign the same score to a wine that is great in its own class.

✔ Number scores tell you absolutely nothing about how the wine tastes.

This last point, for us, is the most important. You might hate a wine that's rated highly — and not only that, but you might end up feeling like a hopeless fool who can't recognize quality when it's staring him in the face. Save your money and your pride by deciding what kinds of wine you like and then trying to figure out from the words whether or not a particular wine is your style — *regardless of the number rating*.

Despite the pitfalls of number ratings, you might be inclined to score wines yourself when you taste — and we encourage you to do that. Numbers can be very meaningful to the person assigning them.

To start, decide which scale you'll use. We suggest a scale with 100 as the highest score, because it is more intuitive than a scale ending in 20. (Most 100-point scales are actually only 50-point scales, with 50 points, not zero, representing the poorest conceivable quality.)

After deciding your scale, create several groupings of points, and write down the quality level that each group represents. It could be something like this:

✔ 95–100: Absolutely outstanding; one of the finest wines ever

✔ 90–94: Exceptional quality; excellent wine

✔ 85–89: Very good quality

✔ 80–84: Above-average quality; good

✔ 75–79: Average commercial quality (a "C" student)

✔ 70–74: Below average quality

✔ Below 70: Poor quality

Until you get the hang of using this system, you might just want to give each wine a range rather than a precise score, such as 80–84 (good) or 85–89 (very good). As you gain experience in tasting wine and rating wine quality, you become more opinionated and your scores will naturally become more precise.

Just remember that like every other critic, you have your own taste preferences that inevitably influence your scores, no matter how objective you try to be. Don't fall into the trap of thinking that all your wine friends should agree with you.

Chapter 20

Marrying Wine with Food

• •

In This Chapter

▶ Predictable reactions between wines and foods

▶ Guiding principles for matchmakers

▶ Classic combos that still work

• •

*E*very now and then, we encounter a wine that stops us dead in our tracks. It's so sensational that we lose all interest in anything but that wine. We drink it with intent appreciation, trying to memorize the taste. We wouldn't dream of diluting its perfection with a mouthful of food.

But 999 times out of 1,000, we drink our wine with food. Wine is meant to go with food. And good food is meant to go with wine.

Matchmaker, Matchmaker . . .

Good. We've settled that. Wine goes with food, and food goes with wine. Any questions?

Of course we're being facetious. There are thousands of wines in the world, and every one is different. And there are thousands of basic foods in the world, each different — not to mention the infinite combinations of foods in prepared dishes (what we really eat). In reality, food-with-wine is about as simple an issue as boy-meets-girl.

The dynamics of food and wine

Every dish is dynamic — it's made up of several ingredients and flavors that interact to create a (more or less) delicious whole. Every wine is dynamic in exactly the same way. When food and wine combine in your mouth, the dynamics of each change; the result is completely individual to each dish-and-wine combination. (Dare we also mention that we each use our individual palates to judge the success of each combination? No wonder there are no rules!)

When wine meets food, several things can happen:

- ✔ The food can exaggerate a characteristic of the wine. For example, if you eat walnuts (which are tannic) with a tannic red wine, such as a Bordeaux, the wine tastes so dry and astringent that most people would consider it undrinkable.

- ✔ The food can diminish a characteristic of the wine. Protein diminishes tannin, for example, and an overly-tannic red wine — unpleasant on its own — could be delightful with rare steak or roast beef.

- ✔ The flavor intensity of the food can obliterate the wine's flavor or vice versa. If you've ever drunk a big, rich red wine with a delicate filet of sole, you've had this experience firsthand.

- ✔ The wine can contribute new flavors to the dish. For example, a red Zinfandel that's gushing with berry fruit can bring its berry flavors to the dish, as if another ingredient had been added.

- ✔ The combination of wine and food can create an unwelcome third-party flavor that wasn't in either the wine or the food originally; we get a metallic flavor when we eat plain white-meat turkey with red Bordeaux.

- ✔ The food and wine can interact perfectly, creating a sensational taste experience that is greater than the food or the wine alone. (This scenario is what we hope will happen every time we eat and drink, but it's as rare as a show-stopping dish.)

Fortunately, what happens between food and wine is not haphazard. Certain elements of food react in predictable ways with certain elements of wine, giving us a fighting chance at making successful matches. The major components of wine (alcohol, sweetness, acid, and tannin) relate to the basic tastes of food (sweetness, sourness, bitterness, and saltiness) the same way that the principle of balance in wine operates: Some of the elements exaggerate each other, and some of them compensate for each other. (See the discussion of balance in Chapter 2.)

Here are some ways that food and wine interact, based on the components of the wine. Remember, each wine and each dish has more than one component, and the simple relationships we describe can be complicated by other elements in the wine or the food. Whether a wine is considered tannic, sweet, acidic, or high in alcohol depends on its dominant component. (See "Describing Taste" in Chapter 2.)

The fifth wheel

Common wisdom was that humans can perceive four basic tastes: sweet, sour, salty, and bitter. But people who study food have concluded that a fifth taste exists. This taste is called umami (pronounced *oo MAH me*), and it is associated with a savory character in foods. Shellfish, oily fish, meats, and cheeses are some foods high in umami taste.

Umami-rich foods can increase the sensation of bitterness in wines served with them. To counteract this effect, try adding something salty (such as salt itself) or sour (such as vinegar) to your dish. Although this suggestion defies the adage that vinegar and wine don't get along, the results are the proof of the pudding.

Tannic wines

Tannic wines include most wines based on the Cabernet Sauvignon grape (including red Bordeaux), northern Rhône reds, Barolo and Barbaresco, and any wine — white or red — that has become tannic from aging in new oak barrels. These wines

- ✔ Can diminish the perception of sweetness in a food
- ✔ Can taste softer and less tannic when served with protein-rich, fatty foods, such as steak or cheese
- ✔ Can taste less bitter when paired with salty foods
- ✔ Can taste astringent, or mouth-drying, when drunk with spicy-hot foods

Sweet wines

Some wines that often have some sweetness include most inexpensive California white wines, White Zinfandel, many Rieslings (unless they are labeled "dry" or "trocken"), and medium-dry Vouvray. Sweet wines also include dessert wines such as Port, sweetened Sherries, and late-harvest wines. These wines

- ✔ Can taste less sweet, but fruitier, when matched with salty foods
- ✔ Can make salty foods more appealing
- ✔ Can go well with sweet foods

Acidic wines

Acidic wines include most Italian white wines; Sancerre, Pouilly-Fumé, and Chablis; traditionally-made red wines from Rioja; most dry Rieslings; and wines based on Sauvignon Blanc that are fully dry. These wines

✔ Can taste less acidic when served with salty foods

✔ Can taste less acidic when served with slightly sweet foods

✔ Can make foods taste slightly saltier

✔ Can counterbalance oily or fatty heaviness in food

High-alcohol wines

High alcohol wines include many California wines, both white and red; southern Rhône whites and reds; Barolo and Barbaresco; fortified wines such as Port and Sherry; and most wines produced from grapes grown in warm climates. These wines

✔ Can overwhelm lightly flavored or delicate dishes

✔ Can go well with slightly sweet foods

Birds of a feather, or opposites attract?

Two principles can help in matching wine with food: the complementary principle and the contrast principle. The complementary principle involves choosing a wine that is similar in some way to the dish you are planning to serve, while the contrast principle (not surprisingly) involves combining foods with wines that are dissimilar to them in some way.

The characteristics of a wine that can either resemble or contrast with the characteristics of a dish are

✔ **The wine's flavors:** Earthy, herbal, fruity, vegetal, and so on

✔ **The intensity of flavor in the wine:** Weak flavor intensity, moderately flavorful, or very flavorful

✔ **The wine's texture:** Crisp and firm, or soft and supple

✔ **The weight of the wine:** Light-bodied, medium-bodied, or full-bodied

You probably use the complementary principle often without realizing it: You choose a light-bodied wine to go with a light dish, a medium-bodied wine to go with a fuller dish, and a full-bodied wine to go with a heavy dish. Some other examples of the complementary principle in action are

✔ **Dishes with flavors that resemble those in the wine.** Think about the flavors in a dish the same way you think about the flavors in wine — as families of flavors. If a dish has mushrooms, it has an earthy flavor; if it has citrus or other elements of fruit, it has a fruity flavor (and so on). Then consider which wines would offer their own earthy flavor, fruity flavor, herbal flavor, spicy flavor, or whatever. The earthy flavors of white Burgundy complement risotto with mushrooms, for example, and an herbal Sancerre complements chicken breast with fresh herbs.

✔ **Foods with texture that's similar to that of the wine.** A California Chardonnay with a creamy, rich texture could match the rich, soft texture of lobster, for example.

✔ **Foods and wines whose intensity of flavor match.** A very flavorful Asian stir-fry or Tex-Mex dish would be at home with a very flavorful, rather than a subtle, wine.

The contrast principle seeks to find flavors or texture in a wine that are not in a dish but that would enhance it. A dish of fish or chicken in a rich cream and butter sauce, for example, might be matched with a dry Vouvray, a white wine whose crispness (thanks to its uplifting, high acidity) would counterbalance the heaviness of the dish. A dish with earthy flavors such as portobello mushrooms and fresh fava beans (or potatoes and black truffles) might contrast nicely with the pure fruit flavor of an Alsace Riesling.

You also apply the contrast principle every time you decide to serve simple food, like unadorned lamb chops or hard cheese and bread, with a gloriously complex aged wine.

In order to apply either principle, of course, you have to have a good idea of what the food is going to taste like and what various wines taste like. That second part can be a real stumbling block for people who don't devote every ounce of their free energy to learning about wine. The solution is to ask your wine merchant. A retailer might not have the world's greatest knack in wine and food pairings (then again, he or she might), but at least he should know what his wines taste like.

The wisdom of the ages

No matter how much you value imagination and creativity, there's no sense reinventing the wheel. In wine-and-food terms, it pays to know the classic pairings because they work, and they're a sure thing.

"A châque son gout" — personal taste rules

We once happened to discuss food pairings for red Bordeaux wine with the owner of one of the five first growths of Bordeaux (see Chapter 10 for an explanation of first growths). "I don't like Bordeaux with lamb," the distinguished gentleman proclaimed. We were confused; "But Bordeaux and lamb is a classic combination!" we said. "No, I don't agree," he answered, holding his ground. After a moment, he added, "Of course, I don't like lamb."

Here are some famous and reliable combinations:

- ✔ Oysters and Chablis
- ✔ Lamb and red Bordeaux (we like Chianti with lamb, too)
- ✔ Port with walnuts and Stilton cheese
- ✔ Salmon with Pinot Noir
- ✔ Amarone with Gorgonzola cheese
- ✔ Grilled fish with Vinho Verde
- ✔ Foie gras with Sauternes or with late-harvest Gewürztraminer
- ✔ Braised beef with Barolo
- ✔ Dry amontillado Sherry with soup
- ✔ Grilled chicken with Beaujolais
- ✔ Toasted almonds or green olives with fino or manzanilla Sherry
- ✔ Goat cheese with Sancerre or Pouilly-Fumé
- ✔ Dark chocolate with California Cabernet Sauvignon

Look for various additional suggestions on wine and food pairings scattered throughout Chapters 10 through 14 of this book.

Wine from Venus, food from Mars

Sooner or later you're bound to experience food-and-wine disaster — when the two taste miserable together. We've had many opportunities to test our solution to food-and-wine disaster, and it works: As long as the wine is good and the food is good, eat one first and drink the other afterwards — or vice versa.

Chapter 21

To Have and To Hold — or To Sell

. . . .

In This Chapter

▶ Deciding how much wine to own

▶ Cataloging your wine

▶ Keeping your wine hale and hearty

▶ Investing in blue-chip wines

▶ The sweet seduction of an older . . . wine

▶ Liquidating your assets

. . . .

*W*hen we first started buying wine, we operated from the gut. Carried away with excitement after a wine tasting, we'd decide to buy four or six — or even 12 — bottles of our favorite wine of the evening. Sometimes, browsing the shelves of retail stores, we'd buy 12 different Zinfandels (see Chapter 14) with the intention of setting up our own comparative tasting, which we didn't always get around to doing.

Our wine consumption couldn't keep pace with our curiosity to try new wines and our passion to possess wines we liked. Before we knew it, we had become wine collectors.

Luckily for us, we didn't make *too* many mistakes along the way. Nonetheless, we came to appreciate the wisdom of having a plan for our wine purchases. Wine, we decided, has something in common with rabbits: The population of bottles can very easily get out of hand.

Which Kind of Wine Buyer Are You?

Most people consume wines very quickly after buying them. If this is your custom, you have plenty of company.

But many people who enjoy wine operate a bit differently. Oh, sure, they buy wine because they intend to *drink* it; they're just not exactly sure *when* they'll drink it. And until they do drink it, they get pleasure out of knowing that the bottles are waiting for them. If you count yourself in this second group, you are probably a wine collector at heart. The chase, to you, is every bit as thrilling as the consummation.

If you're a closet wine collector, developing a strategy of wine buying can prevent a haphazard collection of uninteresting or worthless bottles from happening to you. But even if you never intend to have a wine collection, it's worthwhile to put at least a little thought into your wine purchases.

The first step in formulating a wine-buying strategy is to consider

- ✔ How much wine you drink
- ✔ How much wine you want to own (and can store properly)
- ✔ How much money you are prepared to spend on wine
- ✔ What types of wine you enjoy drinking

Unless you strike a balance on these issues, you could end up broke, bored, frustrated, or in the vinegar business!

The avowed noncollector

You are enthusiastic about wine and you enjoy buying it. But you have no intention of becoming a wine collector — you don't have the space, or you have better things to spend your money on.

In your circumstances, the only way to prevent a wine collection from happening is strict personal discipline. Determine how many bottles of wine you consume in a month (be sure to take entertaining into account) and never have more than that number of bottles on hand. If you drink wine at home two nights a week, for example, and entertain once a month, the number could be somewhere around 12 bottles.

When you buy wine, avoid purchasing robust, red wines that need time to develop. Avoid buying more than two bottles of any one wine unless you don't mind drinking the same wine frequently. Don't buy any wine that is so extraordinary or expensive that you might be tempted to hold it for a special occasion. Resist the urge to subscribe to wine magazines. Do not browse wine-related Web sites.

Is the sky the limit?

Some wine collectors own more than 10,000 bottles! This might be called taking one's hobby to the extreme. We believe that a collection of 1,000 to 1,500 bottles is definitely sufficient to handle *anyone's* needs nicely. Then again, 100 bottles isn't so bad, either!

The small collector

Moderation in wine collecting is as challenging as it is commendable.

Say you decide that a six-month inventory of wine seems reasonable for you. (That's probably about 75 bottles, given the same scenario of entertaining once a month and drinking wine two nights a week at home.)

You've just given yourself license to collect, because with 75 bottles, you could surely manage to devote a *case* (12 bottles) or two to wines that require long-term aging. You could also rationalize a full-case purchase of a wine you particularly like, figuring that you'd drink it twice a month for six months (but will you really?).

Your challenge is first to maintain a balance between maturing wines and drinkable wines, and then to have enough diversity among your drinkable wines that you don't get bored with your selection. To accomplish these two goals, you probably have to keep records of your inventory. You also need to think about the storage conditions of your wine — especially those long-term keepers. (See the "Age-worthy wines" section in this chapter for information about long-term keepers.)

The serious collector

Congratulations! Most wine collectors don't ever really *decide* to become wine collectors; they just keep buying and buying until they *are* wine collectors. By making a calculated decision to own a few hundred bottles of wine, you have the opportunity to develop a collection that truly suits your tastes and your goals, and to avoid common pitfalls of wine collecting.

Your challenge is to set financial and quantity limits, diversify your collection appropriately, and exercise patience in your wine buying. You'll also want to make sure that your wine is stored under optimal conditions.

Strategies for Collectors Great and Small

Unless your intention is to fill your cellar with wines that bring you the greatest return on investment when you later sell them (in other words, unless you aren't interested in actually *drinking* the wines you own), you should *like* a wine before buying it. (We're not talking about all those bottles you buy while you're playing the field and experimenting with new wines — just those that you're thinking of making a commitment to by buying in quantity.) Liking a wine before you buy it sounds like the plainest common sense, but you'd be surprised at how many people buy a wine merely because somebody gave it a high rating!

Balance in your inventory

A well-planned wine inventory features a range of wines: It can be heavy in one or two types of wine that you particularly enjoy, but it has other types of wine, too. Your inventory should also strike a balance between

- Wines that are ready to drink, and wines that require additional aging
- Inexpensive wines ($7 to $15 a bottle) that can be enjoyed on casual occasions, and important wines that demand a special occasion

If you like California Cabernet Sauvignons, for example, you may decide to make them your specialty. But consider that you might grow weary of them if you have nothing else to drink night after night. By purchasing other wines as well, you can have the fun of exploring different types of wine.

Table wines, of course, are the bulk of most wine collections. But it's a good idea to have a few apéritif wines — such as Champagne or dry Sherry — and dessert wines — such as Port or sweet white wines — so that you'll be prepared when the occasion arises. (If you're like us, you'll invent plenty of occasions to open a bottle of Champagne!)

In planning your own wine collection, you'd be prudent to include some age-worthy wines that you buy in their youth when their prices are lowest. Many of the better red wines, such as Bordeaux, Barolo, and Brunello di Montalcino, often aren't at their best for at least ten years after the vintage — and some of them are difficult to find once they are ready to drink. Aging is also the rule for some fine white Burgundies (such as Corton-Charlemagne), better white Bordeaux, Sauternes, German Rieslings and late-harvest wines, and Vintage Port (which usually requires about 20 years of aging before it matures!).

Everyday wines

What you stock as everyday wines will depend on your personal taste. Our candidates for everyday white wines include simple white Burgundies, such as Mâcon-Villages or St.Véran; Sauvignon Blancs from New Zealand and France (Sancerre and Pouilly-Fumé); Pinot Gris/Pinot Grigio from Oregon, Alsace, and Italy; Italian Pinot Bianco; aromatic Italian whites such as Vermentino, Verdicchio, or Falanghina; Gruner Veltliner from Austria and Riesling from Germany, Austria, or Alsace; and Albariños from Spain.

For everyday red wines, we especially like Italian reds such as Barbera, Dolcetto, Montepulciano d'Abruzzo, Valpolicella, and simple (under $18) Chianti. These red wines are enjoyable young, versatile enough to go well with the foods many people eat on an everyday basis (simple, flavorful foods), and sturdy enough to age for a couple of years if you don't get around to them (that is, they won't deteriorate quickly).

Other everyday red wines we recommend include Beaujolais, Côtes du Rhône, inexpensive (under $20) Pinot Noir, inexpensive (under $18) red Zinfandel from California, and lighter-bodied (under $15) Bordeaux.

Age-worthy wines

Here we suggest categories of white and red wines that are suitable for aging. For recommendations of some specific producers, see the section "The best bets for investing or keeping," later in this chapter.

Age-worthy white wines we recommend include

- ✔ Above all, grand cru and premier cru white Burgundies — such as Corton-Charlemagne, Bâtard- and Chevalier-Montrachets, Meursault, and Chablis Grand Crus
- ✔ Better (over $25) white Bordeaux
- ✔ Great German and Austrian Rieslings
- ✔ Alsace Rieslings or Gewürztraminers

See Chapters 10 and 12 for an explanation of these wines.

Among the many long-lived red wines, some likely candidates for keeping (or *cellaring* — the term for letting wines mature) are

- ✔ Fine Bordeaux
- ✔ Grand cru and premier cru Burgundies
- ✔ Big Italian reds, such as Barolo, Barbaresco, Chianti Classico Riserva, Brunello di Montalcino, Taurasi, and Super-Tuscan blends

- From Spain: Rioja, Ribeira del Duero, and Priorato wines

- From California: Better Cabernet Sauvignons (and Cabernet blends)

- From the Rhône: Hermitage, Côte Rôtie, and Cornas

- Portugal's Barca Velha, and other good Douro table wines

- Australia's Grange (Penfolds), the Henschke Shiraz wines, such as Hill of Grace, and other super-premium Shirazes

- The finer Champagnes (usually Vintage Champagnes and *prestige cuvées;* see Chapter 15); oloroso Sherries (see Chapter 16); and the finest dessert wines, such as late-harvest German Rieslings (see Chapter 12), French Sauternes, sweet Vouvrays from the Loire Valley, Vintage Port, and Madeira. (See Chapter 16 for Sauternes, Port, and Madeira.)

Where to draw the line

One of the toughest decisions you'll have to make is *how much* of a particular wine you should buy. When you believe that a certain wine is really exceptional (you love it, it's just received a great rating, and/or the vintage year is reputedly terrific), you'll probably have a natural tendency to buy large quantities.

We know a fellow who refinanced his house in order to buy 60 cases of 1982 Château Mouton-Rothschild! Actually, that decision wasn't as crazy as it sounds because first growth Bordeaux (see Chapter 10) from the great 1982 vintage was a sound investment. Our friend made an incredible profit on that purchase when he sold the wine, as the Mouton probably cost him no more than $600 a case in 1985, possibly less, and its value when he sold it was $7,000 to $8,000 a case!

If you are about to buy a large quantity of a particular wine — say, two or more cases — the first question you should ask yourself is, "Will I be able to sell this wine in the future, if I decide to do so?" (Consult a wine-knowledgeable acquaintance if you're not sure of a wine's resale potential; also, see "Selling Your Wine" later in this chapter.)

If the wine that you are planning to buy in a large quantity has no proven track record for resale, we advise restraint — for several reasons:

- You may grow tired of the wine and end up with a case or more of it.

- Your tastes may change, or (as you gain experience) you may find that the wine you thought was so great doesn't live up to your expectations.

- The wine could age more quickly than you expected (which happens often), leaving you with several bottles of a wine that is past its prime.

The charm of an aged wine

Aged wines are a thing apart from young wines — and some wines don't really reach their full expression until they have aged. Try drinking a highly acclaimed young red Bordeaux, say a 1996 Château Lafite-Rothschild. You taste a mouthful of tannin, and although the wine has concentration, you probably wonder what all the fuss is about. Try it in 10 to 15 years; the aggressive tannins will have softened, a wonderful bouquet of cedar and blackcurrants will emerge from the glass, and a natural sweetness of flavor will have developed.

As a fine wine matures in the bottle, a series of chemical and physical changes occur. These changes are poorly understood, but their effects are evident in the style of a mature red wine:

✔ The wine becomes paler in color.

✔ Its aroma evolves from the fruity aromas (and often oakiness) it had when young to a complex leathery and earthy bouquet.

✔ Its tannic, harsh texture diminishes, and the wine becomes silky.

Fine wines seem to be easier to digest when they are mature. Besides visceral pleasure, they offer a special emotional satisfaction, too. Tasting an aged wine can be like traveling back in time, sharing a connection with people who have gone before in the great chain of humanity.

Except for investment purposes, we suggest that you never buy more than one case of a particular wine, *at the most.* We save "buying by the case" for a very few of our proven favorite wines; most of the time, we limit ourselves to three or six bottles of particular wines that we know we like and we know have potential for long life. If we haven't tasted a wine before (or we're uncertain whether to buy a wine), we buy just one bottle first, and try it.

Except for sure-fire "investment" wines, such as the 1982 Château Mouton-Rothschild, be careful not to overbuy sought-after wines out of fear that they will sell out. There is always more wine to buy! You might regret not buying more bottles of some wine when you had the opportunity, but the truth is that more good wine is being made every year.

Organization Is Next to Peace of Mind

When you are not only a wine drinker but also a wine collector, you become aware that you need to keep track of all your wine so that

✔ You can find a bottle quickly when you're looking for it.

✔ You know what you own. (Many a bottle has gone *over the hill* because the owner forgot that he had it!)

✔ You can show off your wine collection to your friends (something like showing your baby's pictures).

You can keep track of your wine in many different ways. A wine inventory on paper should include a list of the specific wines in your collection, the number of each, and the location.

Cataloging our wine collection by computer turned out to be a lot easier than we expected. We used a database program (Filemaker, specifically) on our Macintosh to create the file. We set up a field for each of the following items:

✔ Vintage

✔ Producer

✔ Wine name

✔ Appellation

✔ Region

✔ Country

✔ Type (red, white, rosé, sparkling, apéritif, or dessert)

✔ Quantity owned

✔ Price paid (per bottle)

✔ Value (the latest estimated worth, per bottle)

✔ Size of bottle (to indicate 1.5-liter magnums, half-bottles, and so on)

Two summary fields provide the total number of bottles in our inventory at any moment (or the total of any *segment* of our inventory, such as our red Bordeaux) as well as the current value of our inventory.

A Healthy Environment for Your Wines

If you are an avowed noncollector who never has more than a one- or two-month supply of wine on hand, you don't need to worry about how your wines are stored. You can keep your bottles lying down on a rack in the den or the dining room or any other room, as long as they are not right next to the radiator or in direct sunlight. Even if they're standing upright, they'll survive for a few months.

If you've decided to collect a few bottles, however — or if you discover that a wine collection is happening to you — please take heed. If your wines are stored poorly, disappointment after disappointment is inevitable.

If you plan to keep wines indefinitely, you really need a wine storage facility with controlled temperature and humidity. This is especially important if you live where the temperature exceeds 70°F (21°C) for any length of time. Without proper storage, fine wine is either consumed long before it reaches its best drinking period (known in wine circles as *infanticide*), or it dies an untimely death in some closet, garage, or warm cellar.

The passive wine cellar

You might be fortunate enough to have conditions suitable for what is called a *passive* wine cellar (if you've recently inherited a castle in Scotland, for example).

If the place where you intend to store your wine is very cool (below 60°F, 15.5°C) and very damp (75 percent humidity or higher) year-round, you can be the lucky owner of a passive cellar. (It's called *passive* because you don't have to do anything to it, such as cool it or humidify it.) Usually, only deep cellars completely below ground level with thick stones or comparable insulation can be completely passive in temperate climates. Passive cellars are certainly the ideal way to store wines. And you can save a lot of money on their upkeep, to boot.

If you don't have a space that's already ideal for a passive wine cellar, you might decide that you can dig one. For instructions on building your own passive wine cellar, see Richard M. Gold's authoritative book, *How and Why To Build a Passive Wine Cellar,* Third Edition (available at Morrell & Company, ☎ 212-688-9370).

If you can't be passive, be bullish on wine storage

Most of us are neither lucky enough to have a passive wine cellar nor fortunate enough to be able to create one without extraordinary expense and trouble (bulldozers, wrecking crews, and so on). But second best — an artificially cooled and/or humidified room — is far better than nothing.

The following are key features of a good wine storage area:

- ✔ A good storage area should be cool — ideally, in the 53° to 59°F range (12° to 16°C).

- ✔ The temperature should be fairly constant — wide swings in temperature are not good for the wine.

✔ The area should be damp or humid, with a minimum of 70 percent humidity and a maximum of 95 percent (mold sets in above 95 percent).

✔ The area should be free from vibrations, which can travel through the wine; heavy traffic and motors cycling on and off — such as in refrigerators or washers/dryers — are detrimental to your wine.

✔ The area should be free from light, especially direct sunlight; the ultraviolet rays of the sun are especially harmful to wine.

✔ The storage area should be free from chemical odors, such as paints, paint remover, and so on.

We built a room in our cellar for our wine storage area. Whatever area you use, as long as it has a climate control unit and is properly insulated (see the following sections in this chapter), your wine will keep well.

Buy a *hygrometer* (an instrument that measures humidity) for your wine storage facility. Our hygrometer gives us both the percentage of humidity and a digital reading of the temperature — information so valuable that we check it almost daily. (Hygrometers are available through wine accessory catalogs, such as *The Wine Enthusiast*, Pleasantville, NY, ☎ 800-356-8466.)

Avoid refrigerators for wine storage. Don't leave good wine or Champagne in the refrigerator for more than a few days; not only is the refrigerator motor harmful, but the excessively cold temperature (as low as 35°F, 1.6°C) tends to numb and flatten the flavors of the wine.

Climate control

Professional cooling units are available. (You'll find them advertised in wine accessory catalogs and wine magazines.) These are climate-control devices that humidify the air of a room as well as cool it. These units come in various capacities to suit rooms of different dimensions. Many require professional installation; they cost from $500 to $2,200, depending on their capacity.

The issue of humidity

Some wine collectors are not particularly concerned with the humidity levels of their cellars. High humidity causes mold, they argue, and disfigures labels. But dry air can cause your wine to either evaporate or leech out around the cork, causing *ullage* (space between the wine and the cork). The greater the ullage, the greater the chance of your wine becoming oxidized.

Because we recommend humidity between 70 and 95 percent, we believe that air conditioners, which dehumidify the air to about 50 percent, are *not* suitable for wine storage areas.

Depending on where you live, you might not need to run your cooling unit all year. We keep ours going from about late May to late September. The additional expense for electricity comes to about $15 to $20 a month (in our area, northeastern U.S.) for four months — well worth it when we consider the value of the wine we are protecting. During the winter months when the air gets dry, we run a humidifier in our wine room.

Wine racks

Racking systems vary from elaborate redwood racks to simple metal or plastic types. The choice of material and configuration really hinges on how much you want to spend, and your own personal taste.

Large, diamond-shaped wooden (or synthetic composition) racks are popular because they efficiently store up to eight bottles per section and make maximum use of space. Such racks also permit the easy removal of individual bottles.

Figure 21-1:
Diamond-shaped wine rack.

© Akira Chiwaki

A rack configuration that gives each wine its own cubbyhole is more expensive; if you're checking out such racks, consider whether any of your oversized bottles (such as bulbous sparkling wine bottles) might be too large to fit the racks. (And consider whether your half-bottles might be too small!)

Some collectors prefer to store their wine in the wines' original wooden crates. (Many classic wines, such as Bordeaux and Vintage Port, come in these crates; you can usually pick up empty wooden crates in wine stores.) The crates are beneficial for storing wine because the wine remains in a dark environment inside the case, and the temperature changes very slowly thanks to the mass of wine bottles packed together in the closed case. Retrieving a bottle from the bottom row of the case can really be inconvenient, though.

Cardboard boxes are *not suitable* for wine storage. The chemicals used in the manufacture of the cardboard can eventually affect the wine. Also, the cardboard boxes become damaged, in time, from the moisture in the air, assuming that you are maintaining a proper humidity in your cellar.

Insulation

Far more important than your choice of racks is your choice of insulation.

We definitely *do not recommend* fiberglass insulation because it will absorb the moisture from your cooling unit. We've heard of cases in which the weight of the moisture inside the insulation actually caused parts of ceilings to come tumbling down, creating quite a mess.

The ideal insulation is a 3-inch thick, thermoplastic resin called *polyurethane*. It's odorless, does not absorb moisture, and makes a fine seal. Even when a cooling unit is not running, temperatures will change extremely slowly in most wine rooms with this kind of insulation.

Wine caves for apartment dwellers

If you live in a house that has either a cellar or a separate area for your wine, consider yourself fortunate. What if you have no space — for instance, if you live in an apartment?

As an apartment dweller, you have three choices:

- Leave your wine in a friend's or relative's house (provided that *he* has adequate storage facilities — and that you trust him not to drink your wine!).

- Rent storage space in a refrigerated public warehouse.

- Buy a *wine cave* — also known as a *wine vault* — a self-contained, refrigerated unit that you plug into an electrical outlet.

We find the first two options barely acceptable because they don't give you immediate access to your wine. It's downright inconvenient to make a trip every time you want to get your hands on your own wine. And both of these options rob you of the pleasure of having your wines readily available in your home where you can look at them, fondle the bottles, or show them off to your friends.

If we lived in an apartment, we'd definitely own a wine cave. Many wine caves resemble attractive pieces of furniture, either vertical or horizontal credenzas. Some have glass doors, and all of them can be locked.

Wine caves range in size and capacity from a tiny unit that holds only 24 bottles to really large units that hold up to 2,800 bottles, with many sizes in between. Prices range from $200 to about $6,000. You'll find wine caves advertised extensively in wine accessory catalogs and in the back pages of wine magazines.

If you're planning to build a wine cellar or buy a wine cave, allow for expansion in your wine collection. Like most waistlines, wine cellars inevitably grow larger with the passing years.

Investment Wines

Some wines do become rarer and more valuable with age, and selling them for profit can be a temptation that's difficult for even the most dedicated wine lover to resist. It's definitely true that (a very small percentage of) wines are great investments. Certain wines are even safer to invest in than stocks or real estate because they only increase in value — they never decline.

Investment wines have certain attributes:

- They have been universally acknowledged by the wine press and the wine trade to be outstanding.
- They have potential for longevity.
- They are from very good to excellent vintages.
- They have been well-stored so that they are in good condition.

Some investment wines also share a *rarity factor* — not many bottles were produced in the first place.

The best bets for investing or keeping

French wines certainly have the monopoly on the wine investment market worldwide. They have a well-established reputation, especially with the British, who more or less invented the wine investment market.

Fine red Bordeaux — with pedigree and reputation for longevity:

Château Pétrus
Château Lafite-Rothschild
Château Mouton-Rothschild
Château Latour
Château Margaux
Château Haut-Brion

Château Cheval-Blanc
Château Lafleur (Pomerol)
Château Trotanoy
Château Palmer
Château La Mission-Haut-Brion
Château Ausone

(The châteaux in the first column are *especially* good investments.)

Fine dry white Bordeaux — with pedigree and reputation for longevity:

Château Haut-Brion (Blanc)
Château Laville Haut Brion
Domaine de Chevalier

Fine red Burgundy — the most highly respected:

Domaine de la Romanée-Conti wines (especially Romanée-Conti,
La Tache, Richebourg)
Domaine Leroy wines (especially grand crus, such as Musigny and
Chambertin)

Fine white Burgundy — the most highly sought-after:

Montrachet (Domaine de la Romanée-Conti; Ramonet)
Ramonet (his other grand cru white Burgundies)
Domaine des Comtes Lafon (Montrachet; premier cru Meursaults)
Coche-Dury (grand and premier crus)
Raveneau (grand and premier cru Chablis)

Sauternes — the crème de la crème:

Château d'Yquem (clearly the *big gun,* investment-wise)
Château Climens
Château Coutet (Cuvée Madame, especially)
Château de Fargues

Italian super-Tuscans and Brunello di Montalcino:

Sassicaia
Tignanello
Solaia
Ornellaia

Masseto
Biondi-Santi Brunello di Montalcino
Soldera Brunello di Montalcino

Vintage Port — the Big Four of Portugal:

Taylor-Fladgate
Graham
Fonseca
Quinta do Noval (Nacional, only)

Spain's most prized wine:

Vega Sicilia Unico

Certain California Cabernet Sauvignons — the rarity factor:

Grace Family Vineyards Cabernet Sauvignon (any vintage)
Beaulieu Vineyards Private Reserve Cabernets (1970 vintage and older)
Heitz Martha's Vineyard Cabernet Sauvignon (1974 vintage and older)

The Big Two from Down Under:

Penfolds Grange (especially older vintages)
Henschke "Hill of Grace" Shiraz

The mortality factor

The inevitable question of your life expectancy, of course, must enter into the equation when you are considering how much wine to buy — unless you don't mind leaving your wine to your heirs.

Our hero is the late, great wine writer, André Simon. When he died at the age of 94, André reputedly had only two magnums of wine left in his once extensive cellar. Now *that's* good planning!

Selling Your Wine

Because wine is a regulated beverage, you can't necessarily sell your wine without complications. But it's getting easier all the time.

Selling your privately-owned wine is now completely legal in many states of the U.S. — California, New York, and Illinois included. In other places, you might be permitted to sell it to a store only, or through a charity auction only. Check with your local beverage control authorities to learn what rules apply in your area.

New York is currently one of the hottest wine auction markets around, thanks to the relatively recent legalization of wine auctions. (You can either sell or buy wines at these auctions.) Four large retail stores lead the crusade: Morrell & Company (☎ 212-307-4200, www.morrellwineauctions.com); Sherry-Lehmann (☎ 212-838-7500, www.sherry-lehmann.com); Zachy's (☎ 914-448-3026, www.zachys.com); and Acker, Merrall & Condit (☎ 877-ACKER-47, www.ackerwines.com). Sotheby's Auction House (☎ 212-606-7050, www.sothebys.com/wine) also holds wine auctions, under the direction of Serena Sutcliffe, MW; Christie's Auction House (☎ 212-636-2270, www.christies.com) is also a major player.

In Illinois, The Chicago Wine Company (☎ 708-647-8789, www.tcwc.com) and Sotheby's Chicago, under the direction of Michael Davis and Paul Hart (☎ 312-396-9513, www.sothebys.com/wine), are the leading buyers of privately-owned wine.

In California, Butterfield's Auction House (☎ 800-223-2854, ext. 3550, www.butterfields.com), The Rare Wine Company (☎ 800-999-4342, www.rarewineco.com), and Christie's Los Angeles (☎ 310-385-2602) will buy your well-stored fine wines.

Most large retail wine stores (where legal) and wine Web sites also buy wine from collectors. Many such wine shops and Web sites run classified ads regularly in *The Wine Spectator* and other wine magazines.

When selling your wine, bear in mind a few factors about most buyers:

✔ They are interested mainly in valuable, prestigious, or rare wines; they're not looking to buy some loser you might be trying to unload.

✔ Wines in good condition are what they really want; some places won't buy wines that aren't at their best — but some will.

✔ All, of course, charge a premium for their services, ranging from 10 to 25 percent of the sale price. Some auction houses pass most of the premium on to the buyer rather than to the seller.

✔ Some outlets pay you only after they sell your wine; others will pay you upfront. Shop around for the best deal.

Part V
The Part of Tens

The 5th Wave   By Rich Tennant

"We had an interesting wine last night at the ball park. I can only describe it as 'vacuum cleaner-like'. It was big and noisy, came with a bag, and definitely sucked."

In this part . . .

This is the place to turn for quick answers and easy solutions. The next time a friend tells you that expensive wines are always better, the next time you're wondering when to drink that special wine, the next time someone tells you that Champagnes don't age — check out the advice in this part.

Chapter 22

Answers to Ten Common Questions about Wine

In our years of teaching about wine and helping customers in wine shops, we've noticed that the same questions about wine pop up again and again. Here are our answers. (We actually have 11 questions and answers; we couldn't resist throwing in another question, about older wines, at the end of the chapter.)

What's a good wine?

This is probably the question customers ask most frequently in wine shops. When they ask this question, they usually mean, "Please recommend a good wine to me," to which the retailer will usually respond with a barrage of questions, such as

- ✔ "Do you prefer red wines or white wines?"
- ✔ "How much do you want to spend for a bottle?"
- ✔ "Are you planning to serve the wine with any particular dish?"

Hundreds of good wines are in every wine shop. Twenty or thirty years ago, there were far fewer — but winemaking and grape-growing know-how has progressed dramatically to the point that there are few poor wines now.

You won't necessarily like every one of those good wines, however. There is simply no getting around the fact that taste is personal. If you want to drink a good wine that's right for you, you have to decide what the characteristics of that wine could be. And then get advice from a knowledgeable retailer.

When should I drink this wine?

Wine retailers frequently hear this question from customers, too. The answer, for most wines, is "Any time now."

The great majority of wines are ready to drink when you buy them. Some of them might improve marginally if you hold them for a year or so (and many of them will maintain their drinkability), but they won't improve enough for you to notice, unless you're a particularly thoughtful and experienced taster.

Some fine wines are an exception: They not only benefit from aging but they *need* to age, in order to achieve their potential quality. For example, assuming that the wines are well stored (turn to Chapter 21 for specifics of wine storage):

✔ You can usually count on 20 to 30 years of life from top quality red Bordeaux wines in good years such as 1982, 1986, 1989, 1990, 1995, 1996, or 2000.

✔ The best Barolos, Barbarescos, and Brunello di Montalcinos can age for 20 to 25 years in good vintages.

✔ The best white Burgundies and white Bordeaux will improve with 10 to 15 years of aging or more, in good vintage years.

✔ Most of today's red Burgundies, with the *possible* exception of the 1995 and 1996 vintages, should be consumed within 10 to 15 years (the less expensive ones even earlier).

For a listing of good vintage years and their approximate stage of readiness, refer to Appendix C. For the names of some specific producers in each category whose wines we recommend, refer to Chapters 10 and 11.

Is wine fattening?

A glass of dry wine contains 80 to 85 percent water, 12 to 14 percent ethyl alcohol, and small quantities of tartaric acid and various other components. Wine contains no fat.

A 4-ounce serving of dry white wine has about 104 calories, and 4 ounces of red wine has about 110 calories. Sweeter wines contain about 10 percent more calories depending on how sweet they are; fortified wines also contain additional calories because of their higher alcohol.

What grape variety is this wine made from?

Many wines today tell you what grape variety they're made from right on the front label — it's often the very name of the wine — or on the back label. Traditional European wines blended from several grape varieties usually don't give you that information a) because the winemakers consider the name of the place more important than the grapes, anyway, and b) because often the grapes they use are local varieties whose names few people would recognize.

If you really want to know what grape varieties make a Soave, Valpolicella, Châteauneuf-du-Pape, Rioja, Côtes du Rhône, or other blended European wines, you'll have to look it up. (See our charts in Chapters 10, 11, and 12.)

Which vintage should I buy?

This question assumes that you have a choice among several vintages of the same wine. Most of the time, however, you don't. Nearly every wine is available in only one vintage, which is referred to as the *current* vintage.

For white wines, the current vintage represents grapes that were harvested as recently as nine months ago or as long as three years ago, depending on the type of wine; for red wines, the current vintage is a date one to four years ago.

Classified-growth red Bordeaux wines (see Chapter 10) are a notable exception: Most wine shops feature several vintages of these wines. A few other fine wines — such as Burgundies, Barolos, or Rhône wines — might also be available in multiple vintages, but often they're not because the quantities produced are small and the wines sell out.

A red Rioja or a Chianti Classico might appear to be available in multiple vintages, but if you read the label carefully, you'll see that one vintage of the Rioja could be a *crianza* (aged two years before release), another might be a *reserva* (aged three years), and another might be a *gran reserva* (aged five years) — so they are each actually different wines, not multiple vintages of the same wine. Likewise, a Chianti might be available in an aged riserva version as well as a non-riserva style.

Most of the time, for most wines, the vintage to buy is the vintage you *can* buy — the current vintage. For the exceptional cases, consult our vintage chart in Appendix C.

Are there any wines without sulfites?

Sulfur dioxide exists naturally in wine as a result of fermentation. It also exists naturally in other fermented foods, such as bread, cookies, and beer. (Various sulfur derivatives are also used regularly as preservatives in packaged foods.)

Winemakers use sulfur dioxide at various stages of the winemaking process because it stabilizes the wine (preventing it from turning to vinegar or deteriorating from oxygen exposure) and safeguards its flavor. Sulfur has been an important winemaking tool since Roman times.

Very few winemakers refrain from using sulfur dioxide, but some do. Your wine shop might carry two or three wines whose sulfite content is so low that their labels do not have to carry the phrase *Contains Sulfites* (which the U.S. government requires on the label of any wine that contains more than 10 parts per million of sulfites).

If you wish to limit your consumption of sulfites, dry red wines should be your first choice, followed by dry white wines. Sweet wines contain the most sulfur dioxide. For more info, turn to the sidebar "The skinny on sulfites," in Chapter 1.

Are there any organic wines?

The new standards of organic agriculture established by the U.S. Department of Agriculture in 2002 contain two categories for wine:

- ✔ *Wine made from organically grown grapes,* whose grapes come from certified organic vineyards.
- ✔ *Organic wine,* which comes from organically grown grapes and is also produced organically, that is, without the addition of chemical additives such as sulfur dioxide during winemaking.

These categories apply to imported wines sold in the U.S. as well as to domestic wines. Many more brands, by far, fall into the first category than the second, because most winemakers do use sulfur dioxide in making their wines. (See the previous section for the reasons.)

But not all wines from organically grown grapes are labeled as such. Some winemakers who are deeply committed to organic farming prefer to promote and sell their wines based on the wines' quality, not the incidental feature of their organic farming. For them, organic farming is a means to an end — better grapes, and therefore better wine — rather than a marketing tool. Also, the fact that a national definition of *organic* did not exist in the past disinclined some wineries from using that word.

Now that formal categories exist, many more producers who farm organically will probably begin using the "O" word on their labels. But the number of wines in the more rigid *Organic wine* category will probably remain small, because of the sulfur dioxide restriction.

What's new oak?

You don't have to read very many wine columns before realizing that many winemakers use *new oak* for their wines, and are proud of it. The term refers to 60-gallon oak barrels (usually French oak but sometimes American oak) that winemakers use to ferment and/or age their better white wines and to age their better red wines.

The amount of oaky aroma and flavor that a barrel is able to give to a wine — and the amount of tannin — is a function of how often the barrel has been used. After several years, the insides of the casks or barrels become encrusted with crystalline acid deposits from the wine so that the wood itself might not even come in contact with each new wine.

Most winemakers who use new oak barrels replace them after just three to five vintages. To avoid being hit with a big expense all at once, winemakers might replace 20 percent of their barrels each year. Their *new oak* is therefore 20 percent brand new, 20 percent one year old, 20 percent two years old, and so on. When a winemaker replaces 20 percent of his oak barrels every year, he might say that he practices a *five-year rotation* for his oak. If he replaces one-third of his barrels every year, he uses a *three-year rotation*.

What is a wine expert?

A wine expert is someone with a high level of knowledge about wine in general, including grape growing, winemaking, and the various wines of the world. A wine expert also has a high degree of skill in tasting wine.

Until recently, most wine experts in the U.S. gained their expertise through informal study, work experience, or experience gained as *amateurs* (lovers) of wine. Although accredited wine courses did exist, they were university programs in *enology* (winemaking) and *viticulture* (grape growing) — valuable for people who plan to become winemakers or grape growers, but scientific overkill for people whose goal is breadth of knowledge about wine.

Today, many people become wine experts through programs of the Wine & Spirit Education Trust (or WSET; www.wset.co.uk), or various professional sommelier organizations, which include examinations at the end of study. Some examinations entitle successful students to use initials after their names, such as CWE (Certified Wine Educator), MS (Master Sommelier) or MW (Master of Wine). MW is the oldest and most difficult credential for wine experts to earn.

How do I know when to drink the special older wines I've been keeping?

Unfortunately, no precise answer to this question exists because all wines age at a different pace. Even two bottles of the same wine that are stored under the same conditions can age differently.

When you have a specific wine in mind, you can get advice in several different ways:

- Consult the comments of critics like Robert Parker, Michael Broadbent, or Clive Coates, who almost always list a suggested drinking period for wines they review in their newsletters and books (listed in Chapter 18); their educated guesses are usually quite reliable.

- Call or write to the winery; in the case of fine, older vintages, the wine-maker and his staff are usually happy to give you their opinion on the best time to drink their wine — and they typically have more experience with the wine than anyone else.

- If you have several bottles of the same wine, try one from time to time to see how it is developing. Your own taste is really the best guide — you might enjoy the wine younger, or older, than the experts.

Do old wines require special handling?

Like humans, wine can become somewhat fragile in its later stages. For one thing, it doesn't like to travel. If you must move old wine, give it several days' rest afterwards, before opening the bottle. (Red Burgundies and other Pinot Noirs are especially disturbed by journeys.)

Older wines, with their delicate bouquet and flavors, can easily be overwhelmed by strongly flavored foods. Simple cuts of meat or just hard cheeses and good, crusty bread are usually fine companions for mature wines.

If you're going to drink an older wine, don't over-chill it (whether it's white or red). Older wines show their best at moderate temperatures. Temperatures below 60°F (15.5°C) inhibit development in the glass.

Decant red wines or Vintage Ports to separate the clear wine from any sediment that formed in the bottle. (For tips on decanting, see Chapter 8.) Stand the bottle up two or three days before you plan to open it so that the sediment can drift to the bottom. An important concern in decanting an old wine is giving the wine *too* much aeration: A wine in its last stages will deteriorate rapidly upon exposure to air, often within a half hour — sometimes in 10 or 15 minutes.

When you decant an old wine, taste it immediately and be prepared to drink it rapidly if it shows signs of fading.

Chapter 23

Ten Wine Myths Demystified

As you leaf through the pages of this chapter, you'll probably recognize several of the myths we mention. They all represent common thinking — and common misinformation — about wine. We set the record straight.

Wine is for experts

True, wine is for experts. Wine involves so much detailed information — vintages, winemakers, winemaking techniques, history, tradition, new trends — that there's plenty of stuff for experts to sink their teeth into. Wine is definitely for them.

But wine isn't *only* for experts. Wine is for anyone who likes the taste of wine, or thinks that it's the perfect drink to accompany dinner.

Wine is a beverage, one of the oldest beverages in history. Millions of people all over the world drink wine without knowing anything about the wine they're drinking other than the fact that it's made locally, it's the wine their brother-in-law recommended, or it tastes good.

Wine is a beverage, plain and simple. It's fermented grape juice, the product of a simple, natural process. The next time you worry that maybe you don't know enough to be a wine lover, consider this: If people in the wine business had to rely on experts alone to drink their wines, they'd have been out of business long ago!

Wine has to be expensive to be good

For wine, as for any other product, the more expensive, the better the quality, generally speaking. But the highest quality wine isn't always the best choice, for the following reasons:

- ✔ Your taste is personal, and you might not like a wine that critics consider very high in quality.

- ✔ Not all situations call for a very high quality wine.

We certainly can enjoy even a $6 wine in many circumstances. At large family gatherings, on picnics, at the beach, and so on, an expensive, top-quality wine can be out-of-place — too serious and important.

Likewise, the very finest wines are seldom the best choices in restaurants — considering typical restaurant prices. Instead, we either look for the best value on the wine list (keeping in mind what we are eating) or experiment with some moderately priced wine that we haven't tried before. (There will *always* be some wines that you haven't tried.)

Quality isn't the only consideration in choosing a wine. Often, the very best wine of all — for your taste, or for a certain situation — will be inexpensive.

Imported wines are better

First of all, imported from where? If you live in Europe, California wine is imported wine; if you live in the U.S., European wine is imported wine. How can they both be better than each other?

We have a friend who drinks only French wine. He insists that all other wines are inferior. We love to serve him a good Italian or California wine *blind* (that is, with the label covered) and watch his reaction when he discovers it's not from France — after he has praised the wine!

Nowadays, every wine region makes some excellent wine. The "Imported wines are better" myth is just a bit of snobbery.

Here's a daring suggestion that flies in the face of the imported wine myth: Discover your own local wines. If you live in southern Pennsylvania, New England, Ohio, Texas, Idaho, Vancouver, or Toronto, for example (not to mention Capetown, Melbourne, or Santiago), people are making wines practically in your own backyard. Try them. How do you think the Burgundians discovered that Burgundy is worth drinking?

White wine with fish, red with meat

As guidelines go, this isn't a bad one. But we said *guideline,* not rule. Anyone who slavishly adheres to this generalization as if it were a rule deserves the boredom of eating and drinking exactly the same thing every day of his life!

Do you want a glass of white wine with your burger? Go ahead, order it. You're the one who's doing the eating and drinking, not your friend and not the server who's taking your order.

Even if you're a perfectionist who's always looking for the ideal food and wine combination, you'll find yourself wandering from the guideline. The best wine for a grilled salmon steak is probably red — like a Pinot Noir or a Bardolino — and not white at all. Veal and pork do equally well with red or white wines, depending on how the dish is prepared. And what could be better with hot dogs on the grill than a cold glass of rosé?

No one is going to arrest you if you have white wine with everything, or red wine with everything, or even Champagne with everything! There are no rules. (We offer a few additional suggestions for possible wine–food pairings in Chapter 20.)

Numbers don't lie

It's natural to turn to critics for advice. We do it all the time, when we're trying to decide which movie to see, when we're choosing a new restaurant to try, or when we want to know what someone else thinks of a particular book.

In most cases, we weigh the critics' opinions against our own experience and tastes. Say a steak house just got three stars and a fabulous review from the dining critic. Do we rush to the telephone to make a reservation? Not if we don't like red meat! When the movie critics give two thumbs up, do we automatically assume that we'll like the movie — or do we listen to their commentary and decide whether the movie might be too violent, silly, or serious for us? You know the answer to that.

Yet many wine drinkers, when they hear that a wine just got more than 90 points, go out of their way to get that wine. The curiosity to try a wine that scores well is understandable. But the rigid belief that such a wine a) is necessarily a great wine, and b) is a wine you will like, is simply misguided.

The critics' scores are nothing more than the critics' professional opinion — and opinion, like taste, is *always* personal. (Chapter 19 tells you more about scoring wine.)

Vintages always matter/vintages don't matter

The difference between one vintage and the next of the same wine is the difference between the weather in the vineyards from one year to the next (barring extenuating circumstances such as new ownership of the winery, or the hiring of a new winemaker). The degree of vintage variation is thus equivalent to the degree of weather variation.

In some parts of the world the weather varies a lot from year to year, and *for wines from those regions,* vintages certainly do matter. In Bordeaux, Burgundy, Germany, and most of Italy, for example, weather problems (frost, hail, ill-timed rain, or insufficient heat) can affect one vintage for the worse, while the next year may have no such problems. Where a lot of weather variation exists, the quality of the wine can swing from mediocre to outstanding from one year to the next.

In places where the weather is more predictable year after year (like much of California, Australia, and South Africa), vintages can still vary, but the swing is narrower. Serious wine lovers who care about the intimate details of the wines they drink will find the differences meaningful, but most people won't.

Another exception to the "Vintages always matter" myth is inexpensive wine. Top-selling wines that are produced in large volume are usually blended from many vineyards in a fairly large area. Swings in quality from year to year are not significant.

Wine authorities are experts

Wine is an incredibly vast subject. It involves biochemistry, botany, geology, chemistry, climatology, history, culture, politics, laws, and business. How can anyone be an expert in all of that?

To compound the problem, some people in authoritative positions within the wine field might have had little, if any, education, training, or background in wine before being given jobs by wine companies or columns by publishers, and "ordained" wine authorities almost overnight.

Also, different aspects of wine appeal to different people. Depending on what they particularly like about wine, people tend to specialize in some of wine's disciplines at the expense of others. (Now you know why it takes two of us to write this book.)

Don't expect any one person to be able to answer all your questions about wine in the most accurate and up-to-date manner. Just like doctors and lawyers, wine professionals specialize. They have to.

Old wines are good wines

The idea of rare old bottles of wine being auctioned off for tens of thousands of dollars apiece, like fine art, is fascinating enough to capture anyone's imagination. But valuable old bottles of wine are even rarer than valuable old coins because, unlike coins, wine is perishable.

The great majority of the world's wines don't have what it takes to age for decades. Most wines are meant to be enjoyed in the first one to five years of their lives. Even those wines that have the potential to develop slowly over many years will achieve their potential only if they are properly stored. (See Chapter 21 for information on storing wines.)

The purpose of wine is to be enjoyed — usually, sooner rather than later.

Great wines are supposed to taste bad when they're young

If this myth were true, wouldn't that be convenient for anyone who made poor wine! "It's a great wine," the winery owner could argue. "It's *supposed* to taste bad when it's young."

In the past, some of the great wines of the world, like red Bordeaux, were so tough and tannic that you really couldn't drink them until they had a few decades under their belts. As recently as the 1975 vintage of Bordeaux, some collectors believed that the undrinkability of the young wines was proof positive of their age-worthiness.

Winemakers today believe that a great wine must be in balance when it's young in order to be a balanced wine when it's old. (Refer to Chapter 2 for a discussion of balance.) Although the tannins in old wines usually soften and/or drop out in the form of sediment, most wines today that are extraordinarily tannic when young don't have enough fruit character to last until their tannins fade.

Of course, for a wine to be in balance doesn't mean that it's ready to drink. A great wine can have enormous tannin when it's young, along with its enormous fruit. It might be balanced, even if it's still embryonic. You may be able to appreciate the wine's balance when it's young; you may even enjoy the wine to some degree, but its true greatness is years away.

Champagnes don't age

We don't know who started this myth; to the contrary, Champagne *does* age well! Depending on the particular year, Vintage Champagne can age especially well. We have enjoyed two outstanding 1928 Vintage Champagnes, Krug and Moët & Chandon's Dom Pérignon, neither of which showed any sign of decline. The oldest Champagne that we've ever tasted, a 1900 Pol Roger, was also in fine shape.

But Champagne demands excellent storage. If kept in a cool, dark, humid place, many Champagnes can age for decades, especially in the great vintages. They lose some effervescence but take on a complexity of flavor somewhat similar to fine white Burgundy. Champagnes in magnum bottles (1.5 l) generally age better than those in regular size (750 ml) bottles.

If you want to try some very fine, reliable, older bottles of Vintage Champagne, look for either Krug or Salon in the 1964, 1969, 1973, or 1976 vintage. If stored well, they will be magnificent. Dom Pérignon is also reliable — the 1961 and 1969 DPs are legendary.

The following houses produce Champagnes known to age well:

- ✔ **Krug:** All their Champagnes are remarkably long lived.
- ✔ **Pol Roger:** Especially Cuvée Sir Winston Churchill.
- ✔ **Moët & Chandon:** Cuvée Dom Pérignon, ageless when well stored.
- ✔ **Louis Roederer:** Cristal, Cristal Rosé, and Vintage Brut all age well.
- ✔ **Jacquesson:** Signature and Vintage Blanc de Blancs.
- ✔ **Bollinger:** All their Champagnes, especially the Grande Année.

- ✔ **Gosset:** Grand Millésime and Celebris.
- ✔ **Salon:** Remarkable Blanc de Blancs; needs at least 15 years of aging.
- ✔ **Veuve Clicquot:** La Grande Dame and the Vintage Brut.
- ✔ **Taittinger:** Their Blanc de Blancs (Comtes de Champagne).
- ✔ **Billecart-Salmon:** The Blanc de Blancs.
- ✔ **Pommery:** Cuvée Louise.
- ✔ **Laurent-Perrier:** Cuvée Grand Siècle.
- ✔ **Philipponnat:** Clos des Goisses.

Recent great vintages for Champagne are 1996, 1990, 1988, 1985, and 1982.

Part VI
Appendixes

The 5th Wave   By Rich Tennant

CHARD

"I want something that will go well
with a retired admiral and his wife,
a best-selling author from the Hamptons,
and a media wonk."

In this part . . .

Here we give you some useful tools of the trade, like a vintage chart, an extensive pronunciation guide to wine terms and names, and a glossary of wine terms. We were going to include a listing of every winery in the world that makes Chardonnay, but we ran out of space.

Appendix A

Pronunciation Guide to Wine Terms

• •

*N*othing will set a wine snob on your case more quickly than a mispro-
nounced name of a famous wine or wine region. In order not to give
snobs their smug satisfaction, we provide pronunciations of dozens of words
here, for easy reference. This list is not exhaustive, however; the pronunciations of other, less common names and terms appear throughout the book.
Accented syllables, if any, are indicated with capital letters.

Name or term = Pronunciation
Aglianico del Vulture = *ah lee AHN ee coh del VUL toor ay*
Albariño = *ahl bah REE nyoh*
Aligoté = *ah lee go tay*
Aloxe-Corton = *ah luss cor tohn*
Alsace = *al zass*
(Alto)-Adige = *AH dee jhae*
amontillado = *ah mon tee YAH doh*
Anjou = *ahn jhew*
Arneis = *ahr NASE*
Au Bon Climat = *oh bone klee maht*
Auslese = *OUSE lay seh*
Auxerrois = *aus ser whah*
Auxey-Duresses = *awk say deh ress*
Barbaresco = *bar bah RES co*
Barbera = *bar BEAR ah*
Barolo = *bah RO lo*
Batard-Montrachet = *bah tar mon rah shay*

Name or term = Pronunciation
Beaujolais = *boh jhoe lay*
Beaulieu (Vineyards) = *bo l'yuh*
Bianco di Custoza = *bee AHN coh dee cus TOEZ ah*
Blanchot = *blahn shoh*
botrytis = *boh TRY tis*
Bougros = *boo groh*
Bourgogne = *boor guh nyuh*
Bourgueil = *bor guh'y*
Brouilly = *broo yee*
Brunello di Montalcino = *brew NEL lo dee mon tahl CHEE no*
brut = *brute*
Cabernet Sauvignon = *cab er nay saw vee nyon*
Canaiolo = *cahn eye OH loh*
Carmignano = *car mee NYAH no*
Chablis = *shah blee*

(continued)

Name or term = Pronunciation

Chardonnay = _shar doh nay_

Chassagne-Montrachet = _shah san yuh mon rah shay_

(Château de) Fieuzal = _fee oo zahl_

(Château) Grillet = _gree yay_

(Château) Haut-Brion = _oh bree ohn_

(Château) Lafite-Rothschild = _lah feet roth sheeld_

(Château) Margaux = _mahr go_

(Château) Mouton-Rothschild = _moo tohn roth sheeld_

(Château) Petrus = _peh troos_

(Château) Trotanoy = _trot ahn wah_

Châteauneuf-du-Pape = _shah toe nuf dew pahp_

Chénas = _shay nahs_

Chenin Blanc = _shen in blahnk_

Chevalier-Montrachet = _sheh vah lyay mon rah shay_

Chianti = _key AHN tee_

(Chianti) Rufina = _ROO fee nah_

Chinon = _she nohn_

Chiroubles = _sheh roob leh_

Clos du Val = _clo dew val_

Colheita = _col YAI tah_

Condrieu = _cohn dree uh_

Corton-Charlemagne = _cor tawn shahr luh mahn_

Côte de Beaune = _coat deh bone_

Côte Chalonnaise = _coat shal oh naze_

Côte d'Or = _coat dor_

Côte de Nuits = _coat deh nwee_

Côte de Nuits-Villages = _coat deh nwee vee lahj_

Côte Rôtie = _coat roe tee_

Côtes du Ventoux = _coat due vahn too_

cuvée = _coo vay_

Name or term = Pronunciation

Dolcetto = _dohl CHET oh_

(Domaine) Leroy = _lay wah_

Eisele Vineyard = _EYE seh lee_

Entre-Deux-Mers = _ahn truh duh mair_

Fleurie = _fluh ree_

Fourchaume = _for chahm_

Friuli-Venezia Giulia = _free OO lee veh NETZ ee ah JOO lee ah_

Galicia = _gah LEETH ee ah_

Garrafeira = _gar ah FAIR ah_

Gattinara = _gah tee NAH rah_

Gavi = _GAH vee_

Genevrières = _jen ev ree aire_

Gewürztraminer = _geh VAIRTZ trah mee ner_

Gigondas = _jhee gohn dahs_

Givry = _jee vree_

grands crus classés = _grahn crew clas say_

Graves = _grahv_

Grenouilles = _greh n'wee_

Grüner Veltliner = _GREW ner VELT lee ner_

halbtrocken = _HAHLB tro ken_

Haut-Médoc = _oh may doc_

Hermitage = _er mee tahj_

Juliénas = _jool yay nahs_

Languedoc-Roussillon = _lahn gweh doc roo see yawn_

Les Clos = _lay cloh_

Les Forêts = _lay for ay_

Les Preuses = _lay preuhz_

Liebfraumilch = _LEEB frow milsh_

Listrac = _lee strahk_

Loire = _lwahr_

Name or term = Pronunciation	Name or term = Pronunciation
Mâcon-Villages = *mac cawn vee lahj*	Pays d'Oc = *pay ee doc*
Malvasia = *mal va SEE ah*	Penedés = *pen eh DAIS*
Margaux = *mahr go*	Pernand-Vergelesses = *pair nahn vair juh less*
Médoc = *meh doc*	Perrier-Jouët = *per ree yay joo ett*
Menetou-Salon = *meh neh too sah lohn*	Pessac-Léognan = *pay sac lay oh nyahn*
Mercurey = *mer cure ay*	Pfalz = *fallz*
Merlot = *mer loh*	Pinot Bianco = *pee noh bee AHN coh*
Meursault = *muhr so*	Pinot Blanc = *pee noh blahnk*
Moët = *moh ett*	Pinot Grigio = *pee noh GREE joe*
Mont de Milieu = *mon deh meh lyew*	Pinot Gris = *pee noh gree*
Montagny = *mon tah nyee*	Pinot Noir = *pee noh nwahr*
Montepulciano d'Abruzzo = *mon tae pul chee AH noh dah BRUTE so*	Pinotage = *pee noh TAHJ*
Monthélie = *mohn teh lee*	Pouilly-Fuissé = *pwee fwee say*
Montlouis = *mon loo wee*	Pouilly-Fumé = *pwee foo may*
Montmains = *mon man*	premier cru = *prem yay crew*
Montrachet = *mon rah shay*	Priorato = *pree oh RAH to*
Mosel-Saar-Ruwer = *MOH zel-zar-ROO ver*	Puligny-Montrachet = *poo lee nyee mon rah shay*
Moulin-á-Vent = *moo lahn ah vahn*	Qualitätswein = *KAL ee tates vine*
Moulis = *moo lees*	Quincy = *can see*
Müller-Thurgau = *MULE lair TOOR gow*	Quinta = *KEEN ta*
Muscadet = *moos cah day*	Regaleali = *ray gah lay AH lee*
Muscat = *moos caht*	Regnie = *ray nyay*
Nahe = *NAH heh*	Reuilly = *reuh yee*
Nantais = *nahn tay*	Rheingau = *RYNE gow*
Nebbiolo = *neb bee OH lo*	Rheinhessen = *RYNE hess ehn*
Neuchatel = *NOI sha tel*	Rías Baixas = *REE ahse BYCE ahse*
Niebaum-Coppola = *NEE baum COPE poh lah*	Ribera del Duero = *ree BEAR ah del doo AIR oh*
Niederosterreich = *nee der OZ ter ryke*	Ribolla Gialla = *ree BOHL lah JAHL lah*
Nuits-St.-Georges = *nwee san jorg*	Riesling = *REESE ling*
Orvieto = *or vee AE toh*	Rioja = *ree OH hah*
Pauillac = *poy yac*	Rueda = *roo AE dah*

(continued)

Name or term = Pronunciation	*Name or term = Pronunciation*
Rully = *rouh yee*	Torgiano = *tor gee AH no*
Saint-Amour = *sant ah more*	Tre Venezie = *trae veh NETZ ee ae*
Saint-Aubin = *sant oh ban*	Trebbiano = *treb bee AH noh*
Saint-Nicolas-de-Bourgueil = *san nih coh lahs deh bor goye*	Trentino-Alto Adige = *tren TEE noh-AHL toh AH dee jhae*
Saint-Romain = *san ro man*	trocken = *TRO ken*
Saint-Véran = *san veh rahn*	Vacqueyras = *vah keh rahs*
Sancerre = *sahn sair*	Vaillons = *vye yon*
Sangiovese = *san joe VAE sae*	Valais = *vah lay*
Saumur = *soh muhr*	Valmur = *vahl moor*
Sauvignon Blanc = *saw vee nyon blahnk*	Valpolicella = *val po lee CHEL lah*
Savennieres = *sah ven nyair*	Vaudésir = *voh deh zeer*
Savigny-lès-Beaune = *sah vee nyee lay bone*	Vega Sicilia = *VAY gah see SEAL yah*
Scheurebe = *SHOY reb beh*	Vendange Tardive = *vahn dahnj tahr deev*
Semillon = *SEM eh lon* (Australian)	Veneto = *VEN eh toh*
Sémillon = *seh mee yohn* (French)	Verdejo = *ver DAY ho*
Sèvre-et-Maine = *sev'r et mehn*	Verdicchio = *ver DEE key oh*
Soave = *so AH vay*	Vernaccia di San Gimignano = *ver NOTCH cha dee san jee mee NYAH noh*
Spanna = *SPAH nah*	Vinho = *VEEN yo*
Spätlese = *SHPATE lay seh*	Vinho Verde = *VEEN yo VAIRD*
spumante = *spoo MAHN tay*	(Vino) Nobile di Montepulciano = *NO be lay dee mon tay pul chee AH no*
St-Estèphe = *sant eh steff*	Viognier = *vee oh nyay*
St-Julien = *sant jhoo lee ehn*	Vosne-Romanée = *vone roh mah nay*
St.-Emilion = *sant ay meal yon*	Vouvray = *voo vray*
Steiermark = *STY er mark*	Wachau = *va COW*
Tempranillo = *tem prah NEE yoh*	Weissburgunder = *VICE boor gun der*
Tinto = *TEEN toe*	Wien = *vee EN*
Tocai Friulano = *toe KYE free ou LAH noh*	Willamette (Valley) = *wil LAM ette*
Tokaj-Hegyalja = *toe KYE heh JAH yah*	

Appendix B

Glossary of Wine Terms

● ●

*H*ere, for handy reference, are definitions of dozens of the most common wine terms and wine-tasting terms.

acidity: A component of wine, generally consisting of tartaric acid (a natural acid in grapes) and comprising approximately 0.5 to 0.7 percent of the wine by volume.

aerate: To expose wine to air in preparation for drinking it, usually with the intention of allowing off-odors to escape from an older wine, or softening the harshness of a younger wine.

alcohol level: The percentage of alcohol by volume that a wine has; most white wines have an alcohol level between 9 and 14 percent, and most red wines have an alcohol level between 11 and 14 percent.

American oak: Oak wood from a U.S. forest, of the species *quercus alba,* and the barrels made from such wood; some winemakers in certain wine regions (such as Spain and Australia) favor American oak for aging their wines.

ample: A descriptor for wines that give the impression of being full and expansive in your mouth.

AOC: Abbreviation for *Appellation d'Origine Contrôlée,* sometimes shortened to *Appellation Contrôlée* and abbreviated as AC; translates to *protected place name;* France's official category for its highest-ranking types of wine, whose name, origin,

grape varieties, and other defining factors are regulated by law.

appellation: Name; often used to mean the official geographic origin of a wine, which is part of a wine's official name.

aroma: The smell of a wine. Some purists use the term *aroma* only for the straightforward, youthful smells of a wine, and use the term *bouquet* for the more complex smells of an aged wine. But we use *aroma* as a general term for all wine smells.

aromatic: A descriptor for a wine that has a pronounced smell, used particularly in reference to fruity and floral smells. Some white grape varieties are also dubbed *aromatic* because the wines made from them tend to be extremely strong in aroma.

aromatic compounds: Those substances in wine — derived from the grapes, from winemaking, or from aging — that are responsible for a wine's aromas and flavors.

astringent: A descriptor for the mouth-drying, mouth-roughening tactile character of some wines, caused by tannin, acid, or the combination of both.

attack: The first impression a wine gives you when you taste it. A wine's attack is usually related to sensations in the front of your mouth, especially the tip of your tongue, which is usually the first place the wine touches.

balance: The interrelationship of a wine's alcohol, residual sugar, acid, and tannin; when no one component stands out obtrusively on the palate, a wine is said to be well-balanced; a prized characteristic in wines.

barrel: A relatively small wooden container for fermenting and/or aging wine, generally 60 gallons in size and generally made of oak.

barrel-aged: A term that applies to wines that are fermented in containers of inert material, such as stainless steel, and subsequently placed into wooden barrels for a period of maturation; the term also applies to the maturation period of wines that also fermented in the barrel.

barrel-fermented: A term that applies to white wines that are fermented in oak barrels; the oaky character of such wines is generally more subtle than that of wines that have been merely barrel-aged.

big: A general descriptor for wines that are either very full or very intense.

black fruits: A general term for wine aromas and flavors that suggest blackberries, blueberries, black cherries, blackcurrants, or other black fruits.

black grapes: Wine grapes that have a reddish or blue pigmentation in their skins; used to make red wine.

blend: To mix together two or more individual lots of wine, usually wines from different grape varieties (but also applies to wines from different vineyards, different regions, or different vintages); a wine derived from the juice of different grape varieties is called a blend.

bodega: A winery in Spain; also the Spanish word for a building where wine is stored.

body: The impression of a wine's weight in your mouth. A wine's body is generally described as light, medium, or full.

bottle-age: Maturation of a wine after it has been bottled; most wines undergo a short period of bottle-age at the winery before release, while fine wines require additional bottle-age from the consumer.

bouquet: Evolved, mature aromas.

bright: Indicates a wine whose characteristics are perceived vividly by the senses. A wine can be visually bright, or it can have bright aromas and flavors; in both cases, the opposite is dull.

cask: A relatively large wooden container for making or storing wine.

castello: Italian for *castle;* refers to a wine estate.

cedary: Having aromas or flavors that resemble the smell of cedar wood.

character: An anthropomorphic attribute of wines that give the impression of having substance and integrity.

charry: Having aromas or flavors that suggest burnt wood or charred wood.

château: A French name for a grand winery estate, commonly used in the Bordeaux region as well as other regions.

classico: An Italian term applicable to certain DOC or DOCG wines whose vineyards are situated in the original, classic part of the territory where that particular type of DOC/DOCG wine can be made.

clone: A subvariety of a grape variety; a vine, or set of genetically identical vines, that exhibits characteristics specific to it as compared to other vines of the same variety.

colheita: Vintage, in Portuguese.

commune: A village.

compact: A descriptor for wines that give the impression of being intense but not full.

complex: Not simple. A complex wine has many different aromas and flavors, and "has a lot going on."

concentrated: A descriptor for wines with aromas and flavors that are dense rather than dilute.

concentration: A characteristic of wines whose flavors or fruit character are tightly knit as opposed to being dilute or watery.

cosecha: Vintage, in Spanish.

crisp: A wine that feels clean and slightly brittle in your mouth; the opposite of "soft." Crispness is usually the result of high acidity, and crisp wines therefore are usually relatively light in body and go well with food.

decant: To transfer wine from a bottle to another container, either for the purpose of aerating the wine or to pour a red wine off its sediment.

depth: A characteristic of fine wines that give the impression of having many layers of taste, rather than being flat and one-dimensional.

dilute: A descriptor for wines whose aromas and flavors are thin and watery, as opposed to concentrated.

district: A geographic entity more specific than a region and less specific than a commune.

DO: Abbreviation for *Denominación de Origen,* which translates to *place name;* Spain's official category for wines whose name, origin, grape varieties, and other defining factors are regulated by law. Also an abbreviation for Portugal's highest official wine category, *Denominação de Origem,* translated similarly and having the same meaning.

DOC: Abbreviation for *Denominazione di Origine Controllata,* which translates to *controlled place name;* Italy's official category for wines whose name, origin, grape varieties, and other defining factors are regulated by law.

DOCG: Abbreviation for *Denominazione di Origine Controllata e Garantita,* which translates to *controlled and guaranteed place name;* Italy's official category for its highest-ranking wines.

domaine: A French term for wine estate, commonly used in the Burgundy region.

dry: A wine that is not sweet. The word *dry* can also describe the texture of a wine that feels rough in your mouth, as in *dry texture* or *dry mouthfeel.* But when it is used alone, it refers specifically to lack of sweetness.

dull: A wine whose expression is muddled and unclear. This term can apply to a wine's appearance, to its aromas and flavors, or to its general style.

earthy: Having aromas and flavors that suggest earth, such as wet soil, dry earth, certain minerally aromas, and so forth. This term is sometimes used as a general descriptor for wines that are rustic and lack refinement.

elegance: An attribute of wines that express themselves in a fine or delicate manner as opposed to an intense or forceful way.

estate: A property that grows grapes and produces wines from its own vineyards; wines labeled *estate* are made from vineyards owned by (or in some cases, under the direct control of) the same entity that owns the winery and makes the wine; use of the term is regulated by law in most areas.

fermentation: The natural process by which the sugar in grape juice is transformed into alcohol (and the juice is thus transformed into wine) through the action of yeasts.

finish: The final impressions a wine gives after you have swallowed it or spat it out.

firm: A descriptor for wines that are not soft, but are not harsh and tough; generally relates to the tannic content of a red wine or the acidity of a white wine.

flabby: A perjorative term used to describe wines that are too soft.

flavor compounds: Organic substances in grapes responsible for many of the aromas and flavors of wines.

flavor intensity: The degree to which a wine's flavors are pronounced and easily observable.

flavors: Aromatic constituents of a wine that are perceived in the mouth.

fleshy: A descriptor for a rich textural or tactile impression of some wines.

fortified wine: A wine that has had alcohol added to it.

French oak: Oak wood from the forests of France, of the species *quercus robur,* considered the finest type of oak for aging most white wines; the barrels made from such wood.

fruit character: Those characteristics of a wine that derive from the grapes, such as a wine's aromas and flavors.

fruity: Having aromas and flavors suggestive of fruit. This is a broad descriptor; in some cases the fruity aroma or flavor of a wine can be described more precisely as suggestive of fresh fruit, dried fruit, or cooked fruit, or even more precisely as a specific fresh, dried, or cooked fruit, such as fresh apples, dried figs, or strawberry jam.

full: A descriptor for wines that give the impression of being large in your mouth. A wine's fullness can derive from high alcohol or from other aspects of the wine.

garrafeira: A Portuguese term for a reserva wine with specific aging requirements — for red wines, at least three years of aging in oak and bottle before release.

generous: A descriptor for wines whose characteristics are expressive and easy to perceive.

gran reserva: On Spanish red wines, a term indicating a wine that has aged at least five years in oak and in bottle before release.

grape tannin: Those tannins in a red wine that come from the grapes from which the wine was made.

grape variety: A type of grape within a species.

harmonious: A descriptor of wines that are not only well balanced but also express themselves in a particularly graceful manner.

herbal: Having aromas and flavors that suggest herbs, such as fresh herbs, dried herbs, or specific herbs (rosemary, thyme, tarragon, and so forth).

intense: A descriptor for wines that express themselves strongly. When used in reference to a wine's aromas and flavors, this word describes the volume of those aromas or flavors — how strong the smell of lemon is in the wine, for example. When used in reference to a wine's total expression, this word describes an impression of general forcefulness that the wine gives.

lees: Grape solids and dead yeast cells that precipitate to the bottom of a white wine following fermentation.

length: A characteristic of fine wines that give a sustained sensory impression across the length of the tongue.

maceration: The process of soaking the skins of red grapes in their grape juice to leach the skins' color, tannin, and other substances into the juice.

malolactic fermentation: A natural conversion of harsh malic acid into milder lactic acid, which softens the total acidity of a wine; an optional process in white wine production.

maturation: The aging period at the winery during which a wine evolves to a state of readiness for bottling; the process of development and evolution that fine wines undergo after they are bottled.

medium sweet: A term to indicate the perceived sweetness level of wines that are sweeter than medium-dry, but not fully sweet.

medium-dry: A term to indicate the perceived sweetness of wines that are very slightly sweet.

minerally: Having aromas or flavors that suggest minerals (as opposed to organic substances such as plants or animals). This is a broad descriptor; in some cases the minerally aroma or flavor of a wine can be described more precisely as suggestive of chalk, iron, steel, and so forth.

New World: Collective term for those winemaking countries of the world that are situated outside of Europe.

new oak: An imprecise term for oak barrels that are brand new (also called "first year oak") as well as barrels that have been used approximately one to four times previously.

nutty: Having aromas or flavors that suggest nuts. This is a broad descriptor; in some cases the nutty aroma or flavor of a wine can be described more precisely as suggestive of roasted nuts, toasted nuts, nut butter, or cashews, almonds, hazelnuts, and so forth.

oaky: Having characteristics that derive from oak, such as toastiness, smokiness, a charry smell or flavor, vanilla aroma, or a higher tannin level than the wine might ordinarily have. Usually these oaky characteristics occur as the wine ages in oak barrels, but in very inexpensive wines they might have been added as an actual flavoring.

off-dry: A generalized term for wines that are neither fully dry nor very sweet.

Old World: Collective term for the winemaking countries of Europe.

old oak: Oak barrels or casks that are old enough to have lost most of their oaky character, generally five years old and older.

old vines: An unregulated term for grape vines whose fruit quality presumably is quite good due to the fact the vines are old — generally 40 years old or older — and therefore produce very little crop.

palate: A term used by wine tasters as a synonym for "mouth," or to refer to the characteristics of a wine that become manifest in the taster's mouth.

petrol: Having aromas or flavors that suggest diesel fuel.

phylloxera: A parasite louse that feeds on the roots of Vitis vinifera grape vines, resulting in the vines' premature death.

plummy: Having aromas or flavors that suggest ripe plums.

plush: A textural or tactile descriptor for wines that feel luxurious in your mouth.

powerful: An anthropomorphic descriptor for wines that convey an impression of strength and intensity.

pretty: An anthropomorphic descriptor for wines that are attractive for their delicacy and finesse.

primary aromas: Fresh aromas in a wine that derive from the grapes used to make that wine.

red grapes: Wine grapes that have a reddish or blue pigmentation in their skins; also called black grapes.

region: A geographical entity less specific than a district, but more specific than a country; for Italian wines, the term "region" applies to the political entity as well as to the wine zones within that area.

reserva: On a Spanish wine, a term indicating that the wine has aged longer at the winery (usually some specified combination of oak aging and bottle aging) than a non-reserva version of the same type of wine; red reserva wines must age at least three years before release. On a Portuguese wine, a wine of superior quality from one vintage.

reserve: A designation for wines that are presumably finer than the non-reserve, or normal version, of the same wine; use of the term is unregulated in the U.S. and in France.

residual sugar: Sugar remaining in the wine after fermentation.

rich: A descriptor of wines that offer an abundance of flavor, texture, or other sensory perceptions.

riserva: Italian word for "reserve," indicating a wine that has aged longer before release from the winery than a non-reserve version of the same type of wine, and suggesting higher quality; the period of time a wine must age to earn the term "riserva" (and sometimes the conditions of that aging) is defined by individual DOC regulations for each wine.

round: A descriptor for wines that are perceived to be neither flat nor angular. Roundness relates to the wine's structure — that is, its particular makeup of acid, tannin, sweetness, and alcohol.

second-label wine: A less-expensive, second wine (or a second brand of wine) made by a winery from grapes or wine not considered worthy of the winery's primary label.

sediment: The solid residue in a bottle of red wine that forms as the wine matures.

serious: A metaphorical descriptor for a wine that is of high quality.

silky: Having a supple, smooth texture.

single-vineyard wine: A wine that is made from the grapes of a single (presumably exceptionally good) plot of land, and that usually carries the name of the vineyard on its label; the term is unregulated in that "vineyard" is not defined as to size or ownership.

skin contact: The process during which the juice of grapes rests in contact with the grape skins; in red wine, the process by which the wines absorb color, tannin, and other substances; not normally used in white wine production, but occasionally used to enhance the aromatic character of the wine.

smoky: Having aromas or flavors that suggest smoke or smoked wood.

smooth: Descriptor for a wine whose texture is not rough or harsh.

soft: Textural descriptor for a wine whose alcohol and sugar (if any) dominate its acidity and tannin, resulting in a lack of hardness or roughness.

stemmy: Descriptor for red wines that give the impression of having dry, raspy, woody tannins, as if from the stems of grape bunches.

stems: The woody parts of a grape bunch, which are high in tannin; usually the stems are removed and discarded prior to fermentation.

stony: Having aromas or flavors that suggest stones. In some cases the stony aroma or flavor of a wine can be described more precisely as suggestive of wet stones.

structural components: Principally, a wine's alcohol, acid, tannin, and sugar (if any).

structure: That part of the impression a wine conveys that derives from perception of the wine's structural elements.

style: The set of characteristics through which a wine manifests itself.

supple: A descriptor for wines that seem fluid in texture in the mouth, without roughness or sharpness.

süssreserve: German for *sweet reserve;* unfermented grape juice that is added to a white wine to increase the wine's residual sugar and sweetness.

sweetness: The impression of sugary taste in a wine, which can be due to the presence of residual sugar or to other sweet-tasting substances in the wine, such as alcohol.

tannic: A word used to describe wines that seem to be high in tannin.

tannin: A substance in the skins, stems, and seeds of grapes; a principal component of red wines, which — unlike white wines — are made using the grape skins. Tannin also is a component of oak barrels.

tarry: Having aromas or flavors that suggest fresh tar.

tart: A descriptor for aromas or flavors of under-ripe fruit. This term can also apply to a wine that is too high in acid.

taste: A general term for the totality of impressions a wine gives in the mouth; more specifically, the primary tastes found in wine: sweetness, sourness, and bitterness.

terroir: A French word that is the collective term for the growing conditions in a vineyard, such as climate, soil, drainage, slope, altitude, topography, and so on.

texture: A wine's consistency or feel in the mouth.

thin: A word used to describe wines that are lacking in substance.

tight: A descriptor for wines that seem to be inexpressive. This term can apply to a wine's aromas and flavors, or to its structure.

underbrush: Aromas or flavors that suggest wet leaves, dampness, and slight decay.

varietal character: The characteristics of a specific grape variety; the characteristics of a wine that are attributable to the grape variety from which it was made.

varietal: A wine named for the sole or the principal grape variety from which it was made.

vegetal: Having aromas or flavors that suggest vegetables, such as green peppers or asparagus.

vin de pays: French phrase for *country wine;* legally, a category of French wine that holds lower status than AOC wines.

vinification: The activity of making grape juice into wine.

vintage: The year in which a wine's grapes grew and were harvested; sometimes used as a synonym for the grape harvest.

viticulture: The activity of growing grapes.

Vitis vinifera: The species to which most of the world's wine grapes belong.

weight: The impression of a wine's volume in the mouth.

wood tannin: Those tannins in a wine that are attributable to the barrels in which the wine aged, as opposed to the grapes.

yeasts: One-cell microorganisms responsible for transforming grape juice into wine.

Appendix C

Vintage Wine Chart: 1982–2001

- -

*A*ny vintage wine chart must be regarded as a rough guide — a general, average rating of the vintage year in a particular wine region. Remember that many wines will always be exceptions to the vintage's rating. For example, some wine producers will manage to find a way to make a decent — even fine — wine in a so-called poor vintage.

WINE REGION	1982	1983	1984	1985	1986	1987	1988	1989	1990	1991
Bordeaux										
Médoc, Graves	95c	85c	70d	85c	90b	75c	85b	90c	90b	75c
Pomerol, St-Emil	95c	85c	65d	85c	85b	75d	85b	90c	95b	60d
Sauternes/Barsac	70c	90b	70c	80c	90a	70c	95a	90b	95a	70d
Burgundy										
Côte de Nuits-Red	75c	80c	75d	85c	70d	80d	85c	85c	90c	85b
Côte Beaune-Red	75d	80d	70d	85c	70d	80d	85c	85c	90c	70c
Burgundy, White	80d	80d	75d	85c	90c	80c	80c	90c	85c	70d
Rhône Valley										
Northern Rhône	85c	90c	75d	85c	80c	80c	90c	95b	90b	90c
Southern Rhône	70d	85d	70d	80c	75d	60d	85c	95b	95c	65d
Other Wine Regions										
Alsace	80d	95c	70d	90c	80d	75d	85c	95c	95c	75c
Champagne	95c	80c	NV	90c	80c	NV	85b	85c	95c	NV
Germany	80c	90c	65d	85c	75c	75c	85c	90c	95c	80c
Rioja (Spain)	90c	80c	70d	80c	80c	80d	85c	90c	85c	75c
Vintage Port	80c	85c	NV	85b	NV	NV	NV	NV	NV	90a
Italy										
Piedmont	90c	75d	65d	90c	85c	80c	85b	95a	95c	75c
Tuscany	80d	85d	60d	95c	85d	75d	90c	70d	90c	75d
California North Coast										
Cabernet Sauvignon	75c	70d	85c	90c	80c	85c	75c	80c	90c	95b

WINE REGION	1992	1993	1994	1995	1996	1997	1998	1999	2000	2001
Bordeaux										
Médoc, Graves	75d	80c	85c	90b	90a	85b	85a	85a	95a	85a
Pomerol, St-Emil	75d	80c	85b	90b	85a	85b	95a	85a	95a	85a
Sauternes/Barsac	70d	65d	75c	85b	85b	85a	85a	85a	85a	95a
Burgundy										
Côte de Nuits-Red	70d	80c	75d	90a	90a	90c	85b	90b	85b	85b
Côte Beaune-Red	80c	70d	75d	90a	90a	85c	80b	90b	75c	80b
Burgundy, White	85c	75d	80d	90b	90b	85c	85c	85b	85c	85b
Rhône Valley										
Northern Rhône	75c	60d	85c	90a	85b	90b	90a	95a	85b	90a
Southern Rhône	75d	80d	85d	90a	80c	80c	95b	90b	95b	90a
Other Wine Regions										
Alsace	85c	80c	90c	85c	85c	85c	90c	85c	90b	90b
Champagne	NV	80b	NV	85b	95a	80b	95a	80b	80b	NV
Germany	85c	85c	90c	85c	95b	85c	85c	85c	85b	90b
Rioja (Spain)	85c	85c	90c	90c	85c	85c	80c	85b	85b	95b
Vintage Port	95a	NV	95a	NV	NV	85a	NV	NV	90a	NV
Italy										
Piedmont	70d	80c	75c	85b	95a	90c	90a	95a	90a	90a
Tuscany	70d	75d	85c	90b	75c	95c	85c	90b	90a	85a

Key:		
100 = Outstanding	70 = Below Average	a = Too young to drink
95 = Excellent	65 = Poor	b = Can be consumed now, but will improve with time
90 = Very Good	50–60 = Very Poor	
85 = Good		c = Ready to drink
80 = Fairly Good		d = May be too old
75 = Average		NV = Non-vintage year

WINE REGION	1992	1993	1994	1995	1996	1997	1998	1999	2000	2001
California North Coast										
Cabernet Sauvignon	90c	85b	95c	90b	90b	90c	85c	85a	85b	95a

WINE REGION	Recent Past Great Vintages
Bordeaux	
Médoc, Graves	1959, 1961, 1970
Pomerol, St-Emil	1961, 1964, 1970, 1975
Burgundy	
Côte de Nuits-Red	1959, 1964, 1969, 1978
Côte Beaune-Red	1959, 1969
Burgundy, White	1962, 1966, 1969, 1973, 1978
Rhône Valley	
Northern Rhône	1959, 1961, 1966, 1969, 1970, 1972 (Hermitage), 1978
Southern Rhône	1961, 1967, 1978
Other Wine Regions	
Alsace	1959, 1961, 1967, 1976
Champagne	1961, 1964, 1969, 1971, 1975
Sauternes	1959, 1962, 1967, 1975
Germany	1959, 1971, 1976
Rioja (Spain)	1964, 1970
Vintage Port	1963, 1966, 1970, 1977
Italy	
Piedmont	1958, 1964, 1971, 1978
Tuscany	1967, 1970 (Brunello di Montalcino), 1971
California North Coast	
Cabernet Sauvignon	1951, 1958, 1968, 1970, 1974

Index

• Ɗ •

• S •

Notes

FOR DUMMIES®

The easy way to get more done and have more fun

FOR DUMMIES®

A world of resources to help you grow

TRAVEL

0-7645-5453-0

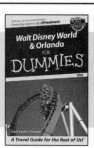

0-7645-5438-7

0-7645-5444-1

Also available:

America's National Parks For Dummies
(0-7645-6204-5)

Caribbean For Dummies
(0-7645-5445-X)

Cruise Vacations For Dummies 2003
(0-7645-5459-X)

Europe For Dummies
(0-7645-5456-5)

Ireland For Dummies
(0-7645-6199-5)

France For Dummies
(0-7645-6292-4)

Las Vegas For Dummies
(0-7645-5448-4)

London For Dummies
(0-7645-5416-6)

Mexico's Beach Resorts For Dummies
(0-7645-6262-2)

Paris For Dummies
(0-7645-5494-8)

RV Vacations For Dummies
(0-7645-5443-3)

EDUCATION & TEST PREPARATION

0-7645-5194-9

0-7645-5325-9

0-7645-5249-X

Also available:

The ACT For Dummies
(0-7645-5210-4)

Chemistry For Dummies
(0-7645-5430-1)

English Grammar For Dummies
(0-7645-5322-4)

French For Dummies
(0-7645-5193-0)

GMAT For Dummies
(0-7645-5251-1)

Inglés Para Dummies
(0-7645-5427-1)

Italian For Dummies
(0-7645-5196-5)

Research Papers For Dummies
(0-7645-5426-3)

SAT I For Dummies
(0-7645-5472-7)

U.S. History For Dummies
(0-7645-5249-X)

World History For Dummies
(0-7645-5242-2)

HEALTH, SELF-HELP & SPIRITUALITY

0-7645-5154-X

0-7645-5302-X

0-7645-5418-2

Also available:

The Bible For Dummies
(0-7645-5296-1)

Controlling Cholesterol For Dummies
(0-7645-5440-9)

Dating For Dummies
(0-7645-5072-1)

Dieting For Dummies
(0-7645-5126-4)

High Blood Pressure For Dummies
(0-7645-5424-7)

Judaism For Dummies
(0-7645-5299-6)

Menopause For Dummies
(0-7645-5458-1)

Nutrition For Dummies
(0-7645-5180-9)

Potty Training For Dummies
(0-7645-5417-4)

Pregnancy For Dummies
(0-7645-5074-8)

Rekindling Romance For Dummies
(0-7645-5303-8)

Religion For Dummies
(0-7645-5264-3)

Available wherever books are sold. Go to www.dummies.com or call 1-877-762-2974 to order direct

FOR DUMMIES®

Plain-English solutions for everyday challenges

HOME & BUSINESS COMPUTER BASICS

0-7645-0838-5

0-7645-1663-9

0-7645-1548-9

Also available:

Excel 2002 All-in-One Desk
Reference For Dummies
(0-7645-1794-5)

Office XP 9-in-1 Desk
Reference For Dummies
(0-7645-0819-9)

PCs All-in-One Desk
Reference For Dummies
(0-7645-0791-5)

Troubleshooting Your PC
For Dummies
(0-7645-1669-8)

Upgrading & Fixing PCs For
Dummies
(0-7645-1665-5)

Windows XP For Dummies
(0-7645-0893-8)

Windows XP For Dummies
Quick Reference
(0-7645-0897-0)

Word 2002 For Dummies
(0-7645-0839-3)

INTERNET & DIGITAL MEDIA

0-7645-0894-6

0-7645-1642-6

0-7645-1664-7

Also available:

CD and DVD Recording
For Dummies
(0-7645-1627-2)

Digital Photography
All-in-One Desk Reference
For Dummies
(0-7645-1800-3)

eBay For Dummies
(0-7645-1642-6)

Genealogy Online For
Dummies
(0-7645-0807-5)

Internet All-in-One Desk
Reference For Dummies
(0-7645-1659-0)

Internet For Dummies
Quick Reference
(0-7645-1645-0)

Internet Privacy For Dummies
(0-7645-0846-6)

Paint Shop Pro For Dummies
(0-7645-2440-2)

Photo Retouching &
Restoration For Dummies
(0-7645-1662-0)

Photoshop Elements For
Dummies
(0-7645-1675-2)

Scanners For Dummies
(0-7645-0783-4)

Get smart! Visit www.dummies.com

- **Find listings of even more Dummies titles**

- **Browse online articles, excerpts, and how-to's**

- **Sign up for daily or weekly e-mail tips**

- **Check out Dummies fitness videos and other products**

- **Order from our online bookstore**

Available wherever books are sold. Go to www.dummies.com or call 1-877-762-2974 to order direct